LAW of the JUNGLE

LAW of the

JUNGLE

The Hunt for Colombian Guerrillas,
American Hostages, and Buried Treasure

JOHN OTIS

WILLIAM MORROW

An Imprint of HarperCollinsPublishers

HarperCollins books may be purchased for educational, business, or sales promotional use. For information please write: Special Markets Department, HarperCollins Publishers, 10 East 53rd Street, New York, NY 10022.

FIRST EDITION

Designed by Jamie Lynn Kerner

Library of Congress Cataloging-in-Publication Data

Otis, John.
  Law of the jungle : the hunt for Colombian guerrillas, American hostages, and buried treasure / John Otis. — 1st ed.
     p. cm.
  Includes bibliographical references.
  ISBN: 978-0-06-167180-7
  1. Howes, Tom—Captivity, 2003–2008. 2. Gonsalves, Marc—Captivity, 2003–2008. 3. Stansell, Keith—Captivity, 2003–2008. 4. Americans—Colombia—Caquetá—Biography. 5. Hostages—Colombia—Caquetá—Biography. 6. Hostage negotiations—Colombia—History—21st century. 7. Fuerzas Armadas Revolucionarias de Colombia. 8. Guerrillas—Colombia—History—21st century. 9. Colombia—Foreign relations—United States. 10. United States—Foreign relations—Colombia. I. Title.
  HV6604.C72H696 2010
  986.106'35092313—dc22

2009039212

---

10 11 12 13 14 WBC/RRD 10 9 8 7 6 5 4 3 2 1

For Alejandra, Martín, and Lawrence of Colombia

The jungle has swallowed them.
—JOSÉ EUSTASIO RIVERA, *The Vortex*

CONTENTS

CONTENTS

LAW of the JUNGLE

CHAPTER 1

AIR AMERICA

If the engine stops for any reason, you are due to tumble,
and that's all there is to it.
—Clyde Cessna, founder of Cessna Aircraft Corp.

As if announcing nothing more momentous than a patch of turbulence, Tommy Janis calmly confirmed the worst. The three-blade prop had spun to a halt. The cataclysmic scenario, the one Janis and the other three American military contractors aboard the aircraft had shrugged off for so long, was now unfolding over Colombia's imposing Andes Mountains. Their single-engine Cessna 208 Grand Caravan, packed to the gunnels with radios, high-tech cameras, and automatic rifles, was going down.

All the crew members could do was buckle their shoulder harnesses and put their faith in Janis, a first-class flyboy with an uncanny knack for survival. A thirty-two-year army veteran who served in the Vietnam War and was awarded a Bronze Star, Janis viewed his job as another way to be a soldier, another way to make a difference. He had earned his stripes in Colombia—and the moniker "ace of the base"—two years earlier when the engine of his Cessna surveillance plane quit over the Caribbean Sea. He simply pointed the plane toward the coastal city of Santa Marta, twenty-five miles away, and began gliding.

"Tommy made it look easy," said Douglas Cockes, a former U.S. Customs Service pilot and private contractor who worked with Janis in Colombia. "If an engine quits right next to an airport, probably half of all pilots would still miss the runway. But Tommy was able to get in there from twenty-some miles out. He made a perfect landing, rolled to the end of the taxiway, then jumped out and lit a cigar."

This time, Janis had two options. He could try to keep the Cessna aloft long enough to clear the mountain ridge and reach their original destination, a nearby Colombian military base. Or if that didn't work, he would have to put her down somewhere in the wilds of southern Caquetá state.

And that would not be good.

Like much of Colombia's Deep South, Caquetá was enemy territory. Home to cattle ranches, cowboys, and twisting, muddy rivers that drain into the Amazon, the region was better known for all the things that ail Colombia. Glossy green coca bushes, the raw material for cocaine, dotted the flatter parts of the landscape. The Colombian government didn't have enough troops in Caquetá to provide much security, which made it possible for Marxist rebels to extort businessmen, kidnap farmers, and manage the local drug trade. But if the rebels' kingdom was vast, their subjects were few. Only a handful of Colombians set foot in these parts and for good reason: Caquetá was Colombia's Sunni Triangle.

The Americans aboard the Cessna were there to help change this dynamic. Though not active-duty military, they were, in effect, the tip of the U.S. spear in the long-running war on South American drugs. They worked for California Microwave Systems, a little-known subsidiary of Northrop Grumman, the Maryland-based aerospace giant which was a major client of the U.S. Defense Department. In the days before the Pentagon began contracting out some of its military and intelligence chores, their work might have been handled by the CIA.

Their missions were classified. As high-tech eyes in the sky, the Americans were supposed to find and photograph cocaine laboratories. The guerrillas were deeply involved in the cocaine trade, thus the data collected aboard the Cessna could also be used for counterinsurgency operations. The contractors were always on the lookout for clandestine airstrips and makeshift river ports used to evacuate bricks of cocaine. From the air, the crew could also spot fifty-five-gallon drums, chemical stains on the jungle floor, and maceration pits where coca leaves were mixed with uric acid and other toxic ingredients to make the white powder. They also had forward-looking infrared. Known as a FLIR, the pod that protruded from one side of the plane could identify heat given off by people, engines, even the microwave ovens drug makers used to dry cocaine. Whenever antidrug agents found a microwave oven deep in the Colombian rain forest, they could be pretty sure the cook wasn't zapping popcorn.

The Americans recorded what they saw on video and digital cameras and fed the data to the fortresslike U.S. embassy in Bogotá. The information was then relayed to Colombian ground forces that would move in to torch the labs and track the rebels. Then, the whole chain of events started again, with peasant farmers planting more coca, Jungle alchemists building more labs, and gung ho drug warriors launching more raids. This self-perpetuating game had been going on for years due, in part, to the overwhelming U.S. focus on cutting off the narcotics supply at its source rather than reducing demand and treating drug addicts at home.

Now Washington was wading deeper into the Colombian war.

These surveillance missions were part of a multibillion-dollar program, known as Plan Colombia, that had made the Andean nation the largest recipient of U.S. foreign aid outside the Middle East and Afghanistan. Much of the $700 million in annual assistance was funneled into programs to eradicate coca fields, blow up cocaine factories, and intercept drug-laden aircraft. Unfortunately, the effort had failed to roll back narco-acreage in any substantial way or to curb the flow of cocaine into the United States. Attacking illegal drugs was like plowing the sea. But Plan Colombia did produce in the early days hundreds of high-risk, high-paying jobs for American contractors.

THE MEN IN THE CESSNA THAT sunny Thursday morning, February 13, 2003, believed they were fighting the good fight. But truth be told, they were mostly in it for the money. Next to Janis in the right seat was copilot

Thomas Howes. A quiet, gray-haired Yankee from Cape Cod, Howes none-theless wielded a sly sense of humor. One of his colleagues compared him to a master doctor "who could give you the needle so expertly that you wouldn't know you'd been jabbed." After a stint flying DC-9 commuter jets out of New York's La Guardia Airport, Tom had gravitated south where he'd gotten hooked on the warm weather, good food, and pretty girls of Latin America. At one point while hanging out in Lima, Peru, Howes missed seven consecutive flights back to the United States. "It was such a change of pace and flavor," Howes said. "I was mesmerized. And I lost that drive to move up the aviation ladder back in the States."

Over the years, Howes had logged thirteen thousand hours flying for private contractors in Guatemala, Haiti, Peru, and Colombia. Along the way he married a Peruvian woman and together they had a boy named Tommy. Howes was thrilled to be earning upwards of $150,000 with California Microwave on a schedule that took him to Colombia for four weeks at a time, with two weeks off back home. Howes sometimes told his friends: "I want to keep these paychecks coming until I'm too old and feeble to read them."

In the back of the plane operating the cameras and the FLIR was Marc Gonsalves. A thirty-year-old native of Bristol, Connecticut, who often wore a goatee, Gonsalves was an eight-year veteran of the air force who worked as an intelligence analyst. As a young NCO, he had married an exotic dancer named Shane whom he'd met at a bar near MacDill Air Force Base in Tampa. The couple had three kids they were raising in the Florida Keys. Though Marc loved his job, the promotion cycle was slow and he was earning only about $28,000 a year. The prospect of putting his kids through college worried him. Thus, when California Microwave offered him a job and a gigantic raise, he eagerly made the switch to the private sector.

Alongside Marc in the back was Keith Stansell, a six-foot-two-inch for-mer marine, avionics whiz, outdoorsman, and self-described southern red-neck. Keith had used his fat salary to climb out of debt and was now enjoying life in his free time by fishing in the Gulf of Mexico or disappear-ing into the Montana outback to hunt deer. Still, he sometimes mused about quitting so he could spend more time with his fiancée and their two young children in rural Georgia. His master plan was to open a crop-dusting business, then kick back on the weekends with his family, his dog, Buck, and a tall glass of Jack Daniel's and Coke. Or was it? Keith, it seems, had built up an exotic, if complicated, parallel life in Colombia. He was dating a Colombian flight attendant and shortly before Thursday's mission he'd found out that she was pregnant—with their twins.

The fifth member of the crew was the so-called host-nation rider, a Colombian sergeant named Luis Alcides Cruz. As a formality, Colombian Army troops rode along on all the flights to put at least a semblance of the Bogotá government's imprint on what were essentially American missions.

When the Cessna accelerated down the runway at Bogotá's El Dorado International Airport at 7:24 a.m., the crew figured they were in for a routine, six-hour sortie, an average day in the war on drugs.

"Just a routine flight," copilot Tom Howes recalled months later. "Everyone was in good spirits. I just got word I was going home a week early to the States, so I was in very good spirits."

But the Americans were heading into the badlands in a bird that was more *Spirit of St. Louis* than AWACS. A stretch version of the Cessna Caravan, the Grand Caravan is the minivan of civilian aviation, and California Microwave had leased two of them for the missions in Colombia. Slow, boxy, and butt-ugly, the aircraft can carry 4,500 pounds of gas, gear, and people and take off and land on tight runways. The plane is a workhorse for bush pilots in Alaska, miners in Argentina, and air-ambulance crews in Third World shit holes. Federal Express runs a fleet of 260 Caravans out of its Memphis hub. Sometimes called a Swiss Army knife with wings, the plane can be found just about any place where there's two thousand feet of dubious grass strip. The Grand Caravan was ubiquitous and in that sense it was perfect, like using a Dodge Caravan on an undercover drug stakeout.

Built in 1994 and purchased secondhand for about $1 million, the Americans' blue-and-white Grand Caravan—tail number N1116G—had initially served as a puddle jumper air taxi in the Caribbean. But since 2000 when the surveillance program kicked off in Colombia, N1116G had huffed and puffed over the Andes Mountains and logged hundreds of hours floating above the Amazon jungle, turning itself into the Little Turbo-Prop That Could.

The weak point of the Grand Caravan was under the hood. The

675-horsepower Pratt & Whitney PT6A turbine engine was a decent-enough power source if the mission was to deliver express mail to Columbia, South Carolina. But Colombia, South America, was a war zone, and when the bullets were flying, one motor might not be enough. Twin-engine aircraft could usually limp home if one side gave out. But a fully loaded Grand Caravan, might glide for a short spell before it eventually began to lose about one thousand feet of altitude per mile.

"Any single-engine airplane by itself over the jungle is dangerous. Any single-engine airplane over the jungle where they're shooting at you is extremely dangerous," said Jorge Sanjinés, an American contractor who flew helicopter gunships—equipped with twin engines—in Colombia. "That's because you only need one, tiny, itty-bitty bullet to take you down."

There had been plenty of warnings, like Tommy Janis's dead-stick landing into Santa Marta on the other Grand Caravan leased by the company. But no one paid much attention because there were no casualties. The Miami-based U.S. Southern Command, the branch of the military that oversaw the surveillance program, was largely unaware of the incident. According to Cockes, Janis had made it look *too* easy. "If he landed on a beach somewhere, then had to get out and fight some guerrillas, then maybe people would have said: 'Well, goddamn, this is dangerous. Maybe we should go to a twin-engine plane.'"

Then, there was the weather. In the frosty, thin air of the Andes, ice sometimes formed on the Grand Caravan's wings. Descending was not an option, yet the Cessna often lacked the power to climb out of the moisture-laden clouds causing the problem. But even in clear skies, the plane was a flying beast of burden that handled like a Hummer.

That's because the back of the plane was usually jammed with rifles, pistols, water, food, books, laptop computers, extra clothes, and survival gear. The Cessna had received a special exemption from the Federal Aviation Administration to fly five hundred pounds overweight. The contractors even brought along thick coils of rope in case they crashed into the treetops and had to lower themselves to the ground. All that was missing, it sometimes seemed, was a guitar and a set of golf clubs strapped to the wing struts.

"You can't put twenty pounds of shit in a two-pound bag, and that's what they had," said Ronnie Powers, the owner who had leased the two Grand Caravans to California Microwave. "It was way too heavy but they learned to fly it like that."

As a result, just getting to their jungle targets was a logistical circus act. The Americans took off from Bogotá with their tanks just half-full of jet fuel because a full load of 335 gallons would have made them too heavy to climb over the mountains that stood between them and the cocaine labs to the south. Once on the other side of the range, they dropped down to Larandia, a Colombian military base in Caquetá, to top off their tanks before resuming their reconnaissance chores in the thicker air of the flatlands.

At a November 1999 meeting, months before the program kicked off, Paul Hooper, one of the California Microwave pilots, complained to his bosses that the Grand Caravan was the wrong plane for the job and suggested upgrading to a twin engine. When it became clear that the company had no interest in trading up, Hooper and Doug Cockes put their concerns in an eerily prescient November 14, 2002, letter. They warned Northrop Grumman and California Microwave that operating a single-engine aircraft invited "a catastrophic aviation mishap." The Grand Caravan, they wrote, "could not reach any suitable landing areas if the engine failed over most of the terrain" where the missions were flown. The two pilots implored the company to consider the Beechcraft King Air, which had a pressurized cockpit, more power to escape icy conditions, and an all-important second engine. But upgrading to King Airs would have cost a couple of million dollars more and California Microwave liked to run things on the cheap, prompting some employees to call their surveillance program Econ-Recon. California Microwave dismissed the warnings and Cockes and Hooper quit a few months later.

"There was a letter that was written by some of the pilots and I did see that after the fact," said Anne Patterson, who was U.S. ambassador to Colombia at the time and is now Washington's envoy to Pakistan. "We use Cessna Caravans here in Pakistan. I fly in them. We put senators in them. The airplane has a good safety record. So would I have changed? No."

But Keith Stansell remained unconvinced. At one point, the company urged him to take a survival training course in case the plane ever went down but he said no. "With this piece-of-shit aircraft we're being asked to fly in, there's no way I'm going to survive a crash. A dead man doesn't need to know how to survive."

It wasn't just the choice of aircraft that raised eyebrows. The missions themselves were becoming more hazardous. At first, the contractors flew only during daylight hours and over flat terrain. But their success at spotting drug labs and cocaine-laden aircraft bred mission creep. If their daylight missions went so swimmingly, the corporate thinking went, why not fly in the cooler nighttime hours when it would be easier to detect the body heat of guerrillas? Soon, the ban on mountain flying also went out the window.

Once again, it had all been spelled out in the letter Cockes and Hooper wrote to company executives. "When pilots and flight crews are successful in mission performance, payload, distance and location are added or stretched to more difficult scenarios," they wrote. "We now are telling you that this mission creep coupled with [the company's] attitude towards safe flight operations has made this mission very dangerous."

Even as Cockes and Hooper raised hell, most of their colleagues at California Microwave viewed the disgruntled pilots as whiners. Three of the four men on the Cessna that Thursday morning were former U.S. military, so it was in their DNA to lean forward, to put aside misgivings and follow orders whether they came from a crew-cut commanding officer or a middle-level manager from Maryland. In the private sector, however, going way out on a limb is usually considered a bad thing.

"But these ex-military guys don't always see it that way," said Peter W. Singer, an expert on private military contractors at the Brookings Institution in Washington, D.C. Instead, they view contracting gigs "like a continuing military mission. They have a can-do attitude: 'OK. This is a bad idea. But sir, yes sir, let's get it done.'"

For the men on the Cessna that day, it wasn't just their inner warrior speaking. At the time—this was just before the 2003 U.S. invasion of Iraq—their high-paying jobs were at the top of the military contracting food chain. Yet it was never made clear to the pilots and crew members how long their contracts would last or whether they would even have jobs next month. Their bosses seemed to be intentionally vague about that and there was nothing in writing. The pilots and the backseaters felt a constant pressure to deliver.

At one point, Cockes got into a shouting match with Janis, who maintained that they were being paid big money to take big risks. Cockes also ripped Gonsalves a new one. Though he had been with the program for just four months, Gonsalves was already urging his colleagues to accept night missions because he feared that some other, more aggressive company could steal away the California Microwave contract.

"I was very new," Marc said. "I did not know about the earlier engine failure. I thought we were safe."

As the Cessna reached a cruising altitude of 12,000 feet and a speed of 165 knots, pilot Tommy Janis turned the Grand Caravan south-southwest toward the city of Girardot, then followed the Magdalena River. Every fifteen minutes, Keith or Marc radioed the plane's coordinates to the embassy and to a Southern Command office in Key West. Approaching the eastern ridge of the Andes, Janis climbed to 14,000 feet, then aimed for the Larandia military base. Everything seemed on track. The pilots were chatting. Keith was in the back reading a biography of Che Guevara. Marc, the new guy, was practicing with his camera gear and a computer. The Colombian sergeant was asleep.

Somewhere north of Larandia, the reassuring, low-pitched purr of the Pratt & Whitney turbine engine came to an abrupt halt.

"Out of the blue, the engine just spooled down," copilot Tom Howes recalled. "The sound we heard was 'bzzzoooh.'"

Howes looked at Janis.

"Sir," Janis said, "that's an engine failure."

Stansell got back on the radio, declaring an emergency and passing along their coordinates from their portable global positioning system.

"Magic Worker, Magic Worker, Mutt 01 is declaring mayday," Stansell said, using code names and still sounding calm. "We have lost engine."

Tommy Janis had a life-or-death decision to make. He could try to repeat his Caribbean heroics by gliding about thirty miles toward the safety of the Larandia base, near the provincial capital of Florencia, which was teeming with U.S. and Colombian troops. But that was a long shot. During his epic glide into Santa Marta, his Grand Caravan was nearly empty. This time the plane, which was now about five thousand feet above the ground, was fully loaded and quickly losing altitude. The other option was to aim for a stretch of road, a cow pasture, or some other clear patch of terrain. However, the Cessna had yet to emerge from the mountains and, peering out of the side windows, the men could see nothing but the tree-covered hills and craggy ravines.

"My gut feeling was: 'Hell no, we'll never make it over the ridge,'" Tom Howes said.

As Keith read a running list of GPS coordinates over the radio, Marc prepared the inside of the aircraft for violent impact by securing loose equipment, which could turn into deadly projectiles, behind a crash barrier in the rear of the plane. The men strapped themselves into their seats. Tom Howes suggested trying to restart the engine in case it might turn over. But the dormant motor refused to stir.

"It looked grim," Howes said. "And then Tommy Janis saw, on his side of the aircraft, a postage-stamp-sized open area of green grass. And he decided immediately that this would be the place."

Stansell got back on the radio, the dire situation now evident in his tone: "We are looking for a place on the ridge to set down." Moments later, monitors at the embassy and in Key West heard one final dispatch from the Cessna, which, after four minutes of gliding, was about to slam into the mountains.

"Down," Keith said. "We are going down now."

But could Tommy Janis hit the target? He had no engine and had lost control of the flaps. And the improvised landing strip was smaller than a football field on a twenty-degree uphill slope that ended at the edge of a cliff. The Vietnam vet maneuvered between the hills, brought the plane low into a ravine just clearing the treetops. Then, with the stall warnings blaring, he pulled back on the wheel just before impact.

"The last thing I remember was a green carpet coming up into my face," Tom Howes said. Then, he was knocked out cold.

CHAPTER 2

EL GORDO

The conventional army loses if it does not win.
The guerrilla wins if he does not lose.
—HENRY KISSINGER

J ORGE SANABRIA GREW UP POOR AMID the potato fields and sheep farms of Boyaca state in northern Colombia. He spent hours in front of the television hypnotized by classic World War II films. He loved *The Dirty Dozen*, in which Lee Marvin plays an independent-minded intelligence officer leading twelve soldiers, who are in the stockade for a variety of crimes, on a top-secret operation in Nazi Germany. Somehow, these cutthroats, misogynists, and oddballs gel into a potent fighting force.

Sanabria's all-time favorite was *Patton*. In the movie's famous opening monologue before a massive American flag, the aggressive general known as "Old Blood 'n' Guts" warns his men not to get caught in a defensive crouch against the Nazis. "Wade into them. Spill *their* blood. Shoot *them* in the belly," he urges. "We're gonna go through 'em like crap through a goose."

"That was inspiring," said Sanabria, who fantasized about leading his own audacious missions behind enemy lines.

In the end, it wasn't Hollywood's version of the gritty warrior that determined Sanabria's career path. Nor was it because his own country was embroiled in a bloody guerrilla war that began in 1964, a decade before he was born. The cold reality was that in Colombia, the army was one of the few institutions that would take in a young hayseed with no money, no connections, and no future, turn him into something, and guarantee a steady paycheck.

The other option was the seminary.

Sanabria had already been saved once by the Church. His father, who worked in an auto engine assembly plant, abandoned the family when Sanabria was a youngster. To provide for her two sons, Sanabria's mother took a job in the farm town of Sogamoso cooking meals and mopping floors for the local Roman Catholic cleric. Padre Roque was something of a whiskey priest. But he had a soft spot for the struggling Sanabrias and let them live in a back room of the San Martín Cathedral that dominates Sogamoso's central plaza. Soon, young Jorge was pitching in, shining the Father's shoes, washing his car, and fetching him green bottles of twelve-year-old Buchanan's Scotch.

Impressed by the boy's dedication, Padre Roque urged Jorge to consider the priesthood. But when Sanabria expressed more interest in the José María Cordova officer-training school in Bogotá, Padre Roque provided him both encouragement and financial support. Sanabria didn't look much like a soldier. An overweight teenager, he earned the nickname El Gordo, or fatso. Even years later when he was photographed in his combat fatigues in front of a chopper, Sanabria looked almost wider than he was tall. But as a youth, he was determined to get in shape for cadet school, so he spent hours hiking along the mountain paths surrounding Sogamoso with a backpack full of bricks. And though he had to take the entry exam twice before squeaking through, the disciplined life of the cadet agreed with him. He didn't mind polishing boots, making beds with military corners, and scrubbing toilets because he'd already done this as a child.

"It wasn't so bad because I had lived and worked in the church," Sanabria said years later as he sat on a bench in the town square facing his old digs at the cathedral. Then, using a Colombian proverb, he smiled and added: "This donkey had already been whipped."

BUT BY THE TIME SANABRIA GRADUATED with a commission as a second lieutenant, the entire Colombian Army was floundering. The guerrillas were handing government troops one embarrassing military defeat after another, killing and kidnapping hundreds of soldiers in the process. Army efforts to strike back weren't working either. During one 1997 operation, dubbed Destroyer II, the military dropped 326 bombs, launched 35 rockets, and fired 84,000 bullets. But the only things the troops destroyed were farmhouses and corn crops and the only casualties were cows.

The grunts on the ground did their best but Colombia's war machine was built to fail. The officer corps was top-heavy with incompetent "chairborne" generals. Elsewhere in Latin America, wearing the uniform was a badge of honor. But in Colombia, the institution was looked down upon as little more than a jobs program for the underclass. To protect their kids from the draft, upper-class parents paid hefty bribes for the laminated military service cards that certified young men had done their duty. Even within the army, the lines were drawn. Recruits with high school diplomas were put in office jobs. The dropouts and the losers who lacked the money to study were dispatched directly to the hot zone where they were often no match against better-trained rebels.

Even with the draft, there were never enough GIs to turn the tide in the war. Fears of coups by military officers, who had overthrown elected governments across South America, prompted Colombia's political leaders to keep the army deliberately undermanned and underfunded. The freshly minted Second Lieutenant Sanabria joined a force of about 146,000 troops, a ridiculously small number of soldiers for a nation the size of Texas and California combined, and where three Andean Mountain ranges and vast tracks of Amazon jungle provided plenty of cover for the guerrillas. In Vietnam, a country one-fifth the size of Colombia, American troop levels at one point topped half a million, yet the United States still lost.

"From the very beginning, we didn't deal with the guerrillas the way we should have," said retired general Jorge Enrique Mora, a former commander of the Colombian armed forces who graduated from officer school in 1964, the year the war started. "The guerrillas were never confronted with the full power of the state."

In the 1960s and '70s, a number of rebel groups sprang up with an alphabet soup of acronyms for names. They included the Marxist FARC, the Maoist EPL, the Castro-inspired ELN, and the upstart urban guerrillas of the M-19. All were fueled by resentment over Colombia's closed, incestuous political system and the huge gap between the rich and the poor, who constituted sixty percent of the population and, like Sanabria, mostly lived in outlying areas. Yet internecine conflicts over ideology, strategy, and tactics kept the rebels from uniting and forming a single, potent insurgency. Often, they clashed with one another.

Most of the fighting took place in parts of the country no one cared about: sparsely populated frontier lands that Bogotá had never really controlled in the first place. There was no rebel noose tightening around the big cities, no final offensive, just occasional raids and ambushes that produced few casualties and didn't seem to add up to full-scale war. Most of the Colombian establishment remained blissfully ignorant. And if they did stop to consider the conflict, they shrugged it off as the military's problem, not the country's problem.

Besides, by the 1980s the country's problem was Pablo Escobar. His murderous Medellín cocaine cartel regularly targeted top government officials while the syndicate's hit men and car bombs were killing and maiming thousands in the cities. And these weren't peasants, draftees, or other no-names. These were senators, ministers, and even presidential candidates. With government troops focused on wiping out the narcos, the guerrillas lay low and bulked up.

"It was the time of Pablo Escobar and bombs in the cities and the deaths of so many people. We had to neutralize the biggest threats of the moment, which is why our attention was distracted" away from the guerrilla war, said retired general Carlos Alberto Ospina, another former armed forces commander.

After the Berlin Wall came down and the Soviet Union collapsed, most of Latin America's guerrilla groups lost their sponsors and their political bearings and either disarmed or were defeated. But the Revolutionary

Armed Forces of Colombia, the FARC, the nation's oldest and largest rebel force, soldiered on. The FARC's origins dated back to 1948 when an outbreak of political violence that eventually killed 200,000 people forced a group of peasants aligned with the country's Communist and Liberal parties to flee to the mountains to defend themselves. For years, the FARC was dismissed by the country's more chic radicals as a collection of backcountry rubes who lacked flair and derring-do. But the FARC emerged as just about the last rebel group standing in Colombia and it did so by surviving long enough to take advantage of the boom in the illegal drug trade. To purists, the cross-pollination of revolutionaries with drug syndicates was akin to mixing vodka with holy water. But the cash provided a steroidal boost that allowed the FARC to triple in size over the course of the 1990s.

Almost by default, the FARC took control of many backward rural zones that nobody in Bogotá cared about. These jungle and mountain plots were perfect for growing coca and opium poppies, which could be turned into heroin. After some internal debates about the morality of drugs, the rebels chucked aside any qualms and began levying taxes on coca and opium growers and charging fees for the use of clandestine airstrips. Eventually, the FARC became directly involved in trafficking cocaine. Adding to its bulging treasure chest, the FARC ratcheted up its campaign of extorting businesses and abducting civilians for ransom. Many rebel targets—small businessmen, cattle ranchers, and plantation owners—received offers they couldn't refuse. They had a choice: either they forked over monthly extortion payments to the FARC or they were kidnapped or killed.

Unlike orthodox narcos who went shopping for mountaintop mansions, BMWs, and cigarette boats, the rebels plowed their newfound wealth back into *la revolución*. They purchased bulk orders of rifles, uniforms, and boots and went on a recruiting spree. That's why Colombian political analysts on both the left and right differentiated the FARC from standard-issue drug cartels. Rebel leaders "are not living at Hilton Hotels," said Daniel García-Peña, a former government peace commissioner. "If they were in it only for the money, why would they bother with all this Marxist-Leninist rhetoric? Why would they live in the mountains and wake up at 5 a.m. to march?"

By the late 1990s, the FARC fielded seventeen thousand guerrillas, which allowed the rebel organization to make a great leap forward from traditional hit-and-run guerrilla tactics to so-called mobile warfare, involving up to fifteen hundred foot soldiers to overrun towns and military bases. Traditional counterinsurgency doctrine held that soldiers should outnumber rebels by at least ten to one. But on the Colombian battlefield, it was often the other way around. Army units were isolated and spread thin, which allowed the FARC to surround and annihilate them.

Many Colombian landowners, politicians, and businesspeople, along with drug traffickers, began sponsoring paramilitary death squads, instead of demanding a better armed forces and putting up the tax money to pay for it. Most businesses in paramilitary-dominated zones ended up contributing to the cause. Even Cincinnati-based Chiquita Brands eventually admitted that it made more than $1.7 million in payments to the paramilitaries patrolling the fruit plantations of northern Colombia, which had been plagued by guerrilla violence and strikes by left-wing unions. And the army, aware that the "paras" were the enemy of its enemy, often worked with the militias. Alluding to the five divisions of the Colombian Army, Human Rights Watch branded the paramilitaries as "the Sixth Division." But rather than taking on uniformed rebels on the battlefield, the paramilitaries usually targeted civilians suspected of supporting the rebel cause. The paramilitaries killed thousands with automatic rifles, machetes, and chainsaws—and they sometimes even stoned people to death. Though effective in their own brutal way, these paramilitary operations created an international outcry that led to a cutoff in some U.S. military aid and further sullied the Colombian Army's wretched reputation.

When Andrés Pastrana was elected as Colombia's president in 1998, he inherited a demoralized, corrupt, undersized military that seemed to be losing the war. Even the number of soldiers was deceptive. The majority of the 146,000 held office jobs or were stuck in fixed positions guarding oil pipelines, roads, and electric plants, leaving only about 30,000 front-line troops, of which only 22,000 were professional soldiers. The rest were poorly trained, ill-equipped draftees. Bullets were rationed. Gasoline for their trucks was hard to come by and they had just two dozen choppers.

Pastrana's army generals told him: "We don't have guns, we don't have men, we don't have uniforms. We are losing."

General Ospina remembered trying to scramble his way to a battle and having to plead with a Medellín contractor to let his men rent a helicopter. Lacking bulletproof vehicles, Ospina's men once built their own armored car following the advice of a tinsmith and instructions from a magazine. Even uniforms and footwear were scarce. Some soldiers went to tire repair shops and asked for discarded pieces of rubber to fix their boots.

"They would tear pockets off their shirts to cover the holes in the knees of their pants," said General Freddy Padilla de León, an up-and-coming officer who was named commander of the Colombian armed forces in 2005.

Things got so bad that Manuel José Bonett, who was Colombia's army chief in the late 1990s and one of the country's more philosophical officers, looked to the ancient Greeks for guidance. He began extolling the antiwar message of *Lysistrata*, Aristophanes' historical comedy in which the title character convinces her female colleagues to refuse to have sex with their husbands until they ended the Peloponnesian War between Athens and Sparta. Bonett went on to suggest that female FARC guerrillas ought to stage their own sexual boycott until peace was at hand.

Was this guy serious?

"I am serious," Bonett, an avid Jimi Hendrix fan, told reporters.

Ignoring the general's advice, the guerrillas multiplied their attacks. Even more than a decade later, Colombian troops winced when they heard the words *Patascoy*, *Miraflores*, and *Mitú*, the names of a string of towns and military bases that the FARC destroyed. It was akin to putting Pearl Harbor, Tet, and Fallujah in the same sentence for an American GI.

In some cases, the army effectively seemed to put out the red carpet for the enemy. In preparing for a raid on the military base at Las Delicias in Putumayo state, a plainclothes FARC militiaman befriended the local army commander. Like Huckleberry Finn and Tom Sawyer, the two men spent lazy afternoons fishing together on the Caquetá River as the rebel queried the army captain on where the guards were posted and the location of arms depots and mortar launchers. Other rebels disguised themselves as farmers and entered the base to sell fruit and vegetables to the soldiers. They took part in army soccer matches and even made a video of the inside of the base. The result was a rout. During seventeen hours of combat, the FARC overran the base, killing thirty-one soldiers and taking sixty prisoners.

Bad as it was, Las Delicias was just a palate cleanser. The worst came during the first week of March 1998 near a jungle village in southern Caquetá state called El Billar. Nestled on the Caguán River in the cocaine heartland, El Billar stood about a hundred miles southeast of Larandia—the military base that the American contractors aboard the faltering Cessna would aim for five years later. The soldiers of the elite Fifty-second Counterinsurgency Battalion of the Colombian Army had been in the area for months, giving away their position. Some had been flirting with local women who turned out to be FARC spies. And they were running dangerously short of supplies. At 5:30 a.m. on March 3, the 154 troops were surrounded by more than 700 guerrillas. As they were picked off, one by one, the soldiers frantically called for backup. But the troops had just one radio for every ten soldiers and in many cases their batteries had died. When they did manage to get through, storm clouds prevented the generals from immediately sending in support aircraft.

By the time reinforcements showed up forty-eight hours later, the battalion had been destroyed. The FARC killed sixty-two soldiers and captured forty-three, who were marched into the rain forest, single file, with cords tying them together by the neck. The carnage ranked as the Colombian Army's worst-ever military disaster, and one that General Ospina compared to Custer's crushing defeat at the Little Bighorn River.

JORGE SANABRIA MISSED EL BILLAR. BUT not long before that pitiful turkey shoot, he got his first taste of action in the mountains surrounding Escobar's old haunt of Medellín. When the bullets began flying, he hid beneath a riverbank, his hands trembling so much he could barely hold his rifle. But Sanabria regained his composure and spent the next six hours shooting at the guerrillas until a helicopter gunship rescued his patrol. "I was never so scared in all my life," he says. "I was breathing like a bull."

Yet the Zen of battle somehow agreed with Sanabria. The danger unleashed a surging waterfall of endorphins. The young officer had been out among the dragons and found that getting intimate with the war god made him feel more awake, more alive. Sanabria began volunteering for risky assignments and was transferred to the northwest state of Chocó. Bordering Panamá and the Pacific Ocean, Chocó was so far off the map that in some areas of the state the only public transportation consisted of stout Afro-Colombians, the descendants of slaves, who for a small fee would carry people along muddy jungle trails on their backs. Like his celluloid idols, Sanabria was determined to be the aggressor. He had joined a battalion so sedentary that its troops hadn't captured or killed a guerrilla in two years. Yet Sanabria recalled leading several risky missions up Chocó's maze of river tributaries. In one battle, he said, his men killed more than a dozen FARC rebels.

"After that," Sanabria said, "[commanding officers] called me one of the best." He was promoted to full lieutenant. Now, El Gordo felt like a hero.

But as he moved along the military stations of the cross, Sanabria sometimes lost his way. Impulsive and bullheaded, he ignored orders and once launched an unauthorized raid up a river to go after a FARC patrol. Sanabria racked up more demerits when, due to a bureaucratic snafu, he reported for duty to the wrong battalion in the wrong town. When he showed up at the correct base three days late, he was nearly kicked out of the army on the grounds that he had deserted.

Still, Sanabria hung on. And so did the Colombian military. Fearing that the FARC had gained the upper hand in the war, Washington boosted aid to the Bogotá government to about $700 million annually, mostly in military assistance. U.S. Special Forces began organizing and training elite battalions. Slowly, the Colombian Army began to turn itself around and take the initiative on the battlefield.

Its first major test came in February 2002. Three years of on-again, off-again peace negotiations between the FARC and the Pastrana government had finally collapsed. Sanabria was part of a massive military force dispatched to reoccupy a Switzerland-sized area of southern plains and jungle—including much of Caquetá—that had been ceded to the guerrillas as a goodwill gesture during the talks. Though it wasn't a rousing military victory—the guerrillas continued to lurk in the countryside—the troops managed to retake several towns and hamlets that had long been in the hands of the rebels. And at least they didn't get their asses handed to them on a platter.

Almost exactly one year after that operation, Sanabria was killing time at the military base in Florencia, the capital of Caquetá, when he saw the TV bulletin: just a few miles to the north, a Cessna surveillance plane had crashed into the mountains. Then came an even more startling piece of news: four gringos were aboard the aircraft.

CHAPTER 3

INTO THE WILD

I am my country's scapegoat, the plausible deniability warrior.
—ANONYMOUS MILITARY CONTRACTOR IN *Licensed to Kill,*
BY ROBERT YOUNG PELTON

THE IMPACT OF THE BLUE-AND-WHITE CESSNA slamming into the hillside snapped off the landing gear and ripped open the fuselage, showering the crew inside with dirt and debris. But the plane kept going, skidding uphill another fifty yards before finally coming to a halt just shy of a steep cliff. Tommy Janis had threaded the needle. He had stuck another heroic landing, this time not on a flat, asphalt runway but on a pitted grid of fractured mountain terrain.

"How the hell he put that airplane in there the way he did is just beyond me," said Jorge Sanjinés, the American helicopter pilot who flew over the crash site shortly afterward.

Despite the pain of two broken ribs, Keith Stansell unbuckled his shoulder harness and got himself out of the back of the crumpled Grand Caravan. He was in the middle of a pasture and a cow was staring at him.

He could see that both Marc Gonsalves and the other crew member, Colombian soldier Luis Alcides Cruz, seemed to be okay. Up front, Janis was moving but had a head injury. Copilot Tom Howes slumped against the Plexiglas window on the right side of the cockpit. Blood streamed from a gash above his left eye. The impact also fractured his nose and broke one of his teeth.

"It was incredible how damaged he was," Keith said. "I didn't think he was going to live."

Within a few minutes, the men heard gunshots. Guerrillas in camouflage uniforms, bandannas, and calf-high rubber boots were firing their rifles as they charged up the hill toward the plane. "I couldn't believe it," Marc said. "We'd survived the crash only to find ourselves in a situation that was arguably worse."

ALTHOUGH THE CESSNA HAD BELLY FLOPPED on top of a guerrilla patrol, the five men on board were just a seventeen-minute chopper ride from safety. Larandia, which was a collection of barracks and firing ranges next to a 6,000-foot-long gravel runway alongside the Orteguaza River, was Colombia's main military base in southern Caquetá state. It was also a bustling outpost of the American empire in the tropics. In the orange-brown mud, dozens of U.S. Army Special Forces troops ran training courses to form elite counterinsurgency units for the Colombian military. These newly formed battalions were to help the Colombian Army take back the initiative in the war and reclaim territory from the FARC. They were also there to ensure that El Billar was remembered as the low point in the long slog to victory rather than as Colombia's Dien Bien Phu.

At the end of their fifteen-hour days, the American trainers went to a separate barracks where they did their own cooking and cleaning and relaxed in the evenings by watching satellite television, surfing the Internet, or downing a few beers in their air-conditioned rooms. They had four days off for every month worked and traveled to Bogotá and other cities to relax. Off base, they were allowed to date Colombian women but were told to be on the alert for guerrilla spies.

"If all of a sudden you have five perfect-ten girlfriends, just remember:

you are not that big of a stud," one Special Forces officer joked to his colleagues as they lunched on fried chicken and flirted with the waitresses at a riverside restaurant on the base.

But these Green Beret macho men—many of whom had seen action in Afghanistan and would go on to serve in Iraq—were also frustrated because they rarely got to see the war zone. To avoid getting sucked too far into the queasy mix of guerrilla and drug war in Colombia, a place few Americans cared about, the U.S. Congress had in the late 1990s limited the number of troops allowed in-country to four hundred, a number that was later upped to six hundred. The Special Forces could train, provide advice and intelligence, and command war games but there was to be no direct involvement in the conflict.

To get around the troop caps and some of the operational restrictions in Colombia, first the Clinton, then the Bush, administrations leaned heavily on private contractors. These were the grease-stained outriders traipsing around Larandia in baseball caps, cargo pants, and hiking boots, and these were the Americans who were taking the biggest risks in Colombia. It could lead to some confusion. Rather than an army of one under a single chain of command there were, in effect, four separate detachments at Larandia, each with its own agenda, its own rules of engagement: Colombian police agents, Colombian Army troops, U.S. Special Forces, and American private contractors. And as word spread at the base that the crew in the Grand Caravan had gone down just outside the wire, the hired guns—not the active-duty American soldiers—were the first to scramble in a desperate bid to save them.

MERCENARIES, OR FREELANCE FIGHTERS, HAVE OFFERED their services to the highest bidder for as long as wars have been fought. But for much of the past century, governments held a monopoly over the use of force. Protecting national security was deemed such a vital task that it became the sole domain of the state. But in the age of globalization and government downsizing, nations began outsourcing everything from health care and tax collection to postal service and prisons. In the name of market-driven efficiency, privatizing military services was the next step. A new generation of for-profit corporations sprang up, offering everything from cooks and drivers to intelligence analysts for Colombia and interrogation teams for the Abu Ghraib prison in Iraq. These private military firms became an essential component of the American war machine.

Many were born at the end of the cold war. Militaries were slimming down. The U.S. armed forces were trimmed from 2.2 million to 1.6 million troops. Yet from Bosnia to Sierra Leone, a new crop of messy conflicts was breaking out. To temporarily bolster their armies when they wanted to intervene, nations could now turn to Blackwater USA, DynCorp International, Halliburton, and others. These firms could provide a surge of specialists in the art of war, folks who wouldn't permanently pad government payrolls. Blackwater, which later changed its name to Xe, could field its own 1,700-man private army with helicopter gunships, armored vehicles, attack aircraft, and remote-controlled blimps. But more often, the contractors were the ones keeping the regular troops battle-ready. They were the men and women washing the uniforms, frying the eggs, and driving the gasoline tankers. The Halliburton subsidiary KBR in 2001 became a de facto quartermaster for the U.S. military when it won a ten-year contract to feed and lodge the troops on short notice. As the world's sole superpower, the United States became its biggest military contractor. Between 1994 and 2002—before the Iraq War accelerated the outsourcing trend—the Pentagon signed some three thousand contracts with private military firms totaling more than $300 billion.

"That is how the modern world works," said Marc Grossman, who was U.S. under secretary of state for political affairs when the Grand Caravan crashed. "If, as a society, we're not prepared to have federal employees do these jobs, then you need contractors."

There was also a widespread, though sometimes inaccurate, perception that contractors were a cheaper alternative to training U.S. troops, keeping them deployed, and paying their retirement benefits. When it came to short-term military engagements, it generally was cheaper to go to the private sector. What's more, the price of the paltry health insurance and death benefits provided for injured or killed contractors was a bargain compared with federal payouts for U.S. troops. Yet there were always hidden costs. For example, so many troops quit for higher-paying posts with private companies that the U.S. military had to increase its reenlistment bonuses to make it more attractive to stay in the army.

So-called sunken costs also had to be factored in. That was the money already invested in military personnel that was suddenly lost. After receiving years of taxpayer-financed training and equipment, many soldiers jumped to the private sector. Working for DynCorp, Halliburton, or other firms, they performed the same jobs that they did in the army, navy, air force, or Marines, but for fatter salaries that, ultimately, were paid by the federal government, which signed and paid for the contracts. Meanwhile, white-elephant projects, no-bid contracts, and cost-overruns racked up by private contractors in Iraq punctured more holes in the cost-savings argument. The abuses led some critics to brand these firms as "the coalition of the billing."

Using these contractors may not have cut *financial* costs but it did reduce the *political* costs when the White House wanted to undertake risky overseas missions. On the front end, the executive branch could avoid the political costs of sending in U.S. troops to dangerous areas while, on the back end, it was easier to skirt the political consequences if something went wrong. Even in Iraq, where their role was well-publicized, contractors obscured the mission's human costs. For years after the fall of Baghdad, the U.S. troop level of 140,000 had been drilled into people's heads as if that was the total American commitment. Few people realized that another 140,000 contractors supported the military mission, people who a generation ago would have been uniformed, gun-toting soldiers. Grim milestones, like when the number of U.S. troops killed in action reached 4,000, caused the nation to collectively shake its head in sorrow. Yet by that time another 1,100 contractors had been killed and 13,000 had been wounded.

The contractors punching the clock in Colombia were even more obscure because few Americans knew the program existed. The Bogotá government was deemed a loyal U.S. ally that was worth propping up, but this conflict had churned on for decades. It was widely believed that direct American involvement would stiffen the resolve of the guerrillas and cause an anti-Yankee outcry across Latin America. By contrast, hiring pilots, intelligence experts, and other privateers was a way to escalate without *appearing* to escalate. In the words of one former U.S. Army intelligence analyst, through the sleight of hand of contracting, the U.S. military was "increasingly everywhere and nowhere."

Using contractors in Colombia "is a lot easier than going before Congress and saying: 'This is a priority for us. We believe it's worth putting American lives at stake,'" said Peter Singer of the Brookings Institution in Washington, D.C. "But if it's such a great idea, how come they don't want to step up to the plate by asking for U.S. soldiers?"

In some ways, Colombia served as a proving ground for many of the contractors who would go on to live, work, and sometimes die in Iraq and Afghanistan. In 2002, about $150 million of the $400 million in American military aid for Colombia was spent on contractors—including $8.6 million for California Microwave and its Cessnas. By 2006, the amount spent on contractors for Colombia had doubled.

Privatizing military and intelligence operations put more power in the hands of the executive branch while the U.S. Congress, the government branch with the power to formally declare war, was often kept out of these decisions. Lawmakers had almost no access to these contracts because private companies considered the documents proprietary information. Congress had more access to information about the CIA than about private military contractors.

One think tank investigator, Sanho Tree of the Institute for Policy Studies, recalled his frustration at trying to find out more about DynCorp International, an Irving, Texas–based company with the most lucrative contracts in Colombia. He said it was like a game of keep-away. "DynCorp said the State Department wouldn't let them talk about it," Tree said. "So I go to the State Department and they say: 'Oh, no. These are private contractors. There are competitive trade secrets involved. We can't tell you anything.'"

WHAT DYNCORP DOES COULD BE SEEN in the peaks and valleys of Colombia's central Andean ridge where rows of opium poppies formed radiant, red-and-green flower beds. For heroin junkies, this was the Big Rock Candy Mountain. But for DynCorp contract pilots, the poppies painted a tantalizing target. Their air raids looked like kamikaze practice. Strapped into his armor-plated cockpit, one of the pilots, who called himself Tato, screamed toward the earth, then leveled off at the last minute and released a cloud of herbicide that saturated a two-acre poppy field. Helicopter gunships hovered nearby to protect the pilots from rebel sharpshooters trying to protect the fields. Still, the planes were always coming home riddled with bullet holes that had to be covered with riveted metal patches. Another rebel trick was to stretch wires between trees and snag the wings of the aircraft. *Soldier of Fortune* magazine headlined its story on the DynCorp pilots "Pray and Spray."

"Someone once asked me if I do extreme sports, like bungee jumping," said Tato, who like most DynCorp pilots refused to give his real name. "But why should I? I have an extreme job."

The DynCorp spray missions, part of a massive aerial eradication program run by the U.S. State Department, were considered far more dangerous than the better-paying California Microwave jobs. Among contractors, orbiting above drug labs at thirteen thousand feet—far above the range of guerrilla gunfire—was considered fairly cushy, if rather boring, compared with the aerial acrobatics of fumigation. Nearly a dozen contract pilots had been killed while spraying drug plantations, including three Americans. During an especially perilous six-month period in 2003, six aircraft were either shot down or hit trees and three pilots were killed. That's why the crop dusters had their own safety net. Helicopter gunships and search-and-rescue choppers, manned by DynCorp and Colombian Army and police crews, were always nearby.

By contrast, the men aboard the Grand Caravan worked for a different company on a U.S. Defense Department contract. They didn't have their own rescue teams but there was an informal understanding that if they ever went down, the State Department contractors at DynCorp would bail out the Defense Department contractors at California Microwave.

"It was a roll of the dice they wanted to make," said John McLaughlin, who was the State Department's Air Wing chief who managed the spray program and the search-and-rescue teams. "The crews on the Caravans were confident we'd get them out."

Among those with the ability—and the cojones—was DynCorp chopper pilot Jorge Sanjinés. A naturalized U.S. citizen born in Peru, Sanjinés was hanging out at Larandia in February 2001 when a mayday call came in. It turned out that Colonel Leonardo Gallego, the hard-charging commander of the antinarcotics division of the Colombian police, was pinned down by FARC rebels fifty miles east of the base. He and his men couldn't get back to their helicopters.

But there was a delay in getting permission from the U.S. embassy to scramble. At the time, Gallego was viewed in Washington as a drug-war hero and the DynCorp crews were itching to save him. But they were not supposed to inject themselves into obvious combat situations. To make sure that U.S. private sector forces wouldn't end up shooting it out with rebels, the copilots and gunners on the choppers had to be Colombians. Only the copilots could give the order to fire, and only in self-defense. But all the rules now went out the window. As the police SOS calls grew more urgent, Sanjinés and his men lifted into the air and went on the offensive.

Using their side-mounted GAU-17 .30-caliber miniguns, the DynCorp chopper crews blasted rebel positions. The timely show of force made all the difference: Gallego and fifteen other police troops managed to scamper back to their birds and escape.

Now Sanjinés was in trouble. Rebel bullets had riddled his chopper, knocking out an engine. Sanjinés was leaking oil and losing altitude. Yet there was still hope because his chopper was a UH-1N which, unlike earlier models of the Vietnam-era Huey, was a twin-engine. By tossing boxes of ammunition and other gear over the side, the crew lightened their load, allowing Sanjinés to limp back to Larandia. Once on the ground, mechanics discovered so many bullet holes in the Huey they quit counting at twenty-five.

DynCorp gave Sanjinés a certificate of appreciation for saving Gallego. Yet officials at the American embassy were livid. Not only had Sanjinés launched without permission, but it was believed, at first, that he had been shot down because he was so late getting back to the base. The firefight appeared to mark the first time that U.S. personnel had become directly involved in a major firefight with the FARC. If Sanjinés had gone missing in action, the incident could have led to demands back in Washington for scaling back the U.S. involvement in the drug war in Colombia.

"The embassy was going bananas," Sanjinés said years later as he stood in the kitchen of his Bogotá house drinking instant coffee from a Lockheed-Martin mug. "I almost got my ass fired."

ACCOUNTS OF WHAT HAPPENED AT LARANDIA on the day the Grand Caravan went down differ wildly. U.S. diplomats and military officers monitoring the situation from Bogotá and elsewhere insisted that they pulled out all the stops to save the Americans. But according to several contractors and American soldiers involved in the operation, rigid protocols for the contractors and rules handcuffing direct action by U.S. troops led to crucial delays.

The Cessna disappeared into the mountains on February 13, 2003, at 8:43 a.m. The final GPS coordinates sent in by Keith Stansell as well as the plane's emergency beacon put the crash site near the village of El Para, just twenty miles northeast of Larandia. But the soldiers and contractors at the base knew every second counted. After all, it was on a stretch of highway not far from El Para where, one year earlier, FARC guerrillas had kidnapped Íngrid Betancourt, a Colombian presidential candidate. Grabbing Betancourt was part of the FARC's strategy to seize high-profile politicians as well as police and soldiers, and then force the government to exchange them for imprisoned guerrillas. If the rescue teams at Larandia didn't bust ass to the crash site, the guerrillas would soon have five new bargaining chips.

Three DynCorp chopper crews scrambled to their Hueys. The plan was for the search-and-rescue chopper to swoop down and pick up the five downed Caravan crew members while the two other aircraft hovered nearby providing protective fire should the guerrillas attack. "We were always ready to launch in a heartbeat," said Keith Sparks, who was DynCorp's program manager in Colombia. "But that day got very complicated."

Larandia was a Colombian military installation, so the base commander had final approval over some of the takeoffs and landings. On that Thursday morning, a Colombian general was on his way to Larandia to inspect the aircraft. According to the State Department's McLaughlin, the base commander wanted all of the choppers in place when his boss arrived. So the DynCorp crews stayed put. McLaughlin said he urged officials at the U.S. embassy to work out new rules with the Colombians that would allow his rescue teams to spring into action immediately. But he said embassy officials "blew off" his request.

Anne Patterson, then the U.S. ambassador in Bogotá, said the contractors launched immediately and she called McLaughlin's assertion "categorically untrue." She said the helicopters were on the scene within thirty minutes.

But Santiago Sánchez, a DynCorp medic and former Green Beret who was at Larandia that day, said he was kept on the ground at gunpoint. When word of the crash spread, he grabbed his medical kit, an M4 rifle, and ten clips of ammunition, and hopped aboard one of the Hueys. Fearing the aircraft would take off without permission from the base commander, a Colombian Army officer ordered twenty troops to surround the aircraft and told the pilot to shut down the engine. On the tarmac, a half dozen American contractors were frantically dialing the U.S. embassy on their cell phones to speed things up, but Sanchez's chopper never got the green light to launch.

"Everybody was saying: 'This is bullshit. We're wasting time,'" Sanchez said.

Finally, McLaughlin said, the Colombian general arrived at Larandia and he promptly cleared the rescue crews for takeoff. But a precious fifteen minutes had been lost.

Two hundred miles east of the crash site, Sanjinés, the DynCorp chopper pilot who had helped rescue Gallego, was on a mission escorting crop dusters. Along with two other helicopters, Sanjinés was ordered to speed to the Grand Caravan crash site. It took them nearly two hours but they still managed to get there before the Colombian Army chopper crews arrived from the Larandia base—just fifteen miles away.

Another group of commandos at Larandia never even made it outside the wire: a crack A-team made up of American Special Forces. Minutes after the plane crashed, their commander, Colonel Kevin Christie, ordered the Green Berets to get ready—just in case.

"Had we gotten there while the crew members were still in the vicinity of the crash site, there's a very good chance that we could have recovered them," Christie said. "Ten or twenty Green Berets would have kicked the rebels' asses."

But Christie didn't control the U.S. helicopters at the base and said he needed embassy permission to launch. And for U.S. diplomats, giving the green light would have signaled a change in the rules of engagement by potentially sending active-duty American forces into direct combat with the FARC. A decision of that magnitude could only be made in Washington.

"We live in a political world," said General Remo Butler, who at the time headed the U.S. military's Special Operations Command for Central and South America. "And I don't think the Colombians would have taken too heartily to a bunch of Americans running a combat operation in Colombia."

In the end, about a dozen Special Forces troops ended up sitting with their backpacks and rifles next to the choppers at the Larandia airstrip as Christie urged embassy officials to spring his men. "We waited about twelve hours or so and nothing happened," he said.

BACK AT THE CRASH SITE, Luis Alcides Cruz, the Colombian Army sergeant and host-nation rider, crawled out of the wrecked Cessna after Keith and Marc. Then Cruz saw the guerrillas rushing for the plane. Several of Cruz's colleagues had been kidnapped by the FARC and he had earlier vowed to his family that he would not allow himself to be taken hostage. Though badly injured in the pelvis, Cruz told the Americans that they all should flee. But their years in the U.S. military had drummed a certain credo into Keith and Marc: no man left behind.

"He [Cruz] was saying: 'That's the FARC! Guerrillas! Guerrillas!' He wanted to run," Stansell said. "I was worried about the plane catching on fire. . . . If the pilots would have burned to death, I don't think either Marc or I could have lived with ourselves."

Keith managed to pull Tommy Janis and Tom Howes from the cockpit but the guerrillas were charging up the mountainside. Although the crew carried with them a bag filled with pistols and an M4 automatic rifle, Keith pitched the sack down the slope. He figured that trying to hold off a platoon of sixty FARC rebels would only get them all killed. Cruz was scared he'd be executed on the spot for belonging to the Colombian Army, and he pleaded with Keith to tell the guerrillas that he was an American.

"We crashed right on top of them," Marc said. "The guerrillas had us in their possession within two or three minutes."

As the guerrillas approached, the men put up their arms and yelled: "*No armas. No armas.*" The rebels were youngsters, between the ages of fourteen and twenty, but they knew how to handle their weapons. They forced Keith, Marc, and Tom down the mountain slope toward a wooden hut. There, the rebels gave the men lemonade and offered Tom a rag to staunch the flow of blood from the gash in his forehead. By then, they had lost sight of Cruz, and Janis was missing.

Inside the hut, the three contractors were forced to strip to their underwear and the rebels frisked them three times looking for tracking devices. They even ran their fingers through the men's hair and between their toes and threatened to shoot them if they found a microchip.

"The little fucks were so young they could have thought that a bit of toe jam was a microchip and opened fire," said Keith, who was already angry because they'd taken his cash and a photo of his son, Kyle, out of his wallet. "They'd sure as shit never seen a microchip before, so how would they know if they'd found one?"

Then Keith heard the sound of a helicopter. A chopper carrying one of the DynCorp search-and-rescue teams—that had been delayed fifteen minutes at Larandia waiting for permission to takeoff—swooped low over the rebel position firing its automatic miniguns at two thousand rounds per minute.

In the chaos, the contractors briefly considered making a run for it before their guards could get fully organized, but the bullets were raining down on their proposed escape route. Then the rebels herded Marc and Tom across a five-hundred-foot clearing and up a hill toward another shack. Keith followed and at one point was caught out in the open between two groups of rebels. Spotting Keith, the chopper pilot began hovering directly overhead, unsure of what to do next. If he tried to land to pick up Keith, the guerrillas would have opened fire and perhaps executed the hostages. But if the rebel gunmen initiated a firefight, the chopper's miniguns would have laid waste to the guerrilla unit. Keith described the scene as a Mexican standoff.

"They were all within range to blast each other, but it was like suicide for both sides," Keith said. "The gunner was looking at me and signaling to me that there was nothing they could do."

When the Colombian soldiers arrived hours later, they found the body of Cruz, who apparently tried to flee. His neck was dislocated and he had been shot in the back. Tommy Janis was also dead. A grainy Colombian Army video of the crash site shows Janis, dressed in jeans, T-shirt, and a leather jacket, lying on his back in the brush, his lifeless body twisted in the bushes, his legs facing up. He was killed with a shot to the back of the head.

His widow, Judith Janis of Montgomery, Alabama, said her husband would have tried to escape at all costs. "The last thing he was going to do was to be taken hostage," she said.

On the ground, FARC guerrillas began herding Keith, Marc, and Tom toward the jungle canopy, beginning a forced march that would last twenty-four days. "I sensed we were all about to enroll in the FARC finishing school, enter into a tear-down and rebuild phase of our lives," Tom said. "I wasn't sure how well suited I was for the task of making it through,"

CHAPTER 4

THE GREAT DIVIDE

Now this is the law of the jungle—
as old and as true as the sky;
And the Wolf that shall keep it may prosper,
but the Wolf that shall break it must die.
—RUDYARD KIPLING, *The Jungle Book*

S HORTLY AFTER THE CESSNA GRAND CARAVAN crashed, Lieutenant Jorge Sanabria and his troops were dispatched to Caquetá, the de facto rebel province of FARC-land, to find the missing gringos. El Gordo, the chubby kid who had grown up in the back of the church in Sogamoso, the hard-charging officer who sometimes went too far, was now in command of Vulture Company, which was joined in the jungle by another company, this one named Destroyer. Both groups, numbering 147 soldiers, were part of the Fiftieth Counterguerrilla Battalion.

In addition to facing the guerrillas, the troops had to fight the jungle and all its mysteries and dangers. They had to face down giant cockroaches, carnivorous ants, and clouds of mosquitoes—flying viral-filled vectors. Hairy brown tarantulas crawled into their hammocks and the soldiers were constantly wielding their machetes and hacking at venomous snakes. At night, ants fell on their faces and the acid from their urine would burn the soldiers' skin. The fecund floor was a damp, moldering carpet of decaying roots, trunks, and slime. Advancing through this spaghetti of vines and undergrowth was like blazing a trail through concertina wire. Overhead, the ceiba, rubber, and palm trees sealed in the humidity, sweat, and stink, but kept out the light, making the men feel they were trapped inside a great pumpkin. The soldiers were just a few degrees north of the equator but hardly saw the sun, and their skin took on the olive hue of the terminally ill. They were in a no-man's-land. Or, as Colombians liked to put it: *en el culo del mundo*—in the asshole of the world.

"It was the hardest mission I'd ever been on," said Corporal Wilson Sarmiento, a nine-year Colombian Army vet. "People were demoralized, but we were being pushed to kill the rebels."

The men plodded ahead, slowly, numbly, like low-altitude sherpas, burdened with Galil automatic rifles, M60 machine guns, bandoliers of bullets, grenade launchers, radios, medical kits, canteens, sacks of rice, bottles of cooking oil, aluminum pots, elastic rope, hammocks, rubber boots, and extra clothes.

Some of the men were also saddled with whimsical first names, a not uncommon custom in the Latin American outback where peasants—perhaps figuring their kids weren't going anywhere in life anyway—became suddenly inventive, historical, and ironic at the hour of birth. The result? Infants, little boys, and old ladies running around with names like Llanta de Milagro (Miracle Tire), Gracias a Dios (Thanks to God), Yusnavy (U.S. Navy), Kotex, Hiroshima, and Hitler. Reflecting influences ranging from the Russian Revolution to Mary Shelley novels, the soldiers from Vulture and Destroyer carried monikers like Lenin and Ilich, Yonid and Yuber, Frudis and Frankistey. One GI was named Nixon while another was called Pobre, which in Spanish means poor. But in the end, they were really just a band of no-names, human driftwood harboring few ambitions. In the contemptuous nomenclature of the Bogotá elite, they were "Indians," dark-skinned lumpen marching and sweating and slicing a path through the rain forest toward the ultimate sacrifice.

And for what? As the mission dragged on, Walter Suárez (a pseudonym he requested to protect his identity), one of the GIs from Destroyer Company, recalled there was a lot of bitching about sticking their necks out and becoming rebel chew toys for the wrong cause. Dozens of GIs were suffering from malaria, dehydration, and diarrhea. The operation had gone on for so long that they had eaten through their rations and were now foraging for food. Running low on hope and calories, they gathered rainwater from banana leaves and hunted vultures, parrots, and spider monkeys to go with their diminishing stocks of rice. *Well, this wasn't much good*, Suárez thought. He'd joined the army so he *wouldn't* go hungry.

At twenty-two, Suárez was one of five sons born to a part-time carpenter and street-corner hot-dog vendor. The family home in the small town of Mesetas in southern Colombia was always tense, with arguments arising from the combination of too many people and too few pesos. Suárez longed to escape. His journey eventually took him to the front lines to fight the guerrillas, but he nearly went over to the other side.

That's because Suárez was born and raised in FARC-land. His hometown, Mesetas, was located about ninety miles northeast of the spot where the Grand Caravan crashed and was part of a vast expanse of flatiron plains and dense Amazon jungle lying south and east of the Andes. The topography was mostly tropical lowlands except for the Macarena massif, a 100-mile-long ridge that mysteriously jutted 7,500 feet above the flats and predated the Andes by millions of years. Largely unpopulated and cut off from Bogotá, the region was teeming with rebels long before Fidel Castro inspired legions of Latin American leftists to rise up in revolt. When famed Harvard ethnobotanist Richard Evans Schultes visited the Macarena ridge where he discovered several new plant species, the local military commander eventually suggested that he clear out; fighting between the army and insurgents erupted shortly afterward. That was in 1951.

When Spanish conquistadors marched through Colombia in the 1500s they largely ignored the south because it lacked gold or anything else worth claiming. Even at the beginning of the twenty-first century, this region, which makes up half of Colombia's territory, is home to just ten percent of the country's 45 million people. Mesetas sat on the ragged edge, a place that was easy for public officials to ignore because there were so few votes to harvest. That's why driving the pitted mud roads could shake loose one's fillings, why there were no antibiotics in the claptrap rural clinics, why courts, schools, and other signs of a functioning government were seldom seen.

Noting that Colombian senators are chosen in nationwide balloting rather than in regional elections, former Colombian lawmaker Luis Eladio Pérez admitted that he hardly bothered to campaign in his impoverished home state of Nariño. He would occasionally hand out bottles of rum and soccer balls in an effort to win the few votes the state had to offer, but he spent most of his time stumping in the big cities. "In just one Bogotá neighborhood, I could get more votes than in all of Nariño," Pérez said. As a result, once he was safely ensconced in the Senate for another four-year term, Pérez largely ignored his home-state constituents.

The guerrillas in Nariño and many other southern states often outnumbered government troops. Casa verde, or the Green House, the long-time headquarters of the FARC high command, was located only a few miles from Mesetas. The guerrillas were the local power brokers, and homesteaders in these areas had little choice but to collaborate with them. To defy the FARC meant expulsion from the community or death.

Besides, some of these peasants—especially coca farmers—viewed the Bogotá government as their sworn enemy. Most of the nation's drug plantations were located south of the mountains, and the crop-duster planes that swooped down to poison their livelihood provided the only real evidence of the state's presence. The guerrillas, by contrast, purchased their coca and pointed their AK-47 rifles at the enemy aircraft. The coca farmers and the FARC may not have been backslapping buddies, but they were loyal business partners.

"These people did not feel like they were citizens of Colombia," said Monsignor Luis Augusto Castro, a bishop for twelve years in the coca-growing southern states of Caquetá and Putumayo. "They were abandoned. And the guerrillas set out to make the people identify with them."

Castro recalled traveling by boat to a tiny village on the Caquetá River and was overwhelmed by the despair and alienation. The people begged the priest to help secure funds for a shelter so the schoolchildren could stay put during the week rather than commuting through the wilderness where they could be attacked by jaguars. They were also concerned about a group of outsiders who had moved into the area and posed a threat to their daughters. The "strangers" turned out to be soldiers. Though willing to construct a military base, the government rejected Castro's proposal to build a hostel for the students. Two months later, FARC guerrillas overran the army garrison.

EVER SINCE THE FARC GAINED A foothold in southern Colombia, this area had been caught in a vicious circle. Classic counterinsurgency doctrine says that victory is achieved by winning over the civilians and isolating the guerrillas. But because the FARC dominated much of the countryside, the Bogotá government—when it bothered to pay attention to the southern wards—focused almost exclusively on attacking guerrilla units and wiping out the drug crops that provided them with so much cash. And a succession of U.S. administrations endorsed the strategy. Since 2000, about 80 percent of American aid to Colombia consisted of military, police, and antidrug assistance. The policy was all stick with just a light garnish of carrot.

U.S. and Colombian officials believed that it made little sense to invest huge sums in health, education, and economic programs when the rebels would simply steal the money, sow mayhem, and drive away investors. And these officials had a point.

During elections, the guerrillas allowed the voting process to go forward, but they rigged the outcome by promoting friendly candidates and forcing independents out of the races. They placed plainclothes rebels in local government posts, giving the FARC access to financial information and influence over personnel decisions. They made mayors promise to donate 10 percent of their budgets to the rebels and to award public works contracts to companies allied with the guerrillas. "If the guerrillas can pass out 100 new houses," said one Colombian Army intelligence officer, "they end up with 100 new friends."

The government managed to institute a few programs designed to convince drug farmers in the south to switch to legal crops. But they were so poorly run that their main effect was to convince farmers that coca was the only realistic way to make a profit. As a result, the number of coca farmers multiplied. And massive aerial eradication, the burning of hundreds of drug labs, and the arrest of growers hardly made a dent. When their fields were fumigated, coca growers would move on to new plots and plant more.

In 2003, the year the Grand Caravan crashed, peasant farmers successfully cultivated 212,420 acres of coca. Five years and hundreds of millions of dollars later, they still raised 200,070 acres of coca, according to the United Nations. Even when authorities registered a reduction in Colombian coca, drug production expanded in neighboring Peru and Bolivia. As a result, on street corners across the United States, cocaine remained potent, cheap, and abundant.

Far more planning, resources, and thought went into military operations even though developing a prosperous legal economy in the southern outback was perhaps the greater challenge. Farmers lacked decent roads or nearby markets to sell legitimate products. They would haul gunnysacks of tomatoes to town on the backs of mules only to reach the market with a sticky mush that resembled ketchup. Cocaine traffickers, by contrast, went door-to-door buying up farmers' coca and paying them far more than the going rate for yucca or plantains.

"We are telling peasants to grow legal crops that must be transported on vehicles they do not have, over roads that do not exist, to sell in domestic and international markets to which they do not have access," said Sanho Tree, a Colombia analyst at the Institute for Policy Studies in Washington, D.C. "These peasants don't stand a chance."

A more sophisticated project was an animal concentrates plant in southern Putumayo state that was built to convince farmers to switch to legal crops. But the peasants were offered just three cents a pound for their yucca, so many went back to coca. After two years, the plant closed down and the machinery was carted away.

Tree, only half-jokingly, talked of putting together a coffee-table book about the failed experiments funded by the U.S. and Colombian governments and the U.N. The "before" photos would feature ribbon-cutting ceremonies with foreign diplomats, gleaming plants, and commemorative plaques while the "after" photos would show rusting equipment, abandoned buildings, and sad-eyed *campesinos*. He planned to call the book *Fiasco!*

Had Tree's book ever been completed, it would have needed several pages for the infamous campaign to turn Putumayo into a haven for hearts of palm. When the United Nations first conceived the idea in 1992, world prices for hearts of palm were soaring. This mildly tart salad vegetable is one of the few products that prospers in the thin jungle soil of Putumayo. But because of cost overruns and construction errors, the plant took six years to build. When it finally opened in 2001, Brazil, Costa Rica, and Ecuador were exporting tons of palm hearts and the price had collapsed. Adding to the madness, U.S.-financed crop dusters aiming for Putumayo's vast coca plantations sometimes missed and hit rows of palm trees.

It was partly the farmers' own doing because they often raised coca alongside their palm hearts, just in case the grand experiment fizzled. As he examined the yellowing leaves of his dying, five-foot-tall palm trees, Manuel Burbano, a portly farmer who also dabbled in coca, frowned and said: "I was just about to harvest these."

The end result was a shortage. During a visit to the canning plant a year after the inauguration, there were hardly any palm hearts to process. When a small shipment arrived, employees wearing T-shirts with the slogan "Without coca we all get ahead" spent two hours cutting the white stalks with paring knives and jamming the pieces into brine-filled cans and jars. Still, plant manager Jorge Yoria was upbeat. He said he'd finally found a solution to the supply problem. He was now buying raw palm hearts from Ecuador.

THE NORTH WAS RICH, THE SOUTH was poor, and the Andes Mountains served as Colombia's dividing line. People living in the more modern and prosperous top half of the country had access to decent clinics and schools, drove along paved highways, and viewed the government as a friendly force. Draft-age lads in the north, like Jorge Sanabria of Sogamoso, went into the army. But young men from Putumayo and other parts of the south, like Walter Suárez of Mesetas, often ended up immersed in the drug trade or joining the FARC.

As the county seat, Mesetas was home to a few government offices and a small police barracks surrounded by sandbags and wrapped in chain-link fencing so that any grenades lobbed at the building would bounce off. Beyond the town limits, the rebels were in control. When boys hit their teens, plainclothes militiamen came around to give them an earful about the revolution. Youths were invited to political meetings where they received a toxic catechism on Marxism, people power, and the creative destruction of the revolution. Most of this went over the heads of these kids, but they liked the smart uniforms, the shiny oiled rifles, and the promise of three meals a day.

True, it was a one-way ticket. Once they joined the FARC, they couldn't go back, and deserters were tracked down and killed. Life had to be supremely wretched to view the FARC as the only path toward upward mobility. But the swelling ranks of the guerrilla army proved that there was a surplus of misery in the Colombian countryside. For boys who were from broken homes or too poor to go to school and were already herding cows and picking coca leaves from dawn to dusk, there were perks to embracing the cause. However twisted, at least it *was* a cause—and it provided a kind of gyroscope for their rudderless lives. Joining the FARC gave these kids instant respect; it was like joining the toughest gang in the barrio.

The rebel army also seemed like a way out for young women. Sick of an abusive stepfather or destined for a life sentence of bearing children, washing clothes, and putting up with a drunken, unfaithful spouse, teenaged girls might see a future in the FARC. Often, these adolescents emerged as camouflaged ninjas who carried guns, sometimes ordered the men around, and were considered valued members of the team. Females made up more than one-third of FARC forces.

Some of them ended up in a sprawling FARC encampment a few hours south of Mesetas. Built during the peace talks in what was once the DMZ, it was one of the largest, most upscale rebel camps in Colombia. Yet the daily routine was tough, monotonous, and often dangerous. Many of the rebels sported scars from shrapnel and bullet wounds. The days began at 4:30 a.m. when the sky was still pitch-black. As the first rebels awoke and struggled out of their wooden bunk beds, they began to softly clap their hands in a stealth rendition of reveille. Soon, the wooden barracks that held 150 bunks was bustling with groggy youngsters pulling on rubber boots and buttoning their camouflage fatigues.

After a breakfast of strawberry-flavored oatmeal and coffee, cooked over woodstoves and served from massive aluminum pots, the rebels marched into the fields where they tended plots of watermelon, banana, and sugarcane. Others fed chicken and pigs while one young guerrilla tossed handfuls of Purina fish chow into a network of artificial ponds and watched as piranhalike cachama attacked the pellets. There was a pharmacy and a photo lab, concrete shower stalls, water tanks, irrigation hoses, and a parking lot paved with a thick layer of asphalt.

Lingering over breakfast, several rebels explained why they joined the FARC. "There is no discrimination and more than enough food," said Olga Lucía, a young black woman who wore dreadlocks and commanded a squad of twelve rebels. "This is real democracy. What I never had in my civilian life, I have here." Another FARC foot soldier, Freddy, sat on the bottom level of a bunk bed adjusting the armband on his camouflage fatigues. He wanted to be a doctor but dropped out of school after fifth grade to go to work and support his parents. Unable to find a decent job, he joined the FARC when he was sixteen. "Things are different when you are from the lower class. If you don't have any opportunities in life, you don't have any aspirations."

The rebel tenderfoots were quick to slam Colombia's ruling class and the way the system seemed slanted against poor folks from the countryside. But when asked about Karl Marx and Vladimir Lenin, many drew a blank. Some of them wore T-shirts depicting Ernesto "Che" Guevara, but they couldn't explain why the Argentine-born rebel who helped win the Cuban revolution had become an icon for leftists around the world. Recruits "do not come here because they are convinced of the revolutionary process," Carlos Antonio Lozada, a FARC commander, said as he wandered around the camp with his three-year-old daughter in his arms. "They come here due to some kind of crisis. Here is where they get their ideology." The basic tenets of Marxism were taught at political classes held every afternoon. There were also literacy courses for those who had yet to learn to read and write. But sometimes the lectures were canceled in favor of American-made movies. The rebels were a bit hazy on the exploits of Che Guevara and some believed that South American independence hero Simón Bolívar— who died in 1830—was still alive. But they were all up to speed with the

Hollywood action hero now projected on the screen before them: Steven Seagal.

IF THE YOUNGSTERS OF MESETAS COULDN'T be won over by the glories of scar tissue and heavy weapons, FARC operatives began leaning on their parents to sacrifice their sons and daughters. If that didn't work, they snatched potential foot soldiers off the streets and press-ganged them into their ranks. And as Walter Suárez approached the age when he should have been joining the Boy Scouts, he faced a pending date with rebel recruiters. "Once you turn thirteen or fourteen, the FARC comes after you," Suárez said years later as he tucked into a plate of fried chicken at a Bogotá restaurant. "I had to leave so the guerrillas wouldn't take me away."

When Suárez turned fourteen, his parents put him on a bus to Bogotá where his grandfather lived in the sprawling slum of Soacha. Once again, money was short. Suárez dropped out of high school and picked up a series of odd jobs. It was a struggle, but at least he wasn't slogging through the mud with the FARC. Then his draft notice arrived. Suárez had escaped the FARC but he could not escape the war.

Yet as he passed through basic training, pulled guard duty, and marched into the countryside hunting guerrillas, Suárez seemed to have found his calling. Like his teenaged buddies from Mesetas who strayed into the FARC, Suárez now wore a camouflage uniform and received three meals a day. He also felt his first twinges of patriotism. The guerrillas had taken control of his hometown and much of the rest of the nation. He had nearly been transferred to a southern jungle town called Miraflores shortly before the FARC attacked its antinarcotics base and kidnapped more than a hundred soldiers and policemen. This was yet another military disaster on a par with El Billar. Amid the burgeoning rebel threat, Suárez decided that a career in the army was a way to bring about a better Colombia. After serving his eighteen months of obligatory service, he re-upped for another four years.

Like Suárez, Hanner Daza was a lost boy from the Colombian countryside who thought he had found safe haven in the military. The youngest of ten brothers and sisters, Daza grew up on his family's ten-acre farm in rural

Cauca state. Although a police station was located just two miles away, the cops rarely ventured into the hills because the area was thick with FARC guerrillas. The rebels would stop by the Daza spread—home to a few cows and patches of corn and beans—chat up the daughters and show off their AK-47s to the boys in a slow-motion recruiting campaign. Carlos Daza, the family patriarch, frowned at the visits and feared that Hanner, who was only thirteen, would disappear into the hills with the guerrillas. But he couldn't do much about it.

"I scolded my kids and told the guerrillas that I didn't want them to recruit my sons," said Aura Gómez, Hanner's mother. "They were even letting my daughters hold their rifles."

"But we had to learn to live with whatever group was in power because the area was completely abandoned by the government," Carlos Daza added. "When the guerrillas came by, we had to greet them and give them coffee and send them on their way with a smile."

But in the late 1990s, right-wing paramilitaries who were funded by wealthy landowners began moving in to cleanse the zone of guerrillas. The gunmen had heard about the constant rebel visits to the Daza farm and decided that the family must have been collaborating with the FARC. It was a lose-lose situation. As the paramilitaries began rounding up local farm boys and executing them for their alleged ties to the rebels, Hanner's parents abandoned the land they had worked for thirty-two years and moved to the southern city of Popayán.

Hanner had been saved from the paramilitaries but he still ended up on the front lines. He had never been much of a student and dropped out after the eighth grade to go to work. But after he spent a few backbreaking years laboring as a field hand for wealthy hacienda owners, the Colombian Army seemed like a decent career option. After being drafted and serving his obligatory eighteen months, he became a professional soldier and soon found himself alongside Walter Suárez marching into the heart of FARC-land.

"It seemed like a good option for him because he hadn't completed his studies," said Yaned Daza, Hanner's older sister. "His dream was to make the rank of sergeant."

But now, as the mission to find the Americans dragged on, Daza, Suárez, and some of the other troops fumed. For a monthly salary of $171, they were tiptoeing through minefields, ducking ambushes, and swallowing simian stew all in the name of finding a trio of gringos who had spurned their own armed forces for six-figure contracts as soldiers of fortune.

"It was just rice and monkey for breakfast and dinner," Suárez said. "We were fighting and staving off hunger for these guys who weren't even Colombians. But others were saying: 'Like it or not, this is our duty.'"

Lieutenant Jorge Sanabria fell into the second category. The commander of Vulture Company had gotten to know FARC-land the year before during the operation to take back territory ceded to the rebels for the peace talks. He relished the challenge but was under no illusions. He knew that Caquetá was the stomping grounds of one of the FARC's most feared units, the Teófilo Forero Mobile Column. These fighters were not the green cannon fodder from Mesetas. They were the very best, commandos who could hold their own in the wilderness and pull off daring raids in the cities. These were the insurgents who effectively put Colombia back on the warpath by pulling off one of the most audacious kidnappings in the country's history.

On February 20, 2002, four rebels skyjacked a commuter plane and forced it to land on a stretch of rural highway in southern Huila state. To clear space for the wings on the narrow, improvised runway, another squad of rebels posing as maintenance workers scaled the broad, leafy saman trees lining the road and trimmed their branches with machetes. They even managed to recruit municipal employees from a nearby town to lend a hand. Once the plane was on the ground, the rebels grabbed one of the passengers, Colombian senator Jorge Géchem, forced him into a pickup, and drove into the mountains where he became yet another bargaining chip for a future prisoner exchange. Twelve hours later, the Colombian government called off the peace talks and ordered the army to retake Caquetá.

A year later, rebels from the same mobile column watched the Cessna Grand Caravan crash almost on top of them and pounced on the five-man crew, executing Tom Janis and Luis Alcides Cruz, and capturing Keith Stansell, Marc Gonsalves, and Tom Howes. Now, as the hungry, demoralized Colombian troops tramped through the rain forest in pursuit of the kidnappers, Sanabria tried to buck up his men for what lay ahead.

"It was an anthill full of guerrillas. We knew there was going to be combat all the time," Sanabria said. "I always urged my troops to never sur-render, to fight, fight, fight like a wounded animal. I told them: 'Boys, all we can do is help each other and try to cover ourselves with glory.'"

In that sense, the jungle land before them was a field of opportunity. Sure, it was a long shot. But if Sanabria and his men somehow managed to rescue the three Americans, they'd be war heroes. Lying in his hammock next to his Israeli-made Galil automatic rifle, Sanabria dreamed of the splendorous aftermath, the ribbons and medals and television interviews. The people at the U.S. embassy would be so pleased they'd issue him a coveted American visa so he could visit Miami and New York. Just in case Vulture Company did find the Americans, Sanabria had instructed one of his men how to use his Canon point-and-shoot so there would be photos of the lieutenant and the newly freed hostages to accompany the newspaper headlines. Hell, they might even make a movie.

CHAPTER 5

GOD'S LITTLE GIFT

The best indicator of future behavior is past behavior.
—Dr. Phil

KEITH STANSELL WAS A REAL-LIFE ACTION figure. He was never the type to punch the clock at a desk job or to pore over books in his spare time. Growing up in south Florida he loved to disappear into the Everglades on fishing trips. Straight out of high school he enlisted in the U.S. Marine Corps—rather than the army or navy—because he knew jarheads were the toughest. Whenever he was on home leave from Colombia, he liked nothing better than to march into the woods to stalk deer with a bow and arrow. Always an athlete, he had bulked up in the gym and was fit enough for a triathlon. But he was also a team player. He'd learned the value of solidarity while in the military, and as a backseater on the California Microwave missions, he was deeply loyal to the rest of the crew.

But Keith had picked up some other habits that might not play as well for him as a hostage in the Colombian jungle. For one thing, he was a serial womanizer, and the only females around him now were wearing camouflage and pointing guns at him. Military life had made him a clean freak, and he often took two showers a day. He also had a streak of vanity. He wasn't a clotheshorse, but his hair had to be styled just so—usually in a Marine brush cut. And he couldn't walk past a mirror without checking himself out. But the main problem for Keith was the pain and guilt of yet another family breakup.

Cancer had taken his mother when he was an adolescent and he hadn't spoken with his estranged father in years. Stansell's marriage had imploded and now he was being held hostage, leaving behind his fiancée, a teenaged daughter, an eleven-year-old son, and a Colombian girlfriend and their soon-to-be-born twin boys.

Keith Donald Stansell was born on September 17, 1964. He never knew his birth parents, who immediately put him up for adoption. Gene Stansell, a high school teacher in the Miami area, and his wife, Jane, spotted the three-month-old Keith at the adoption agency and were immediately smitten. "He was as cute as could be and very, very active. We just immediately fell in love with him," Gene said. "He was a hyperactive kid, always crawling and running around, but he was very intelligent. He always liked animals, snakes, and worms. He also had a big tarantula that he kept in a glass cage. It was huge."

Later, the Stansells adopted a second boy, Frank. They lived in Davie on the outskirts of Miami, still a rural area back then that offered the Stansell kids plenty of space to get into mischief. When Keith wasn't beating the crap out of Frank, the boys would fish, build model airplanes, ride horses, and scoot around the neighborhood on skateboards. Gene made the boys a twelve-foot-tall half-pipe and crowds gathered to watch Keith zip up one side, stop in midair, then come crashing down the other side.

"He always had to have that adrenaline rush," said Frank, who was four years younger than Keith. "He always had this energy encircling him. I think he had attention deficit disorder and was taking some medication for hyperactivity."

From early on, Keith was attracted to flying, and Gene took the boys to air shows at the nearby Homestead Air Force Base. They once met Gregory "Pappy" Boyington, the legendary Marine Corps aviator who commanded the Black Sheep Squadron during World War II. As it turned out,

Pappy had logged a few years as a military contractor, flying in China for an American company called CAMCO that later put together the famed Flying Tigers. He was also captured by the enemy and spent twenty months in a Japanese POW camp before returning home to receive the Medal of Honor. At the air show, Keith approached Pappy to sign a copy of his memoirs but was taken aback when the airman tried to charge him for his autograph.

Keith's fondest childhood memories revolved around family camping trips in the southern United States. Rolling down the highway in the middle of the night, with Jane and Frank asleep in the back of their recreational vehicle, Gene would slide over to the right seat and have a drink while Keith, all of twelve years old, manned the wheel in the captain's chair. Still, Keith was much closer to his mother, who doted on him. Jane Stansell was a heavy smoker and her best friend, Lynne, often urged her to give up the habit. So did her doctor, who at one checkup before taking some lung X-rays, told Lynne that he often used them to scare the hell out of his patients. Instead, Jane's films freaked out the doctor. Jane had lung cancer, and within three months her organs shut down and she was gone.

Keith, then fourteen, was shattered. But his mother was barely in the ground when Lynne began dating his father. "My dad hooked up with Lynne very quickly and my brother is like, 'Hey, my mom just died!'" Frank said. "It happened very fast, like the next day. Jane wasn't even buried yet, and they went to the funeral together so my brother was always mad. It really bugged him."

Jealous of Lynne, Keith constantly fought with Gene and eventually moved out of the house and began living with one of his uncles in a trailer court. He bounced around attending five high schools in four years. Keith was smart but let his grades slide. He also played middle linebacker for the football team and threw himself into tennis. He emerged as a nationally ranked amateur player and was offered a scholarship to Nova Southeastern University in Fort Lauderdale. But Keith didn't care.

"I had a chip on my shoulder," Keith said. "I stopped giving a shit about anything after my mother died."

Instead of a free ride through academia, Keith signed up for the Marines. "I didn't object," said Gene Stansell, a former army staff sergeant who served in the Korean War. "I thought it would make him into a better man."

The summer before reporting to boot camp at Parris Island, Stansell took a detour that nearly landed him in jail. By then, his father had moved in with Lynne who lived across the street. One afternoon, Keith and Frank were sitting around their dad's house bored out of their skulls. They decided to break into a neighbor's house to look for money and beer. Days later, when the neighbors returned home, they told the police and Frank received a frantic phone call from Keith. Arguing that the Marines wouldn't take him if he arrived with a rap sheet, Keith begged his little brother to be the fall guy. Besides, he said, the judge would likely let him off with a slap on the wrist. Frank reluctantly agreed. To his shock, the ill-humored magistrate sent Frank to the Miami Juvenile Detention Center where he spent four days surrounded by assorted lunatics and junior varsity thugs.

Keith wanted to be a pilot but needed a four-year college degree. So, his Marine recruiter convinced him to study avionics, or aviation electronics, which includes radio communications, navigation, and monitoring systems. He also learned how to operate a forward-looking infrared, or FLIR, a skill that would later help him secure employment with California Microwave. Keith liked being around aircraft and knew that the avionics guys were just as important as the pilots. On board, it was all teamwork.

"He was someone who would have your back if he was your friend," said Kevin Fox, a fellow marine who moved on to work on the space shuttle program in Merritt Island, Florida. "I once threw a party at a beach house and somebody started to fight with me. I threw some punches and another guy was about to hit me. Out of the corner of my eye, I saw Keith straight-arm this guy. He dropped him."

While stationed at Camp Lejeune near Jacksonville, North Carolina, Keith met Kelly Coady, a part-time college student who had enlisted in the army. Kelly was on a blind date at a bar but spotted Keith while fetching a drink and ditched the other guy. She was quickly overwhelmed by Keith's high wattage. He was full of energy, liked to be in charge, and hated taking orders, which didn't always go over so well in the Marines.

"He would get a haircut but didn't want it short. He wanted it high and tight. He was always getting into trouble for his hair because the Marines wanted it shorter," Kelly said. "I remember coming to visit him on a couple of weekends because he couldn't leave the barracks. I'd pull up and he'd be sitting on the curb painting rocks" as punishment.

When his four-year commitment was up in 1986, Corporal Keith Stansell left the Marines. By then he was married to the nineteen-year-old Kelly and the two settled down in Savannah where Keith joined the Georgia National Guard as a helicopter mechanic and contemplated working for the Drug Enforcement Administration. His brother, Frank, moved in with them for six months and their sibling rivalry picked up anew.

"I'd come home drunk and Keith would shave half my face or lock the cat in my bedroom so it would shit all over my bed. Just for fun," Frank said, grinning. "He was an asshole."

Kelly would come to the same conclusion. One night, Frank recalled, Kelly was fast asleep after a long day at her bank job. He and Keith were watching college football on TV. Even though the refrigerator was a few steps away, Keith hollered at Kelly to get him a beer. Frank offered to go but his brother wanted to make Kelly do it and he kept hounding her until she woke up, wandered into the kitchen, and brought him a beer. As she stumbled back to the bedroom, Keith snapped open his can and barked a second order: now, get Frank a beer.

"He was terrible," Frank said. "He was relentless."

Keith and Kelly had a daughter, Lauren, but becoming parents only added another level of stress to their already cratering marriage. Ever the tomcat, Keith carried on a series of affairs that drove Kelly to despair. They were about to separate when she got pregnant with their son, Kyle. They tried to patch things up but Keith spent many nights sleeping on the couch. After nine years of marriage, the couple finally hit the wall.

"If the split with Kelly bummed him out, Keith didn't show it," Fox said. "I've never seen him depressed. Not that the man is manic happy all the time, but I've never seen him down on himself, which is great for self-preservation."

WITH THE DIVORCE, KEITH LOST HIS wife, his house, and, for a time, his kids. He moved in with Frank, who was studying at a Savannah vocational school to be an air-conditioning technician. Though nearly broke, Keith offered to pitch in for the rent but Frank refused. To make it up, Keith later gave his brother a Russian SKS assault rifle. "I said: 'What the hell am I gonna do with this?'" Frank recalled. "He said: 'Shoot it.' I never even took it out of the box."

He may have been homeless but Keith was rarely by himself. One evening, Keith was hanging out at an Irish bar in nearby Statesboro listening to the band. So was Malia Phillips, a blond, former beauty pageant contestant and an English major at Georgia Southern University. Keith caught her eye, and Malia's girlfriends dared her to approach him.

"I was just tipsy enough, so I strike out across the room and catch him at the bar and asked if I could buy him a drink," Malia said. "He already had one but said I could stay and talk to him. I said: 'Gee, thank you for the honor.' I thought he was very good-looking. I like tall guys and he was tall, very well built, and with a nice smile. And he was kind of a smart-ass."

At thirty-three, Keith was eleven years older than Malia. But the two bonded. Keith didn't have the money to splurge so they made their own entertainment, often driving around in Keith's maroon Toyota pickup, drinking and cranking the radio. Keith had a spotlight in the truck and the two would sometimes cut through the fields at night looking for deer. Every now and then they talked politics. Though his preferred reading material was gun magazines, Keith kept up on current events. A staunch conservative, he supported gun owners' rights and voiced his view that President Clinton was a weenie for ducking the military.

"He was a right-winger and always talking about the left-wing wackos," Malia said. "He was always getting on Gene and Lynne's case because they were very liberal. But I think he just liked to get on their nerves and he did a very good job of it."

When Keith moved to Panama City, Florida, to work on contract for U.S. Airways, he and Malia maintained a long-distance romance. They'd cast for redfish off a small boat Keith owned. He'd chew tobacco and drink Jack Daniel's. Squeamish about baiting the hook, Malia would lie in the front of the boat, soaking up rays and sipping beer. Back at his apartment, Keith would whip up meals of venison, gumbo, chili, or spaghetti for Malia. Keith liked it hot and drizzled Tabasco sauce on everything. Malia said his steady diet of booze and spicy food may have wasted Keith's stomach lining and contributed to irritable bowel syndrome. His guts were always seizing up. Years later, while flying the bathroom-less Grand Caravan to Griffin, Georgia, for a checkup, the pilots had to make an emergency landing on Marco Island on the Gulf Coast of Florida so Keith could scamper to the head.

Though Malia was hired to teach high school in Camilla, Georgia, she often drove down to Florida to see Keith on the weekends, missing her Monday-morning classes and sparking a flash of knowing smiles from her smart-ass students. Keith was still living paycheck to paycheck so Malia loaned him $500 to take courses at Fort Rucker, Alabama, to get the airframe-and-power-plant license he needed to become a certified mechanic. He roomed with Malia's mother, Charlotte Phillips, in nearby Bainbridge, Georgia. She treated him like a son, feeding him country-fried steak, biscuits, corn bread, and other southern specialties.

"I think he felt like I was his mom," Charlotte said. "Every time he'd see me, he'd assure me he was going to take care of my little girl and make her happy."

After getting his license, Keith was hired as a chopper mechanic for DynCorp in Colombia. He also worked as the sensor operator in the backseat of twin-engine OV-10 Bronco aircraft. The job kept him in Colombia much of the time, but the work was good and the paychecks were better. "He could live in a cool, calm atmosphere for a while, but then he would go to Colombia to get the daily adrenaline rush," Frank said. "He had to have it."

Keith and Malia shacked up in Colquitt where she taught English, Spanish, and journalism at the local high school. Keith had joint custody of Lauren and Kyle, and Malia was very fond of the kids. They rented a farmhouse on the outskirts of town, a spread with horses to keep the kids entertained and a stray donkey that seemed to think it was a dog and begged for affection. Lauren, a straight-A student, got into cheerleading and signed up for beauty pageants. Kyle hated school and periodically left town to be with his mother. But in Colquitt, he forged a closer relationship with his father. Keith sometimes took the kids fishing and let them skip school, but he could also be a strict disciplinarian. When Lauren and

Kyle misbehaved, they got the belt or were sent into the backyard to pick up pinecones.

"He was a marine so he was strict," Lauren said. "He always wanted us to do things for ourselves and to never have to depend on anyone."

Malia remembered their days in Colquitt as a rare moment of stability. The DynCorp paychecks helped the family climb out of the hole. Keith was able to pay off some debts and he liked the small-town feel of Colquitt, a racially mixed village of 1,939 people. The schools were decent. People were friendly. Malia's mother helped produce *Swamp Gravy*, a play staged by volunteers that paid tribute to the history and culture of rural south Georgia. Under its masthead, the *Miller County Liberal*—the boosterish local newspaper that could find beauty in the local RV park—carried the slogan: "Pull For Colquitt Or Pull Out."

"Colquitt had a family feel to it. Keith was really missing that family dynamic because of the way that he grew up. His own family fell apart and then he got divorced," Malia said. "My mom was the closest thing to a mother that he had. He thought the sun rose and set on her. So Colquitt is where he wanted to be. He just wanted to live a simple life out in the country, and hunt and fish and have his dogs and drink his coffee and take it easy. And that sounded pretty good to me."

From DynCorp, Keith made the jump to California Microwave as a systems analyst where his familiarity with the FLIR helped seal the deal. In the long-running debate over the wisdom of flying the single-engine Grand Caravan, an argument that had split the California Microwave employees into two camps, Keith sided with Doug Cockes and Paul Hooper, agreeing that it wasn't the best aircraft for the job.

"California Microwave was kind of cowboyish," Keith said. "And we were pushing the limits."

Keith sometimes talked of quitting, going back to Colquitt and being his own boss. But it was hard to walk away from a job that paid him nearly $200,000 a year. Besides, living in Colombia had its perks. By exchanging their American dollars for devalued Colombian pesos, Keith and his coworkers lived extra large. For these gringo kings there were plenty of Colombian queens and Keith emerged as horn dog in chief.

"I was a pretty selfish son of a bitch, truth be told," Keith said. "I figured that since I was a good dad to my kids and a single parent tackling the responsibilities of being a caregiver and provider, the world owed me my little moments of stepping out and finding pleasure wherever I could."

And in the Colombian capital he found instant gratification.

"Bogotá is the good-looking-women capital of the world," said pilot Paul Hooper, who lived downstairs from Keith in a north Bogotá apartment complex. "Keith Stansell was literally God's little gift. I have never seen anyone who attracted women like he did. Women would cross the street or pull their cars over to the curb to talk to him, give him their phone number, or whatever. He was a magnet. He's the only guy I ever knew who had home delivery. Women would just deliver themselves to his apartment."

Or to his seat in first class. Keith met Patricia Medina, a beautiful brunette on an Avianca flight from Bogotá to Panama City. She was a flight attendant stuck back in monkey class but traded places with a colleague working the front of the cabin after spotting a handsome gringo who had settled into one of the plush, wide seats and was nursing a drink. Keith didn't speak much Spanish so Medina switched to English. They began joking and by the time they landed in Panama City, Keith walked off the plane with Patricia's phone number. He called her a week later.

"I felt an attraction that I'd never felt for anyone else in the world," Keith said. "In my heart, I just wanted to be with Patricia."

Patricia, who came from working-class stock, liked that Keith valued people for who they were, not how much money they possessed. But there were also some tense moments. Keith let it be known from the beginning that he didn't want any commitments. He also told Patricia to be careful. He liked kids but already had Lauren and Kyle. What he didn't tell Patricia was that he was planning to ask Malia to marry him.

Back in the United States, Keith proposed shortly before Christmas 2002. He led Malia to a jewelry store in Albany, Georgia, and urged her to try on a few rings, including one with a 1.6 carat diamond that he'd previously picked out. She admired it for a few seconds, then Keith dramatically announced that it was hers if she said "yes." From then on, Keith dragged Malia around Colquitt by the left hand so everyone would ooh and ah at the magnificent rock on her ring finger.

"When a woman says, 'I'm engaged,' the first thing people say is, 'Let me see your ring.' He got that," Malia said. "Not a lot of guys get it."

The seemingly happy couple planned to get married on May 31, 2003, aboard a cruise ship in the Caribbean. But something was eating Keith. Shortly after setting the date, Keith said that with the fresh start of marriage he wanted to come clean with his fiancée. After hemming and hawing, he blurted out that he was seeing Patricia in Bogotá. Malia flew into a rage. Keith let her scream, then tried to make peace. He said that he was breaking things off with Patricia and that he wanted to spend the rest of his life with Malia. Though deeply hurt, Malia believed him and the marriage was back on.

But by then Patricia was four months pregnant. Malia found out after intercepting an e-mail from Patricia requesting money. "I asked him: 'Do you mind explaining this to me?'" Malia said. "I showed him the computer screen and that's when he told me she was pregnant."

"Then he said: 'With twins.'"

Talking fast, Keith claimed to have it all figured out. He had talked to an attorney. He told Malia that he would provide financial support to his growing family in Colombia but other than setting up a Miami bank account, he would no longer be involved. His family was Malia, Lauren, and Kyle. He told Malia that he thought Patricia had stopped taking her birth-control pills so she could bag a wealthy gringo.

And once again, Keith talked of making a fresh start. He wanted to marry Malia. His contract with California Microwave expired in March 2003 and rather than re-up in Colombia he would settle down in Colquitt. He even mused about getting into law enforcement. Sometimes Keith dropped by the police station to hang out with the boys while one of the officers, Jason Wells, lived next door. Jason remembered his neighbors spending most of their time with the kids, and said Keith rarely talked about his job. But the night before Keith left for Colombia—three days before the Grand Caravan crashed—the two men had dinner together and Jason asked what would happen if his surveillance plane ever went down.

"He said all you do is call in the coordinates," Jason said. "He carried a nine-millimeter Baretta and a survival pack and said he'd try to hide until help arrived. But I think he was starting to get concerned. I could tell it was bothering him. He said this was going to be his last tour."

CHAPTER 6

BLADE CREEP

In modern war there is nothing sweet nor fit in your dying.
You will die like a dog for no good reason.
—ERNEST HEMINGWAY

A S GUESTS OF THE FARC, KEITH, Marc, and Tom were immediately hustled out of sight, forced to march for twenty-four straight days, each step taking them deeper into the jungle-covered mountains. It was slow-motion torture. Keith had broken several ribs in the crash and his injuries, combined with the incessant marching, led to chronic diarrhea and vomiting. Tom suffered a concussion. Marc struggled with back and hip pain. They were dressed in T-shirts, and the jungle became so cold at night they had to huddle together to stay warm. Every time they stumbled and grabbed a bush, vine, or tree to steady themselves, they came away with a hand full of spines. Tom wore tennis shoes, Keith had a pair of Timberlands, and Marc sported what he called mall-walking boots with no grip. As the guerrillas pushed them forward, they were constantly slipping on leaves, rocks, and trail mud and on algae-covered rocks as they crossed rivers and streams.

"The jungle is beautiful, but it's harsh," Keith said. "It's not user friendly. Everything bites. Everything sticks. Nothing's clean. The jungle makes the simplest things difficult."

Unable to keep food down, Keith grew so weak that the guerrillas fed him with intravenous drip bags. Near the end of the march, when Keith was at the point of completely shutting down, the rebels tied a hammock to a tree limb and carried him up the mountain trails as if they'd just bagged a jaguar. Later, three teenaged female guerrillas stripped a chagrined Keith down to his underwear and gave him a sponge bath. Keith slowly improved, but with each passing day, the Americans realized that the likelihood of being rescued diminished.

"The fact that the FARC were jungle rats, expertly navigating a maze of their own making, did not help our hopes for a quick rescue," Keith said. "If some troops were on the ground trailing us, I had to trust that they were the stealthiest the Colombian Army had."

THE COLOMBIAN ARMY HAD SENT SOME of their best men to hunt for the Americans, but their frantic search effort had gone horribly awry. By the time the DynCorp search-and-rescue teams and the Colombian Army units from Larandia reached the crash site the Americans had disappeared. Meanwhile, it took a full twenty-four hours for Colonel Kevin Christie's Special Forces to receive authorization to leave the base. In kidnappings, the first hours are crucial because there is still a chance to set up security perimeters and block hostage-takers from moving out of the area. But all the Special Forces could do now was stand guard as agents from the FBI and the Bureau of Alcohol, Tobacco and Firearms inspected the destroyed Grand Caravan.

Even so, it was widely believed, at least in the first few weeks, that the Colombian Army knew, in general, which way the FARC kidnappers were taking the hostages. About 150 Green Berets and U.S. civilian personnel were airlifted to Colombia to assist in the search operation while General Remo Butler, who was in charge of all U.S. Special Forces in Latin America, worked alongside the Colombian Army setting up blocking operations.

It turned out that neither the Colombians nor the Americans had any decent intelligence on where the hostages were located. In addition, a shortage of helicopters slowed down the moving of troops around the jungles of Caquetá. The FARC rebels knew the rugged terrain better than the GIs and relied on a network of civilian supporters to help them smuggle the hostages out of the area. They stayed off their radios, spread false rumors to send the search parties in the wrong direction, and staged diversionary attacks to throw off their pursuers.

"We kept getting all these conflicting details: 'They're going east! They went west! They went south!'" said one State Department official. "But I don't think we ever knew, within many miles, where they were located."

"We set up five to ten different blocking operations," General Butler added. "But these guys were very good. The FARC maintained radio silence. They did not divulge their information. They knew what they had and they were intent on keeping the hostages."

As hopes of an immediate rescue slipped away, U.S. officials in Washington debated how to respond. Two scenarios emerged. The more muscular plan involved launching U.S. air strikes on top guerrilla commanders and rebel fronts as well as dispatching some American ground forces to Colombia. The operation would have been legal because the cap on American troop levels and restrictions on direct involvement in the conflict did not apply when U.S. hostages were involved. But ultimately, American officials figured that coming in hot would only get the hostages killed. Going all Chuck Norris wasn't going to solve the problem.

Plan B called for the Bush administration to continue its military assistance programs designed to upgrade the Colombian Army and let these troops take the lead in any search-and-rescue attempt. Besides believing that U.S. military strikes wouldn't work, American diplomats were concerned that the hostage issue would overwhelm the broader relationship with the Bogotá government, Washington's closest ally in Latin America. President Álvaro Uribe was a full-throated backer of the war on drugs. The Colombian Army was making some progress against the FARC. Uribe was also attempting to disarm thousands of right-wing paramilitaries and he was pushing for a new trade agreement with the United States.

Or in the words of Thomas Shannon, who later became the top U.S. diplomat for Latin America: "We wanted to make sure that while we worked to win the release of the hostages that it didn't become the only focus of our activities in Colombia."

AT ANY OTHER MOMENT IN TIME, the abduction of U.S. military contractors in Colombia would have provoked a wave of press coverage. There would have been bouts of soul-searching about the legal gray area occupied by the growing number of American privateers performing dangerous duties on the Pentagon's behalf. There might have been congressional hearings and perhaps calls for a reappraisal of the American aid program in Colombia. And there would have been intense political pressure to bring the boys home.

Instead, a funny thing happened.

Nothing—at least in the view of the hostages' families.

The Cessna crashed on February 13, 2003, five weeks before the Bush administration launched Operation Iraqi Freedom and nearly all eyes were on Baghdad. Some U.S. reporters in Latin America had been pulled off their beats and sent to Iraq, and those who did write about Colombia saw their stories buried. "Every time we started to get a little traction with the media, it was always overridden by some other event," said Malia Phillips, Keith Stansell's fiancée. "The guys were kidnapped and then three weeks later we invade Iraq and it goes straight to the back burner."

By then, America had became infatuated with another POW. Jessica Lynch, a nineteen-year-old supply clerk, was captured by Iraqi troops three days after the start of the U.S. invasion. Her Humvee made a wrong turn in the southern city of Nasiriyah and was ambushed by Iraqi troops. Lynch's M16 jammed and her injuries occurred when the vehicle crashed. Yet after American commandos rescued Lynch from the Iraqi hospital, her Pentagon handlers massaged her story, claiming she had bullet and stab wounds and had been slapped around by her Iraqi captors. The media swallowed it whole and soon Lynch was transformed into a full-blown war hero. Later, she would protest the way her story was manipulated. But by then she had made the cover of *Time* magazine, signed a book deal, and appeared on *The Today Show*. By then she had helped rally a nation behind the war in Iraq.

If the government and the media could team up to turn a scared accident victim from West Virginia into a female Rambo, they could also perform another neat trick. They could turn a potential hostage crisis in Colombia into a nonstory. Not only was the media focused on Iraq to the near exclusion of other world events, but the U.S. State Department advised the families of the hostages to keep mum.

The gag order made sense for two reasons. One obvious benefit was that it would help the government and Northrop Grumman keep the lid on an embarrassing foreign policy fiasco, one that had been loudly predicted by two of the California Microwave pilots. For another, it might protect the hostages. It was unclear what they were telling the FARC about their work, whether the rebels knew that Keith and Marc were military vets, or whether the guerrillas would demand ransom payments for their release. Any sensitive information that leaked out about the three men or the efforts to find them could work against them. Not helping matters was conservative columnist Robert Novak, who would later come under fire for outing Valerie Plame as a CIA agent. Writing in the *Chicago Sun-Times*, Novak blithely stated that the three men were part of a "covert CIA operation."

American officials also feared that making a yellow-ribbon fuss over Keith, Marc, and Tom would only raise their value in the eyes of the FARC and convince the rebels to hold on to them until they could extract major concessions from the U.S. government.

So, the families were told to keep their heads down and their mouths shut and to let the professionals handle it. But it was frustrating advice. Out of necessity, the relatives were told very little about U.S. efforts to help free the hostages. To them, nothing seemed to be happening.

"We had a meeting with the State Department and one of the things they cautioned us about was saying things to the media," said George Gonsalves, Marc's father, as he sat on a sofa in the living room of his rural Connecticut home. "They said, 'You don't want to give the FARC any information they don't need.' I followed that whole line of crap, because they said they were working on it. So for the whole first year, we were sitting around, all hunky-dory, thinking they were working on it."

But the Iraq War and the campaign to keep the FARC in the dark were not the only reasons this story stayed out of the public's consciousness. Keith, Marc, and Tom were civilians rather than active-duty soldiers, and for many Americans they were a separate species. Private contractors were widely perceived as cowboys who signed up for big paydays and the big risks they entailed. Soldiers were seen as patriots whereas contractors were seen as profiteers. Thus, the killing, maiming, or capture of private-sector security guards, truck drivers, pilots, and intelligence analysts failed to ring the same emotional bells as photos of flag-draped caskets, the names of dead GIs in Iraq listed in the newspapers, or even decades-old POW horror stories from the Hanoi Hilton. Working as a contractor "means you're expendable. I didn't like that but I always understood it," Keith said. "And then the Iraq War kicks off. So it was kind of like a double fucking."

"If you had three active-duty troops taken, they wouldn't be forgotten. Their capture would be page-one news," said Peter Singer of the Brookings Institution. "But with these guys, the original newspaper stories were on page A26."

In the twelve months following her rescue, Jessica Lynch was written up in more than a thousand newspaper and magazine articles. During the same period, the names of the American hostages in Colombia appeared in just thirty stories. On TV, there was a virtual blackout. When Dan Rather and 60 Minutes II finally got around to reporting the story seven months after the crash, the resulting segment was called "The Forgotten Hostages." Had the three men been uniformed members of the military, there would have been full-throttle efforts to rescue them—a Colombian sequel to Black Hawk Down. Instead, they were three luckless nobodies in a downed Cessna.

IF A DISASTER INVOLVED ACTIVE-DUTY MILITARY personnel, there was a clear chain of command for investigators to follow, including established mechanisms for assigning blame, meting out punishment, and making amends. But if private contractors, subcontractors, and subsidiaries were involved, the process was messier. The added degrees of separation facilitated bobbing and weaving and passing the buck. Pinning down responsibility was like nailing jelly to a wall.

That's what Representative Dan Burton, an Indiana Republican, found when he tried to get to the bottom of another midair mishap. In April 2001, a CIA surveillance aircraft directed the Peruvian air force to shoot down a civilian floatplane suspected of transporting cocaine. But the aircraft was actually carrying an American missionary and her infant daughter and both were killed in a hail of gunfire as the plane crash-landed in the Amazon River. It later emerged that the people running the surveillance systems were employees of Aviation Development Corp., a private company that had been subcontracted by the CIA.

A month later, Burton conducted a hearing to figure out what went wrong and tried to bring together officials from the CIA, Customs, the State Department, and the military's Southern Command. But the CIA agents refused to testify and everyone else at the hearing stonewalled. Burton nearly screwed himself into the floor in frustration.

"A plane was shot down. Americans were killed. It was a plane that was a civilian aircraft," he said. "This is not a national security issue. Why is it classified? Why is it you guys can't tell us that? Speak to me!"

Contracting also meant less accountability for the U.S. military. Indeed, shedding responsibility for performance, supervision, and oversight— and therefore liability when things went wrong—was one of the main attractions of outsourcing. "This was clearly one of the government's intentions when it entered into its contract with Northrop Grumman/California Microwave," said a U.S. Navy investigation that was published five months after the Grand Caravan crash.

Could Washington, in good faith, simply wash its hands of the bungle in the Colombian jungle? Had government employees done the job, things would have been different. Despite infamous cases like that of GIs being sent to Iraq without body armor, the U.S. military hewed to a far longer list of standard operating procedures than did private contractors and tended to invest more in big-ticket items, like aircraft. Had CIA, navy, or air force personnel carried out the Colombia surveillance program, there would have been dozens of pilots and crew members flying twin-engine or larger aircraft. But the costs would have been higher and outsourcing was another way the U.S. government aimed to trim expenses. And by proposing Cessnas rather than more expensive, safer aircraft for the Colombia program,

California Microwave was able to low-ball its bid to $8.6 million and win the contract.

Steve Schooner, a government procurement expert at George Washington University, said that the U.S. government sends certain signals to contractors about what level of investment it wants to make. "It's easy to blame the contractor for doing it on the cheap," he said, "but the government is the one paying."

But trying to blame the contractor could reveal another frustrating shell game. Northrop Grumman owned California Microwave which leased from a Georgia businessman the Grand Caravan manufactured by Cessna that housed the suspect engine which was built by Pratt & Whitney.

Huh?

In theory, free-market forces should have prompted a Fortune 500 company like Northrop Grumman to guarantee a high level of safety standards for the Colombia surveillance program if only to protect its corporate image. But other market forces were at work. At the time, the business of military outsourcing was growing so quickly that major corporations, whose bread and butter had long been weapons systems, began snapping up small military service companies to get a bigger piece of the outsourcing pie. Yet they often failed to provide much oversight or to put the company stamp on their new acquisitions.

"My sense is that if you shook awake the CEOs of these companies at night and said, 'Name all the businesses in your conglomerate,' they'd get four or five," said Peter Singer. "It wouldn't surprise me if they didn't even know about the smaller outfits."

After the crash, Northrop Grumman continued to pay the salaries of the three hostages and stayed in touch with their families. But having been warned by pilots Doug Cockes and Paul Hooper about the dangers of flying a single-engine Cessna over Colombia, and facing the prospect of a drawn-out hostage situation and public relations nightmare, Northrop Grumman was anxious to distance itself from California Microwave and the surveillance program.

Northrop Grumman simply dissolved its troublesome subsidiary and gave up the contract. A new company arose in place of California Microwave. Called CIAO Inc., the firm consisted of the same supervisors and managers and the same pilots and intelligence analysts—now minus the four downed Americans—who were tasked to carry out their missions, using the one remaining Cessna Grand Caravan. Months later, the name of the new company, which means "goodbye" in Italian, would come back to haunt the three American hostages. The problem was those first three letters: C-I-A.

TWO THOUSAND MILES TO THE NORTH, Ronnie Powers was fuming. Powers operated an airplane boneyard in Griffin, Georgia, just south of Atlanta, and a tour of the site could give even the most grizzled globetrotter fear of flying. Ailerons, stray wings, chipped props, and mangled cockpits were splayed about the compound. The junkers had been transported from their crash sites to Powers's aircraft salvage and parts business located next door to the Griffin municipal airport. Powers held on to the high-priced remains as lawyers and insurance companies worked out settlements. Later, the planes were cannibalized for parts because Piper, Beechcraft, and Cessna had stopped making many of their older models. Powers also owned the two Cessna Grand Caravans that had been leased by California Microwave. But it wasn't the loss of the plane in Colombia that was eating him up inside. It was the loss of his three buddies, Keith, Marc, and Tom.

Part of Powers's arrangement with California Microwave was a maintenance contract for the two Grand Caravans, thus the Bogotá-based pilots and crew members often flew to Griffin for equipment tweaks and major inspections. Knowing that the men basically lived in the plane, Powers and his grease monkeys took extra care to redo the seat configuration and clean the cockpit to make it more comfortable. Over the years, the guys from Bogotá and Griffin bonded. The crews often stayed at Powers's apartment next to the airport hangar, and when the workday was over, they grilled burgers or went out for dinner. Keith's girlfriend, Malia, drove up from Colquitt and they sometimes looked after the Powers children. "It was like the annual visit from your cool relatives," Powers recalled.

Yet ever since Tom Janis's motor had suddenly conked out over the Caribbean on June 10, 2001, Powers wondered about the Pratt & Whitney engines inside his two Grand Caravans. Janis had been flying a 1995 model, tail number N5512B. The pilots called it Bravo to distinguish it from the other Caravan, N1116G, known as Gulf. After Janis's near catastrophe, Bravo's engine was taken apart and put under the microscope. The failure resulted from a phenomenon known as blade creep and it was the human equivalent of a full-on coronary.

In the combustion section of the Cessna's PT6A engine, fifty-eight one-inch metal blades were arranged around a platter called a compressor-turbine disk. Hot air at the scalding temperature of 750 degrees centigrade would blow through the blades spinning the disk and giving the engine its power. But under too much stress and heat, the blades could crack and tear away from the disk. With the disk spinning at 3,600 rpm, the loose bits of blade could ricochet around the inside of the housing, tearing the engine apart and making it stop.

The effect "is like a hand grenade going off," Powers said, "and the pieces get spit out the front of the engine."

With the original engine shot, Pratt & Whitney sold Powers a new one for Bravo. About a year later, the crew, including Keith Stansell, returned to Griffin for a routine checkup. It was January 2003, just a few weeks before the other Cessna, Gulf, would crash in Colombia. Powers and his crew suspended Bravo's engines from chains and were astounded by what they found. The blades on the compressor turbine disk were already starting to tear. After just one year and twelve hundred hours of flight time, Bravo's engine was on the cusp of another catastrophic failure.

When Powers put the engine back together, he discovered that the temperature gauge was off. It read about fifty degrees centigrade lower than the actual temperature. Without meaning to, the pilots may have been running the engine too hot, which could have contributed to the deterioration of the blades. But when Powers traveled to Quebec to meet with Pratt & Whitney officials, no one would level with him about the engine. This infuriated Powers, who pointed out that Gulf, his other Grand Caravan, was flying over rebel territory every other day and could also be at risk.

"My exact words were: 'We have another airplane flying in Colombia, and if we need to stop flying it we will. You are the engine manufacturer. You tell me what to do,'" Powers said. "But there was absolute dead silence."

With no guidance from Pratt & Whitney, Powers didn't think he had the qualifications or the evidence to make a big stink with Northrop Grumman and the U.S. embassy about grounding the Grand Caravans. So Bravo was outfitted with its third engine and returned to Colombia. And Gulf kept flying.

Later, an independent laboratory hired by Powers confirmed that Bravo's engine had developed blade creep. But the report came back on March 3, 2003, and by then the engine on Gulf—the plane carrying Keith, Marc, and Tom—had already failed, the three contractors were in the hands of the FARC, and Janis was dead. After recovering Gulf's engine from the crash site in Colombia, Pratt & Whitney officials broke it down and issued a report on what went wrong. The verdict: blade creep.

AFTER THE CRASH, THE SURVIVING CALIFORNIA Microwave pilots and crew members gathered for the memorial service for pilot Tom Janis. As a contractor, Janis had been an anonymous worker bee in the South American drug war. But as a Vietnam vet, he was accorded a final resting place befitting a Bronze Star winner. Janis was buried in Arlington National Cemetery, Section 65, Site 3-4, surrounded by streets named after Omar Bradley, George Marshall, and Douglas MacArthur.

One of the mourners was James "Butch" Oliver, a Griffin native and the son of an aircraft mechanic for the U.S. military. Oliver had dreamed of being a pilot since he was eight years old. For a short spell, he flew corporate jets. But the money wasn't very good, so he took a job working as a mechanic for his old friend Ronnie Powers. Later, Powers sent Oliver to Colombia to look after his two Grand Caravans in the surveillance program. After Douglas Cockes and Paul Hooper, the whistle-blowing pilots, resigned, California Microwave found itself shorthanded. The company hired Oliver even though he had no experience flying Cessna Grand Caravans.

"I tried to fly with Butch in the Caravan and really couldn't get him to check out," said Powers, also a pilot. "He just couldn't fly it to the point where I felt like I could turn him loose."

But Oliver was good enough for California Microwave. It seemed like another case of the company either forgoing standard operating procedures or not having very many in the first place. The firm had already made a number of questionable personnel decisions. The company's site manager had been fired for smoking marijuana while some of the pilots and crew members claimed that their program manager was a raging alcoholic.

"It was out of control," Keith Stansell said.

Oliver signed his paperwork on February 10. Three days later, the Grand Caravan carrying Keith, Marc, and Tom crashed and the FARC executed Janis. After the emotional funeral, the newly minted California Microwave pilot was having second thoughts. But the thirty-nine-year-old Oliver needed the money. He had bought a house and was remodeling. He had racked up credit-card debts, had taken out a second mortgage, and owed $12,000 in car payments. Powers called him "a walking bankruptcy."

"I begged him not to go [to Colombia]," said Albert Oliver, Butch's father. "I told him I'd give him every penny I had, that anytime he felt he was running short I'd make it up for him."

Besides earning money to pay his debts, Oliver had a personal incentive to go south. He and the program's remaining pilots and crew members were anxious to bring back their buddies from the jungle. Given what they viewed as the halfhearted rescue efforts the day of the crash, they figured the only chance to save Keith, Marc, and Tom was to do it themselves.

By mid-March, Bravo, California Microwave's one remaining Cessna Grand Caravan, had been repaired. But the plane now had a disconcerting track record for engine problems, while the cause of the February 13 engine failure and crash of Gulf had yet to be determined. Officers at the Joint Inter-Agency Task Force–South, the Key West–based military agency that coordinated the plane's flights, lobbied to keep the surveillance program grounded until they could find out more about the Caravan engines. But they were overruled. The U.S. Southern Command decided to reactivate the program on March 14.

"The reason it got up and running is because, one: we had a mission to do on counternarcotics surveillance," said Anne Patterson, who was at the time the U.S. ambassador to Colombia. "And two: we were hunting for the hostages. Basically, every asset we had was thrown into hunting for the hostages."

By then the pilots and crew members had reassembled in Bogotá, after their contracts were transferred to the new company, CIAO. There, rookie Butch Oliver would serve as copilot with Tommy Schmidt, a former Vietnam chopper pilot. Schmidt, however, was in no better shape than Oliver to climb aboard Bravo.

After getting out of the air force in 1990, Schmidt had flown for United Airlines, but after his experiences in Vietnam, he found the work as boring as driving a bus. Later, he was hired by California Microwave in Colombia, but something didn't feel right. While tracking a plane suspected of transporting cocaine, his Grand Caravan was hit by several bullets. The incident left Schmidt badly shaken. It was the first time he'd been fired upon and couldn't shoot back. He stewed for a few days, then resigned and returned to California.

Two months later, Schmidt's teenaged son was killed on a camping trip when the pickup truck he was in rolled over. Though still grappling with shock and depression, he was rehired by California Microwave, but he returned to Colombia a changed man. "By the end of 2002, Tommy Schmidt was a spent round," Hooper said. "He looked horrible."

But Schmidt had vast experience in search and rescue. While in Vietnam, he was shot down five times and each time was saved by his military colleagues. He also had extracted others from the jungle.

"I know Tommy's commitment to his guys," said his wife, Sharon Schmidt. "It was just one of those things. You just can't leave them and do nothing. He thought that if they could pinpoint the hostages, then the U.S. government would *have* to go get them."

When the flights resumed in March, most of the missions were launched in the cool night hours when it would be easier for the FLIR on Bravo, the one remaining Grand Caravan, to detect the body heat of the guerrillas. If they actually found the FARC units holding the hostages, however, the FLIR was no help in distinguishing the good guys from the bad. What's more, night flying over the mountains and jungles increased the risks because the pilots had to rely on their instruments and no longer had any visual cues to warn them of danger. Thus, as the quality of the pilots deteriorated, the risk of their missions increased. And when it came to fly-ing, the difference between night and day was just that: night and day.

"It was absolute lunacy to send Bravo out to look for us," Stansell said. "They could do nothing for us."

Night flying was especially hard on Schmidt. He was a morning person who was up before dawn drinking coffee, exercising, and running around like a gerbil. At night, by contrast, he complained that he could hardly see and he was unable to catch up on his sleep during daylight hours. But when the new company, CIAO, relaunched the surveillance flights in March, Schmidt began flying nights. He was also charged with the task of breaking in Butch Oliver. On their second flight, Oliver flew into the middle of a thunderstorm. Schmidt was livid, but he decided to give his copilot one more chance.

"It was Tom Schmidt's tenth night mission in a row," Cockes said. "He had to be a walking zombie."

On March 25, Schmidt and Oliver departed for Larandia along with crew member Ralph Ponticelli in the back to operate the cameras. Against protocol, they took to the air without the required Colombian host-nation rider. They landed safely just after sunset at 6:15 p.m. After refueling, the three Americans took off at 7:00 p.m. with Oliver at the controls and Schmidt serving as instructor. As the Grand Caravan gained altitude, Oli-ver steered the aircraft southwest, unaware that he was aiming directly for a rising mountain ridge.

They almost cleared the peak. But fourteen minutes after takeoff, the left wing of the Caravan clipped the top of a sixty-foot tree. On impact, the plane corkscrewed around the trunk, then plummeted to the ground. Oliver, Schmidt, and Ponticelli died instantly. Colombian troops stationed nearby heard an explosion as the nearly full fuel tanks ruptured. The wreckage burned through the night.

A U.S. Navy investigation speculated that Schmidt, rather than paying full attention to Oliver's maneuvers, may have been distracted by a prob-lem with the aircraft's transponder. In conclusion, the navy investigators blamed California Microwave/CIAO for poor management and supervi-sion as well as "unprofessional, unsafe and undisciplined practices" by pi-lots and crew members. But the report said nothing about the wisdom of teaming an exhausted, burned-out pilot with an untrained rookie with only three hours flight time in Colombia in a plane he hardly knew on a night mission over guerrilla territory in the Andes.

"The stupidity to do that is almost a world record. And no one is ever held liable," said Cockes, who heard about the crash while on a motorcycle trip through South America. "Butch Oliver, that poor guy, they were able to kill him on his third flight in-country."

CHAPTER 7

THREE GRINGOS

Saddam stole it from the sheiks. I have no problem
stealing it from Saddam.
—Major Archie Gates in the Gulf War gold-heist film
Three Kings

FOR LONG STRETCHES, THE TROOPS OF Vulture and Destroyer companies were punching through the snarled jungle foliage of southern Caquetá state as part of a massive operation to encircle the guerrillas holding the three American hostages. In many ways, it seemed like a death march. On some days land mines, heavy rains, and the undulating piedmont prevented them from advancing for more than a few miles. This was April 2003, and the soldiers were hungry, exhausted, and ill.

They were, however, inching steadily closer. The FARC was a mostly invisible enemy, but signs of rebel activity were everywhere. In an area known as El Coreguaje, the soldiers of Vulture Company discovered a handful of rebel laboratories stocked with piles of green coca leaves and drums of chemicals used to make cocaine. A little farther along, they came upon a hanging bridge fashioned of rope and wood planks that spanned a rain-swollen river. After careful inspection, they saw that it was booby-trapped and removed the explosives. The troops scampered across and their metal detectors began to make the whining sound that meant that rebel ordnance was buried all over this area. Clearly, there was something here the guerrillas were intent on protecting.

Then came a hail of gunfire as the men came under attack from the FARC. Eager to capture the kidnappers, Lieutenant Jorge Sanabria, the rotund, gung ho commander, wanted to press forward. But amid heavy rebel resistance, El Gordo received instructions over the radio to stay put until the seventy-five soldiers of Destroyer Company, bogged down a half mile away, caught up with his men. Sanabria told his troops to advance anyway.

"I got pissed off," Sanabria said. "I was convinced that if they let me go ahead, we could find the three Americans."

The FARC reacted by launching powerful homemade bombs fashioned out of cooking gas canisters and packed with nails, glass, bits of metal, and other deadly shrapnel. But the explosives were notoriously inaccurate and fell harmlessly by the wayside. After about two hours of combat, Vulture Company had fought its way to the top of a hill and the shooting suddenly stopped. The rebels had melted away. But Sanabria feared the FARC was trying to suck his men into an ambush. So he halted the advance, set up a security perimeter, and waited for Destroyer Company. While Sanabria was catching hell on the radio for his aggressive tactics, his men searched the area and discovered an abandoned guerrilla encampment, a semipermanent facility that seemed more like a rebel country club than a rustic bivouac. There was a massive kitchen, wooden hooches, and even a volleyball court outfitted with sand hauled up the hill from the nearby Pato River.

Sanabria interrogated a peasant woman who admitted that about 150 FARC rebels had occupied the area and were holding several prisoners who were *monos*—the local slang for people of light complexion. Sanabria also found a plastic-covered hut with reading material in English and a wooden pole marked with notches, as if someone had been counting the days. Had this been the temporary prison of the Americans?

Sanabria's troops continued rooting around and stumbled upon a stash of rifles and ammunition as well as plastic drums filled with toothpaste, deodorant, shampoo, soap, and skin cream. They also found an underground warehouse packed with camouflage uniforms, rain ponchos, bras, underwear, and flashlights. Finally, the troops had something to smile about. The booty was their first war trophy, their first concrete triumph of the two-month-long operation. Denying the enemy weapons and other provisions was nearly as important as taking rebel prisoners or running up the body count.

The grubby GIs eagerly divvied up the personal hygiene products, then stripped down to their underwear and took turns bathing in the river. Yet as they tried to scrub away the organic stench of mud, mold, and sweat from their bodies, the men fretted about their own supply line. The triple canopy forest, the torrential rains, the sketchy radio communications, the lack of helicopters, and the indifference of their superiors had the men of Vulture and Destroyer companies feeling frustrated and on their own.

It didn't seem fair. Under pressure from Washington, the Colombian high command had gone all out for the abducted U.S. contractors. Despite critical delays on the day the Grand Caravan went down, helicopters were in the air within twenty minutes and troops were on the ground at the crash site within two hours. But when the Colombian GIs now tracking the Americans were badly in need of food and other supplies, their superior officers scrambled a fleet of . . . donkeys.

The officers back at battalion headquarters argued over the radio that stormy weather and the thick tree cover made a helicopter resupply effort impossible, and instead they dispatched choppers to the nearest hamlet every ten days or so and sent in the supplies with local farmers on mule trains. But sometimes the peasants were so worried about rebel reprisals that they refused the work. And as the operation dragged on and the troops marched deeper into the wild, the overloaded beasts could no longer reach them. To feed themselves, the soldiers aimed for macaws with their slingshots. They killed *borugos*, a kind of Amazon rodent that looks like a cross between a squirrel and a rat and is a popular source of jungle protein. They also bagged monkeys, which they would stew for hours before braising over a fire in an attempt to cook away the gamey taste. But the meat was stringy and tough and as they gnawed on the primates' tiny arms and legs, some of the soldiers felt like they were eating their young. Others couldn't keep anything down. They were suffering from malaria and dysentery, and dozens of troops had the Hershey squirts and were constantly dashing for the bushes. An army fights on its stomach but their guts were in full-on mutiny.

"It wasn't normal," said Corporal Wilson Sarmiento, the nine-year veteran from Destroyer Company. "We were very demoralized. Only an animal lives like that."

General Carlos Alberto Ospina, the Colombian Army commander at the time, denied that Vulture and Destroyer companies had been left in the lurch. He pointed out that officers who deliberately fail to feed their troops can be court-martialed. He blamed the delays in resupply on bad weather, the shortage of helicopters, and the intrinsic army bureaucracy.

"This happens a lot in the army, but these are professional soldiers who sign up voluntarily. They know what they are getting into and they know it's not easy," Ospina said. "As a soldier, I went through many periods where we suffered from hunger and somehow we had to feed ourselves. Sometimes, it wasn't because the choppers couldn't reach us. It was because there *were* no choppers. And as a soldier I've seen much worse. Once, we had to evacuate some injured troops and we couldn't save them because the helicopters developed mechanical problems. While they were being repaired, the soldiers bled to death."

The battalion commander finally dispatched a chopper to El Coreguaje, but only after an NCO, who was an antiexplosives expert, stepped on a land mine and blew off part of his foot. As the badly injured sergeant screamed in pain, a handful of soldiers rushed to clear a landing pad with chainsaws and machetes. But the pilots had launched so quickly in order to save the soldier that there was no time to pack the helicopter with supplies for the rest of the troops. Once on the ground, the flight crew picked up the injured soldier and the captured guerrilla weapons but refused to evacuate any of the ailing troops. Sanabria was livid.

"We needed food, drugs, and ammunition," Sanabria recalled. "But they said that the choppers couldn't get in there. I said it was an outrage, that we had sick people, that we were running out of ammo, that we didn't have anything. At least get us some food. At least get us one meal per day. I never thought the army would turn its back on us."

WAS IT THE WATER? OR THE wild monkey? Either way, the improvised Amazon chow was playing havoc with Walter Suárez's innards. Suárez, the soldier from Mesetas who years earlier had nearly been press-ganged into the FARC, was part of Destroyer Company, which had finally caught up to Sanabria's men at the abandoned guerrilla encampment. Drifting in the netherworld between sleep and consciousness, Suárez twisted and turned in his hammock until he finally popped awake in the early-morning light. His stomach was about to detonate.

Suárez made his way past his colleagues in search of some privacy. Adding to the indignity of the moment, he'd run out of toilet paper, so he tore off the sleeves of a tattered T-shirt in his backpack. He squatted behind a tree and, to help balance himself, used both hands to drive his machete into the ground, but something didn't feel right. As the blade pierced the soil, the metal struck something hard that gave off a hollow thud. Intrigued, Suárez finished his business, hitched up his pants, and began rooting around with his hands. The dirt was loose, mixed with leaves, and easy to brush away. After burrowing down about one foot, he discovered the top of a blue plastic five-gallon container. Then, he froze. Whatever the guerrillas had hidden could be booby-trapped. "I got really scared," Suárez said. "I thought I'd be blown to bits."

But his curiosity got the best of him. Besides, if he found another rebel arms cache, he'd win points with his superiors. Suárez pried off the lid. Like foam in a beer stein, a white substance topped the thirty-inch-tall barrel. Was it cocaine? Suárez plunged his hands into the powder, which turned out to be ant poison. But instead of finding pistols and grenades underneath the powder, he pulled out block after block of blue-and-white 20,000-peso bills.

Suárez's heart raced. Each plastic-wrapped packet contained a thousand banknotes, or 20 million pesos—the equivalent of nearly $7,000. His wallet had never held more than petty cash, but now he was stuffing his uniform pockets with thick wads of currency. It wasn't easy because his whole body quaked with the snap realization that he, Walter Suárez, a $44-a-week anonymous soldier condemned to a mission impossible, had just won a kind of ad hoc lottery.

There was no question that the money was the evil lucre of rebel drug deals, extortion rackets, and ransom payments made by the desperate relatives of hostages. By some estimates, such scams earned the FARC $500 million annually. And since the guerrillas couldn't very easily open high-interest bank accounts, the rain forest became the FARC's safety-deposit box.

But knowing that these riches were tainted didn't stop Suárez.

"I was so happy. I'd never seen so much money," he said. "It was like the Virgin had appeared before me."

Divine or otherwise, some transcendental trail guide seemed to be steering the GI. Not only had Suárez survived the grueling trek into the shadowy heart of FARC-land, but the path led him into a tropical emporium where the world suddenly seemed shiny and bright and flush with possibility. In his search for a stopgap latrine, he'd found El Dorado.

Suárez took as much money as he could yet he barely made a dent in the pile. It was like drinking from a fire hydrant. So he hastily covered up the treasure chest with leaves and dirt, then staggered back to camp. Flopping into his hammock, Suárez did the math and came to some quick calculations. He'd never drag the entire contents of the barrel out of the jungle by himself without being caught. If he was going to get rich, he would have to share the wealth.

And why not? His buddies in Destroyer Company could use a boost. None of them earned enough that they even qualified to pay income taxes. Besides, as he rocked back and forth chewing it all over, Suárez was too agitated to keep the incredible news bottled up inside. He had to let the secret out. He needed advice. He needed coconspirators.

But when Suárez told two of his closest friends camped nearby, they barely stirred from their hammocks. *Mierda*, they said. Bullshit, pure and simple. The equatorial heat, they said, must have poached the man's brain. Suárez grinned. Then he reached inside his backpack and carefully dropped a cluster bomb of bills into their laps.

. . .

THERE WERE APPROXIMATELY 147 VERSIONS OF what happened over the next three days because Suárez, it turned out, was not the only soldier who found the guerrilla riches. And in the fog of war, or perhaps in this case the hallucinogenic haze of an unfolding free-for-all, memories failed, tellers of the tale added and subtracted, molded and twisted. But as the novelist and Vietnam veteran Tim O'Brien observed, soldiers tend to embellish their accounts with the mundane rather than the fantastic. They do so to establish credibility because in many cases, true war stories simply could not be believed.

"Often," he wrote, "the crazy stuff is true and the normal stuff isn't because the normal stuff is necessary to believe the truly incredible craziness." So, in the various renditions that emerged from FARC-land, the outlying details sometimes clashed, but the surreal center held.

"Each witness had his own truth. Each had a different story," said Héctor Alirio Forero, a Bogotá attorney who later represented more than a dozen of the soldiers. "They wouldn't tell everything that happened, not even to their lawyers."

Camped down the hill from their brothers in Vulture, multiple soldiers from Destroyer Company began finding their own barrels of cash. And like Suárez, they couldn't keep the secret. As word of the fantastic riches spread, more and more troops began scouring the jungle floor, hacking at the earth like overcaffeinated grave diggers. Their frantic excavations were aided by a treasure map of sorts. They noticed that the bark of certain trees was etched with symbols—"X," "Y," or "+"—indicating the location and position of the plastic drums. The blue barrels bulged with Colombian pesos but they also found yellow containers that were even more intriguing. They were filled with U.S. currency: twenty-, fifty-, and hundred-dollar bills.

The giddy GIs quickly forgot about the search for Keith, Marc, and Tom. As Suárez later explained, they had already found three gringos: Andrew Jackson, Ulysses S. Grant, and Benjamin Franklin.

How much was there? Months later, a report by the office of Colombia's inspector general, which was in charge of investigating government corruption, estimated that the containers held $14 million in U.S. and Colombian currency. But in the same report, several troops testified that the final haul exceeded $43 million. One government investigator said the figure was much higher—more than $80 million.

"When I got my hands on money, I looked at it. I counted it. And I looked at it again and counted it again because I just couldn't believe it," said soldier Fredy Alexander Rojas. Another soldier said all the cash infused him with an overwhelming sense of liberation, "like letting a dog run free."

Yet almost immediately, the money became a millstone. Rumors of the fantastic riches soon reached the top of the hill where the men of Vulture Company realized they were being shut out. Their true enemy was the FARC, yet now some of the GIs turned on one another, with the have-nots demanding a share from their nouveau riche colleagues.

According to one version of events, Lieutenant Fernando Mojica, commander of Destroyer, contacted Lieutenant Sanabria, the head of Vulture, on the radio and the two met halfway up the rise to devise a way to restore order. As rival officers, the two lieutenants despised each other. But in rebel-dominated patches, they had learned to work together in the name of survival. Now, Mojica realized that another nonaggression pact was in order. His men couldn't keep all the money or the troops from Vulture would rat them out or worse. So the two officers decided to share the riches, passing out packets of pesos and dollars to all 147 men in the two companies.

Sanabria, however, painted a slightly different scene. He claimed that troops from both Vulture and Destroyer came across the buried treasure. He first suspected that his men were camped above a guerrilla ATM when his troops found a FARC notebook, its pages filled with columns of numbers. Later that evening, a soldier stopped by his hammock and told him, "I've got a present for you, Lieutenant." Then he dropped several million pesos onto Sanabria's lap. The soldier explained that he was scouring the jungle floor for rebel munitions and food when his metal detector began to whine. As the GI brushed away the dirt to uncover and deactivate the land mine, he found a barrel of cash. He led Sanabria to the spot. Later, the lieutenant gathered ten of his best soldiers and informed them of the find. "If there's one," he said, "there must be more." And there were.

"It was like what Ali Baba says: 'Open sesame,'" Sanabria said. "There was such happiness. Many of my men had never seen one million pesos (about $350) together at the same time."

Sharing the riches seemed in order because of the 147 soldiers, many of whom were pulling guard or KP duty, only about 30 GIs actually dug money out of the ground. No one had the vaguest idea yet how much was at stake. Under Colombian law, had the soldiers reported their find, they would have been entitled to keep between ten and thirty percent of the final haul to split among them. But as the tally rose neither Sanabria nor Mojica, the two commanding officers, seriously contemplated doing the right thing.

Under this unique set of circumstances, the right thing could be explosive. They were on their own and out of touch. No one was looking. Euphoria mingled with expectation, tension, and suspicion. Sanabria figured that if they turned in the money, higher-ranking officers would give his soldiers three-day passes, then start filling their own pockets. Wasn't that what always happened? It was like that scene in the Clint Eastwood flick *Kelly's Heroes*, where the preppy American captain warns Big Joe and his exhausted foot soldiers that the punishment for looting is death even as he considers the logistics of loading a German yacht aboard a B-17.

"You know how the story goes," said Wilson Sarmiento, an NCO from Destroyer Company who found one of the barrels. "If we would have reported the money, much of it would have been 'lost.' If the military finds one billion pesos, they report that they found 400 million."

Sanabria thought about his men, how they all came from poor families and had given everything to the army only to be abandoned. In that light, the cash was karmic payback. He and Mojica also realized that demanding scores of hungry and exhausted yet suddenly elated troops to return what they'd fairly and squarely found in the jungle could spark a backlash. One of them could end up "eating dirt," Colombian slang for getting fragged.

"The situation was unprecedented," Sanabria said. "It was difficult to maintain order amid the chaos. Should I have reported the money? I'm not sure. Sometimes I think that if I had, those sons of bitches would have killed me. So the decision that I took was the best I could have made."

The two lieutenants had pretty accurately read the minds of their men. Suárez, who by now had forgotten about his upset stomach and had made several trips back to the barrel with his buddies, said that if their officers had insisted on reporting the find, there would have been an uprising.

"You begin to become attached to the money," he said. "You start thinking: 'I won't let them take it from me. How many years have I been killing myself in the jungle?' There would have been problems so there was huge pressure on our commanders. And if it spun out of control, you just don't know what the reaction would have been. But it would have been bad."

So Sanabria and Mojica gathered their men and laid out a new set of ground rules. All the troops would get a cut, with officers and NCOs taking a bit more than the grunts. There would be a pact of silence. And to avoid calling attention to the companies, there were to be no self-inflicted wounds or sudden sicknesses as a way of getting a free ride back to civilization.

They would all dip in and they would all shut up about it. But there were a few Boy Scouts among them. One soldier, an Evangelical Christian, refused to take his share of the money. "People were glaring at him," Suárez recalled. "They kept saying: 'Take it. Take it. Take it.' And he said: 'No. No. I don't want it.' We were all staring at him with really angry faces."

BUT WAS THE MONEY THEIRS FOR the taking?

Making off with other people's possessions had been a part of every conflict since ancient times. Until recently, pillaging and requisitioning food to sustain armies was an accepted part of the deal, a way to compensate for the risks and losses of carrying out invasions. Later, new technologies, such as the canning of food, meant that armies could carry their own supplies, limiting the need to swallow up everything in their path. The 1907 Hague Convention and the 1949 Geneva Convention outlawed looting during wartime. But that didn't stop the practice.

During World War II, the Nazis plundered paintings and sculptures from nearly every territory they occupied, with some objects destined for the never-built "Fuhrer Museum" commissioned by Hitler, a frustrated art-ist. Serb paramilitaries stripped Croatia and Bosnia of virtually all durable goods. After invading Kuwait in 1990, the Iraqi Army made off with mil-lions in gold bullion, fleets of luxury cars, and even amusement-park rides.

Then there was the case of U.S. Army sergeant Matt Novak, a deco-rated Gulf War hero who was sent back to Iraq for the 2003 invasion. He found $200 million in American $100 bills in one of Saddam's safe houses, pocketed what he could, then sank the rest in a canal, planning to retrieve it later with scuba gear. Novak, who confessed but was still kicked out of the army, said the invading troops were conditioned to take whatever they found.

"We'd come in the front door and it was a free-for-all. Whatever we needed we took. If there was money it was taken. If there was jewelry it was taken. Military stuff, of course it was taken. . . . People used to tell me that when I got back I was going to have to have counseling because otherwise I'd walk into Wal-Mart and just take what I wanted."

What happened in FARC-land, however, fell into a gray area. Looting implied plundering goods from their rightful owners. But the rebel stash had already been stolen by gun-toting bandits performing cashectomies on the good people of Colombia. The troops reasoned that these banknotes now had no legitimate proprietors, and so they weren't committing a crime, they were performing a public good. They were cheating the cheaters out of money that would otherwise go toward grenades and guns, making the guerrillas stronger and, ultimately, perpetuating the war.

Rather than being castigated, the thinking went, they ought to be deco-rated. There was also a sense among the troops that the cash was a seren-dipitous payoff for years of dangerous duty protecting the homeland. And if that wasn't enough, it was Easter week, the holiest time of year in Colombia. Many soldiers viewed the treasure as nothing less than a gift from God.

CHAPTER 8

THE LION'S DEN

*The solitude, desperation and fatigue lead hostages to constantly
contemplate taking their own lives.*
—Martha Lucía Aristizábal, *How to Survive a Kidnapping*

Jo Rosano had begged her son, Marc Gonsalves, to reject Northrop Grumman's princely offer to work as a systems analyst on antidrug air missions over Colombia. "Marc, it's not worth it," Jo told him. "They will shoot at your airplane."

Jo had always been a ferocious den mother around Marc. Once, after some punk at school punched her son, Jo marched up to the kid and warned him that while she might be too small to retaliate, she had a posse of beefy Italian-American nephews who would be only too happy to even the score. Years later, she spotted a tearful Marc walking home from American Legion baseball tryouts. He'd been cut. Jo fumed and later gave the coach hell because she knew that the boys who came from more prominent families in Bristol, Connecticut, made the team.

Jo developed her toughness and tribalism amid her own difficult upbringing. Giuseppina Teodoro—everyone called her Jo—grew up in Salerino, Italy, one of four brothers and sisters. Her mother lavished attention on her older sister and paid for her to go to university. She insulted Jo or simply ignored her. Her father was a furniture maker who built and sold tables, chairs, headboards, and bedroom sets. But he was just scraping by and sometimes his clients paid him with eggs or chickens. So, in 1956, he moved the family to New Britain, Connecticut, where he found construction and factory work. Speaking only Italian, eight-year-old Jo felt like an outcast in the New World. She cried constantly. But Jo learned English and made a few friends. And as she blended in, she shed her innate shyness.

After high school, Jo did the Connecticut thing, working a series of jobs for banks and insurance companies. She also began dating George Gonsalves, a banker who later worked in information technology. The two were married and moved to Bristol, an ethnically mixed city of 61,000 known for its colonial-era clockmakers—it housed the American Clock and Watch Museum. But Jo and George constantly clashed and, after twenty years, the marriage expired.

Marc lived for a few years with Jo, then, at age sixteen, he moved in with George, who had by then remarried and relocated to rural Connecticut. If Jo was protective, George was the drill sergeant who lit a fire under Marc's butt. Marc had a lot of friends and made the high school wrestling team, but in George's view his son never pushed himself.

"Youthful ambitions? He didn't have any. He was a B student. He was a B individual," George said. "He could do very well if he applied himself, but he had a tendency to be lazy."

After graduating, Marc figured he'd punch the clock at the local Walgreens while he figured out what to do next. But George was having none of it. Marc could either attend the nearby community college or join the military, but he wasn't going to goof off all summer. As a young lad, George had also been adrift. Fearing that he'd be sent to Vietnam if he got drafted, George joined the air force—and was promptly sent to Vietnam. "It was entertaining at night because we'd watch the rockets come in and run for the bunkers," said George, who worked as an air traffic controller. Though at times harrowing, the experience helped George mature. And when Marc followed his father's footsteps into the air force, George was pleased.

"It's funny how a kid makes decisions," Marc said. "I had just seen that movie *Top Gun*. That was cool. Tom Cruise, the motorcycle, the hot-looking instructor. It was sexy. So I'm thinking: '*Top Gun*! I can be a pilot!'"

Except he needed a college degree to qualify for flight training. So, this time picturing himself as James Bond, Marc decided to become a spy. As a young NCO, Marc trained to be an image interpreter at MacDill Air Force Base in Tampa. It was classified stuff, involving the deciphering of satellite photos and other images of tanks and artillery in places like Iraq. Sometimes the air force sent him down to Bogotá to analyze the images that the California Microwave crews brought back from the jungle. The pay wasn't great—just $28,000 a year—but at first money wasn't an issue. Marc was nineteen and single, a free man in Florida. But not for long.

While moonlighting as a bartender in Tampa, Marc met an exotic dancer with big blond hair who had her name, Shane, tattooed across the top of her left hand. Shane was raising two boys from a previous relationship but wanted to make a fresh start with Marc. The once aimless teenager suddenly knew exactly what he wanted. Without telling his parents, Marc and Shane were married in a ceremony that was so hastily arranged the wedding planners got Marc's name wrong. The lettering on their cake read: "Congratulations Shane and Jim."

"I know it was a stupid decision because Shane and I didn't know each other very well," Marc said. "But the only way to live off base with her was by being married. And married couples earned a housing allowance. That was why we got married so quickly."

Never one to keep her feelings bottled up, Jo clashed with Shane from the beginning and pleaded with her son to reconsider. She was desperate to save Marc from a situation she described as "a hillbilly movie."

"One year she had blond hair. The next year she had red hair," Jo said. "She wore layers and layers of gold, like Mr. T."

But Marc was in love. And unlike his mother with her explosive personality, he was go-along, get-along. He moved his new family to the Florida Keys where he was assigned to a military base in Key West. Marc assumed responsibility for Shane's two kids, Joey and Cody, and the couple had a daughter, named Destiney. Marc loved to play with the children and to cook for them, often calling Jo for her chicken recipes.

But there were strains in the marriage. According to Marc, Shane was a big spender with a taste for expensive purebred dogs. In one of their fights, they came to blows. The oven-hot summers in Big Pine Key were also getting to Marc, who talked of buying a nice spread back in Connecticut. But that wasn't going to happen on his air force paycheck. Marc had already asked his mother to loan him $8,000. So Marc posted his résumé on Monster.com and was soon doing the same work he did in the air force for a private military contractor in Key West at twice the salary. Then Marc received an even better offer. While in Bogotá, he'd made friends with one of the California Microwave crew members who recommended Marc for a job. It meant living in Colombia but it also meant a massive salary bump. Jo protested vigorously, telling her son that if he was going to leave the service for the private sector, he should consider a safer job, like becoming an air traffic controller. But his mind was made up.

Marc was an innocent abroad. Before his first sojourns to Colombia, he'd never ventured farther afield than Canada or the Mexican border. When Marc arrived in Bogotá, his initial reaction was to marvel at how much a few Colombian pesos could buy. He'd call Jo to report that for five bucks at lunchtime, restaurants would feed you half a cow. The job wasn't bad, either: four weeks on, two weeks off, and $150,000 a year. Marc's plan was to work three years in Colombia, save $50,000 per year, and then put a down payment on the Connecticut dream house. Never one to make waves, Marc ignored the warnings of pilots Doug Cockes and Paul Hooper about the single-engine Cessna.

"I was young and new and that's what my attitude was," Marc said. "I just wanted to be successful at the mission."

But after just four months on the job, the Grand Caravan crash-landed in the jungle and Marc was missing. "Right now," said Jo, as she lit a Virginia Slims in the living room of her Bristol home, "he's probably thinking, 'I should have listened to my mom.'"

AFTER YEARS OF OBSERVING THE JUNGLE through digital cameras from an altitude of ten thousand feet, Keith, Marc, and Tom were getting a feel for what their high-powered lenses never registered. Some of their new neighbors were coral snakes and tarantulas. From the treetops, monkeys would fling their feces on passersby. They witnessed dark tapestries of ants moving across the forest floor and watched as spiders, frogs, and salamanders scampered out of the way of the coming swarm. And the jungle was loud.

"There's a constant chorus of crickets and birds chirping and monkeys screaming," Marc said. "The only time it stops is for the split second after a bomb hits. Then everything goes quiet for just a nanosecond. And then they start up again."

The Americans moved slowly across this strange new landscape. They were still recovering from the aches and pains of the crash and Keith's feet were a mess. The guerrillas gave the hostages Wellington boots but Keith was a size eleven and a half and the rebel logistics men didn't have anything close. They cut off the tips of his rubber boots so his toes could stick out, but he was constantly stubbing them on roots and rocks. His guts were finally on the mend, though no thanks to the FARC's prehistoric medical techniques. At one point, two stout guerrillas began violently massaging Keith's stomach, then turned him upside down and shook him as they tightened a tourniquet around his belly.

"They were literally squeezing the shit out of me," Keith said.

Psychologists who treat former hostages say the initial months of captivity are the most stressful because prisoners are often still in denial, spending more time fighting their circumstances than accepting them. But for Keith, Marc, and Tom, the main problem was the uncertainty and the mental anguish as they considered the impact the kidnappings must be having on their families back in the States.

Then there was the boredom. After living extraordinarily hectic lives—juggling family obligations, traveling overseas, and working long hours at high-tech jobs—suddenly they were thrust into a kind of black hole, with no duties, no gadgets, and far more hours in the day than they knew how to fill. Time, that precious commodity in the modern world, became a curse.

To kill a few hours, Marc stared at spiders spinning their webs and meticulously cleaned the treads of his boot with a toothbrush. Keith escaped by trying to remember every moment of his life. Daydreaming about Cape Cod, Tom tied fishermen's knots.

"I would count bugs on my tent top," Tom said. "I would look at the trees, look at the toucans. I would try to build houses and motorcycles in my mind."

The three men learned how to make peashooters out of plants and whittled a set of weights out of logs to equip what they called their "Flintstones gym." But just as they'd get comfortable in their daily rhythm, the FARC would break camp and force the men to hike through the mountains once more. Also throwing them off were the ever-changing camp rules. Sometimes they were allowed to roam free. Then, for no apparent reason, they would be locked down at night inside wooden boxes with chain-link doors.

Even worse, there were long stretches when Keith, Marc, and Tom were not allowed to talk to their guards or among themselves because the FARC feared they might plot an escape. Thus, they could only whisper to one another in passing on the way to breakfast or the latrine. For a time, they lost their voices due to lack of use—a common symptom among hostages.

Luis Eladio Pérez, a Colombian senator who was later held alongside the Americans, recalled how the forced silence caused half of his face to become temporarily paralyzed. He borrowed a mirror from a rebel and performed facial exercises to recover the movement of the atrophied muscles. He also held lengthy, one-way conversations with trees.

Another Colombian political hostage, Óscar Tulio Lizcano, was not allowed to talk to anyone, not even to his guards, for most of his eight years in captivity. To keep his brain from completely shutting down, the onetime university professor created ten imaginary students out of sticks and branches. "We would study for three hours a day," Lizcano said. "I gave them classes in philosophy and history." The guerrillas thought he had gone mad.

Keith, Marc, and Tom were completely cut off from current events because the FARC did not allow them to listen to radio news programs. They went from the information age to the Stone Age. Once, Keith overheard something about Tiger Woods at the Masters Tournament on a rebel's short-wave radio. The Americans talked about Woods for the next three days. When an old newspaper made its way to their camp, they were delighted to spot an ad for a Dell computer. But it wasn't much to hang on to.

"I had never wanted to be a priest or a monk but I was gaining some appreciation for what the life of quiet, solitude and faith must be like," Marc said. "But I hated living in my own head exclusively. It got too crowded in there."

Controlling the mind was imperative. With little to do but chew over the past, daydream, and fantasize about the future, their spirits dipped, their brains spun in all directions.

Terry Anderson, who was the chief Middle East correspondent for the Associated Press when he was kidnapped in 1985 by Islamic extremists, believed that after several years in chains he had become an expert at mind control. But one day he began beating his head against a wall trying to make it all stop. As the blood ran down his face his guards raced in to save him.

Lapsing into depression could be a form of slow-motion suicide. Hostages sometimes stopped eating or became careless during marches and hurt themselves. In backwoods areas with little access to antibiotics and other medicines, minor injuries could quickly turn into life-threatening code reds. A few desperate prisoners provoked their guards into shooting them. Pérez, the kidnapped Colombian senator, twice contemplated killing himself. A diabetic, he pushed aside his food figuring he would develop hypoglycemia and lapse into a coma. When that didn't work, he was set to gash his veins with a nail clipper when a guard approached and asked if he could borrow the device.

Tom, the eldest of the three American hostages, sometimes grew so frantic he got the dry heaves. He didn't dare think about his young son, Tommy, back in Merritt Island because it was simply too painful. "I would wake up in the morning and want to put a bullet in my head," he said.

Marc's darkest day nearly did him in. He had a dream about his daughter, Destiney, and was ecstatic to be with his family. But then he woke up and realized he was still a prisoner. He became so melancholy that he couldn't even lift his head. Keith and Tom noted Marc's state of depression and wrapped their sobbing colleague in a bear hug.

"But something happened that day," Marc said. "There was a rainbow and the three of us, we had our arms around each other, and we were looking at it. And I held that rainbow. I took it [to mean] we were going to live and we were going to go home. . . . I just never knew when."

Emotionally vulnerable, Keith, Marc, and Tom sometimes allowed themselves to believe their guards' optimistic forecasts that freedom was just around the corner. They interpreted the arrival of FARC higher-ups at their camps to mean that a prisoner exchange was in the works. Once, the Americans were told that they would be taken to an airplane and speculated about being home in time for family birthdays and the Fourth of July. But "the plane" turned out to be the wreckage of an old Cessna where the FARC had set up one of their camps. After a handful of false alarms, the hostages eventually realized that the guerrillas were either lying or clueless. And as their weeks of captivity stretched into months, there were disconcerting signs that their jungle odyssey was only just beginning.

One day, a rebel nicknamed Pollo, which means "chicken" in Spanish, gave the hostages a year's supply of soap, razors, and toothpaste.

"I never would have guessed that knowing how many bars of soap I had at my disposal would have such an influence on my outlook," Keith said. "But when Pollo dumped those things at our feet and told us they'd be in short supply, he might as well have been dumping our hearts into the ground."

Their lodgings also began to take on a more permanent feel. Instead of latrines, one camp featured an outhouse with a manual flush system. At another, they were housed in a three-room shack of chainsawed wooden planks topped with a corrugated metal roof. Rats had built a nest in the rafters and their constant movement showered the men with debris. Underneath the floorboards, pigs rooted in the mud. At night, vampire bats fluttered in circles around the hostages.

For the Americans, survival was job one, but that required keeping up their morale. So they looked for small victories anywhere they could find them. One defense mechanism was a sense of humor, and among their targets was a veteran FARC commander named Martín Sombra.

The Americans first met Sombra after they were marched out of the mountains and into an area known as the Yarí Plains in southeast Caquetá state. There, they were handed over to a group of about two hundred rebels under the command of Sombra, who joined the FARC in 1968 and was nearly sixty years old. Sombra was old school. For every jungle illness, he claimed that soup was the cure. He would kill ocelots and boa constrictors, cook them over a fire, and feed the broth to the hostages—though their normal diet was a monotonous, carb-heavy mix of rice, pasta, yucca, and beans, and occasionally armadillo, caiman, monkey, or fish.

"I came to love fish heads," Tom said. "I'd eat the brain, the tongue, the cheeks, the eyeballs, everything. I'd get annoyed if I got a fish head without an eyeball."

Thanks to extra helpings, Sombra had packed on the pounds and the gringos took to calling him Fat Man. They also delighted in pulling his leg. At first, Sombra was afraid of the Americans. He had been told by his commander that they were Special Forces and that if they ever got their hands on him they would rip him in half. But they didn't know much Spanish so Sombra tried to teach them, starting out with simple words like "food" and "water." As the Americans warmed up to Sombra, Tom began calling him "Son of a Bitch," which Sombra figured was a term of endearment.

"I liked to talk shit with the gringos," Sombra said later. "My belly hurt from laughing so much."

Keith focused on the Spanish swearwords. As his vocabulary improved, he jokingly called one of his guards an "ill-born son of a bitch." The rebel frowned and pulled Keith aside, explaining that the phrase was the worst thing he could possibly say and that if he uttered the insult to another sentry he might be repaid with a bullet.

Keith replied with a smile. "All right, I won't say it again . . . you ill-born son of a bitch!"

JO FOUND OUT ABOUT THE GRAND Caravan crash and Marc's kidnapping on her fifty-fifth birthday. For the next two months, all she did was stay in her house "crying and losing my mind." But then she got mad. She couldn't fathom why rescued POW Jessica Lynch had been transformed into a war hero and yet no one had ever heard of the three Americans lost in the Colombian jungle.

So despite the State Department's urgings and Northrop Grumman officials' requests that she lie low, Jo went public. She called a reporter at the *Hartford Courant* and gave the first of what would turn out to be hundreds of interviews about the hostages in Colombia. Jo lashed out at the

Bush administration and questioned why the United States had gotten sucked into Colombia's conflict. But driving her despair was a deep longing to reconnect with her son.

Then she received a phone call. Victoria Bruce, a documentary filmmaker, was on the line and she asked Jo a question: Would you like to send a message to Marc?

CHAPTER 9

BONFIRES

It is the bitter fate of any idea to lose its royal form and power, to lose its "virtue" the moment it descends from its solitary throne to work its will amongst the people.
—JOSEPH CONRAD, *Nostromo*

THE GUERRILLAS WERE FREEZING THEIR HIND ends off. It was February 2000—three years before the FARC kidnapped the U.S. contractors—and the rebel leaders had just arrived in Switzerland as part of a European trip put together by the Colombian government to promote peace negotiations. But the bus picking them up at the Geneva airport had stalled. So the rebels and the Bogotá officials they were trying to overthrow teamed up to push the vehicle down the icy highway. Later, they unwound around a cozy fireplace where they broke open several bottles of wine and took turns singing boleros. Sworn enemies, they were now harmonizing.

The trip was part publicity stunt, part transatlantic Hail Mary. The idea was to salvage the 1999 peace negotiations that had quickly descended into diplomatic burlesque. The two sides didn't clash over whether the negotiating table should be round or rectangular, but they went in circles when the subject turned to essential points, like a broad cease-fire. It was almost like they were speaking different languages.

For the government, ending hostilities meant stopping armed attacks and war crimes, like kidnapping—which made sense. But the FARC regarded the state's failure to guarantee decent living conditions for the poor as a "hostility." In other words, the guerrillas would stop chaining innocent people to trees only after all 45 million Colombians had decent jobs, schools, and health care. All the dithering convinced some participants that the FARC had no intention of signing any paperwork.

"We could go on like this forever," said Alfonso López Caballero, one of the envoys from Bogotá.

To break the impasse, government negotiators decided to break the FARC leaders out of their isolation. Manuel Marulanda, the FARC's founder and maximum leader, had been hiding in the hills since the late 1940s. He hadn't been to the movies since World War II and had never even seen the ocean. The hope was that the guerrillas would visit several European capitals and realize that in the post–cold war world, left-wing leaders didn't need bullets; they could take power through the ballot box. And maybe they would take these lessons back to Colombia and be more willing to give peace a chance.

But these guerrillas were not the slow-witted doofuses the government sometimes made them out to be. They were focused and patient and viewed the peace talks as a way to buy time while they ramped up their war machine. They played along with this European tour because it seemed harmless enough. And in an ironic twist, it was the Bogotá sophisticates who sometimes came off like the rubes. When dining in Rome, Simón Trinidad, one of the few FARC leaders from the upper class, had to explain to some of the confused government types that instead of a dominant main course, they would be served a series of dishes—*antipasti*, followed by a *primo* and a *secondo*.

During the twenty-three-day trip, the guerrillas, dressed in donated business suits and ties, visited Spain, France, Italy, Sweden, and Norway— where on the last night they took a sleigh ride through the woods to a restaurant. At each stop, European politicians urged them to cash in the FARC's awesome military power for a stake in the country's political system. And at every news conference, the rebels made increasingly moderate remarks. By the end of the trip, this motley band was photographed with grins on their faces and airport duty-free shopping bags in their arms.

"It was, in many ways, the high point of the whole peace process," said Jan Egeland, a Norwegian who served as the UN secretary-general's special adviser on Colombia and accompanied the rebels on the trip.

But there were signs that the traveling revolutionaries hadn't swallowed the European Kool-Aid. They were obsessed with buying lightweight souvenirs, like pen flashlights, that would be useful in the jungle. At the end of the trip, they gave away their enormous wheeled suitcases, since roller luggage would not work so well in the rain forest mud. And FARC leader Marulanda made them renounce whatever conciliatory hooey they'd spouted in Europe. He also demanded that they hand over their wool and polyester suits, which were inspected for tracking devices. Then, the shirts, pants, underwear, socks, vests, jackets, and ties were placed in a pile and set on fire.

THE PARANOIA AND MISTRUST THAT RAN so deep within FARC ranks had also been key to the organization's longevity. Manuel Marulanda is the one who most personified this insular, survivalist worldview.

They called him Tirofijo, Spanish for Sureshot, a nickname he had picked up during his early days in the mountains when it was said that he never wasted a bullet. During the ill-fated peace negotiations, the last time outsiders had a close-up look at the reclusive rebel commander, Marulanda exuded a quiet authority. "When he shows up it's like the arrival of Ho Chi Minh," said Caballero, the government envoy. "He has the final word on everything."

Yet Marulanda didn't exactly suck the oxygen out of the tent. In his seventies, he seemed more lugubrious than lethal. His girlfriend, a rebel in her late thirties named Sandra, sometimes cut his food into little pieces for him. He wore a pistol on one hip, a machete in a fringed leather holster on the other. The bill of his field cap was always flipped up at a dorky angle and, in the style of Colombian plainsmen, he draped a towel over his right shoulder to wipe away sweat and swat mosquitoes. In Colombia, he was a legend. Yet he lacked the intense charisma of Che Guevara or the oratorical flourishes of Fidel Castro. Instead, the paramount leader of Latin America's largest, most powerful guerrilla army came across like Marlon Brando's end-stage Godfather, a thickening and weary warrior emeritus who just might tip over into the flower patch.

"He looked like an old granddad in the countryside in his Wellington boots and his dirty towel," Egeland said. "It was hard to understand the power of Marulanda except that, at times, you could feel how ruthless the guy could be."

Many people back in Bogotá thought of Sureshot and his rebel band as failures because they were still fighting after four decades without ultimate victory. But for the FARC, the wrinkles, potbellies, and age spots of many of its leaders were badges of honor. Other guerrilla groups, impatient for glory, burned out or faded away. But for Marulanda, war was a marathon, not a sprint, and he had a knack for pacing himself.

Countless times over the past half-century, Colombian troops claimed to have killed him. But with a better grasp of his surroundings, Sureshot always managed to escape. Over the years he outfoxed scores of generals and outlasted more than a dozen presidents. He was old, yes. But he was the world's oldest guerrilla.

He was also a details man. During the peace talks, he invited a pack of reporters to lunch and—as if taking stock of the enemy—went to great lengths to get the correct body count. The next day, rebels in SUVs escorted a convoy of press vehicles twenty miles down a dusty road to a red-brick bungalow with tile floors and white plastic furniture. There, a staff of cooks served huge bowls of *sancocho de gallina*, a stew of chicken, potatoes, yucca, and plantains, along with fried sweetbread and shots of Chivas Regal. With Sandra at his side, Marulanda bent over his food, gripping his spoon in his fist like a six-year-old. Afterward, as some of the FARC's most cunning and deadly bloc commanders helped clear the table and wash the dishes, Marulanda turned to address the journalists.

"I never went looking for war," he began. "The war came looking for me."

The eldest of five children, Marulanda grew up in Génova in the coffee-growing state of Quindío. He was born Pedro Antonio Marín but later assumed his nom de guerre in honor of a slain Communist union leader. As a teenager, he dreamed of becoming a tango dancer or playing the violin. But he dropped out of school after fifth grade to help his working-class family. He was a math whiz and had a knack for cutting deals as he traveled the back roads selling lumber, meat, and bread. In Marulanda's telling, he would have led a quiet life as a country merchant were it not for the events of April 9, 1948. On that day, Jorge Eliécer Gaitán, a Liberal Party presidential aspirant beloved by the Colombian underclass, was shot down on the streets of Bogotá by a deranged killer. But the Liberals blamed the rival Conservative Party, which considered Gaitán a dangerous radical. The two parties had fought several wars in the last century but this feud reached a new level of senseless barbarity. A combination of political rivalries, religious fervor, and class resentment led to a horrific outbreak of killings, rapes, looting, and land grabs. Over the next decade, more than 200,000 people perished in what became known as La Violencia.

Some of the bloodshed was outright banditry under the guise of political grievances. But it was also fueled by frustration in the countryside over unequal land distribution, unemployment, and the lack of education. Historian David Bushnell pointed out that had the countryside been a little more developed, a little less feudal, the sheer intensity of the violence would have been unthinkable. "Only a semi-literate peasantry with the vaguest notions about what was happening at the national level could be made to believe that members of the other party were somehow in league with the devil," he wrote. "And only in small towns of utterly grinding poverty would control of the local government, with a yearly budget amounting to something under a thousand dollars, be sufficient motive to go out and kill people."

Among those targeted by Conservative gunmen was Marulanda's Liberal family in Génova. In 1949, after gangs burned down his store and killed one of his uncles, Marulanda and fourteen cousins formed a rural self-defense group. The anarchy and violence provoked mass displacements. Homeless and on the run, a handful of Colombians drifted into the mountains to join Marulanda's tiny band of gunmen, which included disgruntled Liberals and, soon afterward, members of the Communist Party.

By 1955, Marulanda's malcontents had set up a clandestine agricultural commune on the rugged Andean slopes of southern Tolima state, an area known as Marquetalia. They divided up the land and prevented the army and the Conservative-dominated police from penetrating the zone. Olinda Losada, whose boyfriend was a guerrilla, learned to read at Marquetalia and sewed clothes for the rebels. "It was very well organized," she said. "We had bullfights and beauty pageants."

The movement was more about survival than anything else. Marulanda studied military texts, not Marx. Still, he was impressed by the Communists' discipline, their military skills, and their organizational abilities. They also provided an ideological framework for the burgeoning conflict. Marulanda came from Liberal stock, but by then the party had worked out a power-sharing pact with the Conservatives. To end the violence, the two parties agreed to divide up everything from mayoral posts to ministries and alternate in the presidency. But the arrangement shut out all other political organizations. Feeling betrayed by the Liberals, Marulanda threw in his lot with the Communists.

Sureshot's arsenal didn't amount to much. The men at Marquetalia were armed with pistols, shotguns, and homemade grenades, and in one low-tech ambush, Marulanda recalled, his troops used spears. They once fired on a bus that was supposedly carrying government troops but ended up killing two nuns. Even their looting seemed amateurish. After taking over one town and robbing its bank, the fighters commandeered a grocery store and filled their pockets with candy.

For the first few years, it was hard to take them seriously. But in 1959, Fidel Castro seized power in Cuba, an event that inspired a generation of left-wing rebel groups. It also provoked a Red scare, and Colombian politicians began denouncing Marquetalia as an "Independent Red Republic" in the Andes. With the help of U.S. military advisers, the Colombian Army in 1964 sent thousands of troops into peaks and valleys surrounding Marquetalia. The rebels escaped through a network of Indian trails but historians described the fallout as profound. The attack was deemed as the beginning of Colombia's modern-day guerrilla war because it convinced Marulanda to scrap his self-defense doctrine and create a more aggressive insurgency that would fight on behalf of the poor and install a Marxist government in Bogotá. Two years later, he christened the movement the Fuerzas Armadas Revolucionarias de Colombia (Revolutionary Armed Forces of Colombia), or FARC. Its initial strength: 350 men.

OVER THE NEXT TWO DECADES, THE FARC grew in fits and starts and at one point the government wasn't even sure the rebel outfit still existed. One of the main problems was money. Though linked to the Communists, the FARC never received much funding from the party nor, for that matter, from Castro or Eastern Bloc countries. So, at a conference of top rebel leaders in 1982, the FARC took a historic decision. The group would create a war economy to finance a massive expansion of its forces.

To fill its coffers, the FARC began collecting taxes for every kilogram of coca paste—a rough form of cocaine—exported from rebel-held territory and levying takeoff and landing fees on drug dealers who used clandestine airstrips in guerrilla zones. Critics quickly cast the FARC as a drug cartel. Lewis Tambs, the U.S. ambassador to Colombia in the mid-1980s, had the FARC in mind when he coined the term *narco-guerrillas*. But there was a key difference. For the narcos, the objective was to get rich. For the FARC, the drug business was a means to their revolutionary ends.

The other key decision made at the FARC conference was to start kidnapping en masse. The FARC had long condemned abductions, bombings, and other terrorist acts pulled off by rival rebel organizations. But the easy money from kidnappings was too good to pass up. Much of the countryside was beyond the state's control, making it relatively easy to abduct plantation owners, businessmen, and other big-time capitalists and to extract huge ransoms for their release. Sure, it was a crime against humanity, but the guerrillas viewed pained arguments about human rights violations as drawing-room debates for the bourgeoisie that didn't apply to them. Besides, kidnapping was already part of the national fabric. By the mid-1960s the practice was so widespread that the government had established a national commission to investigate kidnappings. Often just the threat of kidnapping was enough. Business owners and landlords were given the option of forking over wads of cash or taking a lengthy eco-tour with the rebels.

When Panamerican Beverages, Colombia's main distributor of Coca-Cola, refused to pay the FARC, the rebels burned forty-eight of the company's trucks, kidnapped eleven workers, killed seven, and robbed the firm's installations and vehicles more than four hundred times. Thus, many Colombians decided it was easier to open their wallets. The owner of a Bogotá trucking company, for example, admitted to paying a local FARC front $300 a month to allow his vehicles to pass unmolested along an eighty-mile stretch of highway that crossed rebel-held territory. "I can operate in peace for $300," he said. "If that's the way to avoid bigger problems, why not?"

The payments became known as *vacunas*, vaccinations, because the monthly installments inoculated the victim from being hauled into the hills. Disbursements could also be made in the form of food, medicine, boots, uniforms, ammunition, radios, and, later, prepaid cell phone cards. Óscar Beltrán, who ran a poultry farm near the guerrilla-infested town of Viotá, recalled turning over hundreds of chickens to the guerrillas as well as 1.25 million eggs.

But the FARC also targeted major companies, like the U.S. coal giant Drummond Co., Nestlé, Halliburton, and 3M. A 1998 Colombian government report estimated that oil companies turned over more than $40 million annually to the guerrillas in extortion payments. The rebels preferred extortion because ransoms were subject to drawn-out negotiations and the amounts were unpredictable. By contrast, extortion payments were usually fixed amounts paid at the same time every year, which helped the FARC draw up their financial plans, like corporate executives.

Over the next fifteen years, money from the drug trade, kidnappings, and extortion helped the FARC expand to seventeen thousand foot soldiers and evolve into a kind of revolutionary-industrial complex thought to be raking in $500 million annually. But self-financing and the resulting autonomy created their own set of problems. Whereas Nicaragua's Sandinistas and the Farabundo Martí rebels in El Salvador relied on fervent political support in the countryside to survive and turned to Fidel Castro for both military training and behavioral guidelines, the cash-rich FARC had no need for outsiders. It followed its own skewed moral compass.

In 1999 alone, the group kidnapped 965 people, among them taxi drivers, bakers, and small-scale farmers. The FARC's criminal behavior made the group deeply unpopular, but the leadership didn't seem to care. Why bother with the slow, difficult, precinct-by-precinct process of winning the support of the peasants when you could bully them into collaborating? Conceived amid the fires of La Violencia and raised on the revolutionary ethos of the 1960s, the FARC had became so enmeshed in drug deals, assassinations, and criminal conspiracies that by the turn of the century the organization seemed more like some twisted protuberance from the family tree of Pablo Escobar.

FROM TIME TO TIME, THE BOGOTÁ government extended an olive branch. But the FARC's steady influx of cash dulled any sense of urgency. Other rebel groups, like the EPL and M-19, eventually disarmed, but the FARC claimed these rivals had been bought off for diplomatic postings, scholarships, and other perks. In the FARC's lexicon, perestroika remained an unpronounceable foreign word. In its rarefied mythology, disarming and embracing peace was more dangerous than war. And the group's iron-clad insistence on hanging on to its weapons was solidified during the rebel group's only stab at legal politics.

In 1984, FARC leaders agreed to a cease-fire and formed their own party, called the Patriotic Union. If the party gained legs and turned into a viable political force, there would no longer be grounds for an armed uprising and, in theory, the FARC would disband. Bogotá officials, in turn, promised to protect the new party from reprisals. But neither side played it straight.

To make their intentions clear, other guerrilla groups disarmed before jumping into politics. But the FARC and its Communist Party backers wanted it both ways. The Communists clung to Vladimir Lenin's theory of commingling legal and illegal methods on the road to revolution, a concept synthesized by the phrase "the combination of all forms of struggle." In other words, the FARC would entwine war with civilian politics. The Irish Republican Army and the Basque separatist group ETA had mixed the two and gotten away with it. But that was in genteel Europe. In Colombia, with its history of bloody vendettas, civil wars, and death squads, the fusion was a recipe for disaster.

As a few high-profile members of the FARC put down their rifles to organize the Patriotic Union and run for office, the bulk of the rebels continued with their plan to topple the government. In private, rebel leaders viewed the Patriotic Union as the ideal vehicle to spread their message to the cities and recruit more fighters.

But no one told the idealistic Colombians who flocked to the party's headquarters to sign up. Most rank-and-file party members leaned left but hated guns and saw the experiment as a way to end the war, not expand it. They began winning congressional seats and mayoral posts. But much of the Colombian establishment and the military viewed the Patriotic Union as the FARC's Trojan horse. Party members were assumed to be guerrillas in disguise and, thus, legitimate targets.

The backlash was furious. Between 1984 and 1992, illegal right-wing paramilitaries slaughtered more than two thousand party members and completely gutted the Patriotic Union. The dead included everyone from office secretaries and mayors to two presidential candidates. Human rights groups called it political genocide. The killing spree also wiped out some of the FARC's most capable political cadres. Those losses would haunt the FARC and help explain why its leaders would later make so many wrongheaded decisions.

The government bore much of the blame. Bogotá officials often denounced Patriotic Union members as rebels—in effect putting a big red bull's-eye on their backs—then did little to stop the killings, which were often carried out by death squads in collaboration with the military. Yet in a perverse way, the party served its purpose for the FARC. Forever after, Marulanda's minions could hold up the extermination of the Patriotic Union as Exhibit A in their argument that the only path for leftists to reach political power in Colombia was the warpath.

BY THE LATE 1990S, THE FARC was present in thirty-one of Colombia's thirty-two states, the only exception being the Caribbean island of San

Andrés 450 miles offshore. The army's string of battlefield disasters had convinced the war-weary population that the only way out was by cutting a deal with the guerrillas. The FARC found itself in an ideal position to extract major givebacks from the government.

Thanks to the nation's long string of guerrilla wars and peace negotiations, Colombia was loaded with talented people schooled in the history and folkways of the FARC. Yet the designated deal-maker was a last-minute convert to the cause of peace. Like many sons of ex-presidents, Andrés Pastrana—whose father, Misael Pastrana, served as president from 1970 to 1974—seemed to think that following in his footsteps to the national palace was a birthright. A former TV journalist and Bogotá mayor, Pastrana had a sunny disposition. He spoke perfect English and boasted of close ties to Washington power brokers. He also campaigned on an anticorruption platform that appealed to Colombians following the debacle of his predecessor, Ernesto Samper, who was accused of winning the presidency with the help of $6 million from the Cali drug cartel.

Yet Pastrana was widely viewed as an intellectual lightweight and somewhat tone deaf. He once toured the coffee-belt city of Armenia, which had been devastated by an earthquake, wearing a pink golf shirt. For most of his political career, Pastrana paid scant attention to the guerrilla war raging in the countryside. But in seeking an edge during the 1998 presidential election, he repositioned himself as the man who would make peace with the guerrillas. Then, a week before the vote, Pastrana pulled off a masterstroke. He sent an emissary into the jungle to meet with FARC leaders who declared that they would be willing to negotiate with Pastrana, but not with his opponent, Horacio Serpa, a former government minister. It was a major coup that helped Pastrana score a narrow victory.

Perhaps as a result, Pastrana, if not willing to give away the entire bodega, was set to grant the FARC enormous concessions. As a goodwill gesture that would ensure the rebels' security during the negotiations, he also agreed to create a demilitarized zone. But rather than designating a rural township or a cow pasture on some farmer's back forty, Pastrana redrew the Colombian map. He agreed to pull government troops from sixteen thousand square miles of territory in southern Colombia, an area the size of Switzerland totaling four percent of the national territory. True, the region was already a rebel stronghold. But now the few police stations and the lone army base in the zone were closed down even as the guerrillas got to keep their guns. They were now the official overlords of the DMZ.

When the talks kicked off on January 7, 1999, Pastrana invited hundreds of dignitaries, including the U.S. ambassador, Sandinista leader Daniel Ortega, and the writer Gabriel García Márquez. In San Vicente del Caguán, the largest town in the DMZ, they were treated to the bizarre spectacle of a FARC honor guard set up for Pastrana's arrival, as if he were a visiting head of state of a foreign country. During the ceremony, Pastrana was supposed to shake hands with Marulanda, who would be seated on the stage next to him. But the FARC leader was a no-show because of a possible assassination attempt. As the invited guests glumly stared at Marulanda's empty chair, a guerrilla stand-in read his speech, a bitter tirade that ignored the history of the moment and instead recounted a long list of FARC grievances, including the 1964 army attack on Marquetalia that killed Marulanda's cows, chickens, and pigs. All along, the FARC's three designated negotiators kept their AK-47s onstage.

Pastrana shrugged off the snub and pressed ahead. But the war had yet to run its course. The FARC was at the height of its powers and believed that history was on its side. Its leaders openly spoke of doubling the rebel army's troop levels to 35,000 within five years. Thus, while talking peace the FARC used the DMZ to build up its military machine, grow coca, collect ransoms, and prepare for a general uprising. In fact, just a few hundred yards from the negotiating table, the FARC ran a training camp for raw recruits. Taking it all in was like watching a split-screen television. On one side, negotiators gathered around a white plastic table in an open-air thatched hut where they argued, joked, and smoked cigars as waiters in black ties served bottles of water and fruit cocktail. On the other, bare-chested teenagers hurdled tree trunks on a FARC obstacle course and trotted in unison, chanting: "We are guerrillas, sons of the people. And we are not content with this evil government."

But Pastrana also had a double-barrel strategy. He took the oath of office just as American officials were growing alarmed about the growing chaos in Colombia. Coca production was surging and the FARC was on the rampage. At the urging of President Bill Clinton, the U.S. Congress approved a multiyear package of U.S. aid that would make Colombia the largest recipient of American assistance outside the Middle East. The laundry list included sixty new helicopters, funding to train and equip three elite army battalions, and more spray planes to attack coca plantations. It was all couched in the language of the drug war but the main target was the FARC.

Besides U.S. military aid, the Colombian armed forces received a boost from its mutant offspring. Paramilitary death squads were laying waste to rebel supporters and taking back swaths of territory once dominated by the guerrillas. In a way, this mix of legal and illegal warfare was the Colombian establishment's version of Lenin's "combination of all forms of struggle."

Thus, in the relentless logic of escalation, both the FARC and the government believed they were gaining ground and time was on their side. And the peace talks floundered.

The guerrillas simply dug in and refused to make concessions. On the other side, it was amateur hour. Though more flexible, the government constantly changed the lineup of its negotiating team as if trying to end the war was a game of musical chairs. Then, just as they would get going, some blue-blooded envoy would demand to fly back to Bogotá so he could spend the weekend on his plantation. Other government delegates bitched about the rustic living quarters in the DMZ and scolded the cooks for serving their breakfast eggs hard-boiled rather than soft.

Though Pastrana had staked his presidency on the peace process, "it was unbelievable how bad his people were in planning things, in listening to advice," said Egeland, the UN special envoy to Colombia. "They brought in inexperienced people who trusted nobody."

Sometimes the two sides simply gave up and cracked open a bottle. During one impasse, the rebel commanders tossed a surprise party for the government team, a spread that included vodka, whiskey, hors d'oeuvres, and grilled steak and chicken. A fourteen-piece guerrilla orchestra struck up a tune and the rebel women paired off with the government men. "We were dancing with the enemy," said David Manzur, a well-known painter and one of the government delegates. "It's like Stockholm syndrome. They can kill you. But when you are with them, the guerrillas seem like your best friends. Everyone was hugging and calling one another 'comrade.'"

The FARC also tried to win over the busloads of political tourists who visited the DMZ under the guise of supporting Pastrana's peace process. Marulanda exchanged hugs and baseball caps with Jim Kimsey, the founder and president emeritus of America Online. Queen Noor of Jordan also dropped in for a chat, as did Richard Grasso, the chairman of the New York Stock Exchange. As if the guerrillas were exotic zoo animals, teachers brought their students on field trips to the DMZ. But they could be a tough audience. At one point, a gaggle of sixth-graders surrounded a FARC commander named Ívan Riós and grilled him about the hostages. "Why do you keep them in a cage?" one youngster asked. "I saw it on TV."

LIKE DESPERATE GROUPIES AT A MUSIC festival, throngs of sweating men and women crushed up against a chain-link fence in a pitiful bid for contact with the headliners. Relatives of more than three hundred police and soldiers kidnapped by the FARC, they had traveled from all corners of Colombia to FARC headquarters in the DMZ. They wore straw hats and T-shirts bearing photos of their loved ones and they were here to plead for their liberation.

Nearby stood two Soviet-style billboards depicting the smiling face of Marulanda. And suddenly, there he was in person, the great leader himself. Sureshot walked over to greet the crowd, which by then had turned into an angry mob. "These soldiers are not from the oligarchy," one woman yelled. "They are from the working class. Don't torture them anymore." Sensing he was outnumbered, Marulanda simply walked away.

Still, there was room for hope. With the peace talks bogged down, the FARC focused on what it really wanted out of the negotiations: a prisoner exchange. In the late 1990s, Marulanda had hit upon a plan to secure government recognition as well as fresh blood for his forces. The FARC was growing so fast that the rebel ranks needed more midlevel commanders to lead the rookie foot soldiers. And hundreds were sitting in Colombian prisons.

More important, trading prisoners would make the rebels appear to be full-fledged equals of the State and confer a certain political legitimacy on the guerrilla organization. So the rebels announced that they would capture and hold government troops until Bogotá agreed to swap them for experienced FARC cadres sitting in Colombian prisons. The FARC would later add to this group of so-called exchangeables two dozen kidnapped politicians as well as the three American contractors.

"The FARC was testing the waters to see how Colombian society and the government would react," said Francisco Santos, a newspaper editor who was later elected vice president. "They were seeing how much they could pull the cord."

Pastrana, who hoped to be nominated for the Nobel Peace Prize, was intent on extracting some concrete benefit from the peace talks. And for all his yuppie sensibilities, because he had been one, he did feel a special solidarity with the hostages. In 1988, just weeks before he was elected mayor of Bogotá, gunmen from the Medellín cartel abducted Pastrana. He was rescued by the police a week later.

"I know about kidnapping," Pastrana said. "And, fortunately, I also know what it means to be liberated, which is nothing less than getting your life back."

So the two sides cut a deal. In exchange for 14 guerrillas, 323 policemen and soldiers who had been held for three years or longer walked out of the jungle during the last week of June 2001. Reaching a clearing where the handover took place, many of the troops had to shield their eyes from the intensity of the sun. The newly freed men hoisted Pastrana on their shoulders and chanted "Freedom! Freedom! Freedom!" Then, as if they could burn away years of suffering, they pulled off their guerrilla-issued trousers and T-shirts, tossed them on the ground, and set them on fire.

CHAPTER 10

COMMUNITY CHEST

And, as his strength
Failed him at length,
He met a pilgrim shadow—
"Shadow," said he,
"Where can it be—
This land of El Dorado?"
—EDGAR ALLAN POE, "EL DORADO"

THE TROOPS OF VULTURE AND DESTROYER companies now had to pull off a delicate extraction operation. They were stealing cash from under the noses of the guerrillas who were definitely going to want it back. Amid the revelry, the ear-to-ear grins, the pure joy, discipline and security remained top priorities. So while a few designated squads sniffed around like bloodhounds for more barrels of money, most of the troops went about their business, reinforcing the perimeter, patrolling the hills, and taking turns cooking and cleaning. Each GI would get a fair share. But it was more than just money. It was financial security. They began to refer to the cash as *la pensión*, the retirement fund.

Yet as the stacks of Colombian pesos and American dollars grew, the math became more complicated. At the exchange houses back in Bogotá, the peso was trading at about 2,900 per dollar. But few of the soldiers had ever changed money before. Many of the GIs had only seen dollars on TV and in the movies and had never actually held one in their hands. Some thought the portrait of Ben Franklin on the $100 bill was South American liberator Simón Bolívar. For folks who had never before held $100 in their hands, it was impossible to wrap their heads around sums of $10,000 or $100,000.

In fact, the troops were far more excited about what was, by comparison, chump change: the Colombian pesos. These banknotes came in 20,000-peso denominations, worth at the time about eight dollars. Most of the American cash came in the form of $100 bills. Yet due to their very foreign-ness, the C-notes seemed like the lesser currency. They were viewed like Monopoly money: worth a fortune, perhaps, while playing the American game, but of dubious value once the board was folded up.

Frankistey Giraldo—yes, his father named him after Frankenstein—one of three Giraldo brothers in Destroyer Company, recalled unearthing a barrel containing four blocks of American currency. Each block held two hundred fifty $100 bills. He was an instant millionaire. But like many of the GIs, he soon became desperate to get his hands on *real* money by trading dollars for pesos. Instead of breaking out calculators and figuring out the exchange rate, however, the troops bartered on the basis of bulk and weight, like commodities, as if the bricks of banknotes were bushels of soybeans. Giraldo traded two blocks of U.S. money to another soldier for several blocks containing a total of 200 million Colombian pesos. Only much later did he realize that in exchange for his half-million dollars, he received the equivalent of $69,000. He'd swapped Boardwalk for Mediterranean Avenue.

"Everyone wanted to fill up their pockets with pesos," Giraldo said. "We didn't know what dollars were. They made me nervous. I didn't know how to manage them, how to change them. I didn't want that shit. I wanted pesos."

Walter Suárez, the GI from Mesetas who was almost recruited into the FARC, said there was a certain logic to trading down for pesos. For one thing, he figured it would be easier for investigators to track foreign currency. And since the troops didn't know American greenbacks from Polish zlotys, there was also concern that the dollars might be counterfeits.

Still, they had to get the money out of the jungle, and that could mean humping on foot for days on end. Every extra ounce in their backpacks counted. In that sense, low-value pesos were deadweight. A one-inch-thick packet containing two hundred Colombian bills in 20,000-peso denominations was worth about $1,380. A one-inch-thick packet of Ben Franklins—or two hundred C-notes—was worth $20,000.

Similar calculations over weight and value had transformed Colombia's illegal narcotics trade. Traffickers started out in the 1970s exporting bulky bales of low-rent reefer, but soon began filling their cargo holds with smaller, more profitable packets of cocaine. There was, after all, no such thing as the Medellín marijuana cartel. Soldiers with a bit more cunning and savvy, like Lieutenant Jorge Sanabria, understood the dynamics and hoovered up all the dollars they could get their hands on. But many of the grunts, by their own volition, lost out. "I was a real idiot because the pesos were so heavy," Suárez said. "Now I think to myself: 'Why did I do that? Why didn't I take the greens?'"

THE SOLDIERS WERE THE LATEST IN a long tradition of treasure hunters. Over the centuries, rumors of underground riches attracted fortune seekers of all stripes to Colombia. Many were after *guacas*, the clay urns used by the region's Indians to bury their most precious possessions. Later, as the expeditions grew, a new verb in Spanish was coined. To search for riches was to *guaquear*. And the people digging in the dirt were dubbed *guaqueros*.

The initial gold rush could be traced to the Muisca Indians. They would coat their newly crowned chiefs with mud followed by a layer of gold dust, then send them on reed rafts into the middle of Lake Guatavita, located in the mountains near present-day Bogotá. The new Indian kings were baptized in the icy waters while precious stones were thrown overboard as offerings to the gods. The ceremonies became the basis for the legend of El Dorado, or "the gilded man," and later prompted several failed efforts to drain the lake. In the vivid imaginations of the Conquistadors, El Dorado became a city of gold. Appearing on early maps of the region, the location of El Dorado shifted depending on the cartographer of the moment. Epic search expeditions were launched by Gonzalo Pizarro and Francisco Orellana. They scoured the Andes Mountains, then moved into the Amazon basin, but came up empty. Although Orellana became the first outsider to navigate the Amazon River to its mouth, his feat was viewed as a meager door prize.

In later years, subterranean deposits of oil and coal would fuel Colombia's economy, but another business would add several more points to the annual gross domestic product. The illegal drug trade generated unimaginable new wealth for people who, like many of the soldiers in Vulture and Destroyer companies, began life on the bottom rung. The biggest capo of them all, Pablo Escobar, started out stealing grave stones, and through a combination of street smarts, business savvy, and ruthlessness emerged as the seventh-richest man in the world, according to *Forbes*. Escobar and his fellow free-spending narco-millionaires created their own myths and urban legends.

The drug lords required temporary spots to stash their bills until they could deposit them in banks, purchase cattle ranches and condominiums, or figure out other ways to make their dirty profits appear clean. Often they built elaborate vaults in the false walls and floors of their luxury homes and apartments. And as the narcos were hunted down and arrested or killed, news of their demise inevitably kicked off a frenzy of freelance search parties. Mobs of bounty hunters tore down ceilings with crowbars, broke up cement floors with sledgehammers, sawed through walls, and excavated front yards.

One of Escobar's contemporaries, Gonzalo Rodríguez Gacha, buried much of his treasure around his country estate near the town of Pacho, just north of Bogotá. A month before he was gunned down in 1989, police stumbled upon $6.2 million of Gacha's money. They figured there was more to be found. Indeed, years afterward, Pacho residents continued to mount makeshift digs. During one particularly rainy year, a nearby river rose and people spotted barrels of cash bobbing in the water. Later, they drained a lagoon after it was rumored that a truck full of gold bars could be found under the water. Believing the rumors, the Colombian Army contracted twenty-three farmers to search for a hidden vault on Gacha's former property that supposedly contained $8 billion.

"It's a strategically built vault that contains arms, jewelry and money," army general Carlos Lemus confidently told reporters.

The demise of Gacha and Escobar and the breakup of the Medellín and Cali cartels were heralded at the time as definitive blows against the drug-trafficking industry. But the old guard was simply replaced by a new generation of mini-cartels. These kingpins were less flamboyant but smarter, and probably even richer, and authorities continued to find huge quantities of buried cash. In 2001, for example, police stumbled upon an underground stash of $35 million belonging to a drug-trafficking duo known as The Twins. It took a five-person team three days to count all the bills.

The most recent case involved Juan Carlos Ramírez, one of the leaders of the Northern Valley cartel, which rose from the ashes of the Medellín and Cali syndicates. Ramírez, known by his alias Lollipop, was thought to be worth nearly $2 billion. As the Colombian authorities hunted him down, using stethoscopes, fiber-optic devices, and tiny cameras inserted into walls, they discovered five hidden chambers where Lollipop stashed a total of $71 million and 309 gold bars. He was finally arrested in Brazil in 2007. Fearing that he would be killed in prison by rival narcos, Lollipop made an offer. If the Brazilian judge handling his case would release his wife from jail and quickly extradite him to the United States, Lollipop would reveal the false walls, underground vaults, and other hiding places where he had stashed another $40 million. The judge turned him down.

Not surprisingly, some authorities were unable to resist the lucrative offers. In recent years, more than a dozen Colombian police and army soldiers were arrested on charges of filling their pockets after discovering subterranean caches. Before Rodríguez Gacha was killed, army captain Álvaro Uscategui and Major Darío Pacheco, with the help of an informant, discovered $19 million in cash and gold bars and divided the riches among the search party. But the pilfering officers were outed after Uscategui complained to authorities that Pacheco and the informant were trying to gun him down in a dispute over how the money was distributed.

"Army units are spread out across the country for months at a time," said Hernando Castellanos, a lawyer specializing in military affairs who would later represent several soldiers from Vulture and Destroyer companies. "What happens out there depends on their honesty."

Now, camped atop a FARC treasure chest, the soldiers of Vulture and Destroyer companies had decided to lay down their rifles and get their hands dirty. Once soldiers, they were now *guaqueros*.

THE TWO LIEUTENANTS, JORGE "EL GORDO" Sanabria and Fernando Mojica radioed back the news to their commanding officers in Popayán about the guerrilla weapons and ammunition stash but omitted any mention of the money. As expected, they were ordered to stay put, which fit right into their plan, giving their men more time to plunder all that was beneath them.

Yet after a day or so of foraging like wombats, the troops began to fidget. They began to feel like they were trapped inside a gold mine with no way to extract the bullion. Their stacks of dollars and pesos added up to nothing because there was nothing to buy: no bars, no brothels, no BMW dealerships. In the outback, their riches couldn't even get them a lukewarm Coca-Cola. "Imagine having so much money and nothing to eat!" Frankistey Giraldo said. When they looked at themselves, they still saw a bunch of hungry, unwashed peasants in the middle of FARC-land. They were fabulously wealthy. Except they weren't.

Yet even in a place where consumer spending never before existed, the rules of the market economy suddenly kicked in. Among the troops, there were a few goods and services that could be bought and sold. And the explosive growth in the money supply, combined with pent-up demand, led to another economic phenomenon: hyperinflation.

Cigarettes, a scarce commodity, sold for as much as one million pesos a pack. The going price for a roll of toilet paper was 100,000 pesos, or $34. In the evenings, the soldiers threw dice and played poker, making massive bets as if they were Vegas vets. Suárez recalled a bidding war that broke out over a transistor radio that finally sold for the equivalent of $12,000. Later, the GI who unloaded the radio complained he'd gotten a raw deal because the salsa music and news reports provided the only relief from boredom. In the mornings, the soldiers took turns in the rustic kitchen boiling water for rice and for whatever edible critter they could scavenge out of the forest and dump in the pot. But now, cooking breakfast became a highly paid skill set. Some of the troops, intent on spending every waking hour looking for money, bought their way out of KP by paying colleagues up to 10 million pesos—or about $3,500—to replace them.

As their treasure accumulated, the GIs killed time by counting and recounting their money, then dreaming up ways to carry it back. If not on par with Carlos Fitzcarrald, the rubber baron who portaged a thirty-ton steamboat between jungle rivers in Peru, the logistics of moving a Brink's truck full of cash through the rain forest were tricky enough. Their backpacks were already jammed with gear and now they were adding heavy bricks of currency that had to be moved one step at a time. If they'd had their druthers, they would have tossed away most of their kit to make room for the money. But the guerrillas were lurking. They needed their guns and ammunition. They couldn't dump their remaining bags of rice because they still had to eat. And they couldn't toss out their boots and uniforms because it would raise uncomfortable questions if they arrived back at base half-naked.

Again, they had to think like smugglers. A few obvious things could go: personal items like socks, boxer shorts, and T-shirts. Envisioning an inspection, some wrapped their money in their most foul-smelling garments. More storage space was created by dumping the water out of their canteens. Some troops jammed pesos and dollars into empty plastic cooking oil bottles. Walter Suárez recalled removing the foam lining from his backpack frame and replacing it with bills. He also rolled up banknotes into tight cylinders, then inserted them, one by one, into the hems of his uniform pants and the collars of his shirts.

Once the money was safely stowed away, their thoughts turned to how they would put it to use. Now that their lives actually seemed to be worth something, dozens planned to quit the army. Either you retired when you had the chance, the saying went, or you would be retired by a bullet. What to do on the outside? Maybe buy a taxicab or a street-corner grocery. Some imagined purchasing homes for their parents and SUVs for themselves. But in the same way that the true value of a $100 bill didn't really register, the soldiers found it hard to think big. Their dreams were small beer. They were like youngsters fantasizing about the candy counter when they could have purchased the entire M&M'S plant.

But Lenin Giraldo, Frankistey's little brother, was Destroyer Company's dream weaver. He was never comfortable in a man's body and many of the troops knew he was gay. He decided to quit the army and invest part of his stash in a chain of beauty shops. Then he would travel abroad, shop around for the best surgeon, and have an operation to adjust the internal plumbing and turn himself into a woman.

THE TREASURE HUNT LASTED THREE GLORIOUS, sleepless, elongated, excruciating days and nights. Then word crackled over the radio that fresh troops were moving in to replace Vulture and Destroyer companies. It wasn't exactly mission accomplished. They'd struck out in their quest for the American hostages. There would be no newspaper headlines, parades, or movies based on Lieutenant Jorge Sanabria's heroic exploits. But the soldiers felt giddy all the same. They had penetrated into a rebel rearguard position, outwitted the enemy, and kept themselves alive. And then there was the money.

But extracting themselves from the jungle would prove far more hazardous than hiking in.

Some of the soldiers got busy cutting a landing pad so the U.S.-made Black Hawk helicopters could touch down and take them back to civilization. Others focused on wrapping the leftovers and cleaning up. Their camp was a mess. They'd burrowed so many holes that the site looked like it had been carpet-bombed. By Sanabria's count, the men unearthed 158 barrels. But they managed to empty out just 70 containers. A few had been punctured and the rain and mud had damaged the cash. But still, the soldiers would be walking away from millions. Though it seemed unlikely that they would ever make it back to this enchanted spot, the troops reburied the untapped barrels and positioned some of the land mines from the rebel arms cache around the perimeter. A few soldiers made Billy Bones–style treasure maps while Sanabria wrote down the coordinates from his GPS.

As the drone of approaching aircraft grew, Sanabria gave his men one final lecture. Stuffing their pockets was easy. But as in most under-the-table endeavors, he noted, the hard part was act two: keeping mum and covering their tracks. He told his soldiers to avoid their hometowns, especially if they lived in rural areas where the FARC might find them. He told them to exercise prudence in their spending, to save for the future. If they planned to resign from the army or just plain desert, he told them to do so gradually, one by one over the coming months, to avoid calling attention to the unit. One screwup could ruin things for everyone. This was a once-in-a-lifetime haul, he concluded. So don't blow it.

Then the helicopters touched down. Then the troubles began.

Apparently, the choppers evacuating the troops were needed for more important endeavors elsewhere. There wasn't enough time for the pilots to airlift the men to the closest military installation in San Vicente del Caguán. So the GIs were extracted from their jungle landing pad and delivered to a gravel road . . . in the middle of nowhere.

As if marching through FARC-land for weeks on end wasn't bad enough, the dirty, exhausted, hungry—and now overloaded—GIs would have to walk the last fifty miles to the base. On the exposed road, they'd be easy pickings for the FARC. With no tree cover, the sun bore down on the dehydrated men, who had no water because their canteens were crammed full of rolled-up Colombian pesos and dollars.

Yet even out here they were a few degrees closer to civilization. Along their route were a few ramshackle mom-and-pop stores where the troops snapped up cases of soft drinks, bags of bread, packets of crackers, and cans of sardines. Spread out along the road, the troops leading the column would buy in bulk, leaving behind bare shelves for the stragglers at the tail end. "We had to rotate our formation," said Walter Suárez, who had been stuck in the back, "because the first guys in line took everything."

Farther down the road, the troops met a woman who raised chickens, pigs, and *mojarra* fish. At first, she was reluctant to cook for 147 famished GIs with wild, feral looks. But after they flashed a few bills the woman got to work. She fried dozens of fish. She killed twenty chickens and made a massive cauldron of soup. Then she slaughtered a hog and braised the pork ribs over an open fire.

A few miles later, they marched into a tiny community called Puerto Amor, which served as a kind of last-chance truck stop for drivers heading into FARC territory. At first several truckers refused the soldiers' requests to take them to San Vicente del Caguán, citing possible retaliation by the rebels for collaborating with the army. But Sanabria took up a collection among the troops and offered 500,000 pesos to each driver. Once again, the money worked its magic. Even better, one of the trucks carried cans of Cola y Pola, a local drink that's half bubble-gum-flavored soda, half beer— perfect for starter drunks. The troops aboard this truck toasted their good fortune and arrived at the base after midnight fully sloshed.

The next morning, the soldiers lined up at the tiny airport in San Vicente del Caguán to board three C-130 Herculeses, the four-engine turboprop transport planes that would take them back to their battalion headquarters in the southern city of Popayán. From there, many of the troops planned to launch their new lives by deserting the army. Freedom was just a forty-five-minute flight away.

Sitting on the bench seats in the forward section of the plane was soldier Darwin Ávila, who'd scored a kilo of marijuana the night before and was smoking doobies right up until the moment he boarded the Hercules. With the plane at twelve thousand feet and approaching Popayán, the combination of dope, fluctuating air pressure, and the tightly packed quarters made Ávila a little paranoid. Shortly before landing, he stood up and made an announcement.

"The guy went crazy," Sanabria recalled. "He said: 'Sons of bitches! Give me back my money!'"

The green military-issue rucksack containing all of Ávila's cash was gone. He berated his colleagues, called them guerrillas, and said he'd kill each and every one of them if they didn't return his booty. The other soldiers told him to shut the hell up, saying that no one had taken anything. Enraged, Ávila grabbed an M26 fragmentation grenade, pulled the pin, and screamed, "I'm going to blow you all to shit!"

If Ávila let go of the safety lever, or the spoon, the grenade would explode in four and a half seconds. The troops scrambled over one another as they pushed to the back of the plane and threw themselves on the floor. "It was a human stampede," Sanabria said. "It was a shit storm." The lieutenant closed his eyes, covered his head, and began counting: 1001, 1002, 1003 . . .

But the blast never came. For all of the soldiers' craven exploits in the jungle, at the moment when an entire army company was seconds away from disaster, a hero emerged. When Sanabria looked up, Corporal Carlos Fernando López was biting Ávila's fingers and wrestling away the grenade while two others tackled the addled GI. All the while, López fought to hold down the spoon. As long as the metal handle was depressed, it would prevent the deadly chain reaction of primer detonating, fuse burning down, main charge exploding, and thousands of bits of razor-sharp shrapnel spraying the kill zone, ripping open the fuselage and cutting into the soft flesh of the soldiers.

Told of the unsecured grenade, the pilots dive-bombed toward the Popayán airport, anxious to put the hulking transport plane on the ground before it was blown to bits. In the back, the soldiers tried to buck up López, urging him to maintain his white-knuckle death grip on the grenade as they readied themselves for an emergency exit. The Hercules hit the runway and pulled to a halt within a thousand feet. The back ramp slowly opened. Sanabria, positioned to be the first out the door, was trampled by his troops who scampered onto the tarmac in the opposite direction of López. Meanwhile, Corporal López calmly walked to the side of the airfield and flung the grenade into a vacant lot, where the roar of the Hercules engines muffled the sound of the explosion.

CHAPTER 11

THE MESSENGER

I'll send an S.O.S. to the world.
—The Police, "Message in a Bottle"

JORGE ENRIQUE BOTERO WAS EATING DIRT. Bombs were falling all around him, causing the jungle floor he was hugging to buckle. A veteran Colombian war reporter, Botero was hiking through rebel territory with a squad of FARC guerrillas on his way to what he thought would be an exclusive interview with hostage Íngrid Betancourt, the Colombian presidential candidate who had been kidnapped along with her campaign manager, Clara Rojas, in 2002. But the Colombian Air Force was now pounding the area and the bombs were hitting just four hundred yards away.

"I was looking for Íngrid and Clara and was this close," Botero said. But due to the growing danger the guerrillas evacuated the journalist the next day.

If any outsider was going to get in to see the FARC's prisoners, it was going to be Botero. A longtime television journalist and writer on friendly terms with the rebels, Botero had also worked for the Cuban wire service

Prensa Latina and would later become information director of the twenty-four-hour Caracas news station Telesur, President Hugo Chávez's left-wing answer to CNN and Fox News. Botero's uncritical posture toward the FARC infuriated some of his colleagues in the media, who viewed him as a rebel propagandist. But the FARC commanders trusted Botero and gave him broad and continued access to the guerrilla group.

In 2000, for example, Botero had been the only reporter allowed to visit the jungle concentration camps where the FARC had penned up more than three hundred kidnapped soldiers and policemen. Just as the guerrillas had envisioned, Botero's gripping images of the sad and sickly troops standing behind coils of barbed wire provoked much hand-wringing back in Bogotá and new demands for a prisoner exchange. Most of those hostages were released the next year when President Andrés Pastrana agreed to free fourteen rebels from the country's jails.

Back in Bogotá after his brush with death in the jungle, Botero waited for another chance. It was July 2003, five months after the Grand Caravan carrying the three Americans had crashed and more than a year since Betancourt had been kidnapped. So far, no proof had emerged that Keith, Marc, and Tom were still alive.

Finally, Botero received the message he'd been expecting. The note instructed him to meet with a FARC contact in southern Colombia and to bring his video camera. Figuring he would be meeting with Betancourt or the Americans, Botero hustled to bring them some news from home. He quickly videotaped an interview with Betancourt's husband. Then he called Victoria Bruce and Karin Hayes, two American filmmakers with whom Botero had collaborated for a documentary about the kidnapping of Betancourt. If the two women could track down the relatives of the Americans and interview them, Botero promised to play the video. In Bristol, Connecticut, Bruce taped a tearful message from Jo Rosano, then e-mailed the file to Botero in Bogotá.

Before setting off, Botero added a few more items to the care package. Scouring his apartment for reading material in English, he found a recent edition of Newsweek and a paperback John Grisham thriller, The Street Lawyer, the tale of a corporate attorney who discovered his humanitarian side after being taken hostage. Finally, Botero printed out copies of news stories, including one about the second Grand Caravan that was dispatched to find the three American hostages but instead hit a tree, instantly killing the three men on board. Once in San Vicente del Caguán—the unofficial capital of FARC-land—Botero met his guerrilla contact and began an eleven-day journey along jungle trails and rivers that left him completely disoriented.

"The sun doesn't penetrate," Botero said. "You don't know whether you are north, south, east, or west."

Finally, Botero and his escorts arrived at a sprawling encampment with wooden huts, a massive kitchen, and lecture halls for political classes. There, he met Jorge Briceño, the commander of the FARC's eastern bloc. Known as Mono Jojoy and widely considered the No. 3 FARC leader, he was a burly man who always wore a black beret. Mono Jojoy was one of the masterminds behind the FARC's strategy to kidnap high-profile hostages and exchange them for imprisoned rebels. He had even threatened to abduct Colombian legislators unless they passed a law formally authorizing prisoner exchanges. After a bit of small talk, Mono Jojoy told Botero: "We're going to show you the three gringos."

AFTER 130 DAYS IN CAPTIVITY, THE Americans were suddenly uprooted from their camp and put aboard an aluminum boat. They spent the next three days motoring along a river to another bivouac, where they were given haircuts, new clothes, and fed huge portions of rice and canned tuna. What was going on? Perhaps the guerrillas had secured their DMZ and were about to turn over their hostages, the contractors speculated. They'd also been told that Secretary of State Colin Powell had visited Bogotá and they quickly assumed that his mission was to lobby for their freedom.

But there was no prisoner exchange in the works. Fully engaged in the Iraq War, Powell had not flown to Bogotá. In fact, during his tenure at the State Department he never once publicly referred to the American hostages in Colombia. It turned out that the rebels were preparing Keith, Marc, and Tom for a proof-of-life video. Told that reporters from the international media would interview them, the Americans speculated about which big-name correspondent would show up in the jungle. But once again, they vastly overestimated the world's interest in their drama. Instead of Christiane Amanpour of CNN they got Jorge Enrique Botero from the Chávez News Network.

"We didn't know Botero at all, but the fact that he was allowed inside a FARC camp and his chummy demeanor didn't sit well with us," Marc said. "We knew in some ways we were being used by him, but we also wanted to let our families know that we were okay."

FARC guards positioned the three hostages around a table in a wooden shack, then stood behind them holding AK-47 rifles. Botero pulled out his digital video camera to begin recording, but eleven days of rain, mud, and humidity had rendered the device useless. Luckily, he had packed a backup. For all of the Pentagon's high-tech spyware, Botero's footage, though sometimes jerky and unfocused, would provide the first proof that the Americans were alive and in the custody of the FARC.

On camera, Mono Jojoy confirmed that their only way out of the jungle was through a prisoner exchange. Keith then asked what would happen if President Álvaro Uribe—a hard-liner who had vowed to crush the FARC—refused to negotiate. Could they be stuck in the jungle for five years? Ten years? Mono Jojoy simply shrugged.

During breaks in the interviews, Keith, Marc, and Tom devoured Botero's reading material, but the news was nearly all bad. They were fascinated to find out that the U.S. military had launched an invasion and ousted Saddam Hussein. But the focus on Iraq meant that no one was paying any attention to Colombia. Botero confirmed that their fellow crew members on the Grand Caravan, pilot Tommy Janis and Colombian sergeant Luis Alcides Cruz had been executed shortly after the crash. Then, they read the account of the second Grand Caravan crash, which killed their buddies Tommy Schmidt, Butch Oliver, and Ralph Ponticelli.

"Ralph was killed! Ralph Ponticelli!" Keith said. Marc shook his head while Tom started sobbing, then hid his face behind a newspaper as Botero zoomed in with his camera to capture the moment.

"Thank you for the news. But the first thing you see is that one of your best friends died looking for you," Keith said. "I see one, two, three, four deaths in five and a half months and for what? It's a tragedy."

Keith was also dumbfounded to learn California Microwave no longer existed and that the company's contract had been transferred to a new entity called CIAO. The name was apparently chosen by some knuckle-dragger back in Bogotá. But for Keith, Marc, and Tom—who were trying to paint themselves as hapless civilians, cover up their military backgrounds, and downplay their value as hostages—the moniker was like wearing a sandwich board that said: Spies R Us. Sure enough, a gruff, fiftyish FARC *comandante* glanced at the plane-crash story, then glared at the Americans and announced: "The press says that you are CIA agents."

"It's C-I-A-O," replied Tom, slowly pronouncing each letter. Then, he used the Italian pronunciation. "That's Ciao—C-I-A-O, not C-I-A."

The mix-up might have seemed inane but it wasn't the first time an unfortunate company name had waylaid Americans. In 1994, Thomas Hargrove was working as an agronomist for the Cali-based International Center for Tropical Research, known by its Spanish acronym CIAT. After stopping Hargrove's car on a rural highway, FARC rebels—teenagers with fourth-grade educations—scrutinized Hargrove's employee ID card. In his diaries, he described what happened next.

"'I work for CIAT,' I tell them. No response. 'Do you know what CIAT is?'
"'CIA,' a teenager says. 'That's the intelligence agency of the United States.'
"'No!' I cry. 'Not CIA. CIAT.'"

But it was too late. Convinced that Hargrove, an expert on high-yield rice varieties, was a certified American intelligence agent, the rebels dragged him into the mountains where he was chained for the next eleven months.

Keith, Marc, and Tom were even further off the grid than Hargrove. They were in a place where children carried the names of monsters and dictators, a place where, for their barely literate guards, the damning first three letters of their company's name outweighed the evidence of the final consonant. Back home, they were low-on-the-totem-pole contractors largely forgotten about by the American public. But in enemy territory a spook was a spook. Among the FARC prisoners, the gringos, along with Íngrid Betancourt, were the crown jewels.

THE TAPING HAD A FEW ALICE IN WONDERLAND moments. At times it seemed as if the hostages had walked onto the set of a daytime TV talk show in which gangsters had replaced Oprah. At one point, a Dutch woman who had joined the FARC, spoke perfect English, and served as a translator began questioning the hostages. Oozing empathy, she asked them: "Where do you get the strength to go through this?"

When Botero played the video message from his mother, Jo Rosano, Marc had to bite his lip to keep from crying.

"I hated that this journalist was manipulating us," Marc said later. "But we decided that we had to go along with what the FARC were having us do—not for the good of them but for our families."

Questioned by Botero and the FARC translator, Keith, Marc, and Tom had to be very precise with their answers. This was their one chance to describe their situation to their employer and to the U.S. and Colombian governments. They wanted to be honest, but they didn't want to upset their families or say anything that would piss off the FARC. As a result, all three men enthusiastically endorsed the idea of a prisoner exchange.

"I would ask for a diplomatic solution. I would ask to be exchanged," Keith said. "I don't want to be used as an example by some government to prove a point. . . . For me an exchange is victory because it is life. It is life for us. It is life for the Colombian prisoners."

Then they were asked about a possible military rescue attempt. They had constantly fantasized about a snatch operation but the question came shortly after all three men had learned that a group of FARC hostages in northern Colombia had been killed in an army operation. Though in favor of a rescue attempt by U.S. Special Forces, Keith, Marc, and Tom feared the Colombian Army wasn't up to the task.

"I think the likelihood of us being rescued alive is low," Marc said. "This is not a movie. For the three of us, this is real life."

Keith was even blunter.

"We are in the world of the FARC," he said. "There are people around us at all times, just a few feet from us. They carry automatic weapons. You may show up, but when you get here, we're going to be dead."

CHAPTER 12

LAND OF OZ

"And now let the wild rumpus start!"
—Maurice Sendak, *Where the Wild Things Are*

Founded in 1537, the Colombian city of Popayán first rose to prominence as a way station for the Conquistadors as they shipped gold north from Peru on the long trek back to Spain. Called the White City for its whitewashed colonial buildings, Popayán has produced poets, painters, and seventeen presidents. Tourists used to flock to the city of 350,000 people, located in southwest Cauca state, for its lavish Easter processions. But in recent years, Popayán had fallen on hard times. A 1983 earthquake destroyed much of the downtown and the local economy slid into recession. But sitting on the outskirts of the city next to the airport was the headquarters of the Fiftieth Counterguerrilla Battalion, which included Vulture and Destroyer companies. And now that the soldiers had made it home, they set out on a spending spree that, at least temporarily, boosted Popayán's struggling economy.

Darwin Ávila, the frantic, grenade-wielding ganja man who nearly blew apart the Hercules, was hauled off to the base clinic where he was put in a straitjacket and injected with tranquilizers. Later, the base psychologist diagnosed post-traumatic stress syndrome, never realizing that his real problem was something more akin to where-the-hell-is-my-goddamned-money disorder.

As the soldiers discreetly unpacked inside the barracks, they began scheming ways to hide, hoard, or spend their riches. They were anxious to leave the base but they knew they'd get busted if they began spending like the day after Thanksgiving. They needed a battle plan and Lieutenant Jorge Sanabria tried to sketch one out. He secured two-day passes for several of his soldiers and told them to be discreet. He warned his men not to desert. And he suggested that they hide their money in their dirty fatigues, as they'd done in the jungle, to dull the curiosity of the MPs at the gate.

But once his men were outside the wire, Sanabria could no longer stage-manage them. And just as the lieutenant had predicted, the real trick would be pulling off the second act. While on patrol in the jungle, the troops had maintained their bearings even among the guerrillas, land mines, and wild animals. The branches, banana leaves, vines, and spider webs had served as protective cover. Engulfed by triple canopy rain forest, their wealth was untouchable, their secret safe. But in the city, they were exposed. The modern, urban setting dulled their threat-assessment skills. For these backcountry palookas, Popayán was a devil's lair with multiple temptations and flimflam men on every corner. There were a million ways to blow it.

Even if they managed to sidestep the parasites and con artists, how would 147 flush and feckless GIs put their money to work all the while keeping quiet, maintaining their sanity, and avoiding the long arm of the law?

"It was," Sanabria said, "like entering a world that we knew nothing about."

KICKED LOOSE FROM THE BASE, A few of the soldiers, intent on deserting, caught the first bus out of town. Some hooked up with friends and relatives in Popayán to brainstorm ways to invest or hide their money. But many others cast aside Sanabria's warnings about keeping their mouths and wallets shut. It had been a dialogue of the deaf. Enough already with the orders! They were determined to take a victory lap around the city and enjoy the fruits of other people's labor—in Hogarthian proportions.

Just as Dorothy received a new hairdo and the Scarecrow fresh straw at the gates to the Emerald City, the soldiers tried to gussy themselves up before hitting the White City. One group tramped into María Bravo's beauty parlor in downtown Popayán for haircuts and manicures. As she worked their nails, she could tell that these boy kings, with laughing eyes and bulging pockets who smelled like the jungle, weren't ordinary soldiers. For one thing, they tried to pay in dollars. It seemed unnatural, like when Colombia's rough-hewn drug lords—looking for new ways to wash their cash—began snapping up high-priced paintings at Bogotá's art galleries, or when the guerrillas went dashing through the snow on their Norwegian sleigh ride.

"With white-collar people you never notice that they're stealing because they're already rich," Bravo said. "But when poor people come into money, it's obvious."

The unfolding scenario was not lost on Popayán's money changers. Some of them convinced the wide-eyed rustics that each of their dollars was worth 1,000 pesos rather than the true rate of 2,900. Ecstatic and awash in millions, small particulars like the currency markets meant little to the soldiers.

As the troops set upon the shopping malls, store owners quickly surmised that something was amiss. Daniel López, the manager of the clothing store Original Sin, recalled that four soldiers walked in and began trying on sunglasses, jeans, and loafers. They left behind pairs of muddy combat boots in the dressing-room stalls. One of the men bought a $100 leather belt. Another laughed aloud at the prospect of his once-poor "Indian" colleagues roaring around town in spanking new SUVs with the dealer stickers still glued to the windshields. To López, they were too rich to be regular soldiers. He guessed they were guerrillas, paramilitaries, or drug traffickers spreading around their profits. But he and the other merchants were happy to take their money, and no one asked for a receipt.

"It was a time when sales went up," López recalled. "I hope it happens again."

The accessorizing continued at the El Dorado jewelry store where a handful of troops, seemingly intent on sticking out and flaunting their wealth, purchased thick gold-rope chains. But after they spotted the security cameras on the walls above the display counters, they left quickly. All along, they called their parents, wives, and girlfriends to let them in on the secret.

By sunset, many of the soldiers had crowded into the city's bars and bordellos, neon-lit joints with pink walls and beer-stained dance floors where there was never a last call. Whenever the cops showed up, the soldiers handed them 20,000-peso notes and sent them on their way. But that only tweaked the officers' curiosity.

A Popayán taxi driver recalled how a group of three men with crew cuts piled into his car and offered him huge sums for what would have been a five-dollar fare.

"They told me: 'If you take us to a place with hot women we'll pay you fifty dollars,'" the driver said. "I headed toward the edge of the city to a bordello where soldiers always go on the weekends. I knew they were trolling for girls. They checked out the place. Then one of the men came back to the car and, sure enough, he gave me fifty dollars!"

In the jungle, the soldiers drank murky river water or the moisture collected within vines and leaves. Now they had an entire bar to quench their thirst: whiskey, vodka, gin, rum, cognac, wine, and champagne. Where to start? Wage earners usually opted for cheap Colombian *aguardiente*, a licorice-flavored cane alcohol. But this crew demanded aged whiskey and the finest of rums—though they sometimes mixed the two together.

"They got drunk really fast and they tipped the girls with dollars," said Carlos Ordóñez, the manager of a brothel called Punto 30, where about forty soldiers set upon the twenty-one prostitutes. The tall, chesty ladies, accustomed to furtive, half-hour mergers at twenty dollars a pop in one of the six cramped rooms in the back, were suddenly treated like Miss Colombia contestants. They boogied with the soldiers on the black-and-white-checkered floor, pole danced, and shared their whiskey and dreams. Later, some of the pixilated GIs paid triple the normal price to take their dates back with them to motels.

"They arrived smelling of cologne and showing off rings and gold chains," said a report in the Bogotá daily *El Tiempo*. "They were always affectionate with the girls and they never started fights. Some talked of traveling to the United States, of learning English, of buying hot rods and SUVs. But when they remembered fathers and mothers who had passed away, some of them cried."

Yolanda, the madam at Kassandra, said that the soldiers didn't stay long at her body shop because she had only six girls working that evening. "I lost out on a bonanza," she said as she leaned against the bar. Some of the troops moved on to a more upscale whorehouse, Kaliente, where they paid off the police and locked the doors behind them. There, the prostitutes found themselves showered in cash and illusions. The drunken soldiers promised to buy them motorcycles and the finest garments and to pay for their kids to go to private schools. Over the next three days the troops knocked back twelve-year-old Johnnie Walker and knocked up four of the employees.

The soldiers were oblivious to it, but their movable, X-rated Romper Room left behind telltale clues as easy to smell as their collective whiskey breath.

As THEIR FREE-SPENDING COLLEAGUES RAMPAGED, SOME of the more savvy soldiers—those who realized they hadn't come away with enough cash to retire—were figuring out ways to get their money back to their hometowns. There was an express mail service in the city, but sending envelopes stuffed with cash seemed like an easy way to lose it all. Instead, some of the GIs purchased wide-screen TVs, sound systems, and kitchen appliances. Then they yanked out the bolts, wires, and components, replaced them with cash, and sent the high-tech piñatas back to their families.

Others set out on epic road trips. Walter Suárez secured a weekend pass and set out to personally carry his money back to Bogotá. He jumped into a taxi and paid the driver to take him all the way to the capital, an eighteen-hour trip. Married and with two young children, Suárez hugged his wife at the door, then quickly proceeded to the backyard to greet Tuco, a shaggy, black former stray. Suárez crouched down and pushed Tuco's doghouse to one side. Then he dug a four-foot-deep pit, placed his bag of cash in the hole, covered it with dirt, and returned the doghouse to its original spot. "The dog slept there all day," Suárez said. "No one would have ever suspected."

Frankistey Giraldo took a more roundabout route. Opting for the anonymity of public transportation, Frankistey and his soldier-brother Isaac jammed their money into a couple of suitcases and hopped aboard a bus to Cali, where they planned to stay overnight with an uncle. Almost at the same time, another soldier hired a taxi and put his duffel bags of money in the trunk. Both vehicles were immediately stopped at a police checkpoint on the outskirts of the city. The officers frisked the bus passengers but didn't bother opening the luggage compartment. When the police moved on to the taxi, they immediately found the bags of cash. They let the soldier go, but only after stealing half of his money and sending the taxi back to Popayán. The angry GI joined Frankistey and Isaac aboard the bus and cursed all the way to Cali.

At the Cali bus station, the Giraldo brothers had another close call. Moments after checking their bags into storage lockers, they were stopped by police officers for a routine ID check and body search. Later, their uncle picked them up and drove them to his house where Frankistey and Isaac closed the curtains before opening their bags. Shocked by so many packets of currency, their uncle had just one question: "Who did you rob?"

After the Giraldo brothers told him the shortened version of events, their uncle agreed to help them move the money to their hometown of Machetá, just north of Bogotá. Figuring they'd run into dozens of checkpoints along the way, the men went grocery shopping. Back at the house, they sliced open packages of cookies and boxes of cereal and stuffed the money inside. Then Frankistey bought a bus ticket and once again checked his packages into the luggage compartment.

Isaac, meanwhile, hired a taxi, and by flashing a few bills won the driver's cooperation. He agreed to break down his vehicle, prying off the door panels and ripping up the carpet in order to hide Isaac's loot. Like Cheech and Chong's marijuana panel truck from *Up in Smoke*, Isaac's money mobile sailed unimpeded through seven police and army roadblocks because there was nothing to search. Once safely home in Machetá, Isaac ripped the car apart and tipped his driver with enough cash to buy another taxicab.

Then he laid the stacks of banknotes on the kitchen table. Isaac's father, a country veterinarian who was struggling to get by, was so happy he broke down in tears.

"And that's just my money," Isaac told his old man. "Frankie is bringing the rest!"

FOR HANNER DAZA, THE RETURN TO Popayán was a triumphant homecoming. His family had relocated to the provincial capital eight years earlier after fleeing paramilitaries who branded the Daza family as FARC collaborators. Daza was penniless when he went away to join the army but now he showed up on his parents' doorstep on Mother's Day with two fellow soldiers and several laundry bags containing a fortune.

"He said: 'The Virgin appeared before us!'" recalled Hanner's sister, Yaned Daza. "Then he and his friends began laying out packets of cash and hiding them underneath the floorboards."

Yaned and the rest of the family urged Hanner to invest his money in some productive venture, like a store or a taxicab. Instead, Hanner loaded up on clothes, furniture, a wide-screen television, and a fancy sound system. Always a libertine, Daza then disappeared into the bars and brothels. When he resurfaced a few days later, he gave Yaned wads of cash to buy clothes for her three-year-old son. He also begged his parents to take a cut of the money so they could remodel their house, a cramped one-story concrete structure where his mother, a farm girl to the end, raised chickens on the back porch. "Take the money," he said, "or I'll drink it."

"I got very nervous," said Aura Gómez, Hanner's mother. "I told him he should go back and turn that money in. I told him that never in my life had I accepted stolen goods. We've always been honest people. But he said: 'I'm not going back to the military. This is my big opportunity.'"

Lieutenant Jorge Sanabria, who had tucked away mostly dollars, was anxious to confirm that his banknotes were indeed real, so he stopped by an exchange house in Popayán. Without blinking, the money changer accepted several of his $100 bills and shoved fistfuls of pesos back underneath the glass window. Sanabria smiled. His fortune was officially certified.

He jumped into a taxicab. His first order of business was to find a laundromat to wash his filthy uniform, but they were all closed. So he went shopping. He purchased a refrigerator and a television and shipped them home via the express-mail service. He also paid off a few lingering debts. But Sanabria knew people would notice an army officer forking over stacks of cash for a condominium or a Land Rover, so he decided to take his own advice and cut short his buying spree.

Sanabria locked the rest of the money in a suitcase and left it at a friend's house. Later, he bought himself dinner and tossed back a few shots of rum to unwind. But it was hard to celebrate. It had only been a few days since Vulture and Destroyer companies had returned from the jungle, yet Sanabria had the sinking feeling that word of their magnificent find was leaking out. He was right. Back in Bogotá, the army brass was already on the case.

CHAPTER 13

MIRACLE FISHING

And he said unto them, Cast the net on the right side of the ship,
and ye shall find. They cast therefore, and now they were not able
to draw it for the multitude of fishes.
—JOHN: 21, THE HOLY BIBLE, AMERICAN STANDARD VERSION

UNLIKE THE SOLDIERS OF VULTURE AND Destroyer companies, American officials had not gone AWOL in the search for the hostages. Still, some of the stunts they pulled left the relatives of the missing men scratching their heads. Malia Phillips recalled being contacted by the State Department about using a photo of Keith Stansell to put together leaflets offering cash rewards to peasants who came forward with useful information. But in the end the flyers featured photos of barnyard animals instead of the grinning mugs of Keith, Marc, and Tom.

At the suggestion of Northrop Grumman, Malia and some of the other family members put together care packages in the hopes that the Red Cross would eventually gain access to the hostages. Malia boxed up reading glasses, sneakers, medicine, and photos to send to Keith. But later, Northrop

Grumman officials were warned that if the goods ended up in the FARC's hands, they would be violating the Patriot Act, which outlawed providing material goods to terrorist groups.

Some of the State Department handlers had a hard time keeping the names of the relatives straight. They had Kyle Stansell, Keith's son, listed as Kyle Phillips. President George W. Bush had never publicly mentioned the hostages, but he eventually sent Kyle and his sister Lauren one of those generic letters—that could have been sent to a cancer survivor or a campaign donor—lauding their "American spirit." The same letter could have been sent to a cancer survivor or a campaign donor.

"I'd give the U.S. government a D-minus," said Gene Stansell, Keith's dad.

The State Department upped its reward to $5 million, from $340,000, for information leading to the arrest and conviction of those responsible for the kidnappings and the killing of Tom Janis. But the announcement came in October, eight months after the crash.

"We were asking, 'What's going on?'" George Gonsalves, Marc's father, said. "But we couldn't get straight answers from the government. They'd say, 'We can't confirm this. We can't confirm that.' I said, 'Jesus Christ!'"

Behind the curtains a great deal of action was playing out, but none of it led to any breakthroughs. The Miami-based U.S. Southern Command launched the first of several thousand military surveillance flights. The FBI sent crisis negotiators and investigators to Colombia. After his proof-of-life videos were broadcast, Botero claimed a U.S. embassy official promised him a huge payoff to help track down Keith, Marc, and Tom.

"Mr. Botero," the official said, "write on this napkin the amount that you need so you'll never have to work again. We'll give it to you if you help us rescue our compatriots."

Botero refused but, apparently, U.S. officials continued to seek out Colombian reporters. After scoring a rare interview with FARC spokesman Raúl Reyes, journalist Olga Vega said she was approached by FBI and CIA agents. She agreed to help. On Washington's dime, Vega made four trips back into rebel territory to convince Reyes to turn over the Americans. But on one of her journeys she was followed by Colombian troops. When the FARC found out, the group cut off all ties with Vega, who fled with her family to the United States.

The American embassy in Bogotá, a massive gray bunker located on the highway to the airport, displayed framed portraits of Keith, Marc, and Tom in the lobby to remind all visitors of the missing men. But the real action took place farther back in the building where Ambassador Anne Patterson and her replacement, William Wood, set up what became known as the Embassy Intelligence Fusion Center. The center brought together military, law enforcement, and intelligence personnel under a single supervisor from the National Security Agency to focus on the hostages. There were many other American assets involved in the war against drugs and the FARC, but with the Fusion Center up and running, Keith, Marc, and Tom took priority.

Even though Washington's attention was now focused on Iraq, "these guys were not forgotten," said one U.S. investigator. "Within the embassy it was always our number one priority. We had it on our minds every single day. People were dedicated to this and nothing else."

The lack of progress had nothing to do with a lack of will. The problem was a lack of information. The American government had the resources to rescue the hostages, but first it had to find them. General Freddy Padilla de León, who would later be named commander of the Colombian armed forces, pointed out that most high-tech monitoring equipment was designed for deserts or urban settings rather than for equatorial jungle. The thick vegetation formed a kind of cushion that absorbed most electronic signals, preventing them from reaching the jungle floor where the hostages were located. What's more, the target area was so vast that the task was like searching for golf balls shanked into the Everglades.

"We were victims of Hollywood in that we couldn't do all the things that people see U.S. forces do in the movies," added another State Department official. "You might think we could dial in on these guerrillas and drop down on them with the ninjas. But it was impossible to track the guerrillas down, pinpoint the hostages, and get them out."

Other factors led to caution. In those haunting interviews from the jungle, Keith, Marc, and Tom appeared to be dead set against a military rescue operation. Sure, FARC rebels were pointing guns at them as they spoke and the hostages were obviously under duress, but they seemed to be speaking from the heart.

There were also serious doubts about the capabilities of the Colombian military. Washington was providing equipment and training in the hope that an improved fighting force could at some point rescue the three contractors. But its officers were only starting to come around to the concept of small, specialized Special Forces–type operations. All too often Colombian GIs moved into the jungle as if they were on an armed camping trip. Instead of stealthily creeping in, they brought along dogs, made pets out of parrots and monkeys, and built great smoky fires to cook their food. One Green Beret who worked with the Colombians felt their tactics had all the subtlety of a string of beer cans tied to a wedding getaway car.

FROM THE DAY HE TOOK OFFICE amid a fusillade of rebel rockets, Álvaro Uribe was determined to bring about a radical shift in the dynamics on the battlefield. Given to gusts of outrage, twenty-hour workdays, and a wonkish fascination with policy details, Uribe demanded results and had little patience for the FARC. He was, in effect, the anti-Pastrana.

In 1998, Andrés Pastrana had won the presidency by promising to negotiate with the FARC. But rebel attacks amid the peace talks disillusioned millions of Colombians. On the campaign trail, Uribe denounced Pastrana's DMZ and quickly emerged as the candidate with the most hard-line message against the FARC. He won the May 2002 election by a landslide.

"I was elected to make peace," Pastrana said. "Uribe was elected to make war."

Uribe's visceral hatred of the FARC dated back to 1983, when suspected rebel gunmen killed his father in a botched kidnapping attempt. He was elected mayor of the city of Medellín and went on to serve as a senator and governor of Antioquia state, which had been wracked by drug-related violence and guerrilla attacks. For decades, the Colombian conflict had been described as a civil war—a conflict between political factions fighting for control of the government. But since the mid-1990s, Uribe had rejected the term. He argued that Colombia's battle was one pitting the state against an illegitimate terrorist group that enjoyed almost no popular backing. The Uribe Doctrine held that the FARC had to be eliminated.

During the presidential campaign, Uribe was nearly assassinated when the FARC set off a bomb as the candidate's motorcade sped through the northern city of Barranquilla. Uribe emerged unscathed, and the attack only hardened his resolve. On the day Uribe was sworn in, the FARC fired a barrage of mortar shells at the ceremony. Most of the explosives missed their mark but one nicked the corner of the national palace. Inside, a stone-faced Uribe simply carried on, greeting dignitaries, swearing in his cabinet, and refusing to acknowledge the rebel bombardment, which killed nineteen indigents in a neighborhood adjacent to the palace.

A slight, bespectacled man who studied at Harvard and Oxford, Uribe could come across as both the nerdy technocrat and a stern plantation *patron*. He rose at 4:30 a.m. to practice yoga and ride a stationary bicycle before starting the workday, which sometimes lasted until after midnight. Uribe's passion was horseback riding, but during his first four months in office, he took just two days off. His wife complained that he had never learned how to dance. Rather than carousing, he spent his weekends traveling to remote corners of Colombia for marathon town-hall meetings.

During one ten-hour session in the city of Paipa, Uribe skipped lunch and took a single bathroom break as he weighed in on topics ranging from potato farming to the emerald trade. Government ministers rubbed their weary eyes and ducked out of the room in search of coffee and most caught an afternoon flight back to Bogotá. But Uribe answered every last question and adjourned the forum well after dark, making good on his trademark slogan: "Work, work, work."

His most pressing task was national security. The new president promised to double the size of the armed forces, hire thousands of police officers, levy war taxes on the middle and upper classes, and create a network of one million civilian informants to undermine the FARC. He called his military chiefs several times a day and knew the country's topography so well that he would even suggest maneuvers for army troops in pursuit of the guerrillas.

In his quest for security, Uribe sometimes ventured outside normal government channels. As governor, he was a strong backer of a system of rural security cooperatives, which were made up of farmers and ranchers who provided the army and police with intelligence. But many of these groups allied themselves with paramilitary death squads and drug traffickers and the program was finally outlawed in 1997. The paramilitaries openly backed Uribe during his 2002 campaign, and it later emerged that these warlords had intimidated voters into casting their ballots for pro-Uribe congressional candidates. Eventually, more than sixty national legislators would come under investigation for collaborating with paramilitaries. Dozens were imprisoned—including Uribe's cousin—while the burgeoning scandal forced his foreign minister and intelligence chief to resign.

But average folks didn't seem to care. Enraged by guerrilla abuses and frustrated by the army's failure to stop them, many Colombians seemed to view the paramilitaries as performing a necessary, if grisly, public good. Thus, any accusations that Uribe may have tolerated their mayhem made little dent in his popularity. Colombians adored their ballsy, tough-talking president. Polls consistently measured his job-approval ratings at between sixty and eighty percent.

As a result, Uribe felt little need to accede to the FARC's demands for its high-profile hostages. Whenever he savaged the guerrillas in speeches and compared them to Nazis, his popularity soared. Besides, the FARC was demanding yet another DMZ, and that was a nonstarter. Uribe's mandate was to *extend* government control to the countryside, not to roll it back. With Colombia under new management, there would be no more FARC-lands. Instead, Uribe began promoting a far more risky plan to save the hostages.

DESPITE THE POSSIBILITY THAT REBEL GUARDS would execute their prisoners, military rescue missions had always been on the table. It would have been counterproductive to rule them out, because the decision would have taken the pressure off the FARC and encouraged the rebels to take more hostages.

"We were very clear since day one that we would try to rescue them," said Vice President Francisco Santos, who was first elected alongside Uribe in 2002. "A state that does not pursue a rescue policy is just legalizing kidnapping."

Yet for many years Colombian search-and-rescue teams lacked training and intelligence. Just tossing out a few numbers could leave them baffled. When guerrillas took a group of foreign diplomats, including the U.S. ambassador, hostage inside the Dominican embassy in Bogotá in 1980, the rebels assigned themselves odd-numbered names, ranging from one to twenty-nine. Army intelligence agents took the bait and for several weeks operated on the assumption that there were twenty-nine kidnappers inside the building when there were only fifteen. Two decades later, commando units were still floundering. At one point in 2000, army officers became so frustrated by their lack of progress in finding Fernando Araújo, a former government minister kidnapped by the FARC, they turned to a psychic named the Blue Angel. On her advice, the troops marched into the middle of a swamp.

To their credit, highly specialized Colombian police and army antikidnapping units, known as GAULA, put together an impressive record of extracting hostages. But most operations were pulled off in urban settings that played to the advantage of the authorities, rather than in FARC strongholds in the southern jungle where the Americans were being held. When going after hostages, everything had to be perfect. One tiny error could derail the entire operation. That's why Yolanda Pinto de Gaviria was clear that she opposed a rescue attempt following the kidnapping of her husband in 2002.

Guillermo Gaviria, who held Uribe's old job as governor of Antioquia state, was grabbed by FARC rebels along with Gilberto Echeverri, a former defense minister, in April 2002. FARC roadblocks had prevented farmers from getting their coffee crop to market. Gaviria, a student of Gandhi's nonviolent methods, organized a peace march in an effort to persuade the guerrillas to open up the highways. Instead, the FARC grabbed Gaviria and Echeverri, and now had two more high-profile bargaining chips.

Uribe, who was close to Echeverri and to Gaviria's parents, was determined to save both men. He had promised to secure permission from their families before launching a rescue attempt and had on five occasions approached Gaviria's wife. But each time she refused. "I knew," she said, "that if they tried to rescue my husband, the rebels would kill him."

Unwilling to drop the idea, Uribe did an end around. He contacted Gaviria's father who eventually gave his blessing. The president was anxious to move because Echeverri, sixty-seven, was ill. Within Uribe's inner circle, there was also the notion that a bold strike against the FARC would set the tone for his administration. It was part of the president's larger strategy to make life so difficult for the rebels that they would change their tactics, scale back on kidnappings, and consider serious peace talks. To that end, Uribe was willing to put his reputation—as well as the lives of the hostages—on the line for what seemed like the greater good of Colombia.

But on May 5, 2003, the day the rescue operation was launched, the military was still prone to battlefield meltdowns. Intelligence agents had pinpointed the rebel unit holding the men and had cobbled together what was to be a lightning-fast raid. Helicopter-borne troops would rappel down ropes into the FARC camp, surround the rebels, and rescue Gaviria and Echeverri, who were being held along with ten army and marine officers and NCOs. But there were so many miscues and giveaways that the after-action report would read like the chronicle of a fiasco foretold.

Hours before the helicopters took off, support troops aboard twelve military trucks rumbled into the nearby hamlet of Urrao alerting guerrilla militiamen in the village that a rescue operation was under way. Overhead, the commandos aboard one of the choppers were spotted by the guerrillas holding the hostages. The army believed the area around the camp was flat. Yet the commandos descended into hilly, swampy terrain several hundred yards from the hostages. After slogging through the mud for twenty-five minutes, they finally entered the rebel bivouac, shouting through bullhorns for the guerrillas to give up. By then the guerrillas had opened fire on their captives and were long gone. The commandos found the bullet-pocked bodies of Gaviria, Echeverri, and eight other hostages, their faces masked in the gray seal of death. Three soldiers were injured in the spray of gunfire but survived by playing dead.

"We were very naive. We thought that when we arrived, the rebels would flee," said one of Uribe's top aides. "It was a disaster."

THE MASSACRE MADE IT SEEM LIKE the only option for bringing the American hostages back alive was a prisoner exchange. But President Uribe was in no mood to cut deals with the FARC, and the relatives of the American hostages felt utterly helpless. They were quickly learning what many Colombians had realized long ago: that the crime of kidnapping could be nearly as stressful for the family members as for the hostages.

Though it wasn't an option for the three U.S. captives, most FARC hostages were freed after the guerrillas received cash payments. But when, for example, brothers or sisters of the victims took over negotiating chores, it often angered fathers, husbands, and wives. Those putting up the bulk of the cash sometimes castigated relatives for refusing to pony up their fair share of the ransom. Then there was the tricky business of taking care of the hostages' financial assets while they were gone. The ordeal could shatter even the most unified households.

The Americans, at least, had the U.S. government on their side as well as Northrop Grumman, which hired the London-based security firm Control Risks Group for expert advice. But many Colombian hostages came from middle-class families that lacked high-powered connections or the money to hire outside consultants. Unlike Russell Crowe's portrayal of the swashbuckling ransom negotiator in the 2001 film *Proof of Life*, most go-betweens in Colombia were nervous neophytes—brothers, wives, cousins, and close friends who were called upon to save the lives of their loved ones.

"Negotiators are not like Superman," said one Bogotá lawyer who bargained for the release of three abducted colleagues. "We didn't choose this. But if they kidnap your brother, you have to do something."

Relatives wanted to give themselves a fighting chance against these experienced, cold-blooded rebels, so they sought out advice from a loose network of former hostages and amateur go-betweens. And there were many. Colombia was the kidnapping capital of the world. In 2000, the peak year, rebels, paramilitaries, and street criminals pulled off more than 3,500 abductions.

Everyone knew someone who had been snatched, and the crime had transformed President Uribe's cabinet into a family tree of tragedy. There was the president himself, whose father had been murdered during a kidnapping attempt. Vice President Francisco Santos was abducted by the Medellín drug cartel. Though Education Minister Cecilia Vélez had eluded the rebels, her mother and two brothers were abducted and killed by the FARC.

People disappeared in all manner and magnitude. CEOs were dragged from their SUVs. Fourth-grade students were spirited out of school yards. Yeoman farmers were marched away from their cornfields. Urban gangs sometimes snatched people then sold them to the rebels, who could more easily stash them in the jungle. But for maximum impact, rebels turned to mass kidnappings.

In 1999, for example, a squad of ELN guerrillas entered La María church in the city of Cali during a service and abducted 140 worshippers, including children and the elderly. Three years later, FARC insurgents—disguised as army troops and accompanied by "explosives-sniffing" German shepherd dogs—stormed a government building in downtown Cali in broad daylight. Brandishing megaphones and stop signs to block traffic, they announced a bomb threat, then herded twelve state legislators aboard a bus. As the vehicle transported the dozen fresh hostages into the mountains, one of the gunmen announced: "Ladies and gentlemen: We are the FARC."

The rebel roadblock was a less-precise practice but when it worked, it could ensnare hundreds of motorists and scare thousands of others off the highways. FARC guerrillas would halt dozens of cars at a time, then haul away the richest-looking passengers. The gunmen would even extract on-the-spot ransom payments from the most down-and-out drivers who were sometimes forced to empty their wallets and give up their wristwatches. To assist motorists, Colombian newspapers published maps of the safest roads and warned drivers to turn around if no vehicles approached from the opposite direction for more than five minutes. The roadside abductions were dubbed "miracle fishing" after the biblical story in which the disciples, on Christ's instruction, cast their nets into the Sea of Galilee and took home a colossal catch. In Colombia, even scripture became code for kidnappings.

To discourage the criminals, Colombian authorities made it illegal to pay ransoms, but the provision was quickly overturned by the Constitutional Court. Besides, the law was unenforceable. Nearly everyone paid on the sly. There was even a support group for the relatives of hostages, the Foundation for a Free Country, which published a ten-page how-to guide—a sort of *Ransom Negotiations for Dummies*. The pamphlet included a tear-out cheat sheet to help rookie negotiators when the kidnappers phoned in their demands. For example, they were advised to negotiate slowly, that their initial offer should be about 10 percent of the expected final payment, and that they should prepare for multipart payments, since kidnappers often negotiated one price but released their victims only after receiving a second—or third—payment.

For all their preparation, no one could match the guerrillas in experience, cunning, and patience. Unlike distraught family members desperate to spring their loved ones, the guerrillas were in no hurry. They operated on peasant-standard time. They could wait for months until they received the required payment. And if one FARC middleman was unable to squeeze enough money out of a hostage's family, the deal making would be turned over to a second, more hard-line rebel negotiator.

"You have to convince the kidnappers that what you are offering is all that you can give," said Juan Francisco Mesa, who served for a time as the Bogotá government's antikidnapping czar. "The moment they are convinced that they can't extract any more money from you is the moment they liberate the person."

The talks were usually carried out on cellular telephones or two-way radios, but payments had to be made in face-to-face meetings with guerrilla go-betweens. A favorite FARC pay station was the town of Nazareth, located in the frigid mountains three hours south of Bogotá, at the end of a winding dirt track that became known as "the kidnap trail."

During one especially busy morning, a plainclothes rebel had set up a makeshift office by placing a table in the middle of a basketball court on the town square. As he tallied up the final bill of payment for one nervous man, frightened family members of other hostages sat in the bleachers waiting their turns. Once they worked out the details, the relatives were led up a mountain path to hand the kitty over to the local FARC commander.

Striking a deal wasn't always the end of the affair as Jaime Lozada and his wife, Gloria Polanco, found out. Lozada, a senator from southern Huila state, was one of the main targets of a raid pulled off by the FARC's Teófilo Forero Mobile Column, the same rebel unit that abducted Keith, Marc, and Tom. On July 26, 2001, guerrilla commandos stormed his apartment building in the state capital of Neiva. Lozada was in Bogotá so the guerrillas snatched fifteen other residents, including Polanco and the couple's two teenaged sons. Fortunately, the kidnappers never spotted their youngest son, eleven-year-old Daniel. He slept through the assault and woke the next morning to find an empty apartment.

A self-described crybaby with a phobia for snakes and insects that was so extreme she couldn't even watch the Discovery Channel, Polanco now had to live among her demons. In shock, out of shape, and with no sense of direction, she couldn't keep up with her fellow hostages and guards during marches. Sometimes she simply wandered off the trail, forcing the rebels to reel her in.

Back in Neiva, Lozada desperately tried to negotiate a ransom payment to secure his family's freedom. But the negotiations dragged on and Lozada feared his wife and sons might be executed. As the 2002 regional elections approached, Lozada devised a plan. At the time, the FARC was holding three other Huila politicians, including Jorge Géchem, the senator who was dragged off the skyjacked commuter plane. The FARC wanted to exchange the politicians for imprisoned guerrillas, a deal that seemed possible because the Pastrana government had recently won the release of 323 soldiers and policemen by freeing fourteen rebels. Lozada figured his wife and sons might have a better shot at survival if they were grouped among the politicians.

So, even though she was held hostage, Lozada signed up Gloria Polanco as a Conservative Party candidate for the House of Representatives, a maneuver that, inexplicably, was allowed under Colombian law. In a show of solidarity, the citizens of Huila elected Polanco by a huge margin. The sobbing prisoner cowering from the scorpions and tarantulas in the jungle was now a congresswoman. Polanco was heartened by the outpouring of support but also worried that her change of status could make matters worse.

"I knew the election was a big risk, but who could I get angry at?" Polanco said. "If people would have known what was in store for me, they never would have voted for me."

Sure enough, by pulling the lever for Polanco, the voters of Huila had handed the FARC another high-profile bargaining chip. Two days after the electoral results were announced the guerrillas separated Polanco from her sons and marched her to a rough prison camp surrounded by a barbed-wire fence. There she was grouped together with Géchem, Íngrid Betancourt, and the other kidnapped politicians, and would soon meet up with Keith, Marc, and Tom. By then the hard-line Álvaro Uribe had replaced Pastrana in the presidential palace and the campaign to exchange hostages for FARC prisoners ground to a halt. Polanco would not see her sons for another six years.

Though his wife was now a political hostage whose freedom could not be purchased for cash, Lozada continued to talk money with FARC middlemen to secure the release of his sons. Finally, a deal was struck and the two teenagers were liberated nearly three years to the day after they were abducted. But the final price tag was so high Lozada had to pay the FARC on the installment plan. He took out bank loans, borrowed money from friends, sold the family farm, and even offered to give the guerrillas an SUV in lieu of payment. But it was never enough and the guerrillas showed no mercy. On December 3, 2005, FARC gunmen stopped Lozada's Jeep on a rural highway and pumped two bullets into the politician. He died a few days later.

BECAUSE THE FARC WAS NOT ASKING them for money, the relatives of the American hostages were spared the excruciating task of putting a price on the heads of Keith, Marc, and Tom. Yet sitting still and doing nothing was worse. And even without drawn-out ransom negotiations, the stress of the kidnappings quickly began to break down the bonds of family solidarity.

Northrop Grumman officials continued to send paychecks to the families, but the money became a major source of friction. Jo Rosano complained that Marc's wife, Shane, had gone on a spending spree and was tearing through her son's savings. Even with Marc stuck in the jungle thousands of miles away, Jo said, Shane went ahead with breast-augmentation surgery. "And my gosh they're big!" she added. Jo feared that if her son was ever released, he'd come home to a full-figured wife and an empty bank account.

Jo also clashed with other family members. They disagreed with her decision to go public and accused her of trying to become a media star, like Cindy Sheehan, the mother of an American GI killed in Iraq who camped outside President Bush's Crawford, Texas, ranch demanding an audience. But one of the experts from Control Risks, the crisis consulting firm hired by Northrop Grumman, eventually came over to Jo's side.

"He told me I was right to do what I did," Jo said. "If no one had opened their mouth, no one would know about the hostages."

On three occasions, Jo traveled to Colombia to march in the streets with the relatives of other hostages. She was stunned by the natural beauty of the country, while Bogotá's outdoor cafes reminded her of Italy. But the splendor was spoiled by the knowledge that Marc was somewhere out there, far beyond the mountain ridge skirting the eastern flank of the capital.

Jo's public pronouncements sometimes baffled outsiders. She never, for instance, criticized the guerrillas who were responsible for taking Marc away from her. By Jo's calculations, harsh words for the FARC would only backfire and make Marc's life even more difficult. Others believed that there may have been a kind of long-distance Stockholm syndrome at play. Confusion over the true culprit in kidnappings was common. Family members sometimes began to see the guerrillas as the ones feeding, clothing, and protecting their loved ones while the government contemplated risky military operations that could mean death. And because the guerrillas were hidden away in the jungle, it was easier for family members to take out their frustration on more visible targets: like Álvaro Uribe and George W. Bush.

Never subtle, Jo lambasted President Uribe for failing to support a prisoner exchange, called him "the devil" in a radio interview, and accused him of working in cahoots with the paramilitaries. She also blamed the U.S. government for getting involved in a seemingly endless war in Colombia, putting American lives at risk, then turning its back on the hostages.

"My sons are growing up without their father," said Shane Gonsalves, Marc's wife, who was raising their three children in Big Pine Key. "My oldest is shaving. I had to have somebody else teach him how to shave. That's nonsense."

In Colquitt, Georgia, Malia Phillips was struggling to stand by Keith. Three months after the kidnapping, Patricia Medina, Keith's girlfriend in Bogotá, went public, announcing that she was about to give birth to their twins. Some of Keith's best friends, who stayed in touch with Malia, seemed to take the news in stride. And little by little, they let on that Keith had carried out six or seven affairs during their five years together. Malia was furious but there was no outlet for her anger because she couldn't speak with her fiancé. And though she wanted to wait for Keith, it dawned on her that while on duty in Colombia, Keith hadn't really waited for her.

Malia began going out with her girlfriends. One night at a bar she met Ryan Lee, a commercial diver and "deadhead" logger who plunged into rivers to pull up valuable trees that had been preserved underwater. Unlike the controlling Keith—whom Malia called even when he was in Colombia to ask permission to go out with her friends—Ryan urged Malia to be more independent. To Ryan's chagrin, she insisted that if Keith ever came home, they would still get married. But as their relationship blossomed Malia had a change of heart. Keith's children moved back to Florida to live with their mother while the elder Stansells took control of Keith's paycheck. Malia and Ryan were married in 2005 and the bride changed her last name to Phillips-Lee.

"I know outsiders would look at me and say, 'How insensitive can you be? Your fiancé is out in the middle of the jungle!'" Malia said. "But I think everybody who knew the situation and had heard about Patricia thought I was justified in getting on with my life."

Much later, when Keith found out, he was disappointed but not surprised.

"She had hung in there with me when she found out about my affair and I had to give her credit for that," Keith said. "Unfortunately, the three of us had crashed before my relationship with Malia had gone too far down Forgiveness Road."

CHAPTER 14

THE ROUND-UP

*Fortune pays you sometimes for the intensity of her favors by the
shortness of their duration.*
—SPANISH PHILOSOPHER BALTASAR GRACIÁN

IT MAY HAVE BEEN THE GI WITH the shit-eating grin who resigned from the
Colombian Army, then roared off in a shiny new Ford Explorer. Or perhaps it was morning reveille back at the base in Popayán, where the lines
of soldiers seemed a few bodies shy of a battalion—twenty-five the first
morning, sixty the next. Soon there were hardly enough members of Vulture and Destroyer companies left on base to take out the garbage. In sum,
forty-two soldiers and NCOs sought voluntary retirement, fifteen failed to
return from weekend passes, and nine disappeared altogether. The rest
were gallivanting around the city in a drunken stupor. By day three, military commanders sensed that something was seriously wrong.

Jorge Sanabria, the head of Vulture Company, knew things were getting
out of hand when a fellow officer pulled him aside and demanded that Lieutenant Moneybags share some of his wealth. Sanabria pleaded ignorance but

realized that the supposedly drum-tight code of silence had completely broken down. The newly crowned boy kings were acting like brutish, slow-witted beasts.

"They were idiots. Like typical Colombian soldiers, those sons of bitches went out and got drunk and bought gold chains and did a lot of things they shouldn't have," Sanabria said.

Back in Bogotá, General Carlos Alberto Ospina, the army commander, began picking up rumors about free-spending vulgarians staging an impromptu Mardi Gras. The general was familiar with on-the-job temptation. Years earlier, as an army captain patrolling the Caribbean coast, he had spotted a group of smugglers loading a boat with cocaine. The narcos offered Ospina and his troops a box full of cash to look the other way, but he refused the *guaca* and detained the traffickers. But Ospina—who himself would come under investigation much later for allegedly collaborating with paramilitary death squads—admitted that not all of the men under his command were portraits of clenched rectitude.

Ospina ordered an investigation, a military judge issued arrest warrants, and agents began rounding up the culprits. By then, many of the offending GIs realized the party was over or, at the very least, that they would have to take the circus to the next town. So, with their cash-stuffed field packs in hand, they queued up at the Popayán bus station or hired taxis to deposit them on the nearby border with Ecuador. Even so, a few diehards were still swilling whiskey and chatting up B-girls when the MPs showed up to burst their pretty balloons and take the moon away.

One of the first to confess was Wilson de Jesús Artunduaga. One of five brothers from a family of peasant farmers, he admitted that he'd spent about $500 on new clothes. He also took his girlfriend to a discotheque where they blew another $200. But his family eventually convinced him to turn himself in. It was unclear whether Artunduaga had managed to hide any of his cash, but he handed over 19 million pesos, or about $7,000, to army investigators.

For Artunduaga and most of the other soldiers, it had all been a lark, a cartoonish caper that might not last but seemed unlikely to lead to anything more serious than a formal reprimand and a slap on the wrist. In a savage twist, however, army officials were now treating their surreal romp as high treason and acting as if these hooched-up rapscallions were hardened felons. Once detained, they were berated by investigators, given polygraph tests, threatened with years in prison, and forced to spend nights outside on the parade grounds of the battalion headquarters without blankets.

"It made us really sad," said Corporal Wilson Sarmiento, who managed to stash most of his money with an aunt before he was captured. "We fought the bad guys. We gave our best years to the army."

Sanabria said he was handcuffed, denied food—no small issue for the portly lieutenant—and came in for a tongue-lashing. "They called me a miserable son of a bitch. They treated me worse than Sureshot," he said, referring to the maximum leader of the FARC.

Ana Ferney Ospina, an investigator for the attorney general's office who was put on the case to help recover the missing cash, tracked down a nineteen-year-old soldier hiding on a farm near Popayán. In a drunken stupor, he tried to hide by climbing to the top of a tree. "He was screaming like a madman," she said. "He claimed that he'd rather die than go to jail."

Back on the ground, the soldier turned over 25 millions pesos, about $8,600. But several of the fifty-three soldiers arrested in the immediate aftermath carried much more. Second Lieutenant Iván Mauricio Roa was busted with the equivalent of $196,000. Another GI turned over $69,800. Other troops gave up smaller amounts in pesos and dollars ranging from $5,000 to $50,000. Still, investigators believed that the detainees had managed to stash much of their treasure.

As the information poured in, the army brass was aghast. Under President Uribe, the military was supposedly transforming itself into a lethal fighting machine that was going to turn the tables on the guerrillas. But now, just days after the botched army operation to rescue the Antioquia governor had led to the massacre of ten hostages, military commanders were going to have to explain this new embarrassment. Whether tracking kidnappers or unloading misbegotten riches, Colombian soldiers always seemed to lack discretion and savoir faire.

General Ospina knew the press would soon catch wind of the story, so he decided to get out front on the issue by holding a tell-all news conference. Amid the string of scandals, the army could at least come clean and demonstrate to a skeptical public that it wasn't simply an armed engine of government corruption. But how would he spin magical realism? How would he uphold the army's reputation after its noble *Saving Private Ryan* rescue mission had morphed into a Colombian *Caligula*? How would he even keep a straight face?

On May 19, 2003, one month after Vulture and Destroyer companies found the money, Ospina read a communiqué outlining the bare bones of the case. The beat reporters at army headquarters in Bogotá didn't immediately grasp the full dimensions of what the general had just laid out before them. They didn't even ask any follow-up questions. But the story began to gain legs after authorities helpfully paraded some of the offending troops before the media next to a table stacked with piles of confiscated dollar and peso bills. By the next morning, the story was on the radio and splashed across the front pages of the nation's newspapers.

Some members of the Uribe government called for swift and severe punishment. "They betrayed the homeland," said Justice Minister Fernando Londoño, who would later be forced from his post by a corruption scandal of far greater magnitude. "They should be humiliated and subjected to the scorn of their brothers in arms and of the people." It almost sounded like the minister intended to round up the lynch mob, pluck the feathers off the fowl, and bring the tar to boil.

During the previous five years, the number of professional soldiers in the Colombian Army had jumped from 22,000 to 60,000. American aid from Plan Colombia was pouring in. Yet for military analysts and assorted Bogotá thinkocrats, the episode of *la guaca*, as the case became known, seemed like glaring evidence that the Colombian Army, though bigger, was not necessarily better.

Perhaps worst of all, the FARC rebels had inadvertently managed to take out 147 veteran counterguerrilla troops. With every member of Vulture and Destroyer companies sidelined, the military's losses far exceeded the 105 casualties at El Billar, the 1998 FARC ambush widely considered to be the worst defeat in the history of the Colombian Army. And this time, it had happened without a single shot being fired.

DRESSED IN WHITE T-SHIRTS, KHAKI PANTS, and black boots signifying their bottom-rung status as prisoners, several dozen members of Vulture and Destroyer companies now had plenty of time to contemplate fortune's twists and turns. They had tried to go their separate ways. Like pioneers, they had spread out across the land—or at least across the red-light district of Popayán—discovering the new world on a full wallet. Even if they didn't automatically join the ranks of the beautiful people, they believed that money would transform their lives. None of them imagined that the road would so quickly lead them back to where it all began, in this case the mammoth Tolemaida military garrison where the erstwhile GIs were re-united inside the stockade.

Nestled at the foot of the Andes Mountains two hours south of Bogotá, Tolemaida was home to the army's jungle warfare school where many of the detainees had been put through rigorous training courses years before. But it was also home to the military's main detention center where the troops were housed in filthy holding pens next door to troops accused of misdeeds such as aiding and abetting paramilitary death squads. They were allowed just two hours outdoors each day and a few visitors on week-ends. As they awaited trial before a military court, they wrote letters, took bread-making courses, and, depending on how they'd handled their wealth, either beat themselves up for blowing it or brainstormed new schemes for investing their hidden treasures once they were released. In the tropical heat of a Saturday afternoon, one of the soldiers strummed a guitar and composed wistful love songs beneath an awning made from an out-stretched parachute. Others exchanged stories about the sexy sirens of the Popayán bordellos while ruefully pointing out that they were now reduced to getting it on with the Five Daughters of Captain Wrist.

Yet several of the troops seemed relieved that the gravy boat had cap-sized and that they'd washed ashore on familiar ground. Life inside the wire was less complicated than dealing with the world at large. Once their monkeyshines became headlines, once they'd been publicly vilified for leading the life of Riley, everyone from military investigators to FARC guerrillas to drunken uncles knew where to find them and squeeze them.

Within just a few days of General Ospina's news conference, one of the frightened troops turned himself in because he'd received threats from revenge-seeking rebels and needed protection.

"I was ecstatic when we found the cache," said a twenty-three-year-old detainee as he sipped Coca-Cola at Tolemaida and recalled how criminals threatened to kidnap his three-year-old son. "But from that day forward, there has been no peace for me."

Sometimes, the FARC was the least of the troops' problems. After Francy Sanabria, Lieutenant Sanabria's wife, visited the officer at Tolemaida, she returned to the couple's home in a nearby town of Ibague. Shortly afterward, a man with a military-style haircut burst into their apartment, stuck a revolver in Francy's face, and demanded money. Francy's mother, who was also in the apartment, ran outside screaming for help and the gunman escaped. But Francy was so traumatized that she immediately packed up the family's belongings and moved to another city

Another soldier, Giovanny Rodríguez, was targeted by corrupt police officers who began tracking his movements in south Bogotá. One afternoon, Rodríguez and his little brother hopped into a taxi but were quickly pulled over by a police patrol. The cops forced the Rodríguez brothers into a Chevy hatchback, then drove them to a restaurant. Around the table, two of the officers began pressuring Giovanny to hand over his money while the third drove off in the Chevy, turning his little brother into a hostage. The two policemen demanded about $70,000 to free Giovanny's brother. He tried to hold out but eventually called his family and told them to start gathering the money. But his instructions set off alarm bells. His relatives telephoned a nearby police station, the extortionists were arrested, and Giovanny was sent to the stockade at Tolemaida.

Perhaps even more disturbing were cases of family betrayals. Rather than being grateful for the gifts the troops bestowed upon parents, siblings, aunts, and cousins, relatives often angled for more. One disappointed soldier recalled how his father took some of his money and, without so much as a *gracias*, promptly blew it on booze and broads. Another GI said he was kidnapped for twenty-four hours by armed thugs, a gang that included one of his cousins.

"I feel safer in jail than on the outside," he said. "This money was a curse."

Before he was rounded up, Walter Suárez managed to buy a twenty-nine-inch television set that he presented to his parents on Mother's Day. He gifted himself with a video camera, a cell phone, and a leather jacket and, to keep the money coming in, purchased a corner store in the south Bogotá slums where he sold soda, beer, and candy. But it wasn't long before strangers came knocking.

One night, fifteen thieves burst into his rented apartment. Brandishing a grenade, they threatened Suárez and his pregnant wife and began breaking open the floor in search of his money. Finding nothing, they told Suárez he had two days to come up with a huge wad of cash. Unwilling to report the threat to the police, Suárez felt he had no choice. He sold the store and handed the money to the criminals.

Two weeks later came another rap on the door. A group of men flashing ID badges from the attorney general's office burst into Suárez's home. They found Suárez's safe, which contained about $10,000 in Colombian pesos. They also scooped up his laptop computer, a cell phone, and a gold ring. Then they pushed Suárez into the back of a car. Along the way, the men announced they were not from the attorney general's office but instead had come on behalf of Mono Jojoy, the nom de guerre of Jorge Briceño, the FARC's hard-line military strategist. Suárez wasn't sure if he was now a FARC hostage but didn't wait to find out. He rammed an elbow into the side of one of his captors, pushed open the car door, and threw himself into the street.

ISOLATED AT TOLEMAIDA, THE IMPRISONED TROOPS were only vaguely aware of their mounting troubles. In Bogotá, the military was coming under enormous pressure to make examples of the soldiers, though nearly a hundred were still on the lam. A slap on the wrist, it was deemed, would only encourage other far-flung army units to approach the battlefield with shovels and pickaxes along with their automatic rifles in case they too stumbled upon a *guaca*. Rather than sandpaper the rough edges, General Ospina was anxious to put forth all the ugly facts and show that there was no institutional cover-up. But later, even the general would shake his head at the way the hammer came down.

The main complication was that there had never been a case like it before. There was no legal precedent to follow. Cooler heads posited that the soldiers' behavior should be dealt with as a disciplinary issue, with fines, demotions, and a few months in the stockade with heavier penalties for the officers. Instead, the case was turned over to the military's criminal justice system, which accused the troops of embezzling public money. In the dry language of the government's inspector general, "their egotistical desire for riches took precedence over their official duties." If the defendants were found guilty of these charges, they could face between four and ten years behind bars.

But there were other ways to frame the episode, and an army of attorneys, attracted to the soldiers' money, the media limelight, and the bizarre circumstances of the case, descended on Tolemaida to troll for clients. All told, twenty-eight defense attorneys represented the soldiers with about half of them offering to work for free.

It was widely agreed that Lieutenants Jorge Sanabria and Fernando Mojica, the commanding officers of Vulture and Destroyer companies, merited the lion's share of the blame. Still, the lawyers argued that no one had been harmed by their clients' deeds, and therefore, there had been no criminal offense. It was also going to be hard to prove "intent" to commit crimes because the troops had simply stumbled upon the money, then had been, in essence, ordered by their commanders to stuff their pockets.

Ownership of the cash was also in doubt. How could the GIs stand accused of stealing state property when the money had been collected and buried by guerrillas in a patch of territory that the government didn't even control? Besides, no one had come forward to claim the money. Technically, the lawyers argued, the money had been abandoned. One legal expert insisted that unclaimed buried treasure belonged to the citizens of the township where the riches were found, not the government.

Héctor Alirio Forero, a specialist in military law who ran a legal defense organization for soldiers, put forth the thesis that, in spite of the sloppy endgame, the soldiers had served their country by taking millions away from the FARC.

"In the hands of the guerrillas, that money would have been used for very cruel purposes," said Forero, a former army captain. "It would have been used for bomb attacks and to recruit more rebel foot soldiers."

Another lawman who rode to the soldiers' rescue was Jaime Lombana, one of President Uribe's personal attorneys. Though he ran in powerful circles and was trailed by a phalanx of bodyguards, Lombana was immediately drawn to the case, in part because he couldn't stop laughing about it. Lombana's mother helped seal the deal when she asked her son: "What are you going to do for those poor soldiers?"

Lombana did two things. He made a high-profile wager, saying that he would rip up his license to practice law if he couldn't secure a not-guilty verdict. And he also began a concerted public relations campaign, talking up the case to any reporter who would listen.

Across the land, there was already a groundswell of support for the soldiers. About half of all Colombians were straddling the poverty line, and within that demographic it was hard to find anyone who, changing places with the troops, would have dutifully reported the millions to their superiors. This was Colombia, the land of El Dorado, a melting pot of opportunists, black markets, and hot money that had spawned a whole generation of narco-millionaires and where principled public officials were scorned as dim-witted Boy Scouts.

"Luck like that only comes along once in a lifetime," said María Bravo, the Popayán hairdresser who provided haircuts and manicures for some of the soldiers. "And if you don't take advantage, someone else will."

CHAPTER 15

THE EIGHTH PLAGUE OF VALLEDUPAR

The Colombian establishment will not consent to be violently overthrown: pretty much anything else is subject to negotiation.
—DAVID BUSHNELL, *The Making of Modern Colombia*

THE SPRAWLING GUERRILLA CAMP IN SOUTHERN Caquetá state was teeming with teenaged warriors lining up for a dinner of rice, yucca, and gravy. Among them stood a balding, mustachioed FARC commander who, at fifty-one, was old enough to be a father—and in a few cases a grandfather—to some of the young guns. A former cotton farmer, banker, jeweler, university professor, and leftist political organizer, Simón Trinidad—that was his nom de guerre—was one of the few members of the FARC from Colombia's bourgeoisie. Professorial and with a passport full of immigration stamps, he was the savant who had schooled the government envoys on Italian cuisine during the FARC's ill-fated European peace tour in the winter of 2000.

The dead giveaway to Trinidad's blue-blooded origins was his complicated birth certificate. There were no Frankisteys and Miracle Tires among the affluent. Instead, they placed a premium on length, which is why Trinidad was given five names. Born Juvenal Ovidio Ricardo Palmera Pineda, the future FARC negotiator grew up in Valledupar, a city of 350,000 surrounded by cattle ranches at the foot of the Sierra Nevada mountain range in northern Colombia. The son of a country lawyer, Palmera was groomed for a life of relative comfort. He learned French while attending a Swiss-run high school in Bogotá. He briefly studied at the Naval School in Cartagena where he was classmates with Juan Manuel Santos, a future Colombian defense minister. Later, he earned an economics degree at a university in the capital, where, on weekends, he caroused with Andrés Pastrana, the future president. Pastrana remembered Palmera as a clotheshorse and a ladies' man who sometimes used an Americanized nickname: Richard Palmer. He was the first among the student crowd to pay with plastic.

"Ricardo was the most elegant, the best-dressed, the one who went out with the most beautiful girls," Pastrana said. "He was the only one with a credit card so he would pay the bill for the rest of us in the discotheques."

Economics degree in hand, Palmera journeyed to Cambridge, Massachusetts, where he studied on a yearlong fellowship at Harvard University. Back home, he was named manager of the Bank of Commerce and served on the board of the regional branch of Colombia's central bank. He operated the family farm, a five-thousand-acre plantation of African palm and cotton, and mulled over the idea of exporting mangoes to Japan. He married another banker, and the couple opened a jewelry store and raised two children. In his free time, Palmera rode fine horses, danced at the cotillion balls in a black tuxedo, joined the country club, and was an active member in the local arts scene.

Palmera also got to know Gabriel García Márquez, who grew up in the nearby banana plantation boomtown of Aracataca. García Márquez took the stories he'd heard from his superstitious relatives, who spoke of people who could move chairs just by looking at them and make worms emerge from the heads of cows, and transformed Aracataca into the fictional town of Macondo that appears in his novels. Given the pistol duels, the epic floods, and the plagues of locusts described in his memoirs, it wasn't much of a stretch.

"One afternoon," García Márquez wrote, "we heard shouts in the streets and saw a headless man ride past on a donkey. He had been decapitated by a machete during the settling of accounts on the banana plantations, and his head had been carried away by the icy waters of the irrigation ditch."

Palmera's hometown of Valledupar had its own legacy of violence, irrational stories, and outsized characters. Among them was Diomedes Díaz, the country's most popular composer of *vallenato*, the accordion-laced anthems of unrequited love, all-night parties, and the joys and sorrows of life in the backcountry. Díaz lived like the raucous protagonists of his songs. He fathered twenty-two children, had a diamond encrusted in one of his teeth, and, after one cocaine-fueled binge, was imprisoned for strangling his girlfriend and dumping her body in a cow pasture. Free on bail, he fled into the Sierra Nevada Mountains where he was taken in by a paramilitary warlord, nicknamed Jorge 40, who was one of his biggest fans.

Ricardo Palmera wasn't related to Diomedes Díaz, but Valledupar's incestuous power structure meant that, by birth or by marriage, he was tied to just about every mover, shaker, and oddball, and other assorted dramatis personae that city had produced. His kinfolk included an attorney general; an inspector general; the former ministers of culture, foreign affairs, and agriculture; and a state governor, while he was childhood friends with death-squad leader Jorge 40. The place could seem so inbred that outsiders half expected the curlicue tail of a pig to sprout from the hind end of the mayor. And as in the supernatural playground of García Márquez's fiction, calamity struck the town thanks to the paramilitaries and to Palmera, who later became the subject of one of Díaz's songs.

In a move that shocked his family and friends, Palmera sharply deviated from the glide path of the aristocracy. As a rancher and banker, Palmera was aware of the economic struggles of small-business owners and knew it was nearly impossible for peasant farmers to secure loans. His father, in turn, was a sharp social critic who had long been troubled by Colombia's yawning gap between rich and poor. Valledupar was located in northern Cesar state where the land was concentrated in the hands of a few and where a small clique of families dominated politics. Palmera spent marathon sessions discussing the future of Colombia with his father, who admired Fidel Castro and often listened to the nighttime broadcasts of Radio Havana.

Palmera's revolutionary convictions fully synthesized in the mid-1980s. By then, the FARC had launched the ill-fated Patriotic Union political party. The banker became an immediate convert. He also began teaching economics at a local university and organizing protests on behalf of landless peasants. On the rare occasions when they were forced to make contact with the impoverished masses, rich folks might shake hands but would then call for the disinfectant wipes. Palmera was different. He actually believed in their struggle.

"He is an example," Diomedes Díaz, the *vallenato* king, sang of the future guerrilla leader. "And that's why we love Ricardo Palmera so much."

But the backlash against the fledgling leftist movement was swift and brutal. Death squads began assassinating Patriotic Union members, including several of Palmera's colleagues from the university. At one point, Palmera was detained, blindfolded, and held for three days as army interrogators pressed him to admit that he was a guerrilla. Then Palmera received word that his name was on a hit list. He and his wife quit their jobs, sold the jewelry store and the cotton farm, and planned to move with their two children to Mexico.

But Palmera realized that abandoning the country would be an act of cowardice. With the rest of his family safely outside of Colombia, he contemplated moving to Bogotá to continue working for the Patriotic Union. But the circle was closing. Nowhere in Colombia seemed safe for party militants. So on November 6, 1987, at the age of thirty-seven, Palmera bid farewell to Valledupar and disappeared into the mountains.

THOUGH THEY COMMANDED A MOBILE HIT-AND-RUN guerrilla force, the people running the FARC could do a pretty good imitation of sclerotic politburo apparatchiks. They were, after all, Communists, a designation that seemed to require layers of bureaucracy and lists of canons and codes even for irregulars in the mountains. And according to the laws of the FARC, the maximum age for joining the guerrilla organization was thirty. On paper, Palmera was too old for the guerrillas.

But the FARC was willing to make an exception. An army of mostly illiterate peasants, the FARC was always on the lookout for educated cadres who could articulate the gospel. Recruiting them wasn't easy. Lefty intellectuals and university students were attracted to more fashionable rebel outfits, like the M-19, which pulled off spectacular urban raids and enjoyed broad popular support. By contrast, most revolutionaries viewed serving with the retrograde Marxists of the FARC like getting stuck on Planet of the Apes. Thus, Palmera, who adopted the nom de guerre Simón Trinidad in honor of South American liberator Simón Bolívar, was a rare catch. With his thinning hair, banker's mien, and utter lack of combat experience, he didn't look especially lethal. But he brought other skill sets to the table. He was an urban sophisticate. He could explain the enemy because he had lived in their world. He knew the secret handshake.

Trinidad was quickly assigned to the central command of the FARC's powerful Caribbean Bloc, which operated around his hometown. According to urban legend, when Trinidad abandoned Valledupar he made off with stacks of bank records that the guerrillas later used to blackmail the city's elite. True or not, kidnappings jumped, landowners came under new pressure to fork over extortion payments to the FARC, and Trinidad became known as "the eighth plague of Valledupar."

"Because he knew us, he could say how much each of us had," said Hernando Molina, a former governor and member of Valledupar's most powerful political clan who was later imprisoned for collaborating with paramilitaries. "It was a bill come due, but we never understood why, because we had never done anything to him."

Not even family members could catch a break. Perhaps the most infamous FARC kidnapping in the city targeted Consuelo Araújo, the former culture minister whose brother was married to Trinidad's sister. A beloved local journalist and arts connoisseur, she had founded the annual *vallenato* festival and had introduced the young Ricardo Palmera to Gabriel García Márquez. Years later, when Palmera was detained by the military, Araújo helped spring him. Yet once she was taken hostage, Palmera—now known as Simón Trinidad—did nothing to help her. She was sixty-one, ill, and couldn't keep up with her rebel captors. Rather than slowing their pace as they pushed into the mountains with army commandos on their heels, the guerrillas executed Araújo with two shots to the head.

When the FARC and the government opened peace talks, Trinidad trekked south to the newly created DMZ in Caquetá state to join the FARC negotiating team and to face off against his old party pal, President Andrés Pastrana. Trinidad was also tasked with setting up the negotiating site in the hamlet of Los Pozos and schooling rebel foot soldiers in public relations as the media descended on FARC-land.

Although the rebels preached egalitarianism, Trinidad enjoyed the perks reserved for those at the top of the guerrilla pyramid. He roared around in a late-model Toyota four-wheel-drive, often in the company of his girlfriend Lucero, who was twenty-five years his junior and the guerrilla equivalent of a trophy wife. Ensconced in his private tent in the evenings, Trinidad would relax with a book of short stories by Jorge Luis Borges. Or he would open his Toshiba notebook computer that was rigged to a satellite telephone to download his e-mail.

For reporters, Trinidad was a sought-out figure. It was hard to glean very much from the illiterate foot soldiers that made up the rebel ranks, and most of the other FARC leaders were humorless troglodytes. But Trinidad was a master storyteller, especially after breaking out the Chivas Regal. Lacking proper shot glasses, he poured the amber liquid into the cut-out bottoms of plastic water bottles. After a few drams, however, Trinidad transformed into a radical ideologue, and then some. He professed admiration for Joseph Stalin and made it clear that, while peace talks were all well and good, the FARC never intended to put down its weapons.

"Without the guerrillas, we would all be branded on our butts," Trinidad said as he listened to *vallenato* music on the radio inside his tent. "We would all be manservants to the bloody Colombian oligarchy."

And in the name of the revolution, Trinidad could calmly justify everything from recruiting fifteen-year-olds to firing inaccurate homemade bombs that often killed innocent bystanders to kidnapping civilians and holding them for years. He also seemed to relish the idea of drawing the United States directly into the Colombian conflict, which he said would spark a general uprising and bring thousands more volunteers into the ranks of the FARC.

TRINIDAD'S LONG-AWAITED CONFRONTATION WITH THE NORTH would happen a lot sooner than he'd planned. And it would be a long and lonely battle. Nearly a year after Keith, Marc, and Tom were kidnapped by the FARC, Trinidad was dispatched to Quito, Ecuador. It was first thought that he'd traveled there for treatment of prostate cancer or the flesh-eating jungle disease leishmaniasis. But Trinidad later claimed that his true mission was to contact a United Nations representative in order to discuss a prisoner exchange that could lead to the release of the three American hostages.

Colombia's southern neighbor served as a way station for the FARC. Mostly uninhabited jungle, the border provided an easy escape route for the rebels when they were being chased by Colombian troops. The frontier towns were convenient spots to buy food and medicine, while the capital of Quito was full of left-wing politicians who sympathized with the FARC. Indeed, a few military officers had been accused of selling arms to the guerrillas. Yet on the whole there was little stomach in Ecuador for getting involved in Colombia's war. Poking the rebels in the eye would only lead to attacks on the country's military units and the kidnapping of Ecuadorian civilians.

Thus, Trinidad probably had a false sense of security as he roamed downtown Quito on January 2, 2004, in a gray jacket and beret. But Colombian agents, with the help of U.S. intelligence, had been tracking his moves for the past six months. And now, along with a posse of Ecuadorian police officers, they pounced on Trinidad, handcuffed him, and shipped the guerrilla leader back to his homeland. For many Colombians, who were still recovering from New Year's festivities, the arrest sparked a fresh round of celebrations.

During nearly four decades of fighting, FARC *comandantes* had seemed invincible. They moved from the battlefield to the negotiating table and back again and seemed immune to the military's bullets, bombs, and grenades. Even when guerrilla leaders finally expired, the cause of death made a mockery of their adversaries. In 1990, for example, FARC cofounder

California Microwave pilot Thomas Janis earned the nickname "Ace of the Base." After being captured by FARC rebels, Janis and Colombian Army sergeant Luis Alcides Cruz were shot dead.

Keith Stansell poses on one of his many hunting trips. A real-life action figure, he was an avid hunter and fisherman, and his outdoorsman skills helped him survive in the Colombian jungle.

California Microwave pilots and crewmembers in front of the Cessna Grand Caravan that crashed in the Colombian jungle. Douglas Cockes's *(far left)* and Paul Hooper's *(far right)* letters to Northrop Grumman about the dangers of flying a single-engine aircraft over guerrilla territory were ignored.

The Grand Caravan crash-landed on a "postage-stamp-sized" clearing in the jungle-covered mountains of Caquetá state. The crash snapped off the landing gear and ripped open the fuselage of the Grand Caravan.

The bodies of two of the thirty-eight Colombian soldiers killed in a 1999 FARC attack near the town of Gutiérrez, just twenty miles south of Bogotá. In the late 1990s, the Army suffered a string of military disasters at the hands of the guerrillas who killed and captured hundreds of troops.

FARC commander Jorge Briceño, better known as Mono Jojoy, presides over a community meeting in the town of Uribe. Mono Jojoy directed many of the FARC's most devastating attacks and currently heads the FARC's Eastern Bloc, which held captive Keith, Marc, and Tom.

Though his peace negotiations would ultimately fail, former Colombian president Andrés Pastrana met several times with FARC leader Manuel "Sureshot" Marulanda.

Ricardo Palmera (*left*) joined the FARC under the nom de guerre Simón Trinidad. While in Ecuador trying to trade Keith, Marc, and Tom for FARC prisoners, he was captured and charged with kidnapping by the U.S. government.

A FARC squad leader addresses his troops in southern Colombia.

FARC guerrillas relax by playing chess at a rebel camp near the village of La Sombra in southern Caquetá state.

During the 1999–2002 peace talks, the FARC built massive semipermanent camps. This one had a paved parking lot, pools for fish farming, a pharmacy, a photo lab, and concrete shower stalls.

After digging up the FARC money and spending it carousing, Hanner Daza (*right*) was later captured by MPs and tossed in the stockade.

Soldiers from Destroyer Company, one of two Colombian Army units that stumbled upon millions of FARC dollars in the southern Caquetá state.

Five months after they were captured, Keith, Marc, and Tom were allowed to speak with Colombian journalist Jorge Enrique Botero. The interview provided the first proof to the outside world that the three contractors were still alive and in FARC custody.

Policeman John Frank Pinchao (*with shaved head, second from left*) pictured with other Colombian hostages. He spent nearly eight years in captivity.

Proof-of-life images showing the emaciated Colombian politician Íngrid Betancourt caused international outcry and concern that she was on the verge of death.

Desperate to find his wife, Juan Carlos Lecompte rented small airplanes and flew over the jungle tossing out leaflets with images of Íngrid Betancourt's children.

Hanner Daza's family, pictured in their tiny house in Popayán, feared Hanner would join the paramilitaries or be targeted by the FARC.

The soldiers of Destroyer and Vulture companies took over several bars and whorehouses in Popayán and paid the police to look the other way.

Of the 147 soldiers of Destroyer and Vulture companies, only about 50 showed up for their trial at Tolemaida military base on charges of stealing government property. The troops were found guilty and imprisoned, but the trial was later thrown out and the soldiers were freed—only to face new threats.

Gustavo Moncayo's son was a soldier who was kidnapped in 1997. Moncayo marched for hundreds of miles across Colombia to call attention to the hostage crisis.

Relatives of hostages took to the streets to protest Colombian president Álvaro Uribe's refusal to give in to the FARC's demand for territory and the release of imprisoned rebels in exchange for the hostages.

Venezuelan president Hugo Chávez meets with Patricia Medina, Keith Stansell's girlfriend, and their twin boys at the presidential palace in Caracas. The Colombian government briefly asked Chávez to mediate with the guerrillas to try to free hostages.

Luz Marina Chimbaco holds a portrait of her son, Jair, a member of Vulture Company who was held captive by the FARC after purchasing land for his father with the unearthed FARC money. Jair is currently presumed dead.

The Colombian Army formed a group of commandos that proved to be even better than American Green Berets in jungle warfare. In February 2008, the commandos spotted Keith, Marc, and Tom bathing in the Apaporis River near a FARC camp.

Colombian aircraft bombarded Raúl Reyes's camp in Ecuadorian territory, killing the FARC spokesman and breaking the myth of invincibility surrounding the FARC's ruling secretariat.

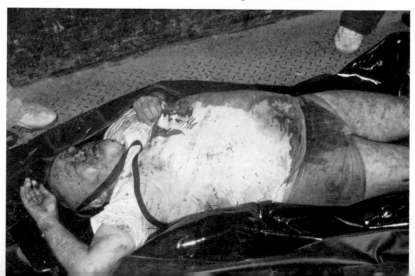

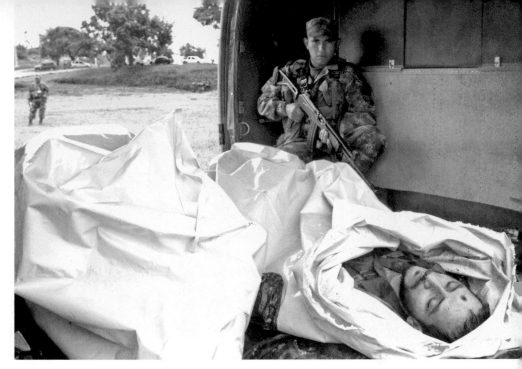

A few days after Reyes's death, FARC secretariat member Iván Ríos was shot in the forehead by his main bodyguard, who then cut off his right hand and turned it over to Colombian officials as proof of the hit.

Colombian policeman John Frank Pinchao was the only hostage ever to escape a FARC camp in the southern Colombian jungle. He became a national hero, and at a May 2007 news conference in Bogotá, Pinchao showed reporters the type of chain and padlock the FARC used to shackle the hostages.

One of the choppers used in the fake humanitarian mission that would rescue Keith, March, Tom, and other hostages. The chopper is flying south one day before the operation and is painted orange and white and decorated with decals of a fake humanitarian organization.

Once all of the hostages were aboard the helicopter, Colombian Army agents pummeled FARC rebels César Aguilar and Enrique Gafas into submission. The hostages piled on and Keith Stansell punched César in the face, bloodying his fist.

Íngrid Betancourt's campaign manager, Clara Rojas, was kidnapped alongside her boss in 2002 and gave birth to a baby boy fathered by a guerrilla.

Pictured alongside Colombian Army commander General Mario Montoya, Tom Howes displays the padlock used by the FARC to shackle him to other hostages.

Paraphrasing Chairman Mao, U.S. ambassador William Brownfield said his approach to freeing the hostages was to "let a thousand flowers bloom." A loyal Texan, Brownfield greeted the newly freed American hostages with bottles of Lone Star beer.

Gerado Aguilar *(center)*, alias César, was tricked into turning over the hostages by Colombian agents. His underling, Alexander Farfán *(right)*, known as Enrique Gafas, served as a kind of prison warden to the hostages.

Shortly after the rescue operation, Colombian president Alvaro Uribe met Keith, Marc, and Tom at a Washington, D.C., ceremony where Gonsalves's mother, Jo Rosano, was granted Colombian citizenship.

Jacobo Arenas was struck down by a heart attack while giving a speech to rebel troops. He was seventy-three. Guerrilla pallbearers solemnly carried his flag-draped coffin along a jungle trail followed by a parade of gun-toting mourners in a ceremony that was broadcast on Colombian television.

But now the balance of power was shifting. Within eighteen months of taking office, President Álvaro Uribe had his first war trophy. The euphoria of the moment and the psychological impact of the arrest were summed up by *Semana*, the country's most influential newsweekly. Atop a cover photo of Trinidad being led off in handcuffs, a boldfaced headline shouted: *Finally!*

"In war, it's not enough to simply advance on the battlefield," the magazine said. "It's essential that the people become convinced they can win. The collective belief that triumph is possible is every bit as important as the territory conquered by the troops."

The arrest of Trinidad would also change the dynamics for the FARC's hostages. The jailed guerrilla was initially set to stand trial in Colombia on forty-five charges ranging from kidnapping to homicide. But Trinidad had also been indicted in the United States for conspiracy to traffic drugs and to kidnap the three American contractors—even though he had no direct involvement in the crime. President Uribe appeared set on dispatching Trinidad to a U.S. prison, but shortly before Christmas 2004, he offered to cut a deal. If the guerrillas would unilaterally release all of their hostages before the end of the year, he would cancel the extradition order. The FARC flatly rejected the proposal.

Meeting with reporters at a high-security prison north of Bogotá a few days before his flight, Trinidad predicted that his extradition would only bring hardship to the hostages. He seemed to have it right. In what would become an excruciating pattern, every time Colombian authorities struck a blow against the FARC, it made life more difficult for the hostages and gummed up the chances for a prisoner exchange.

"Marc, Tom, and I agreed that this wouldn't be a good thing for us," Keith said. "It would piss off the FARC and maybe they'd take their anger out on the Americans."

As the first-ever FARC member to be extradited to the United States,

Trinidad settled into his new home: a six-by-ten-foot cell in the Washington, D.C., jail. He was soon joined in U.S. custody by another FARC guerrilla, a woman known as Sonia who was indicted on drug-trafficking charges. As the two rebels prepared for their trials, FARC leaders back in the jungle came up with a new demand for the release of the three U.S. contractors. Now, they said, if the Americans wanted their precious gringos back, they would have to free Sonia and Trinidad.

AMERICAN OFFICIALS WERE STUMPED. THE LONGTIME U.S. policy stated that American officials would not negotiate with terrorists. Yet the official position could seem a little holier-than-thou. U.S. diplomats would have celebrated had the Colombian government successfully cut a deal to free the American hostages.

"We don't negotiate," said Myles Frechette, a former U.S. ambassador to Colombia. "But there's always back-channel stuff going on. What you have to do is hope that other people, intermediaries, will do something."

Negotiating with the terrorists was how the most high-profile American hostage ever taken in Colombia won his freedom more than two decades earlier. On February 27, 1980, sixteen M-19 guerrillas, their grenades and rifles hidden beneath green jogging suits, stormed the Dominican Republic's embassy in Bogotá during an Independence Day celebration. They seized U.S. ambassador Diego Asencio, the papal nuncio, and fourteen other diplomats. In exchange for freeing the hostages, the guerrillas demanded the release of 311 rebel prisoners plus a $50 million ransom. Trigger-happy Colombian troops surrounded the building and a bloodbath was feared.

Inside the embassy, the rebels seemed unsure what to do next. Thus, Asencio and some of the other ambassadors made friends with their captors and played a major role in the negotiations with the Colombian government. The main rebel intermediary, a woman named Norma, feared that her hotheaded commander would get everyone killed and sought the advice of the diplomats who convinced the guerrillas to tone down their demands and their incendiary language.

At first, the Colombian government refused to budge on the kidnappers' demands, a position fully backed by Washington. This initial inflexibility enraged many of the hostage-diplomats, who insisted that their protection superceded any self-imposed restrictions about dealing with terrorists. Asencio felt like "an afterthought" because his bosses at the State Department were far more concerned about the fifty-two American hostages held by Islamic militants in Iran. In addition, his efforts to negotiate a peaceful solution were, at times, undercut by U.S. officials who believed the kidnapped ambassador had become too much of an activist.

"Looking back, I understand that some of the worst dangers came not from the people who held us at gunpoint but from those who were ostensibly committed to rescue us," Asencio wrote. "Our governments proved to be as much a risk as our captors."

After sixty-one days, the two sides reached a settlement. Instead of releasing guerrilla prisoners, the Bogotá government promised the detainees would receive fair trials with international observers. The $50 million ransom demand was reduced to $1.2 million, which was paid by Bogotá's Jewish community because the Israeli ambassador was one of the hostages. At the time, ransom payments in Colombia were illegal, but officials pointed out that the diplomatic compound was considered foreign territory. On April 27, the hostages were released and the rebels were flown to Havana.

Still, the outcome may have encouraged the M-19 to pull off bolder attacks, such as the 1985 seizure of the Palace of Justice in Bogotá. During that crisis, the Colombian government refused to negotiate and sent in troops and tanks. A fire broke out and the fighting led to the deaths of more than a hundred people, including twelve Supreme Court magistrates. The fallout was a tragic reminder that not all hostages were created equal. Inside the Palace of Justice, the captives were Colombians. Inside the Dominican embassy five years earlier, the hostages were international diplomats, and the Bogotá government could not afford a bloody Black September denouement.

"The only reason they didn't storm the Dominican embassy was because there were a bunch of foreigners in there," Asencio said. "In my view, negotiations are always the right thing to do. The issue is whether you can enter into a negotiation without doing something that might violate your basic principles."

But even the U.S. government has sometimes tossed principles over the transom. In a blunt exercise in realpolitik, the Reagan administration traded arms for the release of American hostages and, in the process, made household names out of obscure figures like Oliver North, Richard Secord, and Manucher Ghorbanifar. Unlike George W. Bush, who seemed oblivious to the plight of the U.S. contractors in Colombia, Reagan couldn't get his mind off the American prisoners in Lebanon.

"Reagan's concern was the release of the hostages, come what may," said Robert McFarlane, Reagan's national security adviser. "He believed that at the end of the day his commitment to releasing the hostages was not only right but . . . politically sound. That Americans would find it defensible to do damn near anything in the world if you could release those hostages."

Abducted in the mid-1980s by the Islamic militant group Hezbollah, the hostages included missionary Benjamin Weir, the Reverend Lawrence Jenco, and Associated Press reporter Terry Anderson. The Middle East had always been front-burner news, and the intense coverage of the kidnappings helped the families of the hostages become an effective lobby in Washington. They were constantly on the news and the TV talk shows. They even sat down with then vice president George Bush while Jesse Jackson and Muhammad Ali took up the cause.

In the end, Reagan's envoys agreed to six separate arms deals with so-called Iranian moderates who pledged to help release the hostages. In his diary, Terry Anderson described the moment when a fellow prisoner, David Jacobsen, was freed.

"Jacobsen's release was the perfect example of the flat, unadorned purchase of an American hostage by the American government. It was exactly what everyone involved, including North, McFarlane, Poindexter, Shultz, Weinberger, Bush, and even Reagan . . . had indicated was unthinkable. The price: a mere 500 TOW antitank missiles."

So, there were exceptions to the "no negotiations" rule in both Washington and Bogotá. Even some U.S. officials believed that a deal involving

Trinidad and Sonia was doable if the FARC was serious about releasing the Americans. But the Bush administration felt no pressure to budge because the hostage ordeal barely registered with the American public. There were hostages but there was no *crisis*. New Mexico governor Bill Richardson tried to intervene but, in terms of media play, he was hardly the heavyweight champ. Perhaps more important, the U.S. government saw no strategic upside in reaching out to the FARC. In the jungle, there were no rebel equivalents of the Iranian "moderates."

Indeed, the lesson from Reagan's arms-for-hostages deals was that it had all been a huge blunder. The profits from the secret arms sales were used to buy weapons for the anti-Sandinista Contra rebels in Nicaragua, and the scandal nearly destroyed Reagan's presidency. And though Ollie North's backroom deals had led to the release of three U.S. hostages, few people remembered that over that same period Hezbollah militants had grabbed six more Americans. Even in humanitarian terms, the net result was a negative.

In the aftermath, the U.S. government settled on a new policy, which was actually a reworked version of the old. Hostages were to be "devalued" in order to persuade the kidnappers that they would get nothing for their efforts. It was also decided that relatives of hostages would never again have access to high government officials. Try as she might, Jo Rosano was never going to get through the gates of the White House. In terms of official emotional capital, that generic White House letter with the likeness of Bush's signature sent to Keith Stansell's two children was as good as it would get.

Yet even if the U.S. government had been willing to negotiate for the release of Keith, Marc, and Tom, there was no guarantee the FARC would keep its end of the bargain. The rebel organization constantly stonewalled and lied about its murderous deeds and criminal intentions. For example, in the only official meeting between a U.S. diplomat and the FARC—a two-day encounter in San José, Costa Rica, in 1998—rebel spokesman Raúl Reyes promised that the guerrillas would not target American citizens. Four months later, the FARC executed three Americans working on behalf of Colombia's U'wa Indians.

"We never got anywhere near" a deal for Keith, Marc, and Tom, said William R. Brownfield, who was named U.S. ambassador to Colombia in

2007. "I don't think the FARC had the least intention of walking down that road."

Most U.S. officials viewed the proposed swap with an astringent eye. Pulling the trigger on a trade, they believed, would endanger U.S. personnel in Colombia because drug lords, rebels, and criminal gangs would realize that one path toward overcoming the extradition of their members to the United States would be to kidnap Americans and then cut a deal. Much as they longed for their freedom, even Keith, Marc, and Tom realized that a trade "was just big pie-in-the-sky thinking."

But to the chagrin of the Americans and the Colombians, the French government would take the exact opposite approach in its efforts to free the most famous FARC hostage of them all: French-Colombian citizen and former presidential candidate Íngrid Betancourt.

CHAPTER 16

JOAN OF ARC

I'm tough, ambitious, and I know exactly what I want. If that
makes me a bitch, okay.
—MADONNA

JUAN CARLOS LECOMPTE PUSHED OPEN THE window on the copilot's side of the single-engine Cessna and tossed out a fistful of leaflets. He had to chuck the laminated flyers in a hard, downward motion so they would miss the rear ailerons. Once in the clear, the papers remained in formation, flickering over the jungle like a covey of white doves. Lecompte was hoping and praying that one would miraculously flutter down to his hostage wife.

The rain of paper was meant for Íngrid Betancourt, a former Colombian senator who was kidnapped by the FARC in 2002 while campaigning for the presidency not far from the spot where the Americans' surveillance plane crashed. Every few months, Lecompte printed leaflets with the images of Melanie and Lorenzo Delloye, Betancourt's two children from a previous marriage, and climbed aboard a small, rented plane in a quixotic attempt to airmail them to his long-lost spouse.

"Her kids make her happy," Lecompte said after a three-hour flight. "This will give her the will to live."

During their seven years together, Betancourt and Lecompte were an odd couple. The pampered daughter of politicians, she grew up in Paris and returned to Colombia determined to save her country by winning the presidency. He was a hyperactive surfing buff, architect, and publicist from the Caribbean coast who had never even voted. They met on a horseback ride, and a few weeks later Lecompte spotted Betancourt on the streets of Bogotá with Lorenzo, who was still just a toddler. He gave them a lift and Lorenzo promptly barfed all over the leather upholstery of Lecompte's BMW. As Betancourt's maid cleaned up the mess, the two struck up a conversation. From then on, they were inseparable.

The vice president and creative director of an advertising agency, Lecompte emerged as the brainchild behind many of Betancourt's ingenious political stunts. In the rare moments when they weren't celebrating another electoral victory or planning the next step in Betancourt's machinations to take over Colombia, the couple skied in Jackson Hole, Wyoming, and took cross-country motorcycle trips. But now, the great river of events had swept Íngrid away. In her absence, young Lorenzo would sneak into Betancourt's closet and hug her clothes so at least he could smell his mother. Lecompte quit his job, sold the BMW, and focused on finding his wife. Now his search had taken him to the jungles of southern Vaupés state.

If not at the ends of the earth, Vaupés was mostly uncharted territory. Located on Colombia's southeast border with Brazil, the state was so far from any governing authority that rubber tappers in the late 1800s managed to enslave many of the local Indians. More than a century later, there were still no roads connecting the capital, Mitú, to any other town. A community of five thousand located on the banks of the Vaupés River, Mitú could only be reached by aircraft or riverboat. In 1998, the FARC bombarded Mitú with homemade rockets, overran the town, and considered declaring it the capital of a breakaway rebel republic. When the Colombian military responded, air force planes had to fly so far from their bases they ran low on fuel and had to land in Brazil to top off their tanks before launching their counterattack.

Lecompte checked himself into the twenty-one-dollar-a-night Mitúsava Hotel. The price was twice the rate at the competing hotel because the Mitúsava sat in an out-of-the-way spot next to the river and was less likely to be hit in the next FARC bombardment. In his green-and-blue polo shirt and tortoiseshell glasses, Lecompte seemed a little out of place in the rustic frontier town, and his mission seemed more than a little eccentric. He spent hours hovering over rebel territory in an aircraft that was even smaller and flimsier than the Americans' Grand Caravan. The target area was a dense, unbroken carpet of trees the size of Bulgaria. Lecompte probably had a better chance of communicating with his wife if he'd used skywriting.

Despite the humanitarian nature of his mission, the police treated Lecompte with contempt, as if he were some yuppie drug lord from Bogotá. Upon his arrival at the Mitú airport, police agents tried to confiscate his leaflets. He had to file a detailed flight plan for every sojourn, and on one trip Colombian military planes mistook Lecompte for a smuggler and flew circles around his Cessna.

On the surface, it seemed like madness. But Lecompte couldn't do much worse than the experts. The bleak science of locating hostages beneath the thick rain forest canopy was so challenging that CIA and Colombian intelligence agents had been completely stumped. So Lecompte acted on his gut. The former adman knew something about saturation coverage and, as he papered the jungle, he made up for his lack of precision with sheer volume.

Recognizable from the hundreds of TV appearances he'd made on behalf of his famous wife, Lecompte was constantly being approached by complete strangers who were full of advice. The guy who ran the cafeteria at the Mitú airport told Lecompte that the hostages were being held along the Papunaua River, fifty miles to the north. On his next flight, Lecompte circled the area. One night, an Indian shaman applied sparkly crimson paint to Lecompte's face and belly, chanted, and invoked the spirits. The next morning, the sleep-deprived Lecompte showed up at breakfast with red streaks across his cheeks and a promise from the shaman that the photos would find Betancourt.

And so he kept at it. On one trip he directed the pilot to land in the tiny hamlet of Carurú where the local army commander asked Lecompte to transport a captured FARC guerrilla back to Mitú. This seemed like a golden opportunity to grill one of his wife's captors. But the prisoner turned out to be a fifteen-year-old Indian who carried his worldly possessions in a black garbage bag. Sobbing in the back of the plane, the teenager said the rebels tricked him into joining the FARC after plying him with beer. He knew nothing about the three American hostages. And he had never heard of Íngrid Betancourt.

THE WORLD MAY HAVE FORGOTTEN about Keith, Marc, and Tom, but the kidnapping of Íngrid Betancourt turned her into an international icon. The families of the other captives grumbled that, by comparison, their loved ones were anonymous low cards. But without Betancourt's face pasted to the tragedy hardly anyone would have taken note of Colombia's hostage crisis.

Betancourt was raised in Paris where her father, a former education minister, served as Colombia's representative to UNESCO. They lived in an enormous apartment where dinner guests included Gabriel García Márquez and artist Fernando Botero, and where the young Íngrid once exchanged verses with Chilean poet Pablo Neruda. In her early twenties, Betancourt fell in love with her first husband, French diplomat Fabrice Delloye, while babysitting for his son. They were married, had two children, and were sent to a series of exotic foreign postings, like the Seychelles Islands. But Betancourt quickly tired of her role as a diplomat's wife. As Colombia descended into a hellish cycle of violence, she left her husband and returned to Bogotá.

"I leave Fabrice, pack my bags, and fly alone to Bogotá," she wrote. "I'm well aware of the suffering that awaits me . . . but I'm sure this is the price I have to pay to finally recover a place among my own people."

Betancourt briefly worked for the Treasury Ministry. But she was outraged by the graft she witnessed within the government, and in 1994 decided to run for a seat in the lower house of Congress. She was a virtual unknown but presented herself as the anticorruption candidate and passed out condoms on the streets of Bogotá as symbolic protection from government depravity. She was elected with more votes than any other Liberal Party candidate. In the ensuing years, she loudly denounced the infiltration of Colombian politics by *narcotraficantes* and received a series of death threats. In 1998, Betancourt won a seat to the Colombian Senate but she made new enemies by declaring that half of her fellow congressional hopefuls were on the payroll of drug dealers. Though she had a point, Colombian lawmakers rolled their eyes.

"Íngrid acted like she was the only pure one, and the rest of us were corrupt. She was so arrogant. It was like you had to walk up a golden staircase just to talk to her," said Luis Eladio Pérez, a senator who served alongside Betancourt. Then, using Colombian slang for "self-regard," he added: "She thought she was the cow that shit the most."

Yet by the time the forty-year-old Betancourt launched her 2002 presidential campaign, she seemed to have lost her edge. She had been a vocal backer of President Andrés Pastrana's ill-fated negotiations with the guerrillas and had even traveled to San Vicente del Caguán, the capital of FARC-land, to urge rebel leaders to stop the cruel practice of kidnapping.

It was a brave performance. But Betancourt was pigeonholed as a naive peace candidate at a time when Colombians wanted their leaders to get tough with the guerrillas. Her self-aggrandizing autobiography, which hit the shelves shortly before her campaign kicked off, didn't help much either. Betancourt painted herself as Colombia's savior and subtitled the English-language version: "My Struggle to Reclaim Colombia." In France, the book was a runaway bestseller and Betancourt was lionized as a courageous heroine doing battle against the forces of evil. In Colombia, the book was panned and the polls indicated that she was headed for a crushing defeat in the presidential race. For most Colombians, Betancourt was a fading voice of protest, more Joan Baez than Joan of Arc.

Seeking to jump-start her campaign, Betancourt set off anew for FARC-land on February 23, 2002. Her big, roll-of-the-dice move came three days after President Pastrana canceled peace negotiations with the rebels and ordered the military to retake the DMZ that he had turned over to the FARC in 1998. The mayor of San Vicente del Caguán belonged to Betancourt's upstart political party and she had promised to stand by with the community if fighting broke out. Her campaign staff met and decided by a twenty-eight to two vote that Betancourt should go.

Adair Lamprea, a campaign worker who accompanied her, said Betancourt didn't consider the trip especially risky because she supported the peace talks and agreed with the FARC's call for political reforms. She sometimes felt more at odds with her corrupt colleagues in Congress.

Betancourt, along with eight campaign workers and two French reporters, flew to Florencia, the capital of Caquetá state. By then, the FARC had set up roadblocks and land mines on the highway, so Betancourt tried to hitch a ride on one of the military choppers transporting journalists, soldiers, and President Pastrana to San Vicente del Caguán. Citing the rapidly deteriorating security conditions, Pastrana had rejected requests from two other presidential candidates to be airlifted to the town, and now he refused to take Betancourt. He wasn't kidding about the risks. After Pastrana's chopper departed for San Vicente del Caguán, the aircraft was hit by a hail of bullets.

In an act of sublime recklessness, Betancourt made the trip overland. The government loaned her a Nissan pickup, but five members of her entourage, including three bodyguards, stayed put. "I told Íngrid: 'I'm freaked out by this. I'm not going,'" said Francisco Rodríguez, Betancourt's press attaché. "But Íngrid is very impulsive."

Thirty miles later, as they approached the town of El Paujil, Lamprea, who was driving the pickup, slowed for a FARC roadblock. The guerrillas had placed a bus across the highway and rigged it with explosives. A group of rebels recognized Betancourt and debated what to do with her. One of the rebels told her to turn around and drive back to Florencia, but she insisted on moving forward. Suddenly, there was an explosion. One of the guerrillas who had wandered off the highway to take a leak had stepped on a land mine. Amid the chaos, Betancourt offered to drive the bleeding man to a hospital. Instead, the angry, agitated rebels commandeered Betancourt's pickup and drove her entire entourage into the jungle.

Hours later, the guerrillas freed Lamprea, along with another campaign worker and a French photographer, but they said Betancourt and her campaign chief, Clara Rojas, would be held until the Bogotá government agreed to release several imprisoned guerrillas. The Colombian people condemned the kidnapping but there wasn't exactly an outpouring of sympathy for the nation's newest hostage. Betancourt's actions seemed so fool-hardy that some Colombians accused her of staging the abduction to gin up interest in her flagging presidential campaign. And it's likely that more than a few politicians, who were no fans of Betancourt, were secretly rejoic-ing at this news.

"IT'S EASY TO CRY OVER SPILLED milk," Clara Rojas later wrote. "But if the president's attitude had been different on that day, we very probably would not have been kidnapped."

Betancourt's family also blamed President Pastrana and claimed that his government wasn't lifting a finger to free her. Yet if there was one prisoner who would not be forgotten it was Íngrid Betancourt. U.N. Secretary-General Kofi Annan, the U.S. State Department, and members of the European Parliament all denounced her abduction. Then there was France, the Betancourt family's deep and loyal ally across the pond.

Because Betancourt had been married to a French diplomat, she had dual citizenship. One of Betancourt's former university professors was Dominique de Villepin, who served as President Jacques Chirac's prime minister and foreign affairs guru. As he looked into the kidnapping, Daniel Parfait, the French ambassador to Bogotá, became so enamored of Betan-court's older sister, Astrid, that he left his wife for her.

Thus while the U.S. government tried to minimize the perceived value of the American hostages, officials at the Élysée Palace declared that free-dom for Betancourt was a national cause. And from day one, French offi-cials put enormous pressure on President Pastrana—and Álvaro Uribe who was sworn in a few months later—to give in to the FARC's demands for a prisoner exchange.

"They were telling us to do deals we weren't willing to do," said Vice President Francisco Santos. "But in turning Íngrid into this important in-ternational figure, it just upped the price for her release."

About a year after Betancourt was kidnapped, an informant told Co-lombian officials that a FARC envoy would be willing to speak with mem-bers of the Betancourt family. Astrid Betancourt spent several days in the jungle along the Colombian-Brazilian border, then contacted the French foreign minister with an urgent request. She apparently told Dominique de Villepin that the FARC planned to release her sister, who required immediate medical assistance. Without informing the Colombian and Brazilian governments, the French dispatched a C-130 Hercules transport plane with a posse of undercover agents to the Amazon city of Manaus. From there, French agents chartered a seaplane and flew farther into the jungle all the while trying to make contact with the FARC. But the operation collapsed when the spies were arrested by the Brazilian police, creating an embarrassing scandal for the French government with its allies in Bogotá and Brasilia.

The French never explained what had made them believe the FARC was suddenly going to hand over Betancourt. But much later, a series of e-mail messages on a computer confiscated from a FARC camp suggested that the mission failed due to a botched ransom payment. In one message, FARC spokesman Raúl Reyes appeared to scold a French mediator—whom Colombian officials had authorized to make contact with the FARC—for turning over a large sum of cash to scam artists impersonating the guerrillas.

By then, France's Colombia policy had become an Íngrid Betancourt policy. Jacques Thomet, a French journalist who wrote a book about the Chirac government's obsession with Betancourt, reported that Paris lost out on $700 million in arms deals with Bogotá because officials at the Élysée Palace worried the transactions might offend the FARC.

Back in Bogotá, officials seethed. In their view, so much attention from the French only played into the FARC's hands by providing the guerrillas with media exposure, a platform for their demands, and a way to slime the Colombian government. They also complained that the Free Íngrid campaign failed to focus on the cruelties of the guerrillas and left the impression in Europe that the hard-line president Uribe—not the FARC—was the villain.

KEITH, MARC, AND TOM FIRST MET Íngrid Betancourt in October 2003, three months after the French rescue mission fell apart. After spending their first eight months in captivity by themselves and completely cut off from the rest of the world—they weren't even allowed to listen to the rebels' transistor radios—the contractors looked forward to being transferred to a larger prison camp that housed six Colombian lawmakers and twenty-seven police and army troops. It was a return to some semblance of society. The new camp was better supplied. There were clothes, books, radios, and better food. But the Americans would quickly realize that living alongside Betancourt and the other prisoners would prove to be almost as challenging as dealing with their prison guards.

Luis Eladio Pérez, a senator kidnapped in 2001, remembered when the Americans trundled into their camp. Reed thin and wearing filthy, raggedy clothes, they looked like walking scarecrows. The FARC had a hard time coming up with pants and shirts big enough for these guys, so they didn't have any extra clothes to change into. "Our reaction was disgust because of the stench," Pérez said. "They smelled horrible."

Then the Americans overheard Betancourt complain that the camp was already overcrowded. She wanted nothing to do with the gringos.

"Can you believe that?" Keith said to Tom and Marc. "The frickin' princess thinks that the FARC built this castle for her alone. How arrogant is that?"

Marc felt like the new kid at school who was trying to figure out who the cool kids were. They viewed Pérez, who had paired off with Betancourt even though both were married, as an insecure man trying to defend his territory amid the arrival of the Americans. At a meeting of all the prisoners, Pérez at one point began screaming, "There are no whores here," as if he thought the Americans were obsessed with getting into the pants of Betancourt and the three other female hostages. Keith and Tom saw Betancourt and Pérez as upper-crust blowhards who had brought their snobbish views with them to the jungle.

Keith, whose parents were Ph.D.s in education, couldn't stomach how the Colombian politicians addressed each other with the honorific "doctor" when not one of them had earned their degrees.

"Are all of you fuckers Ph.D.s?" he once asked in exasperation. "You're all fakes. I'm gonna start calling myself 'Doctor Stansell.'"

In Pérez's telling, the Americans, especially Keith, could be a little overbearing while the guerrillas, for all their anti-imperialist rhetoric, sometimes treated the gringos with deference.

"The resentments could explode over the tiniest thing, like how many potatoes or how much rice you received for lunch," Pérez said. "There were many problems."

The police and soldiers, most of whom came from peasant stock and were housed in a separate barracks, saw the politicians as oleaginous Harvard Yard oligarchs who misruled the country and fanned the flames of the rebel insurgency. They complained that Betancourt and the other captured lawmakers received all the attention from the media while they were ignored.

Some of the soldiers were dignified and went to great lengths to help the politicians by shouldering their gear on marches, treating them when they were sick, and giving them extra food. "The military guys carried the politicians," Keith said, "because the politicians were weak intellectually, physically, and emotionally. They couldn't stand on their own. But the military guys were salt of the earth."

Sometimes the guerrillas became fed up with the bickering and scolded the hostages, telling them they had to learn to get along. "It seemed so absurd that the rebels had to get involved in this, as if we hostages were unable to overcome our rifts," Clara Rojas said.

At other times, the FARC made matters worse by pitting one group against the other. For example, the rebels convinced some of the police and army hostages that the more politicians they kidnapped, the more likely the Colombian government would be to authorize a prisoner exchange. A few of the military men even celebrated when they heard that another politician had been abducted.

The main problem was that many of the soldiers and policemen had been held in the jungle for so long they had simply given up hope. Thus, the kind of *Bridge on the River Kwai* POW discipline that might have stiffened morale and encouraged solidarity never developed. Even as class resentments simmered, military hierarchy went out the window. A corporal was the same as a colonel. And some of the military men, who figured they'd never make it out of the jungle alive, began collaborating with their rebel guards in exchange for extra food or other favors that made their lives a little easier. The Americans took to calling these men "trusties."

Orlando Beltrán, one of the kidnapped lawmakers, recalled how a "trusty" put an end to his escape plans. Beltrán along with two other soldiers planned to climb over the barbed-wire fence surrounding their camp and make a run for it. Though they didn't have much food, they would watch what the monkeys ate, then consume the same seeds and fruits knowing they were not poisonous. They figured that within a few days, the guerrillas would give up their search effort. But all this conspiring was for naught. One of the "trusties" heard about the plan and told the guerrillas.

Afterward, Beltrán approached police colonel Luis Mendieta, who was the highest-ranking officer. "I said: 'Colonel, why don't you organize these men?' But he had been threatened and attacked by some of his own troops. The guerrillas sometimes had to protect him. And they had convinced the colonel that, as a prisoner, he had lost all rank and responsibilities."

Some of the strains were understandable. Spending time as a hostage could be like a never-ending reality show, *Survivor* minus the cathartic act of voting the slackers and half-wits off the island. "In an experiment scientists put a bunch of rats in a small cage," Marc said. "By the end, those rats were eating each other and it's basically the same thing that happens with hostages."

Much of the conflict revolved around Betancourt, who generated all manner of envy. She was attractive, spoke four languages, and, as a former aerobics instructor, could swim better and exercise longer than almost all the other prisoners. In this camp, the prisoners were allowed to listen to the radio, including late-night programs that played messages from family members to the hostages. But the words from Betancourt's mother were nearly always the first to air, while the other hostages had to stay up all night waiting for their loved ones to come on the air. Palpably self-righteous even in captivity, Betancourt drew up a 190-point governing plan to prepare herself for the day she was elected president of Colombia.

"She even offered me a job," Keith said. "She said that when she was president, I could be one of her defense advisers. I said: 'Do you think I'm that stupid that I'll let you manipulate me? Do you think I'm that impressed by you?'"

Amid shifting alliances, the hostages seemed to cleave into two groups: those who were close to Betancourt—like Pérez and Marc who developed a crush on her—and those like Keith, Tom, and some of the military men who loathed her. The dividing line was deep and serious. Keith could never forgive Betancourt for her snotty reception of the Americans and claimed that, in her effort to get the Americans moved to another camp, she even tried to convince the guerrillas that the contractors were CIA agents.

"Whenever I hear her name, my blood boils," Keith said. "I never fell under her spell because I never wanted to sleep with her."

But others felt differently. Marc traded a series of intimate letters with Betancourt but, to his chagrin, she spent much of her time with Luis Eladio Pérez and later paired off with a Colombian Army corporal named William Pérez. The sexual tension led to some surreal moments. One night, Keith recalled, Betancourt and the soldier were together and making a lot of noise. Jealous, Marc rolled over in his bunk plugging his ears. All the while, the prisoners' transistor radio was broadcasting a message from Juan Carlos Lecompte, Betancourt's husband back in Bogotá who was sobbing and telling Íngrid how much he loved her.

Yet even for her detractors, there was a lot to admire about Betancourt. She was one of the few women in the mix—and at times, the only female. The short, stocky female guerrillas were jealous of the tall, svelte Betancourt, while the male rebels sometimes turned into furtive Peeping Toms when she took a bath. Pérez said that the guerrillas sometimes filmed the women at the latrine in order to make rough porno films. There were a few instances of grab-ass, but Betancourt never backed down, never hesitated to take a swing at those who stepped over the line or to plant a firm boot in the crotch of an aggressor.

"The presence of a woman among so many prisoners who have spent eight or ten years in captivity is a problem," Betancourt wrote in a letter to her mother. "I used to love bathing in the river. But I have to go in my clothes—shorts, shirt and boots . . . like our grandmothers."

Luis Eladio Pérez had considered Betancourt unbearable when they served together in Congress, but his admiration for her multiplied in the jungle. A heavy smoker, Pérez suffered from three mild heart attacks and two diabetic comas and each time Betancourt nursed him back to health. When he was an invalid, she bathed him and even washed his underwear.

He thought captivity brought out the best in Betancourt, making her at once more humble—and more courageous.

THE FARC HAD SECURED A DMZ under the Pastrana administration and the rebels would accept no less from Uribe when it came time to discuss a prisoner exchange. Early on, the FARC proposed that Uribe pull troops from Cartagena del Chairá, a jungle village in southern Caquetá state. It was the same area where former president Ernesto Samper had created a DMZ for forty-five days in 1997, allowing the FARC to liberate about sixty captured soldiers and marines.

But the new president said the plan would offend the honor of the army. If granted their own fiefdom, the guerrillas were sure to play host to international delegates, swarms of journalists, and the likes of Queen Noor, creating a three-ring circus that would breathe new life into a movement Uribe had set out to choke. As the impasse dragged on, the FARC upped its demands. The guerrillas began pressuring for a DMZ in Florida and Pradera, two townships located about twenty miles east of Cali, the nation's third-largest city.

The rebels claimed they needed the territory to guarantee their security as they carried out talks on a prisoner exchange. The towns were located at the foot of the central Andean ridge, mountainous terrain that could provide the rebels with a convenient escape route should the ground rules collapse and they came under fire from the Colombian Army. But more important, the act of establishing a DMZ for the rebels meant de facto political recognition from Uribe, the FARC's fiercest enemy.

Despite Pastrana's disastrous experiment with ceding land to the guerrillas, proponents of the new DMZ argued that conditions had changed. The army was stronger, the FARC was weaker. The two townships were small and close to military bases in Cali, which would make it easier to monitor the zone and reconquer the territory once the experiment ended. Some even believed that a successful prisoner exchange could lead to broader negotiations for an eventual peace treaty. And if things fell apart, at least Uribe could say he tried.

"The important thing is to initiate conversations," said Álvaro Leyva, a Bogotá politician and one of the chief backers of the DMZ. "If you don't take the first step, how do you arrive at the fifth step?"

In the jungle, the hostages prayed for a DMZ, and at one point, when it seemed as if Uribe might agree to the rebel's demand, the prisoners celebrated. Marc looked skyward and thanked God. Keith mused about getting home in time for Thanksgiving and strapping on the Stansell feedbag.

"We would have sold our souls to get out of that situation," Tom said.

But the plan never gained traction. Unlike Pastrana's DMZ, which was located in the southern badlands, an area that nobody really cared about, the new proposal contemplated prime real estate. The area around Florida and Pradera was a fast-growing commercial hub, and the heartland of Colombia's sugar industry. Besides, town officials were trying to promote tourism. How were they going to attract outsiders if their communities became known as the new county seats of FARC-land? They pointed out that when the guerrillas briefly occupied the jungle outpost of Cartagena del Chairá in 1997, many foreign travelers mistakenly thought FARC rebels had raided the colonial city of Cartagena, Colombia's best-known tourist destination. Though the two Cartagenas were six hundred miles apart, the damage was done. Travel agencies canceled five charter flights to the more famous Cartagena.

From day one, Uribe and his surrogates ridiculed the plan. Vice President Francisco Santos, a former hostage, took one of the hardest lines against the FARC. Yet Santos was alive thanks to the same kind of deals that he now opposed. A longtime journalist and the son of Hernando Santos, the publisher of *El Tiempo*, the country's leading newspaper, Francisco Santos and several other prominent Colombians were abducted by Pablo Escobar's henchmen in 1990. At the time, Escobar was carrying out a terrorist campaign to force the Colombian government to outlaw extradition to the United States where drug lords faced far harsher prison sentences and could not manipulate the system. Known as the Extraditables, the group had a slogan: Better a grave in Colombia than a prison cell in the United States.

The families of the hostages, who included the daughter of a former president, were so well connected that they were constantly holding meetings with then president César Gaviria and his top advisers. They urged the government to negotiate with Escobar. A group of former Colombian presidents, known as the Notables, also took up the cause by counseling Gaviria to consider Escobar and his accomplices as a political movement rather than a criminal syndicate. Gabriel García Márquez was so moved by the saga that he set aside some half-finished projects to produce his first work of nonfiction in decades: *News of a Kidnapping*. He described writing the book as "an autumnal task, the saddest and most difficult of my life."

Years later, Santos defended his family's easy access to the power dome and recalled that at one of the encounters his father told President Gaviria not to compromise national objectives in order to save his son. Even before he was kidnapped, Santos pointed out, President Gaviria had offered reduced prison sentences and had pledged not to extradite Escobar and other kingpins who turned themselves in, confessed to minor crimes, and cooperated with authorities.

Still, Gaviria had to bend the rules to please Escobar and secure the release of Santos and the other hostages. His government rewrote its non-extradition decree to the drug lord's specifications and built him a five-star prison on the outskirts of Medellín on land owned by one of Escobar's front men. After handpicking the guards, Escobar turned himself in, then promptly remodeled the penitentiary, adding a gym, sauna, lounge, discotheque, Jacuzzi, and fake waterfall. He dined on stuffed turkey and caviar at his birthday party and hosted a wedding reception at the prison, which was soon dubbed Club Medellín. Later, the man responsible for moving tons of cocaine and murdering legions of Colombians was allowed to confess to just one crime: acting as a middleman in a French drug deal. In Escobar's surreal court appearance, the lord of all drug lords identified himself as nothing more than a humble livestock farmer.

So many Colombian governments had bent over backward for the bad guys—there was the $1.2 million paid to M-19 rebels at the Dominican embassy, the legal gymnastics required to secure Escobar's arrest, Pastrana's Switzerland-sized DMZ—that the relatives of Íngrid Betancourt, the three Americans, and the other hostages didn't think converting Florida and Pradera into a rebel haven was unrealistic.

Besides, for all his talk about standing firm against terrorists, President Uribe had earlier withdrawn troops from the township of Santa Fe de Ralito in northern Colombia to begin a peace process with right-wing paramilitaries. And just as the FARC had used its DMZ to traffic drugs and stash hostages, the militias continued to order killings and arrange cocaine shipments from the confines of their fiefdom.

Government officials argued that the paramilitary DMZ opened the door to the demobilization of thirty thousand of the militiamen. By contrast, the FARC had used its demilitarized territory to bolster its war machine. Even so, critics cried foul, accusing Uribe of setting a double standard. They charged that he was willing to make huge concessions to the paramilitaries because the right-wing militias had supported his presidential campaign and had worked in cahoots with many pro-government lawmakers as they took control of rural zones once dominated by the FARC. In the endless debates, the fate of the hostages seemed to be secondary.

"We felt like insignificant pawns," Tom said.

A prisoner exchange "is supposed to be a humanitarian gesture," said Carlos Lozano, editor of Voz, the Communist Party newspaper in Bogotá. "But both the government and the FARC view any concession as a sign of weakness. Yet no one is going to win the war if Íngrid Betancourt is released or if five hundred rebels are let out of jail."

Perhaps more important for the president, holding the line was good politics. Every time Uribe lashed out at the FARC, his poll numbers shot up. It turned out that the constituency of former hostages, the relatives of hostages, and assorted peaceniks pushing for a prisoner swap was no match for the vast majority of Colombians who saw Uribe as a heroic lone ranger, the first Colombian president in ages who was willing to stand up to the rebels and tell them, in no uncertain terms, where they could stick their honey-baked proposals.

"That's vital for a politician," said León Valencia, a Bogotá political analyst and a former guerrilla fighter. "If your poll numbers rise due to a certain policy, why are you going to change? Rather than a humanitarian issue, it becomes a political game. And Uribe has played it well."

JUAN CARLOS LECOMPTE SAW THINGS THROUGH a different moral prism from the copilot's chair in the Cessna high above the jungle gulag where his wife was suffering. He recalled touring Europe and speaking about Betancourt to an audience in Berlin.

"I asked them: 'Can you imagine three thousand Germans being kidnapped? Whether the government was left-wing or right-wing, wouldn't that be the number one national problem?'" Lecompte said. "But here in Colombia, it's not the number one problem or the number two problem or the number ten problem. For this president it might rank as problem number thirty-four."

Lecompte seemed to find temporary solace circling above the rain forest, clutching a green aviation map, studying the winding river tributaries, and directing the pilot to swoop low over sandbars where he thought the hostages might be allowed to bathe. The air raids may have been an arid, hopeless exercise, but it was better than doing nothing. It was better than moping by himself back in the couple's haunted apartment in Bogotá where the Betancourt photos, oil paintings, and campaign posters kept reminding him of all he had lost.

Down to his last wad of pesos in Mitú, Lecompte took up a collection from a couple of reporters so he could pay for one final pass over the jungle. This time the pilot cut south from Mitú toward the Apaporis River, which divided the states of Vaupés and Guaviare—the Colombian equivalents of Mongolia and Siberia. Lecompte spotted a hamlet and the pilot took the aircraft down to nine hundred feet to better aim the leaflets. A group of Indian youngsters burst out of their thatched huts and stared at the paper fluttering their way. Suddenly, a gust of wind knocked the flyers off course and away from the village, and the smiling images of Betancourt's children were swallowed up by the murky brown water of the Apaporis.

CHAPTER 17

THE DIRTY THIRTY

The god I believe in is a god of second chances.
—BILL CLINTON, ABC NEWS, MARCH 23, 1994

OURT CASES IN COLOMBIA THAT INVOLVE just one person can drag on for a decade, so it seemed likely that the young men of Vulture and Destroyer companies would face a drawn-out judicial battle. They felt like hostages stuck in the army's Byzantine legal maze.

Some of them believed they'd been targeted by a military looking for easy scapegoats. After all, overwhelming evidence had emerged showing that scores of army officers had worked closely with paramilitary death squads to plan and carry out massacres. In the bloody aftermath, only a tiny handful of the culprits had ever been punished. But when it came to a victimless stunt involving the grunts, the army brass was more than willing to put on show trials and demonstrate to the public that the military was cracking down on corruption.

After ten months behind bars at the Tolemaida Military Base, the fifty or so troops who had been captured or had turned themselves in were allowed to post bail. Jorge Sanabria handed over the equivalent of $3,000, then went out and did exactly what he'd ordered his flush soldiers not to do back in Popayán: he tied one on. It wasn't exactly a victory celebration. After a decade in uniform, he was no longer a member in good standing of the Colombian Army, an institution to which he still felt an overwhelming sense of loyalty. His wife had been targeted by a masked gunman and more threats were sure to follow. And his future was clouded by the upcoming trial.

Yet in spite of the recent unpleasantness, Sanabria had made it out of FARC-land alive. He had survived the stockade. His family was intact. And he'd managed to hang on to his money. If he hired a good lawyer and played the angles, he could indeed start anew. So, along with his wife and nine-year-old daughter, he moved back to his hometown of Sogamoso. No longer a penniless lost boy forced to take refuge in the Catholic church and to shine the priest's shoes, Sanabria built a house on the outskirts of town. He bought a Ford Ranger and a Toyota SUV, hired a bodyguard, and began sinking his money in cattle and real estate.

A year had passed since the screaming headlines about millionaire soldiers, and Sanabria was able to maintain a low profile and work his deals. Still, he had to invest wisely. Though staggering by the standards of a $400-per-month army officer, the sum total of his FARC loot would not allow Sanabria to suspend his extra-large bulk in a hammock until it was time for liquid Geritol. It did give him some breathing room before he had to find a regular job. But a disgraced soldier with only a high-school education and whose CV highlights consisted of tramping through the mud, shouting orders, and shooting guerrillas wasn't exactly prime material for the executive headhunters. He'd barely qualify for town dogcatcher. Indeed, finding legitimate jobs would be one of the biggest challenges for Sanabria and his men.

Sanabria had more chits to cash in than the other troops—he was one of the few who had stuffed his pants with dollars rather than pesos—yet he was utterly flummoxed by the ways of the investment world. He made some crap deals, and at one point a partner bilked him for $30,000. But denouncing the fraud might have let the authorities know he was moving around large stacks of hot money that he had sworn before military investigators he did not possess. He soon tired of having a bodyguard shadow his every move and let him go. Already corpulent, he began putting on more weight. And every time he saw someone wearing the camouflage uniform of the Colombian Army, he grew wistful. As a civilian on the outside, Sanabria realized that what he really wanted was a way back in.

Restoration began with a telephone call. The man dialing long-distance was a former army sergeant who had been imprisoned at Tolemaida for selling arms to the paramilitaries. Behind bars, he and Sanabria had become friends and the lieutenant had told him the story of *la guaca* and of the eighty-eight barrels of cash he and his men had left behind in the jungle. Now the sergeant had a question for his old jail mate: Would Sanabria be interested in returning to El Coreguaje to dig up the rest of the money?

Sanabria had often fantasized about a jungle do-over. But he knew the operation would work only if carried out with the full backing of the military. The sergeant agreed and contacted Gustavo Álvarez, a well-connected Cali businessman who asked for a meeting with Colombia's interior minister. Sanabria traveled to Bogotá for the encounter but the two men never got past the minister's secretary. So Álvarez got in touch with an old friend, Elmer Arenas, a retired police officer who had been elected to the Colombian Senate and specialized in military affairs. Intrigued by the tale, Arenas agreed to meet with Sanabria.

"When he came into my office, he almost didn't fit into the chair because he was so fat," said Arenas, who found it hard to believe that the supersized figure before him had once been a counterinsurgency point man. "He said: 'Look, Senator, I don't trust anybody. But I want to tell you about *la guaca.'*"

Arenas agreed with Sanabria that it made sense to go after the rest of the money. Keeping millions out of the hands of the FARC constituted a public service. The army had already launched several missions into the same area but only Sanabria had the GPS coordinates with the exact location of the barrels and a croquis showing the position of the land mines that he and his men had placed around the containers. In exchange for his cooperation, Sanabria laid out several conditions. He wanted to take part in the mission alongside his trusted men from Vulture and Destroyer companies. And just as Charles Bronson, Telly Savalas, and the rest in *The Dirty Dozen* were promised moral redemption and legal immunity for carrying out their near-suicide mission, Sanabria wanted assurances that the charges against his men would be dropped. Finally, he demanded a healthy cut of whatever cash they recovered, which was to be split evenly among his troops.

"Obviously, the money was important, but we also wanted to recover our dignity after the army had treated us like dogs," Sanabria said.

At first, there was some pushback. After army officials had publicly denounced Sanabria's men as traitors and thieves who had dishonored the uniform, how could they suddenly reverse course by issuing them new fatigues and rifles so they could take an officially sanctioned stab at the buried treasure that had been the source of so much shame and folly? Though soldiers sometimes patrolled alongside unarmed guerrilla turncoats who served as guides, there was no precedent for outfitting disgraced troops fresh out of the stockade.

To seal the deal, Senator Arenas went to the top. He met with President Álvaro Uribe, who was always game for delivering a stinging blow to rebels in their backyard. Uribe signed off on the operation and sent Arenas to work out the details with General Reinaldo Castellanos, the Colombian Army commander. The decision to go after *la guaca* struck the general as a little strange, but the mission now had the president's seal of approval. Who was Castellanos to object?

Under Colombian law, collaborators who turn over unclaimed riches to the state were rewarded with a cut, and government officials agreed that Sanabria's irregulars would get to share 30 percent of any recovered cash. Arenas promised to pull some strings to get Sanabria and some of his men out of the country under the premise that they were being persecuted by the guerrillas. Álvarez, the Cali businessman, mentioned something about diplomatic passports and setting up foreign bank accounts. Assuming that a legal pardon was in the works, Sanabria jumped at the deal.

Then, in another Hollywood cliché, the disgraced lieutenant embarked on an army-financed road trip to track down his onetime comrades in arms, cajole them into hitting the reset button, and suiting up for one last battle. He drove the length and breadth of Colombia from Bogotá to Popayán, from Cali to Medellín, from Pasto to Cúcuta, to make his pitch. With some of the men, it took a little convincing, and Sanabria sprang for lavish dinners, bottles of whiskey, and coteries of call girls. Eventually, about thirty former members of Vulture and Destroyer companies came on board. Like their commanding officer, many felt rudderless outside of the military and burdened by the ball and chain of the legal system.

"I missed it," said Wilson Sarmiento, a corporal in Destroyer Company and an antiexplosives specialist. "The military runs in my blood. I was one of the first to volunteer."

While Sanabria attempted to recruit two of the Giraldo brothers—the troops who transported their money home by breaking down a taxicab and hiding their cash inside—he was approached by a third person, a curvaceous woman who said she knew him. Sanabria drew a blank so the lady let on that she was the former Lenin Giraldo, the soldier who had used his share of the FARC money for a sex-change operation. She now operated a beauty parlor in Cali, was dating a policeman, and called herself Jenny. For a brief moment, Sanabria considered bringing along Jenny. But then he figured that her fake, size 34B boobs would be too big a distraction.

ONE OF THE MEN SANABRIA FAILED to track down for his military mulligan was Jair Chimbaco, a tough but good-natured soldier from Vulture Company who was on a post-*guaca* mission of his own and seemed to have fallen off the map. One of four brothers and sisters born to sharecroppers, Chimbaco had by age twelve dropped out of school and picked up a machete to join his father in the fields. He was eventually drafted, which seemed like a stroke of luck because it opened the door to a whole new career. Like many of his fellow conscripts, Chimbaco decided to re-up after logging eighteen months of obligatory service. He was sent to Popayán, where he ended up serving under Sanabria, lining his pockets in the jungle and landing in jail. His parents were worried sick. On the day Chimbaco telephoned them with the news of his detention, his mother's cat died. It seemed like an omen.

After posting bail, Chimbaco recovered his money, which he had left in the care of an aunt in Popayán. Then he returned to Pitalito, his hometown in southern Huila state. It wasn't the smartest move. A land of desert, mountains, picturesque coffee farms, and the magnificent prehistoric ruins at San Agustín, Huila was located just across an Andean ridge from FARC-land and the zone was crawling with rebels. FARC units had kidnapped Consuelo González, a congresswoman from Pitalito, who was now being held alongside Íngrid Betancourt and the three American military contractors. And it was just north of Pitalito where the guerrillas kidnapped Senator Jorge Géchem after skyjacking his commuter plane.

But Chimbaco was determined that something good had to come out of his whirlwind journey from sudden wealth and sudden infamy. He was intent on using his riches to ease the burden for his parents. They had spent their lives moving from plantation to plantation, laboring in the tropical heat for a pittance. Through it all, they had never managed to secure a parcel of land to call their own. But in one quick transaction, Jair fixed all that by gifting them five fertile acres on the outskirts of Pitalito. His father put up an adobe house and planted coffee, yucca, cocoa, and tree tomatoes.

But the FARC was already onto Jair. By then, the rebels had formed a special hit squad to target the troops who had made off with their jungle treasure, a task made easier because the soldiers were now walking free and had been identified by name in Colombian newspapers. A member of the FARC's Teófilo Forero Mobile Column, the same group that had captured the three Americans, warned that the rebels had put together a team of thirty commandos.

"They were divided into three groups," the rebel told Bogotá's *El Tiempo* newspaper. "Spies to locate them, people to visit them in their homes, and executioners to even the score."

One evening, just a few months after Chimbaco had purchased the land, two plainclothes rebels showed up at the family's new spread. They demanded a meeting with Chimbaco, but he was attending night school in town. So the rebels dragged his fifty-six-year-old father, José Emilio, out of bed and pushed him into the back of a pickup, still barefoot and in his undershorts. They blindfolded the elder Chimbaco and drove him into the mountains.

When Jair learned of the abduction of José Emilio, he was frantic. The father was now paying dearly for the sins of the son. And as a recently released prisoner and publicly branded as one of the money-grubbing GIs, Jair couldn't exactly dial "911." He was certain the authorities would ignore the kidnapping and try to steal his money. After five days in the dark, a rebel messenger told the family where José Emilio was being held and said that the FARC needed to speak with Jair. He and his mother immediately journeyed into the mountains determined to work out a deal. They pulled into the FARC camp and spotted José Emilio who was tied to a tree and still in his boxer shorts.

Cordial at first, the guerrillas fed the Chimbaco family breakfast. Jair, realizing he had just saved his father, was in a buoyant mood, laughing, smiling, and telling jokes to the old man. He tried to put his parents at ease, saying that if the guerrillas really wanted to kill them, they would have already pulled the trigger.

But the cake was baked. After breakfast, the guerrillas cut loose José Emilio. Then they informed Jair that he was trading places with his father. He was staying put while the rebels investigated his role in stealing millions from the FARC. The date was April 7, 2004. His parents never saw their son again.

Years later, as they sat on the veranda of the adobe house surrounded by hundreds of six-foot-high trees, their branches bursting with burgundy coffee berries, José Emilio and his wife, Luz Marina, said it was impossible to enjoy the pastoral bliss their son had bequeathed to them.

"The dream is always to have a little bit of land," said José Emilio. "Jair was very pleased that he had bought this property. He told us: 'This is land for you to cultivate.' But it doesn't matter how much I have, because I miss my son."

AFTER HIS TWO-MONTH-LONG RECRUITMENT DRIVE, JORGE Sanabria had brought together about thirty troops from Vulture and Destroyer companies. Like the lieutenant, many of the soldiers were itching to get back into uniform. After enduring the humiliation of the stockade, threats from the FARC, and extortion attempts by corrupt police officers, returning to the familiar world of the military—one that provided fraternity, discipline, and protection—seemed like good therapy. And if the legal charges against them were dropped, the scheme would, in effect, allow them to launder the FARC cash they'd scooped up the first time around. They baptized the mission Operation Hope.

Sanabria and his men gathered at a military base in southern Bogotá in August 2005 for three months of training. They were issued uniforms and weapons and spent their days exercising and practicing on the firing range. Each soldier picked up where he had left off. Wilson Sarmiento, the anti-explosives expert, would serve as a sapper. Sanabria, the gung ho lieutenant, would be in command. Though he was massively overweight, he began to shed pounds during the morning runs and to get back in shape.

But they wouldn't be going in alone. The plan called for Sanabria's thirty, the men who knew the lay of the land, to team up with a group of a hundred Colombian Army commandos. Once they closed in on the target, then and only then would Sanabria reveal the exact location of the reburied treasure. As long as he held the GPS coordinates, Sanabria still held some leverage and could call the shots.

But there were delays in launching. Bureaucrats from the Defense Ministry made Sanabria's men sign waivers saying they were voluntary guides and that should anything happen to them, the army was not responsible. The weeks stretched into months and the twitchy troops worried that word would leak to the FARC or that the mission would be canceled. Indeed, some powerful players opposed the plan. General Carlos Alberto Ospina, the overall commander of the Colombian armed forces, thought the operation made no sense. "We had a lot of other priorities," he said. "And I thought for sure that the money would already be gone." But Ospina didn't want to interfere in the tactical decisions of his army chiefs and the planning went forward.

Finally, after three months of training, Sanabria and his men were flown to the military base at San Vicente del Caguán. It was a nostalgic homecoming. Two years earlier, the GIs had been airlifted out of the jungle and had hitchhiked to this same base, arriving high on beer and good fortune just days after finding the FARC loot. Now they were going back for more.

Army intelligence indicated that rebel units were in the region and when the first wave of troops, accompanied by four of Sanabria's guides, entered the zone—arriving at the same helipad they had cut out of the rain forest two years earlier—it was clear that the FARC had been waiting for them. They found camouflaged pits with bamboo spears sticking straight up. Rebels were camped out nearby. Land mines were everywhere.

Two days after the army troops had established a base camp, Sanabria and the rest of his men were airlifted to the site. But on D-Day, the morning when it was agreed that Sanabria would reveal the coordinates so they could extract the barrels of cash, he insisted that the army commandos stay behind. Sanabria said he would only proceed to the sweet spot with his trusted cohorts from Vulture and Destroyer companies along with a civilian inspector from the attorney general's office who was folded into the mission to make sure none of the cash went missing.

As they crept forward, the terrain seemed even more rugged than Sanabria remembered. Their ground game was slow and methodical—three yards and a cloud of mosquitoes. Back at base camp, the operation took a bloody turn for the worse as one of the regular GIs stepped on a land mine and was badly injured. Two other soldiers soon met the same fate. A Black Hawk helicopter touched down to evacuate the wounded and was met by a hail of rebel gunfire. Sanabria could hear the shooting and was worried. He suspected the guerrillas might also be tracking him and were holding off on attacking until he led them to the money. Still, he kept moving. He and his men realized they were getting close when they came across the remains of a FARC rebel who had stepped on one of the mines they had planted to protect the barrels during their original mission.

Accounts of what happened next veered in wildly different directions. Sanabria said the sound of gunfire, the guerrilla corpse, the heat, and the humidity proved to be too much for the civilian inspector, who suddenly came unglued. He began ranting at Sanabria and spouting all manner of gibberish. Fearing that the commotion would let the guerrillas know where they were, Sanabria halted the advance and ordered two of his men to escort the inspector back to base camp. Then the inspector pulled out his satellite telephone and dialed army headquarters in Bogotá where, according to Sanabria, he was connected to the military's operations chief. Not long afterward, an order crackled over the lieutenant's radio: "Abort mission."

Sanabria was livid but he had no choice other than to turn around. Within hours, the soldiers had decamped and were airlifted back to the military base at San Vicente del Caguán. There they stewed for days waiting for another chance but ended up aboard a military transport plane to Bogotá. It was over. Millions of dollars had been at their fingertips but now they would get a 30 percent cut of nothing.

Sanabria tried to piece together what had gone wrong. He later claimed that top army officials were to have secretly received a share of the money, but because the operations chief back in Bogotá had not been cut in on the deal, he pulled the plug on the mission. Army officials dismissed Sanabria's account as pure fantasy. They pointed out that the inspector from the attorney general's office was attached to the mission to prevent another round of looting. They claimed that Sanabria and the rest of the troops were ordered out of the jungle because they failed to locate any of the barrels and because casualties were mounting.

"They tried and it went badly," added General Ospina, the armed forces commander. "I was pretty sure that the money would already be gone."

Senator Arenas, the lawmaker who helped arrange the jungle mission, said he had come across information indicating that two soldiers who knew about the so-called second *guaca* leaked the information to the guerrillas, who moved in to recover the cash. For their troubles, the soldiers were to receive $100,000 from the rebels. Instead, according to Arenas, they were executed by the FARC.

Sanabria's recruits, meanwhile, had been pulled out of FARC-land empty-handed. Worse, they realized they had never received anything in writing about an amnesty. The promise of a pardon seemed to go up in smoke with the unspooling of Operation Hope. Stripped of their uniforms and rifles, the men of Vulture and Destroyer companies immediately reverted to their lowly status as criminal suspects out on bail. And things were about to get worse. In December 2005, the army issued an order that all 147 members of Vulture and Destroyer companies were to report to Tolemaida Military Base where they were to stand trial for the illegal appropriation of government property.

CHAPTER 18

FALL GUYS

I join the ranks of so many others whom history
has and will absolve.
—Simón Trinidad

THE PROSECUTION OF THE GIs OF Vulture and Destroyer companies had
all the makings of Colombia's trial of the century. Yet the outcome was
never really in doubt. The fifty-two GIs who showed up for the trial
quickly realized they were facing a hard-ass when they spotted a statue of
Jesus on the judge's desk. It was made out of grenade shrapnel.

Dressed in white T-shirts and jeans, the troops slouched in rows of
wooden chairs in an auditorium at Tolemaida Military Base. Two large electric fans struggled to cool down the room as the GIs fidgeted and sweated.
Arguments that the soldiers should have faced disciplinary measures had
been cast aside. Instead, the GIs were facing criminal charges and lengthy
prison terms.

And their defense attorneys weren't exactly from the country's top law
firms. The trial attracted a conga line of rank opportunists, the equivalent

of TV dial-a-lawyers who urged folks to drop a quarter if they or a loved one had been wronged in an accident. These counselors envisioned reaping publicity as well as their own cut of the soldiers' cash. But after they figured out that many of the troops had either squandered or surrendered their money, they lost interest and walked out on their clients.

Those who remained served up a mishmash of arguments ranging from the inventive to the absurd. Attorneys argued that at least twelve of the soldiers could not be prosecuted because they had been killed by the revenge-seeking FARC rebels. But the lawyers had no real evidence that the men were dead—and not in hiding—so the judge didn't agree to it.

Lieutenant Jorge Sanabria had no intention of attending what he considered a kangaroo court. Instead, he slipped away from his hometown of Sogamoso, flew to Leticia, Colombia's southernmost city, then crossed the border into Brazil. Another no-show was Lenin Giraldo, the soldier who had undergone the sex-change operation and was now known as Jenny. Out of curiosity, many of the accused were hoping Jenny would grace the proceedings, but she had no desire to provide halftime entertainment for the attorneys and the media mob.

Still, the trial had its moments. The notion that the soldiers had come away with vaults of money was sometimes shot down by eyewitness testimony. After the camouflaged Lotharios hit the bordellos of Popayán, for example, one hooker complained to investigators that she had been stuck with Private Cheapskate. After her date satiated his sizzling loins in an hour-long romp, she was paid the equivalent of $6.89.

Upon hearing her statement many of the troops, who had, at times, fallen asleep during the twenty-six-day trial, burst out laughing. But the judge wiped the smiles off their faces when he issued his ruling. It was like death by a thousand cuts. He took three full days to read the three-hundred-page document listing all the charges against the 147 defendants.

Two of the soldiers were declared not guilty because they were pulled out of the jungle before their colleagues dug up the money. A third soldier was let off the hook because there was clear evidence he had died in a highway accident. The rest of the officers and soldiers were declared guilty and faced prison sentences ranging from three to ten years.

. . .

EVEN THOUGH IT HAPPENED BECAUSE OF unrelated events, one of the top officers involved in the case of *la guaca* would also see his career go up in flames. General Reinaldo Castellanos, the commander of the Colombian Army, had grudgingly green-lighted the ill-fated mission to send Sanabria's men back into the jungle to find the rest of the FARC money. He considered the mission a dubious distraction in the larger war against the guerrillas. At long last, the army was gaining some advantages on the battlefield and the general's star was rising.

Castellanos had been promoted to army chief after leading Operation Liberty, a military campaign that drove the FARC out of strategic Cundinamarca state, surrounding Bogotá. By targeting guerrilla units, plainclothes rebel militiamen, and supply lines, the operation had vastly improved the security in and around the Colombian capital, home to eight million people. The number of abductions dropped dramatically and troops now patrolled the "kidnap trail," the road leading to the town of Nazareth where desperate relatives were forced to turn over ransom payments to the FARC.

The operation was the first of a string of military triumphs under President Álvaro Uribe. And as the military pulled out of its death spiral the improved security opened the door to local and foreign investment. Unemployment dropped and the economy began to grow. Brandishing his soaring job-approval ratings, Uribe convinced lawmakers to amend the 1991 Constitution, which banned presidential reelection, to allow him to run for a second four-year term in 2006, a contest he won in a landslide.

Shortly before they went to the polls, residents of Viotá showered Uribe with praise. This farm town had been a guerrilla stronghold under the Pastrana government even though it was located just twenty-eight miles southwest of Bogotá. Now Viotá was back in government control. On the outskirts of town, soldiers were constructing an army base on land purchased with small donations by local residents. Miguel Sarmiento, a beer distributor who had decorated his warehouse with campaign posters for the president, echoed the views of many Colombians when he declared: "First comes God, then comes Uribe."

Sarmiento wasn't always so upbeat. Back when the guerrillas lorded it over Viotá, a town of about seven thousand people, Sarmiento was forced to hand over thousands of cases of beer to the rebels. Later, the rebels barred him from selling Colombian beer because the country's main brewer refused to make extortion payments to the FARC. Sarmiento was told he could sell only brands from Venezuela, whose left-wing president, Hugo Chávez, openly admired the FARC.

"We were going to leave," Sarmiento said. "But then the army arrived, and the captain told me: 'Don't go because we came here to clean up this town.'"

Ironically, the Colombian military's renaissance began under President Uribe's predecessor, Andrés Pastrana, who left office with his job-approval ratings in the toilet for making so many concessions to the FARC. But Pastrana worked overtime to build up the armed forces. He convinced U.S. lawmakers to support Plan Colombia, a multiyear effort involving billions of dollars in American military assistance designed to improve the nation's security and roll back the cocaine trade. Between 2000 and 2008, U.S. police, military, and antinarcotics-related assistance to Colombia totaled more than $5 billion, while a new policy of domestic war taxes raised billions more.

Within the armed forces, the reforms began with manpower as thousands of conscripts were replaced by professional soldiers. Overall army troop levels nearly doubled to 275,000. After the September 11, 2001, terrorist attacks, the U.S. Congress allowed American advisers to train Colombian troops not just for counterdrug missions but for counterterrorism operations against the FARC. The U.S. trainers helped form special units of Colombian commandos and provided them with, among other things, night-vision goggles, which allowed them to carry out more effective operations after dark. Eventually, these Colombian Special Forces would turn out to be as good as, or better than, the Green Berets in jungle warfare.

"This was a crucial and dramatic shift in the U.S.-Colombian military relationship," said Andrés Villamizar, a former analyst at the Colombian Defense Ministry. "This program was put in place to generate Colombian Special Forces in the true meaning of the term and to bring these commando teams to a whole different level."

Earlier defeats had been chalked up, in part, to the lack of timely rein-forcements. But with a flotilla of 230 helicopters, up from just a few dozen when Pastrana took office, army officers were able to move large numbers of troops around the country to respond immediately to guerrilla attacks. Colombia acquired a fleet of twenty-four Super Tucano light attack aircraft from Brazil, which were considered among the best planes in the world for counterinsurgency operations. The planes could fly lower and slower than jets and stay aloft for patrols of up to seven hours. At higher altitudes, Co-lombian aircraft hovered over the jungle intercepting radio signals and taking detailed photographs, while U.S. AWACS surveillance aircraft, fly-ing out of Ecuador ostensibly for antidrug missions, provided a trove of in-formation on the FARC. Timely "human" intelligence came from hundreds of FARC foot soldiers who, as the war turned against them, began turning themselves in to the army.

Finally, the different service branches began to cooperate. In the past, troops on the ground couldn't communicate with pilots overhead when they came under fire. But under Pastrana and then Uribe, the army, air force, navy, marines, and the police—long plagued by institutional rivalries—made their first serious efforts to mount joint operations.

In the old days, army troops mostly hunkered down in their garrisons. But Uribe launched the Patriot Plan, a four-year-long military operation that sent troops into FARC strongholds for months at a time. There were some unexpected downsides. Because they were now spending so much time in the rain forest, cases of malaria, dengue fever, and leishmaniasis shot up. In fact, far more soldiers were evacuated for tropical diseases than for land mine or bullet wounds. Still, the huge caseload proved a larger point: after many years of *administering* the war, the Colombia military now seemed intent on *winning* the war.

These developments forced the FARC to pull back. In the late 1990s, the FARC had advanced to the point where it could stage semiconven-tional battles, massing hundreds of fighters to overrun army positions and temporarily seize isolated towns. But over the next decade, the Colombian military halted the FARC's advance on Bogotá and other major cities and pushed the rebels into the most remote areas of the countryside where they reverted to traditional guerrilla tactics of hit-and-run attacks and ambushes.

But not all of the military's triumphs were clean, whiz-bang operations. As the army ballooned in size, control and oversight of the soldiers lapsed. The institution had a long history of alliances with paramilitary death squads and officers were reluctant to break ties with the enemies of their enemies. Sometimes soldiers turned on their own men and that's what finally brought down General Castellanos.

In the first months of 2006, a group of soldiers undergoing a jungle survival course were forced to eat animal dung, branded like cattle with the angry end of cigarettes, and sodomized with sticks. The resulting scandal, blamed on rogue NCOs, fit a larger pattern. Every time the Colombian military appeared to be getting back on its feet and gaining momentum, some new depravity would expose the darker aspects of President Uribe's high-octane war machine. When, for example, Destroyer and Vulture companies made off with the buried guerrilla riches, their actions revealed that Colombia's new class of professional soldiers often consisted of underpaid, overworked, and ethically challenged young men. Three years later, the hazing of the troops made army training seem like some sadistic obstacle course designed by prison guards at Guantánamo Bay.

Though Castellanos was not personally involved, the general was forced to resign. His defenestration brought a small measure of satisfaction to Sanabria and some of the other troops who, under Castellanos's watch, had gone back into the jungle for the FARC remainders only to be stiffed on what they saw as promises of legal amnesties. Replacing Castellanos as the new army boss was General Mario Montoya, a close confidant of President Uribe who would be even more successful than his predecessor—and more controversial.

MARIO MONTOYA GREW UP WITH TWELVE brothers and sisters in the Colombian town of Buga, but he escaped his overcrowded, underfunded household by signing up for the army as a teenager. He was a gung ho hard-liner who quickly won promotions and worked closely with Uribe during his stint as governor of Antioquia state in the mid-1990s. But while modern counterinsurgency strategists stressed the importance of territorial control and winning over the civilian population, Montoya seemed stuck in the old Vietnam War mentality that measured progress through body counts.

"He preached it harder than anyone," said one Colombian official. Alluding to possible skeletons in Montoya's closet, he added, "Most of the military commanders worried about him."

Indeed, Montoya's long military career was dogged by accusations of ties to right-wing militias. As far back as 1980, former members of a Colombian Army intelligence brigade charged that Montoya belonged to the Triple A, a secret anticommunist militia that was accused of bombing the Bogotá offices of two left-wing newspapers and a magazine. As the war intensified in the 1990s and the paramilitaries swelled into a potent antiguerrilla force, many army officers viewed the death squads as allies who could be more efficient than government troops. Soldiers had to respect the rights of suspected FARC collaborators who were often set free by judges due to lack of evidence. But the paramilitaries simply murdered the rebel suspects and asked questions later.

"If a junior officer doesn't see his commander coming out strongly against the paramilitaries, he may form alliances with them" to produce better battlefield results, said a retired Colombian Army colonel.

One paramilitary chieftain, Salvatore Mancuso, while recounting his crimes to government officials in exchange for a reduced sentence, recalled meeting with a general at army headquarters in Medellín to plan a 1997 massacre of fifteen peasants in the town of El Aro. Another of President Uribe's favorites, General Rito Alejo del Río, known as "the peacemaker of Urabá," was widely accused of working closely with the death squads to take control of northern Antioquia state. Years later, Del Río was arrested on murder charges.

For all of his venom directed at the guerrillas, Montoya seemed reluctant to take aggressive action against the paramilitaries. His ability to look the other way came into sharp focus in May 2002, shortly before Uribe was sworn in for his first term. At the time, hundreds of paramilitaries moved into the jungles of northern Chocó state to take on the guerrillas. A local priest said he tried to warn Montoya, who was then the commander of the

Fourth Brigade, which was responsible for the area. "But he did nothing," said the Reverend Jesús Albeiro Parra.

The opposing sides met in Bellavista, an Afro-Colombian fishing community on the banks of the Atrato River where most of the houses were flimsy wooden structures built on stilts to escape flooding. As the fighting raged, about 300 men, women, and children sought shelter in the Roman Catholic church. The villagers figured that this house of God, with its sturdy concrete walls, would protect them. Instead, an errant FARC rocket, made out of a cooking-gas canister and packed with shrapnel, crashed through the roof of the building. The blast killed 119 people, including 48 children, in what Colombian authorities described as the worst single loss of civilian life in the four-decades-long war.

Despite the horrible nature of the FARC's latest war crime, and the army's apparent negligence, a boisterous Montoya appeared before a throng of reporters gathered at an army base in Chocó. He always seemed ready to either torment or manipulate the media. After briefing twenty-four journalists and promising to take them to the site of the battle in Bellavista, Montoya announced that he had only one helicopter with space for twenty-three. When the aircraft touched down, a bemused Montoya looked on as reporters shoved, clawed, and climbed over one another to get on board.

Once on the ground in Bellavista, a priest led Montoya into the church, which was littered with broken pews, shattered figures of Christ, and dented copper chalices. On the bloodstained floor, Montoya found a tiny blue tennis shoe belonging to one of the victims. Indignant, he stormed out of the church to show the TV cameras but suddenly seemed to tear up. He walked away to compose himself, then ordered the news crews to hit their "record" buttons for Take Two. This time, Montoya nailed his lines, saying, "This is a terrible massacre!" The reporters were perplexed. Was the general truly shaken? Or was he emulating Douglas MacArthur who, by some accounts, repeated his dramatic wade through the water onto the shores of the Philippines to assure the most dramatic shot for the newspapers?

In the aftermath of the massacre, a United Nations human rights envoy criticized the army for ignoring the presence of the paramilitaries in Bellavista. Yet the election of Uribe, Montoya's old friend from Antioquia, seemed to assure the general's upward trajectory.

After Uribe took office in 2002, he ordered Montoya to clear urban guerrillas from a Medellín slum called Comuna 13. Like many of Medellín's impoverished ghettos, Comuna 13 was a violent area dominated in the 1980s and '90s by ruthless gangsters and drug traffickers. When Pablo Escobar was killed in 1993 and his Medellín drug ring broken up, Comuna 13 became a stronghold for the guerrillas. Dubbed Operation Orión, the joint army-police military assault was deemed a huge success and Medellín would soon gain recognition as one of the safer cities in South America. Thus, when General Castellanos resigned following the hazing scandal, Uribe rewarded Montoya by naming him commander of the Colombian Army.

Yet strong evidence soon emerged that Montoya's troops worked in cahoots with paramilitaries to take control of Medellín. According to a CIA document, Montoya, senior police officials, and paramilitary leaders jointly planned and conducted Operation Orión. Testifying before Colombian prosecutors in 2004, one paramilitary fighter admitted that "all of the authorities who took part in the operation helped us." Rather than fighting side by side, Medellín political analyst Max Gil said, the army and police received intelligence from the paramilitaries on rebel positions. After driving them out, he said, the government forces lacked the troops to occupy Comuna 13, so they relied on the militias. In the six months after Operation Orión, the paramilitaries killed about sixty people, some of whom were cut to pieces and buried in unmarked graves, said Liliana Uribe, a human rights lawyer in Medellín.

During an emotional interview at Colombian Army headquarters Montoya defended his actions in Medellín, proclaiming, "This was a clean operation." Pounding his camouflaged chest with the palm of his hand, he added: "I've done nothing wrong, and that's what gives me strength."

Partly because of concerns about Montoya, Senator Patrick Leahy in April 2007 placed a hold on $55.2 million in U.S. military aid for Colombia. But American officials continued to offer their full-throated backing of Montoya because of his battlefield successes, his close relationship with President Uribe, and the difficulty in proving he had been colluding with death squads. In the words of one State Department official: "There was not enough evidence for us to go and say to the president: 'Your favorite and most successful military commander needs to leave.'"

THOUGH THE COLOMBIAN ARMY WAS IMPROVING, the only headway on behalf of the three American hostages seemed to be taking place 2,400 miles north of their jungle jail. In 2004, Simón Trinidad, the former bank manager and FARC negotiator, was extradited to the United States where he was housed in the six-story salmon-colored Central Detention Facility in downtown Washington, D.C. Two years later, he became the first-ever member of the FARC to go on trial in a U.S. courtroom. And this epic legal battle to convict Trinidad would prove that the U.S. government had not forgotten about Keith, Marc, and Tom.

U.S. prosecutors wielded two key pieces of evidence. In an April 27, 2003, communiqué, the FARC named Trinidad as one of three rebel spokesmen who would attempt to trade the hostages for imprisoned guerrillas. "That reflects the significant role he played in this crime," said Kenneth Kohl, the assistant U.S. attorney who was the lead federal prosecutor in the case. "That was a key part of the conspiracy."

The other evidence came gift-wrapped from Trinidad. After he was captured in Ecuador, he proudly told U.S. and Ecuadorian officials that he was in Quito to deliver a letter from FARC spokesman Raúl Reyes about a possible prisoner exchange to a French government contact and a U.N. mediator. This admission along with the FARC communiqué provided enough of a link for U.S. prosecutors to secure an indictment on one count of conspiracy to engage in hostage-taking and three counts of hostage-taking. Trinidad also faced drug-trafficking charges and one count of providing material support to a terrorist group.

But the families of Keith, Marc, and Tom fretted about the trial. The resulting testimony might answer a few of their questions about what happened to their loved ones. And it would be nice to see someone from the FARC pay for their horrendous crimes. Yet many of the relatives saw the legal proceedings as part of a troubling template in which progress in the military and legal fight against the FARC only meant life-threatening reversals for the hostages.

Army operations, for example, squeezed rebel supply lines, but that made it more difficult to get food and medicine to the hostages. Whenever troops closed in and the guerrillas smelled danger, the hostages were forced to march for weeks on end. And nearly every time a military helicopter came swooping low over the green forest canopy, jumpy FARC guards locked, loaded, and prepared to execute their prisoners.

Yet deep in the jungle, the deteriorating conditions filled the hostages with hope.

"When we saw that there was no food, there were no supplies, and we were hungry, well, we saw that the guerrillas were in the same condition. They were starving too," Marc said. "And that was a good thing because the harder it was for them to hold hostages, the more likely they were to give those hostages up."

Even so, the FARC had linked the fate of the Americans to Trinidad's future. A conviction and lengthy prison term for the imprisoned guerrilla could prompt the FARC to impose reciprocal sentences on Keith, Marc, and Tom.

But Kohl, the chief prosecutor, believed that nailing Trinidad would help the FARC understand that holding American hostages was a dead end. What's more, by the time the trial started in 2006 there had been no progress toward gaining the release of the three contractors. There didn't seem to be anything to lose.

Still, the case was hardly a layup. Kohl's team had to deal with the inconvenient truth that the accused had no direct connection to the abduction of the contractors. Trinidad was nowhere near the mountain ridge in southern Caquetá state when the Americans' plane crashed in 2003. He had no authority over the rebel column that grabbed the three Americans. And Trinidad had never even seen Keith, Marc, and Tom.

In his orange, prison-issue coveralls, the bespectacled, university-educated Trinidad looked more like the former banker that he was than a bomb-throwing radical. He was by far the most articulate member of the FARC, and he had a way of bringing people over to his side. How else to explain one of the members of his legal team? Colombian lawyer Óscar Silva agreed to defend Trinidad even though his older brother had been kidnapped by the FARC and was still missing. "Perhaps I should hate him," Silva said. "But I don't."

Like Jo Rosano and some of the other relatives of the U.S. hostages,

Silva figured that Trinidad wasn't directly involved in the crime. To give their arguments some emotional punch, prosecutors asked Jo to attend the trial and be the grieving mother in the courtroom. But she felt like she was being used and called the proceedings "a joke."

For U.S. prosecutors, and for many Colombians monitoring the trial from afar, Trinidad served as a stand-in for the entire guerrilla organization. Prosecutors never failed to address Trinidad as a "terrorist" or a "narcoterrorist." Kohl, the lead prosecutor, went so far as to compare him to Osama bin Laden.

"How does any guerrilla member take that wire and that chain every night and fasten it around Marc Gonsalves' neck, Íngrid Betancourt's neck, knowing that they have families, mothers, wives, husbands who go to bed each night praying for their release? How?" Kohl told the court. "If the guerrillas who killed Tom Janis and abducted Marc Gonsalves, Keith Stansell and Tom Howes were the paws of the beast, the defendant was its mouth."

Defense lawyers argued that even though Trinidad had not participated in the kidnapping, he was, in a cruel twist, being prosecuted for trying to secure their freedom through a prisoner exchange that even the three American hostages said they supported. In an armed conflict, the policy of taking civilians hostage was considered a crime against humanity. But the defense described the captured Americans as spies who were gathering intelligence on the FARC and were therefore legitimate military targets who should be considered prisoners of war. And rather than a cold-blooded terrorist, they portrayed Trinidad as a lawful combatant, a uniformed member of an insurgent army that had been fighting for more than forty years to overthrow the Colombian government. The defense argued that under the Geneva Conventions—which set the standards for international humanitarian law—taking POWs was not a crime. Therefore, his lawyers said, Trinidad should be declared immune from prosecution.

"This man had nothing to do with the capture of the three Americans," said Trinidad's lead defense attorney, Robert Tucker, who during the trial quoted Shakespeare and invoked Thomas Jefferson's stirring justification of the right to rebel during the American Revolution.

Tucker scored some points, but complaints about the unfairness of

Trinidad's trial sounded rather precious given the FARC's pitiless and unjust treatment of its hostages. And in a post-9/11 environment, the U.S. government wasn't about to cut an accused terrorist any slack. Before the trial started, Thomas Hogan, the D.C. District Court judge presiding over the case, ruled that the FARC would be dealt with as a criminal syndicate rather than a military organization in part because the FARC routinely took civilian hostages. Indeed, the rebel organization had gone out of its way to *avoid* signing the Geneva Conventions, which, among other things, prohibited warring parties from kidnapping civilians. Judge Hogan opined that it was a little disingenuous for Trinidad, who did not feel bound to abide by the laws of war while he was in the jungle, to suddenly claim their protections now that he was in the docket. He also dismissed the assertion that the kidnapped contractors were legitimate military targets because— even though Washington had sent billions in military aid to the Bogotá government—the United States was not formally at war with the FARC and the Americans were clearly civilian contractors.

Even so, prosecutors struggled to close the deal. Trinidad was quickly declared not guilty on the charge of providing military support for a terrorist organization. And after two weeks of deliberations, the jury failed to reach a unanimous decision on the hostage-taking charges. Ten jurors voted for conviction but there were two holdouts. On November 21, 2006, the hung jury forced Judge Hogan to declare a mistrial.

Trinidad, however, wasn't off the hook. A new trial on the same charges began in the spring of 2007, featuring the same cast of characters in what turned out to be an almost word-for-word sequel. Once again, the twelve jurors had a hard time reaching a unanimous decision. But finally, on July 9, 2007, the jury announced its verdict: Trinidad was declared guilty of conspiracy to kidnap the Americans.

At that point, Kohl, the lead prosecutor, announced that he would consider recommending a lighter sentence for Trinidad if the FARC agreed to liberate Keith, Marc, and Tom. "If they were released, say, next week, we would take that into consideration," he said. But there was no response from the FARC.

CHAPTER 19

THE ONE WHO GOT AWAY

Let the great river take me to the main.
—ALFRED LORD TENNYSON

LONG BEFORE ÍNGRID BETANCOURT'S HUSBAND LANDED in Mitú on his quixotic mission, John Frank Pinchao arrived in the southern jungle town to serve as chief accountant at the police station. To other members of the force, a posting to Mitú was like exile to the farthest reaches of the kingdom. But for this young NCO, it seemed a step up in the world.

Born into an impoverished family and raised in a tar-paper shack in south Bogotá, Pinchao managed to graduate from high school. But once he turned eighteen, he faced being drafted into the army, which in the late 1990s seemed like a death warrant. Instead, he enlisted in the police force, not realizing that the job was every bit as dangerous. The FARC was setting its sights on poorly defended frontier towns, and Mitú was especially exposed.

Though the town served as the capital of Vaupés state, Mitú could only be reached by airplane or riverboat. There were no paved streets, no roads connecting the community to other towns, and hardly any vehicles. The place was so sleepy one of the main tasks of the police was to shoo the cows off the airport grass-and-dirt runway as planes approached.

"It was like going back in time," said Pinchao, who arrived in Mitú in March 1997 when he was twenty-four.

At first, all was quiet. Pinchao learned how to use the PC at the police station and started dating a local gal. He was supposed to be promoted to the rank of *intendente*, the U.S. equivalent of a corporal, but the Defense Ministry lacked the money to provide him with the corresponding salary boost. On his days off, he bathed in the Vaupés River, which flowed past the town en route to Brazil, fifteen miles to the east, but Pinchao stayed in the shallows because he didn't know how to swim.

After a few months, the pastoral calm gave way to fear and paranoia. The guerrillas had already routed army troops at El Billar and overrun the poorly defended southern outposts of Las Delicias and Miraflores, and there was talk that Mitú was next on their hit list. Gradually it dawned on Pinchao that Mitú was completely infiltrated by the FARC. When a policeman was injured in an ambush, doctors at the hospital at first refused to take him in because the guerrillas had issued orders not to treat government troops.

By October 1998, Mitú was buzzing with rumors that the FARC was encircling the town. The ninety policemen at the station warned their superiors in Bogotá but their calls for help went unanswered. On Halloween night, one of the policemen dressed up as a clown and Pinchao and his colleagues spent the evening passing out candy and ice cream to children. Shortly before dawn the next morning, fifteen hundred FARC guerrillas attacked Mitú with 50-caliber machine guns and about a hundred homemade rockets.

As Pinchao fought back with his Galil automatic rifle and three hundred bullets, he spotted a twelve-year-old boy who operated a motorcycle taxi. Pinchao had always felt sorry for the lad, who had to punch the clock at such an early age. Now he was in a FARC uniform and blasting the walls of the police station with his Kalashnikov.

After fourteen hours of combat, the policemen ran out of ammunition. The rebels poured gasoline on the partially destroyed police station and threatened to set it ablaze. About forty cops emerged with their hands up. But Pinchao and nine of his colleagues slipped away and hid out in the ruins of a nearby house. They figured they would lie low until reinforcements arrived. But the next morning there was still no sign of help. When the distraught owner returned to her house and found Pinchao and his colleagues hiding inside, she began screaming. The noise alerted the rebels, who surrounded the building and led the policemen away at gunpoint.

Pinchao would spend the next eight and a half years as a FARC prisoner.

From their first day in captivity, Pinchao and the other prisoners dreamed about escaping. But no hostage had ever fled from one of the FARC's southern jungle camps and survived. During forced marches, the prisoners were tethered together by the neck. And once they arrived at their bivouacs, the rain forest proved to be a natural barrier, one so thick and menacing that much of the time the guerrillas didn't even bother fencing in their prisoners.

The great game was not so much breaking away from their captors as navigating the maze of tree trunks, underbrush, waterways, and muskeg stocked with poisonous snakes, malarial mosquitoes, and hungry jaguars. For a desperate runaway, the jungle was a lethal obstacle course.

"Prisoner, do not regret your jail," intoned José Eustasio Rivera in *The Vortex*, his nightmarish novel about indentured Colombian rubber tappers. "You know nothing of the torture of wandering unfettered in a prison like the jungle, a green vault walled in by immense rivers. You don't know the torments of the shadows. . . . The chains that gnaw at your ankles are more merciful than the leeches in these swamps."

Keith, Marc, and Tom constantly talked about this problem. In addition to the jungle barrier, they looked and talked like gringos. Even if they made it out of their prison camp, it wouldn't be long before local peasants tipped off the FARC about three foreigners bushwhacking their way through the forest. At one point, they managed to flip a guard, but he was transferred to another camp before he could help them make a run for it.

"If you're going to try to escape, you have to use your brains, not just your balls," Keith said. "But we never saw ourselves in a spot where the odds were in our favor."

What's more, a failed escape attempt could prompt the FARC to chain up the Americans and place extra guards around them. In their quest to survive, a top priority for Keith, Marc, and Tom was to keep from provoking the FARC and causing the rebels to increase the security around them. They figured the Colombian Army could launch a rescue operation any day. Should that happen, the chains would make it more difficult to get away from the guerrillas, who had orders to execute their prisoners during a rescue operation.

Besides, the Americans were finally growing accustomed to the rhythms of life in their jungle camps. They learned Spanish and taught English to the other prisoners. They also played cards, wrote in their diaries, and worked their way through a collection of books that included *Crime and Punishment*, *The Odyssey*, Sun Tzu's *The Art of War*, and, of all things, Dr. Andrew Weil's *Eight Weeks to Optimum Health*. One of the other hostages loaned Marc a Spanish-English copy of the New Testament which he read, cover to cover, thirty times. Consuelo González, the congresswoman from Pitalito who was kidnapped in 2001, taught the Americans how to sew and helped Marc embroider the names of his three children on his jacket.

Now and again, the guerrillas threw their captives a bone. Sometimes they showed them DVD films on their laptop computers. On special occasions they gave the prisoners a bottle of whiskey or vodka and at one point brought the Americans cans of beer for breakfast. Former senator Luis Eladio Pérez concocted a still to turn *panela*—hard blocks of brown sugar—into an alcoholic potion and sometimes they added the distilled liquor to the mix.

"That was dynamite for both the head and the stomach," Pérez said. "The three Americans got really drunk on the stuff and filled up the latrine. Because of that brew, I think they expelled everything they had eaten during their time in the jungle."

But more important than booze or old movies, Keith, Marc, and Tom were allowed to listen to the radio. To jury-rig an antenna, they tied a piece of string to a battery, flung the cord into the trees, then took apart the steel-wool sponges used for washing dishes and ran the bits of metal up the line.

The trick was to lock onto AM stations, which could usually be heard only at night.

A tiny transistor radio was their all-purpose antitoxin. When they were flagging, they could plug into the world through news programs. When they were bored, they could listen to salsa. They could even deduce their general location depending on what language came out of the tinny speakers. When the deejays spoke in Portuguese, they knew they were in the far south close to Brazil. A more informal Spanish with a Caribbean accent indicated that they were in eastern Colombia near the Venezuelan frontier. And when the Bogotá stations came in loud and clear, they knew they were farther north, perhaps in Guaviare state.

The prisoners' favorite programs were the late-night broadcasts on RCN and Caracol, Bogotá's two biggest stations, that delivered messages to the hostages from their families and friends. Reflecting Colombia's chronic insecurity, a six-hour show called *Voices of Kidnapping* stood as one of the longest-running programs on Caracol. Broadcaster Herbin Hoyos launched the series in 1994 after his own brief stint as a FARC hostage. As he marched at gunpoint through the wilderness, Hoyos's loafers fell apart, but the rebels forced him to keep moving in his bare feet. Along the way, he met another prisoner chained to a tree. The man complained to Hoyos that Colombian journalists never did anything to help the captives or their families. After seventeen days in captivity, Hoyos was rescued by the army. He broadcast the first edition of *Voices of Kidnapping* a few weeks later.

Often the guerrillas burst out laughing at the messages, especially when callers pleaded over the airwaves for the FARC chieftains to show a little heart and release their loved ones. Pérez was shocked by the contrast between the gratuitous cruelty and lack of human feeling among the guerrillas and the reflexive maternal instincts of the animals living all around them—the loving mothers looking after their cubs.

One of the most persistent callers to the radio programs was Patricia Medina, the mother of Keith's identical twins who were born five months after he was taken hostage. Patricia was struggling. Nicolás and Keith Jr. had been born with a speech impediment and required special schooling that Patricia couldn't afford on her salary as an Avianca flight attendant. Another blow was Keith's proof-of-life video recorded by the Colombian journalist shortly after he was captured. Keith nearly broke down in tears as he sent greetings to his fiancée, his two children from his first marriage, and his parents, but he completely ignored Patricia. Not only was she worried he would be killed in captivity, but she also had no way of knowing if he wanted anything to do with her.

Yet as the babies grew into toddlers, they became Keith's reflected glory. Patricia could see him, *feel* him, in the twins' sounds, movements, and facial expressions. Whenever Patricia left a message for Keith on RCN or Caracol radio, she put the twins on the line.

"I didn't want to cause more problems for him. I wanted him to be able to decide if he wanted to be with me or with someone else," Patricia said. "And I told him that, either way, I would wait for him."

Her words and the squeaky sounds of the twins hit Keith like a defibrillator, jump-starting his heart.

"She'd seemingly been able to put aside all the shit I'd done—cheating on her, getting her pregnant, getting pissed at her for getting pregnant, and telling her to forget about any future with me—to let me know how the boys were doing," Keith said. "That took some courage."

Dead air was also a message. There had been no radio contact from Malia, his fiancée in Colquitt, Georgia, whose last name was now Phillips-Lee. Keith figured she must have gotten over him and moved on. Jo Rosano, Marc's mother, who had picked up a few words of Spanish, managed to dial Caracol and RCN and leave recorded messages. But Marc heard only one message from his wife, Shane. And Tom received only sporadic word from his Peruvian wife, Mariana, and openly questioned whether their marriage would survive. And he blamed himself.

"Tom felt guilty because he said that he hadn't been the best husband in the world," Pérez said. "He said his defect was that he was too chintzy and that he was so dedicated to his work that he had abandoned his family. Tom stayed in Bogotá one Christmas because he didn't want to spend money on plane tickets and presents. He told me about this one day while he was crying."

Tom had read *The General in His Labyrinth*, Gabriel García Márquez's fictional account of the last years of South American liberator Simón Bolívar. In García Márquez's re-creation, Bolívar often wrote to his lover, closing his letters with the phrase "I love you resolutely." Later, amid rumors that the guerrillas were going to release one of their prisoners who would be allowed to deliver correspondence, Tom wrote a long letter to Mariana. He signed off: "I love you resolutely."

The Americans found temporary solace in marathon chess matches. Their obsession with the game began one morning when Marc picked up a broken piece of a machete and began carving an elaborate chess set out of cabo de hacha wood. He spent the next three months meticulously sculpting rooks, knights, and pawns, then fashioned a board out of an old cardboard box. When the pieces were ready, all three Americans signed the back of the board. The date was December 10, 2005.

Jorge Géchem, the senator grabbed by the FARC rebels who had skyjacked a commercial commuter flight, was the chess master and gave classes to the Americans. There was no time control and some of the matches lasted for four days.

"We'd sit there in the morning. We're in chains. We're sitting Indian style on a piece of plastic just playing chess and when you're doing that, you're free," Keith said. "Your mind is engaged. You are not a prisoner and that's the game. That's the victory and the guerrillas don't even know it."

AS THE AMERICANS PERFECTED THEIR TACTICS on the game board, Íngrid Betancourt focused on overcoming Mother Nature. Since her capture in 2002, she had tried to flee three times but never advanced more than a few squares across the wilderness. Once, she and Clara Rojas, her campaign manager who was kidnapped at the same time as Betancourt, managed to flee their FARC camp and were sleeping under a tarp when a river began overflowing its banks. Chest-deep in water, the two nearly drowned. During another attempt, the two women were attacked by a swarm of bees and Betancourt's screams of agony gave them away.

The hostages figured that the best way out of the wilderness was to bribe one of their guards into serving as their guide. The FARC, however, had set up an Orwellian system of self-surveillance: the guards spied on one another and reported suspicious behavior to their superiors.

Orlando Beltrán, one of the kidnapped congressmen, recalled how he and two other hostages convinced one of their sentries to help them escape. Everything was set but the guard insisted on bringing along his rebel girlfriend, who turned out to be his secret overseer. As they waited for the right moment to make their break, Beltrán heard a commotion. Several angry guerrillas were dragging the turncoat guard toward the hostages. Then, one of the guerrillas pulled out a pistol and shot the guard in the head. Rather than scolding the hostages for their conspiracy, the guerrillas simply left the guard's crumpled body next to the prisoners' sleeping quarters. For the next four days, vultures circled overhead and the stench of rotting human flesh wafted through the camp.

Still, Betancourt schemed and she convinced her good friend, Luis Eladio Pérez, to escape with her. They began secretly hoarding food and other supplies. But their departure was delayed when Pérez contracted leishmaniasis, a flesh-eating disease spread by sand flies. The guerrillas were under orders to keep their prisoners reasonably healthy. But the treatment for leishmaniasis involved a two-month course of toxic booster shots that provoked severe body aches and left patients bedridden. As Pérez recovered, the guerrillas began building a fence around the prison camp that would make escape more difficult. Although Pérez, a diabetic, was still weak, they headed out of the camp and slipped into a river.

Over the next six days, they swam and floated under cover of night, then climbed ashore at sunrise. To throw off rebel search parties, they hid in the jungle during the day, alternating sides of the river. "We felt like we were swimming to liberty," Pérez said. "It was the most emotional thing."

But euphoria soon gave way to exhaustion. The sky was often overcast so they could never get dry and warm. With their meager food stocks running low, Betancourt caught a few tiny fish. But Pérez, never much of a Boy Scout, used up all of their matches trying to start a fire. Adding to their frustration, they weren't making much progress. As Paul Theroux once observed, rivers can be the most circuitous route between two points. "No river is straight," he wrote. "They only turn and go crosswise and sometimes lead you backward—the nose of your boat heading into the direction you just left. River travel is like forever being turned back and not getting there."

Pérez began to pant and flag. He was suffering from the side effects of his booster shots for leishmaniasis and had developed huge blisters on his feet that slowed him down even more. When a rebel search party approached, Pérez and Betancourt ran to the riverbank and gave themselves up. The rebels motored them back to the FARC camp, a ride that took just thirty minutes. After floundering in the jungle for nearly a week, they'd managed to put just a few miles between themselves and their captors.

The guerrillas were livid. Had Betancourt and Pérez gotten away for good, the rebel guards might have faced execution. The guerrillas lit into their recaptured hostages and chained them up at night. But that didn't stop them from hatching yet another plan. And this time, Betancourt and Pérez teamed up with a prisoner who had endured even longer in the jungle than they had: John Frank Pinchao.

AMONG THE HOSTAGES, PINCHAO WAS A rare bird. He was a loner, and some of his fellow prisoners described him as arrogant and petulant. "John always seemed to be on the fringe of any group," Marc said. "The one person he seemed to communicate with was Íngrid."

Betancourt treated Pinchao like a reclamation project. She encouraged him to pursue his ambitions and schooled him in everything from Colombian politics to the proper way to hold a spoon at the dinner table. She also described her failed escape attempts, which moved something inside the policeman.

"Íngrid was a very important person in my life," Pinchao said. "She taught me how to dream."

By the spring of 2007, Pinchao had been held hostage for more than eight years. In his absence, his girlfriend had given birth to their son, John Alexander. Desperate to get home and with a prisoner exchange seemingly ruled out, he readily agreed to join Betancourt and Pérez on their next breakout.

At the time, Betancourt was teaching French to Pinchao and Pérez and the classes provided the cover to make their plans. The initial dash from their bivouac seemed like the easy part. They were in a camp without fences, and the guards couldn't see much in the pitch-black night. Visibility was so poor that once, after requesting permission to relieve himself,

Pinchao wandered over to a bush and began pissing on the boots of a rebel guard whom he hadn't even noticed.

In theory, the hostages could make more progress by hiking through the jungle. But on overcast days, there was no sun to provide a sense of direction. Even when the clouds parted, sunlight barely penetrated to the jungle floor. The rivers often overflowed their banks, creating swamps that made the going even tougher. Under these conditions, logging a few miles a day could be a challenge. Going overland also meant broken branches, footprints, and other clues that the guerrillas would pounce on. Thus, escaping by river—though maddeningly indirect—seemed like their only choice.

Pinchao had always hated exercise because it made his knees ache. But at the urging of Betancourt and the Americans, he began taking part in their daily routine of sit-ups, pull-ups, steps, and weight lifting. They were camped along the Apaporis River in Guaviare state, where they were regularly allowed to bathe in a deep-water swimming hole. That spring, Pinchao became suddenly obsessed with learning how to swim. Besides demonstrating the high art of sticking a cannon ball, Keith and Tom tried to teach Pinchao how to stay afloat. Though he wasn't very good at it, Pinchao could at least tread water. But just in case, he scrounged a gallon-sized plastic water jug to use as a flotation device.

"I'd been aware that he was up to something," Keith said. "He had been getting swimming lessons and a cigarette lighter from Tom while I'd been giving him navigation lessons. John had asked me if we wanted to go with him. I'd considered it for a few minutes, but the odds were so stacked against us that I didn't think it was the right move."

Instead, Pinchao and his coconspirators found a collaborator among the FARC. It turned out that one of their guards was from Pérez's hometown in southern Nariño state and had met the politician years before. For guiding them out of the jungle, they promised the guard exile in France and huge sums of cash. But like the peasant soldiers of Vulture and Destroyer companies who couldn't wrap their heads around the true value of American dollars, the rebel guard drew a blank at the multimillion-dollar sums Pérez and Betancourt tossed around. So they lowered their offer to about $225,000, and finally got the thumbs-up from the guerrilla.

The rebel had a GPS device to help them navigate and began storing food downriver from their camp. Pérez gathered tarps, mosquito nets, fishing lines, and other supplies. Pinchao began hoarding the heavier food supplies for what they figured could be a journey of up to forty-five days.

Then there was the issue of the chains. Betancourt and Pérez had been chained up as punishment for their earlier escape attempt, as were Pinchao and some of the other military hostages who didn't get along with their guards. Betancourt and Pérez fooled their guards by putting on extra clothes, forcing them to make the loop of chains around their necks a little looser, which allowed them to slip them off at will. Pinchao broke his by twisting a piece of wood through one of the links.

Everything seemed set. But a few days before their planned break-out, Pérez backed out and Betancourt decided to stay put with her fellow politician. So Pinchao gathered up the food and other supplies and, on the night of April 28, 2007, set off on his own.

"He was the mouse of the group," Keith said. "But he had the biggest balls of anybody."

CONDITIONS THAT EVENING HAD BEEN PERFECT. A downpour created a symphony of noise. The guards held plastic tarps over their heads, which kept them dry but also obscured their vision. To make his break, Pinchao figured he had seven seconds, the amount of time it took the guard to pass by his bunk, walk in a circle, and return. When another prisoner asked permission to take a leak, which distracted the guard, Pinchao dove into the mud and crawled toward the Apaporis River.

The Apaporis was a blackwater river that meandered fourteen hundred miles southeast into Brazil before joining the Amazon. As recently as the 1940s, no outsider had ever navigated the entire length of the waterway, in part, because explorers feared they would be set upon by cannibals. Downstream, the river narrowed and dropped, forming treacherous cataracts.

"I didn't know it was the Apaporis," Pinchao said. "But I knew that every river pours into a bigger river and that rivers run into the sea. And I figured at some point along the river there had to be people. So I swam as much as I could and then would get out and walk when I was tired."

As he was sucked downstream, Pinchao couldn't always be sure if he was swimming or drowning. He had tied his plastic jug inside his shirt but the water forced the life preserver up into his throat, making it hard to breathe. Extracting himself from the monster current required a hard, desperate kick toward shore. The first time he worked his way to the shallows, the riverbank was covered with thorny cat's-claw bushes, making it impossible to climb out of the water and forcing him back into the churn.

Like Betancourt and Pérez before him, Pinchao figured he would hide by day and swim by night. But while resting on shore on day two, Pinchao thought he spotted a guerrilla search party. In a panic, he thrashed his way deeper into the jungle. When he finally stopped to rest, the rebels were gone but Pinchao was disoriented. Where was the river?

Pinchao spent the next six days wandering in circles in a desperate search for the Apaporis. He followed tributaries that led nowhere. He disturbed a colony of monkeys who began pelting him with branches. One night, he scampered up a tree as a jaguar prowled nearby. He gashed his hand and worms took up residence in the infected tissue. Before escaping, he had secretly hoarded *fariña*, toasted yucca flour that was a jungle staple, but his supply was now drenched and rotting. He complemented his diet by splitting open small palm trees for their fibrous white hearts. Once, he found a bird's egg on the ground and immediately sucked it dry. At night, he built rough shelters out of the foliage and he jammed leaves underneath his clothes to protect himself from bug bites. But he rarely slept as nighttime downpours forced him to jog in place to prevent hypothermia.

Hungry, exhausted, and desperate, Pinchao had to find the Apaporis. Otherwise, he was doomed.

BACK AT THE FARC BIVOUAC, THE guards discovered that Pinchao was missing about six hours after he had fled. Fearing that Pinchao would tip off the military about their location, the guerrillas began to break camp. Within a few days, they relayed some bad news to the hostages. Pinchao was dead. He had been dragged underwater by an anaconda.

But at just about the same time, intercepts of FARC radio messages tipped off authorities in Bogotá that a hostage had escaped and was somewhere in the southern states of Guaviare or Vaupés. Colonel William

Ruiz, commander of the antinarcotics police unit for the region, figured the fugitive would opt for a water route. So he positioned a joint police-army rescue team in Pacoa, an Indian community on the Apaporis River located 120 miles southwest of Mitú.

Speed was essential. Officials feared the runaway would be recaptured or would stumble upon a village full of rebel sympathizers and be turned back over to the FARC. The troops formed a box around the area where they thought Pinchao might be located and began closing the square. To disrupt FARC units hunting him, jungle commandos tried to engage them in combat while after dark they lobbed random mortar shells at rebel positions. All along, search-and-rescue helicopters swooped low over the Apaporis.

After fifteen days, the police and soldiers had come up empty. But Colonel Ruiz didn't want to pull out just yet. He was convinced that the escaped hostage was on the Apaporis and would likely wash up in Pacoa, one of the few villages on that stretch of the river. And he still couldn't tell which way the village leaned.

Off-the-map outposts like Pacoa, a collection of wood plank and thatch-roof huts, were fertile recruiting grounds for the FARC. Except for a part-time human rights advocate, there were no government officials in the Indian community. Hardly anyone spoke fluent Spanish. There wasn't even a cash economy. People traded chickens and eggs for plantains and fish. Colonel Ruiz tried to win over the locals by distributing bags of rice and by airlifting sick Indians to the hospital in Mitú. He also made friends with the human rights advocate who had a radio and could contact authorities in Mitú in case Pinchao showed up. Finally, on the morning of May 15, 2007, the colonel reluctantly ordered the chopper pilots to fire up the Black Hawks and head home.

PINCHAO WAS LOW ON FOOD AND hope and his left hand was badly infected, but he was very much alive. After nearly a week of floundering in the jungle, a dark and desperate period, some unseen force had brought him back to the Apaporis. He vowed that he would never let the river out of his sight again.

To move faster, he considered building a raft by strapping together branches and driftwood with vines. But he couldn't pull the logs out of the swift current. On the eleventh day, a military plane circled overhead. Pinchao jumped up and down, screaming. He also used a tiny mirror to send a signal to the aircraft but the rescue team never arrived.

On the fourteenth day, Pinchao thought he heard the voices of guerrillas on patrol. Desperate for any kind of human contact, he began screaming, but the voices faded away. Then, he spotted a fisherman in a canoe. He called for help and the man agreed to hide the ragged policeman in the bottom of his boat as he paddled downriver.

At dawn on the seventeenth day of Pinchao's odyssey, Colonel Ruiz was in Pacoa ordering his troops onto the Black Hawks. They couldn't all fit so the pilots planned to fly the men to Mitú in two shifts. After dropping off the first batch of troops, the Black Hawks sped back to the village. In a few more minutes, the last government troops would be gone and Pacoa would revert to its former status as a no-man's-land. Suddenly, Colonel Ruiz's satellite phone rang. One of his agents was calling from the banks of the Apaporis.

"I've got Pinchao," he screamed. "I've got Pinchao!"

CHAPTER 20

SIDESHOW HUGO

It is not the chains we wear around our necks that torment us.
It is the anger produced by the perversity of the bad
and the indifference of the good.
—COLOMBIAN POLICE COLONEL LUIS MENDIETA, HELD HOSTAGE BY THE
FARC SINCE 1998

H E LOOKED LIKE AN EMACIATED CASTAWAY. After surviving the equivalent of a seventeen-day Iron Man competition on a diet of yucca flour, palm hearts, and river water, John Frank Pinchao washed into Pacoa clinging to a log and tipping the scales at eighty-eight pounds. The policemen embraced the waterlogged survivor, then bundled him aboard one of the Black Hawks bound for Mitú. For Pinchao, it was a brief and emotional homecoming at the scene of the crime. As he was led through the rebuilt town and taken past the exact spot where the FARC had captured him, Pinchao burst into tears and began screaming the words that he'd been waiting to get out of his system for eight soul-numbing years: "Ill-born guerrilla sons of bitches!"

Shortly before boarding an airplane for Bogotá, Pinchao sat down with Colonel William Ruiz, the head of the search-and-rescue operation. By now, Pinchao seemed almost hyperactive as he described his capture and escape. He pleaded with Ruiz to go back up the Apaporis River to save the others.

"He grabbed my arm and said: 'I know where they are! Go! Go! I'll take you there. That's where Íngrid is. That's where the Americans are,'" Ruiz recalled. "Then, he drew a perfect map of the river and said: 'This is where I was.' He had it all memorized in his head."

Hours later, Pinchao landed in Bogotá for a tearful reunion with his family, including bear hugs for John Alexander, the eight-year-old son he had never met. At the national palace, Colombia's newest hero demonstrated to an awestruck President Álvaro Uribe the way the guerrillas wrapped chains and padlocks around the prisoners' necks and how he had managed to break free.

Pinchao was also able to give the U.S. and Colombian authorities the first real breakthrough in tracking the American hostages. He told investigators that Keith, Marc, and Tom were being held by the FARC's First Front, a unit based in southern Guaviare state that was commanded by Gerardo Aguilar, who went by the alias of César, and Alexander Farfán, who was known as Enrique Gafas.

"Pinchao was able to narrow the search geographically," said one U.S. investigator. "So, instead of having a hundred guys looking in a hundred places, you had a hundred guys looking in one place."

U.S. ambassador William R. Brownfield, who assumed his duties in Bogotá shortly after Pinchao's escape, described him as an unusually observant and perceptive man, perhaps due to his police training. Pinchao offered vivid details on the mental and physical state of the hostages and on how the FARC shuttled them between different units to make sure that guards would not become too close or comfortable with any of the prisoners. He described how long the guerrillas stayed in each camp and how often they required resupplies of food and other provisions. He was able to pinpoint FARC camps in Guaviare and Vaupés states and the dates he'd been held at each spot. He also clued in authorities to the FARC's habit of leaving behind rough camp buildings and food stocks so they could move around for a few months, then return to the same spot without having to build new lodgings each time.

Soon afterward, Colombian Army patrols pushed into the jungle and found abandoned rebel bivouacs at the same coordinates Pinchao had indicated.

"The guy was a treasure trove," Brownfield said. "Once we began to accumulate intelligence, we could actually start to think operationally. . . . Pinchao's information did not allow us to plan a specific operation but it allowed us to build the database."

Pinchao also provided the families of the Americans with the first hard information about their loved ones in four years. While he was still recovering in a Bogotá hospital, he received a visit from Patricia Medina, Keith's girlfriend, who was relieved to learn that the father of Nicholás and Keith Jr. had not forgotten about her. Then, in a meeting arranged by Northrop Grumman, Pinchao flew to Florida to brief the Stansells, Jo Rosano, and other relatives in a conference room at a Fort Lauderdale hotel.

Pinchao described the hostages' daily routine and used a napkin to draw a diagram of the sleeping arrangements.

"Meeting Mr. Pinchao was a very emotional experience for us," said Lynne Stansell, Keith's stepmother. "John was on a mission to talk to as many of the hostages' family members as possible. It was as though they were all members of a fraternity and he was trying to do right by those he left behind."

To Jo Rosano, Pinchao seemed reasonably well-adjusted and healthy—his gleaming white teeth were perfect—which gave her hope that Marc would survive. Pinchao also told Jo that Marc constantly read the Bible and expressed pride in his mother. "I came out of that meeting feeling very joyous," Jo said.

But deep in the jungle, conditions were only getting worse. Keith, Marc, Tom, and the rest of the hostages were living on boats as the FARC moved them up and down rivers and tributaries to keep their distance from army troops who they figured were retracing Pinchao's path to freedom. Seventeen days after Pinchao escaped, the hostages, who still believed the rebels' story that he'd been killed by a snake, were finally put ashore. When they switched on their transistor radios, they heard newscasters describe his triumphant return to Bogotá. Luis Eladio Pérez, the former senator, broke into a huge smile.

"We all began to yell: 'Pinchao! Pinchao! Pinchao!'" Pérez said. "Then the guerrillas began to shoot at our feet. They told us: 'Shut up, you sons of bitches!' But we kept chanting: 'Pinchao! Pinchao! Pinchao!'"

AT HIS BOGOTÁ NEWS CONFERENCE, PINCHAO confirmed one of the most explosive rumors about the hostages. On April 17, 2004, Clara Rojas, Íngrid Betancourt's campaign manager, had given birth to a baby boy fathered by a guerrilla.

At first, the episode struck many Colombians as far-fetched. Getting pregnant was a cardinal sin within the FARC. While male and female guerrillas often paired off, women who were expecting were often forced to have abortions. Those who persuaded commanders to let them have their babies were usually evacuated to towns and villages for a few months, then ordered back to the jungle, and the newborns were left with family members or handed off to local peasants. Sexual relations between hostages and guerrillas, in turn, were strictly forbidden and punishable by death for offending rebels.

But Rojas, who was single and thirty-eight when she was kidnapped, had long dreamed of becoming a mother and felt her biological clock ticking. Although having a baby in the jungle was a huge gamble, the hostages lived with risk every day. According to hostage Luis Eladio Pérez, she asked Joaquín Gómez, one of the top FARC commanders, for permission to have sexual relations. Afterward, according to one former hostage, FARC guards were free to sleep with her. Months later, Rojas confirmed her state with a drugstore pregnancy test. Martín Sombra, the commander of the FARC camp, congratulated Rojas and suggested that she should massage her belly with jaguar oil to avoid stretch marks.

"On the one hand, I was profoundly happy to know that I was going to have a baby," Rojas said much later. "On the other hand, I was deeply worried to realize that I was going to become a mother in the middle of the jungle."

As the months passed and she began to show, some of the hostages became openly hostile. Why, they asked, would Rojas risk her own life and that of her baby by giving birth in the jungle? Her newborn would become the world's youngest hostage. Others could not fathom how Rojas could voluntarily sleep with the enemy. Rojas had argued with her rebel captors that giving birth in a FARC camp would be a high-risk operation, and some of the hostages viewed the entire affair as a ploy to secure her freedom.

When Rojas was seven months pregnant, the tensions became unbearable. The Americans, concerned that their partners back home would get wind of the pregnancy and blame them, demanded that Rojas reveal the name of the father. Finally, Rojas asked to be separated from the rest of the hostages, saying that they were acting "like hyenas." The rebels placed her in a plastic-covered manger next to a chicken coop and a pigsty, nothing fancy but at least she had some privacy. Betancourt, who had quarreled with Rojas and had not spoken with her for months, softened up amid the pregnancy and sewed clothes for the baby. As the due date approached, the rebels refused to evacuate Rojas to a clinic. Instead, they sent for a doctor. Rojas went into labor but over the next thirty-six hours she failed to dilate. The rebel physician never showed up. Instead, the medical team included farmhands with experience in helping cows give birth.

"Clara was going to die because the baby wouldn't come out," said Sombra, the camp commander. "I know a bit about nursing and realized we had to perform a cesarean section. We found a medical book, studied how to do it, and then I said to Guillermo, one of my troops: 'We're going to have to cut her open.'"

With a 100-watt lightbulb swinging over her stomach, the last image Rojas remembered was of the rebels sterilizing their scalpel blades over a candle. Then, the operation began.

Though competent in patching bullet holes, the guerrillas had a harder time bringing a new life into the world. Rojas lost so much blood that a swarm of flies gathered over the red-stained sheets. While extracting the baby boy, they broke his left arm. The newborn also inhaled amniotic fluid so rebel midwives frantically sucked on his nose and mouth to unblock his breathing passages. Finally, the boy turned pink and began to cry. Rojas called him Emmanuel, which in Hebrew means "God is with us."

But now, the mother was crashing. Rojas developed an infection and became so swollen that she thought she had another baby inside of her. It was five days before the rebels were able to supply her with antibiotics. In the meantime, she lost custody of her newborn. The sick Rojas was unable to nurse and made numerous rookie mistakes, like failing to test hot baby formula on her wrist before giving Emmanuel his bottle. Thus, the female guerrillas took over caring for the baby and allowed Rojas to see Emmanuel for only a few hours a day.

"During the day, Clara would stand at the fence shrieking in agony," Keith said. "At night, we would hear the haunting sound of Clara singing lullabies as loud as she could to her absent child."

When it finally looked like both mother and child were out of the woods, army helicopters began circling the FARC camp. As the guerrillas evacuated, they had to carry the still-weak Rojas through the forest in a hammock. Her stitches popped open, and Sombra, the rebel leader, sewed her back up without anesthesia. Later, as an army patrol approached, the guerrillas had to cover the baby's mouth to stifle his screams. They also took to sedating Emmanuel.

"Even with those drugs, the little guy cried most of the time from the obvious pain he was in," Keith said. "When he wasn't crying, he seemed to just stare vacantly. . . . The kid barely responded to any stimulus at all."

At the next camp, Clara and Emmanuel were together for about six months, though the baby spent most of his time in the guerrillas' care. Some of the rebels treated Emmanuel like a prince. During marches, a female guerrilla carried him in a kangaroo harness and, at the end of the day, they prepared his food first. They were constantly hugging and kissing Emmanuel and, for his first Christmas, the rebels gave him a toy telephone.

But in January 2005, when Emmanuel was eight months old, a sand fly bit him on the cheek. He developed leishmaniasis and the boil on his face would not close. So, the rebels informed Rojas that they would move the baby to another area so he could be treated for the disease. They assured the mother that her infant would be back in her arms within fifteen days.

Rojas would not see her boy for another three years.

GIVEN THE FARC's CRUELTY, THE INTRANSIGENCE of the Uribe government, and the indifference of average Colombians, it sometimes seemed as though the hostages were nonperishable goods rather than desperate and decaying human beings. But Emmanuel brought the holy mess into sharp focus. The madness had gone on for so long that a second generation of hostages had emerged in the jungle. Born into captivity, snatched from the arms of his mother and raised by guerrillas, Emmanuel added a helpless baby boy to the tragic equation.

"If Emmanuel dies this country is screwed," wrote Colombian novelist Héctor Abad. "If he doesn't go to school and doesn't grow up healthy and strong we will have become the most savage nation on Earth."

The campaign to free the hostages gained more momentum during a six-hundred-mile cross-country march staged by Gustavo Moncayo, a high school teacher whose son, army corporal Pablo Emilio Moncayo, was taken prisoner by the FARC in 1997. A father of five, Moncayo wanted his son to study electronic engineering but he didn't have the money to send him to college. And on principle, he refused to bribe army officers to allow Pablo Emilio to skip the draft.

Moncayo, a short man with a goatee and a crop of salt-and-pepper hair, visited FARC camps during the 1999–2002 peace talks to plead with rebel commanders. But years later, his son was still in captivity. The desperate teacher wrapped himself in chains and planted himself next to the national palace, but no one paid attention to his protest. So he took to the highways, walking from his hometown of Sandoná across two mountain ranges, through the Magdalena River valley, then up into the Andean mesa holding Bogotá. Like the hostages, Moncayo wore several feet of chain links around his neck. He was joined on the road by thousands of Colombians who saw in Moncayo a righteous pilgrim with a staff in his hand, blisters on his feet, and a message of peace. He seemed like a Colombian Gandhi.

But not everyone was smitten. Fernando Londoño, the former interior minister who came across in his newspaper columns like Bill O'Reilly's cranky South American uncle, lambasted Moncayo's son as an inept soldier and branded the teacher as a Marxist. Yet by the time Moncayo reached Bogotá, so many people had joined his cause that Uribe felt compelled to meet with him. Moncayo unveiled a petition with 2.5 million signatures collected along his route calling for a DMZ in the towns of Florida and Pradera to hold a prisoner swap. But Uribe refused to change his policies while his aides dismissed the petition because the signatures had not been notarized.

"Who is dying in this war?" Moncayo said following his long march. "Not the sons of politicians. They are studying abroad. It's the sons of the peasants and the Indians. They are the ones joining the guerrillas or the army. . . . I can assure you that if Uribe's sons were kidnapped, he would withdraw troops from Florida and Pradera and from the rest of Colombia and in less than a week they would be free."

Moncayo's march wasn't in vain. The huge crowds that joined Moncayo, the collective hand-wringing over Emmanuel's birth, and the growing international campaign to free Íngrid Betancourt combined to produce a steady drumbeat of media coverage and declarations from world leaders about Colombia's hostage crisis. After four years of silence, even President Bush weighed in on the fate of Keith, Marc, and Tom, telling a Colombian TV station: "I'm deeply concerned about their fate."

As pressure mounted, Uribe finally came through with a bold, if confusing, initiative. At the urging of French president Nicolas Sarkozy, he agreed to unilaterally release nearly two hundred imprisoned guerrillas who agreed not to return to the hills to fight. He also freed Rodrigo Granda, a high-ranking FARC member who, it was hoped, would act as a mediator in talks on a prisoner exchange. But the FARC dismissed Uribe's goodwill gesture and Granda fled to Venezuela. Colombians were left scratching their heads. Out of the blue, Uribe had made a series of concessions that the FARC had not even asked for while refusing to budge on the guerrillas' principal demand—a DMZ in Florida and Pradera. Uribe seemed to be making things up on the fly.

Yet the Colombian president was proving to be far more flexible than the FARC. And as this impasse continued into the summer of 2007, the recklessness of the FARC's bullheaded stance on the hostages would be driven home to devastating effect.

Among the FARC's political hostages were the twelve state legislators snatched in 2002 during the fake bomb scare in downtown Cali. By June 18, 2007, the lawmakers had spent 1,894 days as hostages. On that morning, a rebel patrol from another FARC unit inadvertently stumbled upon the guerrilla squad that was holding the lawmakers. In the confusion, the two sides exchanged fire. The guards thought they were being attacked by the Colombian Army and panicked. Fearing the hostages would be scooped up by the soldiers, they raised their AK-47 rifles to their shoulders and began pumping bullets into their captives. When the shooting stopped, eleven of the twelve lawmakers lay dead. Later, forensic experts examining the bodies counted fifty-five bullet holes.

Keith, Marc, and Tom nearly met the same fate. Once, when the buzz of approaching helicopters filled the air, FARC sentries, spaced five yards apart, surrounded the prison camp. Then, another set of rebels entered the bunkhouses with one executioner assigned to each prisoner.

"Don't gun us down like a pack of cowards," Keith screamed. "If you're going to shoot me, do it straight up. Just look me in the eye and then do it."

Then, the choppers flew away and the order arrived for the firing squad to stand down. The prisoners stood in stunned silence as the trigger-men filed out of the barracks.

THE MASSACRE OF THE STATE LEGISLATORS put even more pressure on President Uribe to find a solution. But for more than five years, the FARC had refused to deal with his designated peace commissioner. With no communication, there could be no progress. Thus, Uribe had little choice but to seek the services of an envoy whom the FARC trusted, which, by definition, implied a figure whom the president distrusted. Uribe's first move was to reach out to Piedad Córdoba, an outspoken Afro-Colombian and Liberal Party senator who had once been kidnapped by paramiltiaries. She accepted the assignment but urged Uribe to enlist the father of all Latin American leftists.

Venezuelan president Hugo Chávez fancies himself as a latter-day Fidel Castro. The boisterous former paratrooper became a household name in Venezuela in 1992 when he led a failed military uprising and was tossed in prison. But he was pardoned a few years later, jumped into legal politics, and quickly gained a wide following. Chávez, who was born in a mud hut on the plains of western Venezuela, claimed to speak for the poor majority, and in 1998 ran for president on an anticorruption platform. He easily defeated a slate of more mainstream candidates.

Chávez, whose idol is Simón Bolívar, promised to carry out what he called a "Bolivarian Revolution" and he moved his government sharply to the left following a 2002 coup that briefly removed him from power. U.S. officials had praised the putsch and that enraged Chávez, who took an almost perverse delight in power hosing George W. Bush with insults, calling him everything from "the devil" and "Mr. Danger" to "a donkey" and "a drunkard."

The Americans saw Chávez as a tropical Sideshow Bob, a potentially dangerous jester with malice in his heart and petrodollars in his pockets. They urged Uribe to break with his Venezuelan counterpart. But trade between their nations was booming, and the two leaders had mutual security interests. Although Chávez sympathized with the FARC, the rebels pulled off numerous kidnappings and killings inside Venezuela. Besides, if Chávez could help bring an end to the Colombian conflict, it would boost his stature around the world. Although Uribe was wary about giving up ownership of the hostage issue, he couldn't deny that the earthy, charismatic Venezuelan had the ear of the FARC.

"The FARC guerrillas that I met see in Chávez their ideological leader," said Fernando Araújo, a former government official who was held hostage by the rebels for six years, and later served as President Uribe's foreign minister. "They are constantly studying Chávez's biography, they watch documentaries about Chávez on television, and there is a sense of excitement among the guerrillas when they hear Chávez speaking on the radio."

Chávez embraced his new role. And in a surprise move, he reached out to the relatives of the American hostages by inviting them to a meeting at the Miraflores presidential palace in downtown Caracas. Northrop Grumman chartered a jet and flew the grateful delegation south. So after more than four years of suffering, anxiety, and perceived neglect from the Bush administration, the relatives of Keith, Marc, and Tom finally received red-carpet treatment from the government—the government of Washington's number one nemesis in South America.

Chávez also extended the invitation to Patricia Medina, Keith's girlfriend and the mother of their now four-year-old twins, and dispatched the presidential jet to Bogotá to pick her up. "I never felt the same support from the Colombian government," she said. "They didn't even know my telephone number. But Chávez sent his jet!"

Once in Caracas, the rambunctious Nicolás and Keith Jr. helped turn what could have been an awkward first encounter between Patricia and Keith Stansell's parents into a joyous family reunion. In one of the ornate palace salons decorated with burgundy curtains and oil portraits of Jesus Christ and Simón Bolívar, Gene and Lynne Stansell embraced Patricia and their two grandchildren. Kyle Stansell, Keith's fifteen-year-old son who also made the trip, recalled that any doubts about his father's role in the making of the twins were quickly dispelled.

"They looked exactly like my dad when he was their age," Kyle said. Four years earlier, he had been crushed to learn of his father's infidelities, but now he was enchanted by the results. "They are my brothers," Kyle said.

The visitors, who included Marc's father, George Gonsalves, and Tom Howes's wife, Mariana, had heard stories about the bombastic, anti-American caudillo, but Chávez worked his magic. He plied the twins with candy and ice cream and gave them soccer balls and red caps featuring the president's grinning visage. He showed the boys the location of Colombia and Venezuela on a globe. And when they finally ran out of gas, he let them nap in a palace bedroom.

But Chávez's main message was that he would not stop working until all of the hostages were free. Before the relatives left for the airport, Chávez embraced Kyle Stansell and solemnly pledged: "You will see your father."

IN THE SPACE OF A FEW WEEKS, Chávez and Córdoba appeared to make more progress on behalf of the hostages than four years of efforts by the Uribe government. Chávez secured a promise from the FARC to provide him with proof-of-life photos and letters from the hostages—many of whom hadn't been heard from in years. Meanwhile, Córdoba convinced Simón Trinidad, the FARC negotiator imprisoned in Washington, to write a letter to the rebel high command stating that he did not want his incarceration to hinder any possible deal.

Successful negotiations, however, usually required secrecy and discretion and the gregarious Chávez was a pathological talker. His Sunday afternoon call-in TV program often lasted for five hours. During marathon news conferences, Chávez would sing songs, talk baseball, and discuss his upcoming vacation plans. Córdoba could also be a showboat. After meeting with several FARC commanders in rural Venezuela, for example, the senator allowed herself to be photographed wearing a Che Guevara–style beret and holding a bouquet of red roses as if she had joined the struggle.

But more troubling to the Colombian government was that the two intermediaries seemed to be going rogue. Chávez started lobbying for a face-to-face meeting with FARC maximum leader Manuel "Sureshot" Marulanda in the Colombian jungle to discuss broader peace talks. Later, he and Córdoba held a news conference with FARC *comandante* Iván Márquez on the steps of the Miraflores Palace. It marked the first time in history that a FARC leader had appeared in public alongside a foreign head of state.

Back in Bogotá, President Uribe stewed. He had spent his entire presidency trying to delegitimize the FARC and now its leaders were being received as heroes in Caracas. But that was partly the president's own doing.

"If the two sides had sat down three or four years ago and agreed to a prisoner swap, not only would the hostages be free but the FARC would have no political momentum," said Camilo Gómez, who was the lead government negotiator during the 1999–2002 peace talks with the rebels. "But now the FARC is gaining ground. President Uribe has turned the FARC into the fundamental axis of Colombia's foreign policy."

But Uribe would soon turn the tables. In late November 2007, Córdoba called Colombian Army commander General Mario Montoya to update him about her efforts. Although Uribe had earlier advised Chávez not to speak with his military chiefs, the Venezuelan leader asked Córdoba to pass him the telephone. The conversation lasted a few minutes as Chávez asked Montoya about the number of soldiers held hostage. When Uribe found out, he abruptly dismissed Chávez and Córdoba as official mediators. That decision sparked a long-distance shouting match. Uribe accused Chávez of lending political legitimacy to terrorists, while Chávez, who had invested a great deal of time, resources, and personal prestige in freeing the hostages, called Uribe a "shameless" liar.

Though wary of Chávez—Keith referred to him as "that leftist red-shirt-wearing bastard"—the American hostages had pinned their hopes on his efforts and were crushed by the bad news, which arrived via transistor radio on November 22.

"Happy fucking Thanksgiving to us," Keith said. "What these politicians forgot was that their actions, their finger-pointing and their manipulating all kept us in chains."

For many watching the drama play out, Chávez's violation of protocol seemed like a minor faux pas and a flimsy pretext to abort the talks with the FARC. It had been widely understood from the get-go that the FARC would reap a temporary political and publicity windfall. That, however, seemed like a small price for liberating dozens of hostages.

Though he felt burned, Chávez refused to give up. And shortly after he was "fired" by Uribe, more evidence emerged that the Venezuelan leader had been making headway. The guerrillas had dispatched two couriers from southern Guaviare state to Bogotá with the proof-of-life materials Chávez had requested. The plan was to hand off the photos, videos, and letters to another rebel contact who was to bring the packet to Caracas. But the rebel envoys had been followed by army agents and were arrested in Bogotá. It was a major breakthrough for the army and evidence that military intelligence operations were vastly improving.

At a late-night news conference, Colombian officials displayed the proof-of-life materials, including a video of a shockingly wan and wasted-looking Íngrid Betancourt who refused to even look up at the camera. An accompanying letter stood as a heartbreaking yet elegant epistle from a hostage who appeared to be giving up hope. Her letter described forced marches, meager rations of rice and beans that caused constant diarrhea, loss of appetite, and clumps of her hair to fall out. She wrote of waking up at 4:00 a.m. to listen to the radio in the hope of hearing her mother's voice. But the reception on her broken transistor radio was so bad that she had to guess what her mother, Yolanda Pulecio, was saying.

"*Mamita*," she wrote. "I am tired, tired of suffering, I have tried to be strong. These almost six years of captivity have shown me that I am not as resistant, nor as brave, intelligent and strong as I had believed. I have had many battles, I have tried to escape at several opportunities. I have tried to maintain hope, as one keeps one's head above water. But, *mamita*, now I have given up. I want to think that one day I'll get out of here, but I know that what happened to the state legislators which hurt me greatly, could happen to me at any moment. I think this would be a relief for everyone."

Semana, Colombia's equivalent of *Time* magazine, shocked readers with a cover juxtaposing an earlier photo of the glamorous, ready-to-devour-the-world politician with the proof-of-life shot of the cadaverous, mourning hostage—which seemed like a synthesis of Mary Magdalene and a Treblinka survivor.

Almost overlooked in the ensuing fuss over Betancourt were videos of Keith, Marc, and Tom, the first proofs-of-life of the contractors to surface in four and a half years. But the Americans still felt they had been manipulated years earlier during their first proof-of-life video, and this time, Keith and Marc refused to utter a word. Though his face was noticeably thinner, Keith wore a sleeveless black T-shirt that displayed his muscular arms, indicating he was still working out. In his video, Marc stared sullenly into the camera and swatted mosquitoes. Luis Eladio Pérez, the former senator who was being held alongside the Americans, had urged Marc to at least send a message to his wife. But Marc had heard nothing from Shane since he'd been captured and suspected their marriage was over. "What am I supposed to say to her?" Marc said. Later that day, Pérez spotted Marc sobbing.

But Tom Howes, now fifty-four, jumped at the chance to communicate with his family. He had long believed that he would not hold up for more than five or six years in the jungle and, in his video, he seemed to acknowledge that he might never see his wife again.

"I love you very much," Howes said, addressing Mariana, as he stood next to a wooden table with the rain forest as a backdrop. "Please send my best to the family. I've got a letter for you and a will, and a last testament."

CHAPTER 21

THE MASKED AVENGER

And where the offense is, let the great axe fall.
—WILLIAM SHAKESPEARE, *Hamlet*

O N THE SAME DAY THE COLOMBIAN military judge sentenced the troops of Destroyer and Vulture companies to three to ten years behind bars for stuffing their uniforms with guerrilla cash, a film about the hard-luck soldiers debuted in movie houses around the country. Lieutenant Jorge Sanabria had fantasized about finding the American hostages and turning his exploits into a Hollywood film. Instead, a Colombian actor portrayed Sanabria in a surreal, black comedy about the rise, fall, and incarceration of the cash-rich GIs. Titled *Soñar No Cuesta Nada*, or "Dreaming Is Free" —the English-language title was *Temptation Trumps Duty*—the film was a huge box-office hit and was Colombia's submission in the Best Foreign Film category for the 2007 Academy Awards.

Re-creating the moment he found the money, an actor playing Walter Suárez was shown leaving a steaming pile behind a bush, then stabbing his machete into the ground and hitting the sweet spot. Sanabria was depicted as a flawed but humane player-coach, counseling his young bucks to be prudent only to watch them lose their money faster than bottom-tier investors in a pyramid scheme.

But the director also took some artistic license. In the movie, most of the troops learned about the money when a mine beneath one of the barrels of cash exploded, showering the GIs with shredded dollars and pesos. And after returning to Popayán, Suárez—a solid family man in real life—was portrayed as proffering a garbage bag full of cash to a high-class hooker only to wake up the next morning to a vacant bed and an empty wallet.

After watching the film in a Cali movie theater, Hanner Daza and his girlfriend, Stefania Ortiz, did their customary Siskel-and-Ebert debate thing. Stefania argued that with a quarter teaspoon of common sense, the dunderheaded troops could have gotten away with their tomfoolery. Daza disagreed, then shocked his girlfriend by saying, "It wasn't like that." The couple had been dating for three years and Stefania knew that her boyfriend had served in the military. But this was the first time Hanner let on that he had been a member of Vulture Company. He was one of those camouflaged chumps up there on the big screen.

"He told me that he didn't regret anything that had happened," Ortiz said as she peddled tomatoes, onions, and red bell peppers from an open-air stall in a market in Cali. "He told me, 'I never hurt anyone.'"

Hanner Daza was the eighth-grade dropout who had nearly been press-ganged into the FARC, a conflict that aroused the wrath of paramilitary death squads and forced his family to abandon their farm. He was the soldier who had buried part of his money underneath the floorboards of his parents' house in Popayán, then urged them to take a cut for themselves before he blew it all on *aguardiente* and sluts. Within a few days, military investigators caught wind of the caper, and Hanner disappeared.

It was an agonizing time for the Daza family. Hanner's father, a farmer and electrician, had always urged his ten children to do the right thing. But now, word was spreading in their working-class barrio in Popayán that the Dazas were adding a second story to their modest concrete house with dirty money from the famous jungle bonanza. One afternoon, a team of policemen burst in the door and began tearing the house apart looking for Hanner's stash. A relative of the Daza family who worked in the police department came by and demanded that the officers show their search warrant. They shrugged and disappeared. Yaned Daza, Hanner's older sister, worried that the family would be targeted by extortionists and feared that criminals would try to kidnap her three-year-old son.

"We spent our whole lives fleeing from danger only to find new dangers here," she said.

She also feared that Hanner, who was now on the lam, would try something desperate. After saving young Hanner from execution at the hands of paramilitary death squads, the family now worried that he would end up joining the right-wing militias because they might guarantee him protection and a steady income. But Hanner was simply lying low. Eventually, he settled in Cali and invested some of his cash in a vegetable wholesale business that he managed with Stefania and her father.

Hanner's older brother Carlos, who worked for the attorney general's office in Cali, tried to convince the younger Daza to surrender. "But he said, 'I'm not guilty of anything,'" Carlos Daza recalled. "He said, 'Why do they have to prosecute me?'"

On February 5, 2007, bandits held up an armored car and police were setting up roadblocks around Cali to catch them. When Hanner and Stefania pulled up to a bank on Hanner's motorcycle, Stefania went inside to pay the electric bill. The cops spotted Hanner waiting outside, frisked him, and asked for his ID. They quickly discovered who he was and put him in jail at a nearby military base in the town of Palmira. The one stroke of good fortune in Hanner's life had followed him like a curse.

WHILE LIVING IN TABATINGA, A TOWN on the Colombian-Brazilian border, Lieutenant Jorge Sanabria had heard about the guilty verdicts and of his ten-year prison sentence. It seemed wholly unjust. But by then, Sanabria was tired of running. Missing his family and homesick for his country, he slipped back into Colombia and returned to Sogamoso, where he opened a restaurant. But he was an easy mark. The onetime counterguerrilla commando had ballooned to 360 pounds. Within a month, police officers tracked him down and slapped on the cuffs. Later, when Sanabria saw himself on TV being led away by the authorities, it hit him that he was heading for prison and he felt a sharp pain in his chest. He was having a heart attack.

Doctors at the Sogamoso hospital managed to revive Sanabria, but they also suggested that he come back for a gastric bypass operation in order to slim down. Elective surgery seemed out of the question because Sanabria was destined for the stockade. But thanks to another abrupt turnaround, his time behind bars would be brief.

On June 4, 2007, a military magistrate declared that there had been serious flaws in the soldiers' 2006 trial. Their legal defense had been compromised because the original judge had moved ahead even though some of the lawyers for the GIs failed to show up during several days of the trial. In addition, the prison terms handed down by the judge were weighted to the amount of money that individual troops had made off with. But those figures could never be accurately determined. Taking these factors into account, the magistrate declared a mistrial. The soldiers were to be furloughed until a new trial on the same charges could be convened.

Two days later, scores of soldiers lined up at the gates outside of Tolemaida and boarded buses back to their hometowns. To avoid being identified by the throng of reporters waiting outside the gates, some of them pulled ski masks over their faces.

When Hanner Daza walked out of the military stockade in Palmira on June 7, he seemed like a new person. He emerged with a somber mien and vowed to take advantage of this unexpected, second chance. He would study for his high-school diploma, marry Stefania, start a family, and put some real flesh on his life plans.

But Hanner also fretted. In the stockade, a guerrilla militiaman in an adjacent cell had learned why he was being held. And Hanner knew that the FARC-issued fatwa to take down the soldiers who took off with the rebel cash still held.

"He was afraid after he got out," said Yaned Daza, Hanner's sister. "He said that he felt safer in jail."

Ten days after he was freed, Hanner and Stefania hopped on his motorcycle and drove from Cali south through the Cauca River valley to Popayán, his parents' adopted hometown and the scene of the soldiers' original binge. The Dazas had planned a family reunion on Father's Day and eight of the ten brothers and sisters showed up. It was a magical moment. After a picnic, they splashed around in a Popayán swimming hole. Laughing and singing, the Daza party made such a spectacle that complete strangers joined their group to soak up the merriment. A photo of the event caught the inebriated Daza brothers, arm in arm, next to their father before a table filled with empty beer bottles. But Hanner struck a contemplative pose.

The next morning his nerves were all a-jangle. He popped open a beer to anesthetize his hangover and his relatives suggested he and Stefania stay for lunch before hitting the road for Cali. "He didn't want to go," said Aura Gómez, his mother. "He said, 'I'm nervous.'"

Once back in Cali, Hanner and Stefania resumed their day jobs as vegetable wholesalers at the market, which was located in a tough, southside neighborhood surrounded by hardware stores, pool halls, and meatpacking plants. On Wednesday, June 20—thirteen days after Hanner had regained his freedom—a man wearing a black ski mask burst into the stall. Hanner tried to stop him by pushing the door shut but it was too late. Stefania intervened, offering the gunman her kangaroo pouch filled with cash and the keys to the motorcycle parked out front. But the intruder pushed her aside, pulled out a pistol, and pumped a bullet into Hanner's midsection. Then he dashed into the crowded streets and disappeared.

"Hanner yelled, 'Take me to the hospital! I'm dying!'" said Nancy Valencia who ran a fruit stand next to the Daza business.

Stefania flagged down a taxi, which took the bleeding Hanner to a clinic. "I thought he was going to live," she said, recalling the chaotic scene at the hospital. "But they told me the bullet destroyed the whole left side of his abdomen." Though no one was arrested, investigators and the Daza family figured it was a FARC hit. Common criminals out for money didn't wear face masks because it only made them stand out. And the shooter wasn't interested in money. He simply took aim and fired.

Hanner Daza died on the operating table at 10:15 a.m. on June 20, 2007. He was twenty-four.

CHAPTER 22

NECK AND NECK

It always seems impossible, until it's done.
—NELSON MANDELA

JOHN FRANK PINCHAO HAD PREDICTED THAT after his great escape, the conditions for the hostages would deteriorate. He was right. Pinchao was able to break his chains because the links were small and thin. But after his getaway, the guerrillas secured their remaining prisoners with long lengths of heavy chain made up of thicker, one-inch links. In addition, the hostages were now chained together twenty-four hours a day. Keith was connected to Marc by a sixteen-foot length of steel chain that looped around their necks and was fastened in place with clunky padlocks. Tom was shackled to Luis Eladio Pérez, the former Colombian senator.

"They made you feel like you were being choked," Tom said. "Every time I swallowed, my Adam's apple rubbed against the steel."

Tom had once gotten into a fistfight with Pérez, but the two men made amends and for the next nine months lived like Siamese twins. If Pérez snored, Tom plugged his ears. If Tom rose at dawn to exercise, Pérez grudgingly rolled out of bed. If one had to go to the latrine, the other followed. And when crossing streams on rustic foot bridges made out of tree trunks, they had to pull off a delicate high-wire act. If one prisoner slipped and fell into the water below, the other had to follow him off the same side of the bridge to avoid being strangled by the chain.

All the while, their prison warden, a ready-to-blow psycho known as Enrique Gafas, kept close watch over the hostages. Gafas claimed to have been a small-town mayor before taking up arms and was a second-tier commander of the FARC's First Front, which operated in the states of Guaviare, Caquetá, and Vaupés.

"Enrique Gafas was bitter and resentful, a total shit," Pérez said. "He fancied himself a politician because that gives you a little more status within the FARC. But he was always very aggressive and threatening to shoot people. . . . Of all of the guerrillas, he was the worst."

Gafas would blather on about the revolution, social justice, and equal rights, then wrap chains around the hostages and treat his guerrilla underlings like servants. One night, Gafas broke out his laptop computer and put on a DVD so the hostages could watch a movie. But Gafas sat front and center on a makeshift throne with his girlfriend lounging between his legs. His troops were scared to death of him.

"I developed a severe distaste for this commander," Tom said. "I would get him in front of his troops and try to make him look bad. And he was a mean guy. He once took out his gun and made a cocking sound and said, 'I'm going to kill you.' Then he said, 'Well, I'm not going to kill you, but I'm going to ruin your day. I'm going to shoot you in the foot.' I said, 'Well, it's going to be tough to march.'"

Rather than pulling the trigger, Gafas opted for a slower kind of torture. He removed Keith's chain and wrapped it around Tom, an additional necklace to the sixteen feet of steel links he was already wearing. That day, Tom marched through the jungle with eighteen pounds of chain, as if he were wearing a steel turtleneck sweater.

In some ways, these tougher conditions united Keith, Marc, and Tom. More than ever, they counted on one another to survive. And they vowed to cash in on their ordeal and split the profits three ways if they ever made it out of the jungle. One night Pérez overheard the three contractors doing the math. They had decided they'd sell their story to the filmmaker Oliver Stone for $3 million. Keith, Marc, and Tom then signed a document spelling out the details and asked Pérez to witness the pact.

BY THE TIME WILLIAM R. BROWNFIELD arrived in Bogotá to present his credentials as the new U.S. envoy to Colombia, Keith, Marc, and Tom had been held for four and a half excruciating years and there was no end in sight.

"We counted the days," said one U.S. official working on the case. "We hit 444 days. Then 1,677 days. . . . As each new year arrived it was like, 'You gotta be kidding me. With all the resources and technology we have we can't find these guys?'"

Worse, American officials were sharply split over how to approach the problem. Hard-liners at the intelligence agencies and the State and Defense departments dismissed the possibility of a prisoner exchange and shook the pom-poms for a rescue mission. Their counterparts argued for a negotiated solution with the FARC even though cutting deals with terrorists ran against official U.S. policy.

"The two sides were digging in," Brownfield said. "Even within the embassy we were torn between those who said, 'If we try a military operation, we're just going to get them killed,' and others who were saying, 'Then why are we here? Why have we put tens of millions of dollars' worth of equipment and assets and people down here to try to chase this down? Why the hell are we here?' It was a perfectly legitimate question."

But Brownfield, a short, intense figure with reddish hair, a folksy demeanor in public, and a talent for cultivating the press, was a veteran survivor of difficult foreign postings. After graduating from Cornell University with a history degree, the Texas native hit the road, busing, training, and thumbing around the world. It was a yearlong sojourn with a low budget and loose itinerary that included a toe-touch in Gaddafi's Libya, winter work on an Israeli kibbutz, and a journey down the Silk Road to Afghanistan where he marveled at the giant Buddha statues of Bamiyan. His wayfaring was brought to an end by a case of hepatitis that he'd picked up on the Nepalese border, but by then Brownfield had become hooked on world affairs.

He entered the U.S. Foreign Service and was promptly assigned to Georgetown, Guyana. The year was 1979 and the former British colony in South America was reeling from the mass suicides of more than nine hundred mostly American followers of People's Temple cult leader Jim Jones. Brownfield reckoned he'd be spending all his time processing the return of bodies from Jonestown to the United States. He wouldn't even learn a foreign language. So he pleaded with his assignment officer who took pity on Brownfield and sent him to Maracaibo, Venezuela. It was the first in a series of Latin American assignments that included war-ravaged El Salvador and postings as ambassador to Chile and Venezuela where Hugo Chávez tried to make him his whipping boy.

From afar, Brownfield had tracked the hostage issue. His predecessor in Bogotá was William Wood, an old friend and a member of Brownfield's wedding party, and the two conferred regularly on Colombia. Wood had helped set up the embassy's Intelligence Fusion Center to focus all assets on finding the hostages. But when Wood was transferred to Afghanistan, Keith, Marc, and Tom seemed no closer to freedom.

The changing of the guard "could only be good for us," Tom said. "Wood only seemed to talk about drugs and counterdrugs, saying nothing about us hostages. Brownfield was different. . . . He made it clear that he knew about the three of us and that he was hopeful a solution could be worked out."

Brownfield's arrival on September 1, 2007, coincided with a big turnover in the Bogotá embassy staff, and the envoy tried to step back and take a new look at an old problem. Brownfield was a freethinker: he was game to try anything as long as it wouldn't get the hostages killed. If Chávez, Senator Piedad Córdoba, or some other mediator held the key, the embassy would support their efforts. If there were breakthroughs on the military side, the ambassador would listen carefully. Paraphrasing Chairman Mao, Brownfield said his approach was to let a thousand flowers bloom.

Among the strategies bearing fruit was the Colombian military's five-year offensive against the FARC. Army operations were cutting off rebel supply lines and communications. Rebels in the north now had a hard time giving orders to fellow fighters in the south. The FARC seemed to be losing its central nervous system. In the words of Deputy Defense Minister Sergio

Jaramillo, it was as if the rebel organization was suffering from Parkinson's disease.

Many of the military's advances were chalked up to vast improvements in intelligence. In the past, jealousies between Colombia's service branches prompted intelligence officers to hoard sensitive data. As a result, army troops would receive tips from the police but hold off launching risky operations until they could gather their own intelligence. By then, the bad guys would be gone.

"What I did was to create a different structure in which all intelligence had to be shared," Defense Minister Juan Manuel Santos said. "If I discovered that someone had information that had not been shared, that person was out of the armed forces the next day."

Adding to the FARC's woes was a team of FBI agents based in Miami who launched an infiltration effort dubbed Operation Alliance. It began with a phone call to Miami by Nancy Conde, the FARC's regional finance and supply chief. She was in charge of getting uniforms, medicine, arms, and food to FARC fronts in the south. Conde was also the wife of alias César, the commander of the FARC's First Front and the boss of Enrique Gafas, the cruel warden of the American hostages. Conde was calling her contacts in Miami about purchasing satellite telephones and other supplies for the guerrillas. But the FBI was listening to her conversation and arrested her rebel contacts in Miami, who agreed to cooperate in their investigation. The collaborators provided Conde wire-tapped satellite telephones, SIM cards, two-way radios, and other compromised communications gear.

Over the years, the operation allowed U.S. and Colombian officials to listen in on more than five thousand phone calls by the guerrillas. Brownfield called Operation Alliance a preliminary process that would evolve into a long-running campaign by both countries to manipulate and deceive the FARC.

"The FARC is extremely sophisticated in their own communications in terms of what they'll say, how much is in code, and where they'll communicate from," Brownfield said. "We had to learn those lessons."

Fearing their communications were compromised, FARC commanders often stayed off their radios and telephones and began sending instructions on USB memory sticks carried by human couriers. But the runners often required days or weeks to move from one spot to another, making it difficult for guerrilla units to coordinate their attacks. With rebel leaders incommunicado and boxed in, the FARC was forced to drastically scale back its Ninth Conference. Held every five years or so, the FARC conferences brought together the seven-man secretariat and the thirty-one-member general staff to determine the rebel organization's broad strategic guidelines. But the Ninth Conference, held sometime in early 2007, was limited to an exchange of e-mail messages.

The glory years of the FARC now seemed like a distant chapter of history. As more rebels deserted or were killed, the lack of front-line insurgents forced the FARC to move their militiamen out of the cities and into the countryside to fight. Army operations greatly reduced the FARC's ability to kidnap and extort civilians while rebel units were pushed out of some drug-producing regions. With less income and ragged supply lines, deliveries of everything from food and medicine to toothpaste and underwear were sporadic. Rather than expensive camouflage uniforms, many guerrillas went into battle wearing black T-shirts and sweatpants.

One rebel with a close-up view of the breakdowns was a Cartagena native who went by the nom de guerre Camilo. He joined the FARC when there was plenty of food and ammunition. Camilo's job was to teach Marxism to green recruits and when he wasn't working he relaxed in villages under rebel control, called home regularly, and sent his mother the equivalent of $150 a month. But by 2007, the FARC had cut off the monthly stipends and, for security reasons, Camilo wasn't allowed to use his cell phone. His rebel girlfriend was gunned down by the military, while the twelve surviving guerrillas from his platoon of twenty-four fighters were reduced to stealing chickens from local farmers to survive.

"We had become nothing more than delinquents and thieves," said Camilo, who deserted a few weeks later.

A government program offering cash rewards for guerrillas who ratted out their superiors spread fear and paranoia. In one rebel unit of seventy foot soldiers, twenty-six were executed on charges of collaborating with the army. Even so, a steady flow of guerrillas abandoned the FARC, which created a snowball effect. The exodus demoralized the remaining guerrillas, while the information provided by the turncoats allowed the army to destroy more

FARC units—all of which spurred more desertions. In 2007, some fifteen hundred rebels turned themselves in, including two hundred who had spent at least a decade in the FARC. One of the most high-profile FARC fighters to demobilize was alias Karina, a one-eyed female commander and a twenty-five-year war veteran for whom the Colombian government had offered a huge reward.

"There were a lot of combatants by my side," Karina said. "But some may have been thinking about how much money had been put on my head."

The army attacks, the supply breakdowns, and the intercepted communications fed rumors among the guerrillas that their every move was being monitored by a team of highly trained super spies. It was said that these commandos survived in the wilderness for months at a time, dressed like Spider-Man, and darted through the trees like Tang dynasty warriors from the *House of Flying Daggers*. The stories freaked out some of the teenaged guards pulling night duty, who flinched at every shadow. The rebels began referring to these forest ninjas as "the solitary men"—and they would turn out to be more fact than fiction.

AMID THE CHANGING CIRCUMSTANCES IN THE ground war, Colombian president Álvaro Uribe advanced a new plan. He figured that if dejected rebel units holding hostages could be located and isolated, perhaps they could be talked into turning over their prisoners. Rather than bursting in guns a-blazing, troops could encircle the rebels, then lean on their leaders to give up their prisoners in exchange for cash rewards, exile overseas, or other benefits.

Uribe called the maneuver a "humanitarian cordon," but the plan was met with great skepticism in Colombia. Critics believed Uribe was simply tossing out desperate proposals to get the international community off his back. They saw the cordon as the worst of both worlds, a risky military operation that stood little chance of bringing about freedom for the hostages and might even prompt the guerrillas to execute their prisoners. In Colombian parlance, the plan was *ni chicha ni limonada*—neither booze nor lemonade.

But the more Ambassador Brownfield chewed over the idea, the more it seemed to make sense. The scenario seemed similar to one in which authorities surrounded a bank and convinced the kidnappers inside to let their hostages go. Brownfield figured that U.S. and Colombian troops would be in a far better position to make it work if they were putting constant pressure on local FARC commanders. What's more, the plan seemed to occupy the fertile middle ground between those who favored a military rescue and those pushing for a prisoner exchange.

"The concept," Brownfield said, "was to stress the FARC, stress the local commanders with the expectation that at some point they'd be willing to open up, talk about, or just release the hostages. We would try to make it in their interest to let the hostages go. And it had the additional benefit of tying together the two extremes in the U.S. government."

Next, Brownfield tried to get the relatives of Keith, Marc, and Tom on board. After meeting with President Chávez in Venezuela, the family members were flown to Bogotá by Northrop Grumman where they met with President Uribe and the American ambassador. Brownfield told the family members that if a negotiated solution would spring their loved ones, he would explore that route. But with President Uribe's humanitarian cordon in mind, he also used the meeting, as well as a second encounter in Fort Lauderdale, to urge the families to go along with the plan.

"I told them that I would never intentionally approve, endorse, or support an operation that in my judgment put their family members' lives at risk,'" Brownfield said. "But my pitch to them was: 'Don't lock out any options.'"

IT WAS CALLED OPERATION EMMANUEL. AND as the name implied, the mission centered on the now three-year-old boy who was born to Clara Rojas, the hostage and onetime campaign manager of Íngrid Betancourt.

Rojas had not seen her child in nearly three years but the FARC claimed he was still in rebel custody. And although the Bogotá government had abruptly removed Hugo Chávez from his role as a go-between, the FARC was keen to boost the Venezuelan leader and embarrass President Álvaro Uribe. So, on December 18, 2007, the FARC made a startling announcement. The rebels promised to turn over Emmanuel, Clara Rojas, and Consuelo González, a former Colombian lawmaker, to delegates of the Venezuelan government. If the FARC made good on its pledge, it would mark the FARC's first unilateral release of hostages in a decade.

Standing before charts and grids as if mapping out the conquest of New Spain, Chávez went on national TV to explain the three stages of the elaborate humanitarian mission. He also invited what seemed like the full plenary of the United Nations to observe the operation and to make sure the Colombian Army didn't sabotage the handover. Besides members of his own government and the International Red Cross, the delegates included officials from Bolivia, Brazil, Cuba, Ecuador, France, and Switzerland as well as Nestor Kirchner, the former president of Argentina. It all seemed to be playing into the FARC's hands. The rebels were reaping press coverage and international attention. Chávez's star was rising while Uribe, the FARC's mortal enemy, appeared to have lost control of events.

On December 29, the delegates flew from Venezuela to the Colombian city of Villavicencio, located just south of Bogotá where the Andes Mountains gave way to the plains and, eventually, the Amazon jungle where the hostages were being held. Once the FARC provided the coordinates, a smaller group would be airlifted on Venezuelan helicopters to the pickup point, then fly with the hostages to Caracas.

Following the events over the radio, Keith, Marc, and Tom were thrilled to learn about the FARC's decision. But then they heard a report that Chávez had invited Oliver Stone to film the mission. Instead of making a movie about the Americans, the director of *Platoon* and *Born on the Fourth of July* seemed set on bringing Hugo Chávez's exploits to the big screen. "I think it was their hardest day since they were kidnapped," said former senator Luis Eladio Pérez, the designated witness of their three-way movie pact. "But the rest of us were dying of laughter. They were so bummed out that they'd lost their business deal."

But like his postulations about the Kennedy assassination in *JFK*, Stone's assessment of the FARC was a blending of fact and fancy.

"I do think that by the standards of Western civilization, [the FARC] goes too far; they kidnap innocent people," Stone said. "On the other hand, they're fighting a desperate battle against highly financed, American-supported forces. . . . I think they are heroic to fight for what they believe in and die for it, as was Castro in the hills of Cuba."

Inexplicably, the FARC kept Team Chávez waiting for three days in sweltering Villavicencio, a cowboy town with few options for tourists except beer and eight-ball in the cantinas. Finally, on New Year's Eve, the rebels released a communiqué explaining that the handover had been delayed because Colombian military operations were disrupting the evacuation of the hostages.

At that point, President Uribe, who had been following the spectacle on the TV news from his cattle ranch in northern Colombia, had seen enough. With Chávez, Kirchner, and some journalists blaming his government for throwing up roadblocks and Stone describing the FARC as more honey than sting, Uribe flew to Villavicencio and called the guerrillas' bluff.

As if the saga of Clara Rojas and Emmanuel wasn't strange and tragic enough, Uribe provided an operatic coda. The real reason the FARC had failed to release the three hostages, he suggested, was that Emmanuel was no longer in rebel custody. He then revealed that a boy with characteristics similar to Emmanuel's had been living in a state-run foster home in Bogotá since June 2005. The boy had scars on his left arm—the same one broken during Emmanuel's birth—and had suffered from leishmaniasis, a disease common among jungle dwellers.

Chávez quickly accused Uribe of trying to derail the mission while Kirchner upbraided the Colombian leader for spreading unconfirmed rumors. But Uribe had it right: DNA samples taken from the boy and from Rojas's mother and brother showed that there was a "high probability" he was Clara Rojas's son.

It turned out that when the guerrillas took Emmanuel away from Rojas in January 2005, they left the baby in the care of José Gómez, a coca farmer and FARC collaborator in Guaviare state. Gómez later told investigators that FARC rebels had simply knocked on his door and handed him the infant.

"I already had five children. My wife was not very happy about this," Gómez said. "But if I refused, I knew I would have problems" with the FARC.

The rebels supplied a can of baby formula and a package of diapers, then disappeared. Within a few months, the child developed a severe case of diarrhea, forcing Gómez, who presented himself as the boy's great-uncle, to take him to the hospital in the nearby state capital of San José del Guaviare. Suffering from malnutrition, malaria, and a mangled right arm, Emmanuel was in such bad shape that the government's Family Welfare Institute placed him in a Bogotá foster home, though officials had no clue of his true identity.

In November 2007, as the FARC prepared to release Emmanuel, a rebel tracked down Gómez and demanded that he produce the boy. Soon afterward, Colombian officials were tipped off that the boy, registered under the name Juan David Gómez, might be the son of Clara Rojas and that a fraudulent effort was under way to whisk away the child.

Not only was the episode incredibly embarrassing for the FARC, it seemed to reveal a rebel organization in a state of steep decline. Command-and-control breakdowns had left the FARC in such disarray that its leaders couldn't even keep track of one of the group's most high-profile hostages.

To REPAIR ITS TATTERED IMAGE AND to keep Hugo Chávez in the spotlight, the FARC decided to make good on its pledge to liberate Clara Rojas and former congresswoman Consuelo González. On January 10, 2008, the FARC finally gave the GPS coordinates of the pickup point to the Venezuelan government. Chávez dispatched two Russian-made MI-17 helicopters, painted white with orange trim and plastered with logos of the International Red Cross. Among others, the pickup crew included a Red Cross delegate, Venezuela's interior minister, the Cuban ambassador to Caracas, and reporters from the state-run Caracas TV station Telesur, which provided live coverage.

After the choppers touched down near La Libertad in Guaviare state, Rojas and González emerged from the bush surrounded by ten gun-toting rebels. The Telesur news team scurried about, interviewing the newly freed hostages and filming the guerrillas. Once the passengers were belted into their seats, the helicopter crews dropped off a cooler of iced soft drinks for the guerrillas, then fired up the engines and flew back to Venezuela.

In Caracas, Rojas learned that her now three-year-old son was in the custody of her family. "I'm alive because of Emmanuel," she told a news conference.

The handover stood as vivid proof that the FARC did not need a DMZ in order to safely carry out a prisoner exchange. More important, the rebels had given up two hostages and, beyond a little media attention, they had received nothing in return. It was an act of one-downsmanship that was viewed in Bogotá as vindication of the Uribe government's hard-line stance.

But the liberations also brought new demands from the hostages' relatives for Chávez to be officially reinstated as a mediator with the FARC. Political intrigue notwithstanding, Chávez possessed the secret sauce. In less than six months, he had ironed out the knotty particulars and pulled off the kind of deal Uribe had failed to manage in six years.

"Uribe didn't do anything except to not shoot down the rescue aircraft," said Gene Stansell, Keith's father.

A few weeks later, lobbying by Chávez led to another FARC announcement. Still chained neck and neck to Tom Howes, Luis Eladio Pérez heard over the radio that he was one of four more political hostages set to be released by the FARC. Tom looked at Pérez, then, using the politician's nickname, began yelling: "Lucho! Freedom! Lucho! Freedom!"

The next day, a rebel guard abruptly unchained the two men, and Pérez, along with three other hostages, headed home after seven years in captivity. He then embarked on a 14-day, 150-mile journey along rivers and through forest, savannah, and pasturelands. Pérez realized he was getting closer to civilization when he and his guards reached the outskirts of the riverside village. It marked the first time since his capture that Pérez had seen regular civilians. There were no police or army troops in the hamlet so, when Pérez grew thirsty, the rebels took him to a pool hall for a soda. Accustomed to the shadows and the indirect light of the jungle, Pérez had to shield his eyes from the neon glare.

That same evening Pérez was reunited with the other prisoners— Colombian politicians Jorge Gechém, Orlando Beltrán, and Gloria Polanco— and all four were handed off to a new set of guards. This rebel group was in an especially diminished state. Despite the orders to fatten up their prisoners for the release, the new guards fed them only plantains for breakfast, lunch, and dinner. And the guerrillas hovered around the hostages like buzzards at a garbage dump, waiting to pick off their hammocks, mosquito nets, and ragged clothes once they were liberated.

The next day, the same white-and-orange helicopters from the first operation touched down to pick up the newly freed hostages. Back in the Venezuelan capital, they rushed across the tarmac into the open arms of their family members. Then, the entire contingent was whisked to Miraflores Palace for a meeting with Hugo Chávez.

"There are a lot of things I don't like about Chávez," Pérez said later. "But without him we never would have been liberated. So if President Chávez said to me, 'I want to make love to you,' well, shit, I'd pull down my pants for him."

By contrast, there was no love from the Colombian government. Not a single member of the Uribe administration showed up at the Bogotá airport to welcome home the hostages. But a throng of well-wishers turned out, including Patricia Medina, Keith's girlfriend. When Pérez realized who she was, he grabbed a rose from one of the bouquets he'd been given and handed it to Patricia. Keith had wanted to tell Patricia that she was a special woman in his life, but his exact words got twisted in translation.

"I have the most beautiful message that anyone can bring to a woman," Pérez said as he looked Patricia in the eye. "Keith told me to tell you that if you're willing, he wants to marry you."

CHAPTER 23

EYES ON

Sometimes a breakdown can be the beginning of
a kind of breakthrough.
—CHERRIE MORAGA, PLAYWRIGHT

IN JANUARY 2008, U.S. AND COLOMBIAN officials received the clearest signals yet on the whereabouts of Keith, Marc, and Tom. The FARC's First Front was holding them in northeast Guaviare state, not far from the area where Luis Eladio Pérez, Clara Rojas, and four other hostages were turned over to the Venezuelans. Figuring that Colombian troops would flood the zone soon afterward, the FARC began moving the Americans south toward the Apaporis River, the waterway that was John Frank Pinchao's yellow-brick road. But rebel radio operators were getting sloppy while the Colombian agents monitoring the airwaves were getting better. And when the guerrillas lapsed into fairly simple code, army agents were able to track their every move.

"That's what kicked things off," said U.S. ambassador William

Brownfield. "For the first time, we thought we had very good intelligence. We were in advance of them."

Brownfield and Defense Minister Juan Manuel Santos agreed to move ahead with a sophisticated, joint operation, one designed to avoid a head-on confrontation. Between nine hundred and a thousand U.S. Special Operations Forces were dispatched to Colombia. Because these commandos were hunting for American hostages, all limits on the use of U.S. troops, aircraft, and equipment in Colombia went out the window. With the consent of the Uribe government, the Americans could mount a mini D-Day.

In past operations, American military advisers had never been deployed farther forward than a battalion headquarters. But now U.S. troops were embedded with the Colombian Army at the platoon and squad levels. In some cases, these joint jungle patrols consisted of six Colombians and six Americans. The U.S. presence would give the embassy real-time information and allow the troops, if necessary, to immediately call in U.S. aircraft, which were a cut above Colombia's and could operate more efficiently after dark. And though it went unsaid, there were some lingering suspicions about the quality of the Colombian troops.

As it turned out, the Colombians displayed an eat-nails toughness. Ever since 2002, when the U.S. mandate was widened to include counterterrorism training, American advisers had helped to build an elite battalion of about three hundred Colombian commandos. They learned all sorts of tricks from the Americans, like the navy SEAL practice of blowing into their uniforms to create air pockets that could serve as makeshift life jackets. But while American Special Operations Forces were more versatile— they could drop into woodlands, desert, or sea and wreak havoc—they hadn't been involved in a prolonged bush war since Vietnam. The Colombians, by contrast, were well into their fifth decade of fighting. By 2008, training Colombian commandos in the art of tropical warfare was like sending a jaguar to jungle school.

"Our guys had more trouble operating in the jungle than the Colombians," Brownfield said. "The fundamental lesson was that the Colombians were a hell of a lot better than we thought. Christ, these guys were probably the premier jungle special operations forces in the world."

These new units of Colombian commandos were the stealth troops, the "solitary men" who the paranoid guerrillas believed could live in the trees and monitor their every move. They carried night-vision goggles and satellite radios. To avoid being detected by the guerrillas' pet dogs, they smoked their uniforms over open fires before setting out and they never bathed during operations so they would take on the fetid smell of the jungle. Regular troops cooked over gas stoves and had to be resupplied by choppers every ten days. But these units could operate on their own for months at a time. They carried a Colombian version of the American Meal, Ready-to-Eat, or MRE. But while the U.S. troops often consumed two or three MREs per day, the Colombians made do with one. Hammocks left rope marks on trees and could help the rebels count the number of enemy troops in the zone, so the commandos dozed on plastic ground sheets. Rather than hacking their way through the jungle with machetes, they pushed through the foliage with their arms. They never marched in single file, and they moved across rough jungle scrub to avoid leaving a trail.

The radio intercepts indicated that the rebels would soon be heading up the Apaporis between the hamlets of Cornelio and Dos Ríos, a well-traveled route that had also been identified by John Frank Pinchao, the escaped policeman. To make full use of the advanced warning, the U.S. government supplied the Colombian commandos with three cameras that could feed video and stills back to the embassy via a satellite connection. Wired to sensor devices, the cameras would begin snapping pictures at the first sign of movement. The trick was getting the cameras in position.

To avoid tipping off the guerrillas, the helicopter-borne troops rappelled down cables into the wilderness, then spent four days hiking into the zone. At the river, they came upon a set of rapids known as El Venado where the rebels and their hostages would be forced to get out of their boats and portage for about three miles along the north bank. They also found prepositioned stocks of food and gasoline that seemed to confirm that the rebels were headed in their direction. It was the perfect spot to hide the cameras.

Brownfield was antsy for images. He wanted to confirm that the FARC group they were tracking had custody of Keith, Marc, and Tom. He wanted an exact body count of hostages and rebels, as well as information on the quality of their arms, the amount of food and other supplies they were carrying, and the speed at which they were traveling. And though he suspected the brutish and depraved Enrique Gafas was the ringleader, Brownfield wanted hard evidence. All of these clues would help in the planning of a snatch operation or a more complicated cordon maneuver.

But the cameras had been designed for more hospitable, open-air settings—like the Iraqi desert—not the pounding rain and equatorial heat of the jungle where the thick canopy blocked the satellite signal. To work out the kinks, the Colombian troops spent another four days retracing their path to the El Venado rapids. But the cameras still didn't work. So the troops had to hike back a third time.

"It took a phenomenal amount of work to get them deployed and they offered no value," said a frustrated Brownfield, who by that time was ready to drop-kick the faulty photographic gear into the Amazon. "We could never get the damned things to work."

But old-fashioned persistence paid off. On February 16, one of the twelve-man commando teams heard people laughing, shouting, and cutting down trees. A Colombian sergeant and a corporal crept to the river's edge where the Apaporis formed a hairpin curve about ten miles downstream from the El Venado rapids. On the opposite bank, where the water narrowed to form a sandy beach, they spotted six people in dark blue sweat suits. Later, a group of twenty-five men arrived at the river and began stripping off their clothes to bathe. These men carried rifles.

Lying on their stomachs and peering through binoculars, the two NCOs tracked every detail of the FARC camp. A female cook ordered three rebels to help her carry an aluminum cooking pot down to the waterside. One guerrilla recharged a battery with solar panels as several colleagues lazily tossed fishing lines into the current. At lunchtime, the rebels disappeared. Then, at about 1:30 p.m., three rebels marched five men at gunpoint down to the beach. The prisoners stripped off their T-shirts and waded into the water.

Three of the detainees were bigger and had lighter complexions than the others. They were speaking English and one of them shouted: "Hey, Marc!"

"I carried photos of the hostages and double-checked," said the sergeant. "They were the Americans."

After forty minutes, the rebels marched the hostages inland and the soldiers withdrew to their bivouac on the opposite side of the river to radio the news to Bogotá. The operation marked the first time Colombian troops had ever managed to sneak up on a FARC camp and observe how they handled their hostages.

Over the next three days, the two soldiers monitored the site from a steep embankment about fifteen feet above the water. Every day, Keith, Marc, and Tom came down to the river to bathe. Once, Marc swam two-thirds of the way across the stream and came within 150 feet of the commandos. On another afternoon, the sound of a hunter's rifle put the rebels on high alert. They ordered the hostages to hide, but instead of scampering to the north side of the river where the army commandos were positioned, they retreated to the south side.

The commandos fantasized about grabbing the hostages, then laying down protective gunfire until rescue helicopters could pick them up. But their mission was to gather intelligence. Any rescue attempt involving the American hostages required approval from the Bush administration. Besides, the twelve-man commando team was badly outnumbered. Perhaps a hundred rebels were holding the Americans as well as twelve other hostages at two camps separated by a short pathway on the south side of the river. The sergeant figured that one false move would provoke a massacre.

"It was very frustrating," he said. "We were so close but we couldn't do anything for the hostages."

The Americans had no clue they were being watched but often imagined the scenario.

"I would scan the vegetation while taking a piss," Tom said. "And I would wonder: 'Is anybody out there?'"

BACK IN BOGOTÁ, U.S. AND COLOMBIAN authorities had to act fast before the rebels decamped. American commandos were in-country and capable of mounting a blitzkrieg rescue mission. But the reconnaissance team was on the wrong side of the river and could not penetrate the FARC camp to describe the layout, the position of the guards, and the physical location of the hostages.

Besides, "it wasn't real-time information," Brownfield said. "There wasn't a man on the radio saying: 'I'm watching the hostages right now.'"

So a snatch operation was temporarily ruled out. That left the option of the so-called humanitarian cordon, President Uribe's plan for encircling the guerrillas, tightening the noose, then talking the guards into turning over the hostages. But that sort of mission had never been tried before anywhere in the world. It was unclear how long the effort would take, how many troops would be required and how the negotiators would open up communications with the hostage-takers.

The final blueprint seemed like a twelve-step crapshoot. It called for helicopters to drop about 250 Colombian troops, accompanied by a few dozen U.S. commandos, about fifteen miles from the FARC camp. Rather than taking the water routes that would give them away, the troops had to walk overland, covering just a few miles per day. It would take about a week to home in on the guerrillas.

After the troops had surrounded the FARC camp, aircraft would zoom over the site dropping leaflets explaining that the rebels were trapped but would not come under attack. Dry runs indicated that the plane would be audible from the ground for less than thirty seconds, thus planners figured the rebel guards would be unlikely to panic and shoot the hostages. Next, a helicopter with broadcast capabilities would fly in circles announcing what radio frequencies the rebels could use to contact the army. All other frequencies would be jammed to prevent the rebels from consulting with the FARC secretariat. One hour later, approaching troops speaking through bullhorns would deliver the same message. Amid the barrage of army communications from all sides, the rebels would realize they were surrounded. Finally, another aircraft would drop by parachute a satellite telephone so the rebels could open up talks with Colombian hostage negotiators accompanied by FBI agents.

The plan was spectacular, audacious, unprecedented . . . and Brownfield gave it little chance for success. He didn't think the hostages would be killed. But he knew the difficulties involved in inserting a battalion into the jungle without being detected. And how would they prevent the rebels from slipping through their ring of fire power in dense forest where it was almost impossible to see or hear another person just fifty feet away?

Still, he harbored a filament of hope. The cordon plan seemed like the least bad of a bunch of not very good options. Besides, after five years of failure, the Americans finally had some hard intelligence on the whereabouts of Keith, Marc, and Tom. Brownfield explained the enterprise to officials at the Defense and State departments who, in turn, informed national security adviser Stephen Hadley, who signed on to the plan. It was time to throw the dice.

The helicopters launched and about nine hundred troops began slogging through the swamps and tangled undergrowth at a snail's pace heading for the Apaporis. But the rebels were already breaking camp. The Colombian sergeant and the corporal, who had been spying on the guerrillas for five days, watched as rebels filled several boats with food and camping gear, then sped away. The next day the hostages were put aboard the vessels and motored upriver toward the El Venado rapids. The first soldiers taking part in the military's cordon operation reached the empty FARC camp two days later.

Though Brownfield later claimed that the Bush administration approved the operation within twenty-four hours of receiving confirmation of the American hostages' whereabouts, one Colombian official involved in the planning vented his frustration.

"One of the reasons the February operation failed was because of the slow decision-making process in the United States," he said. "Everything had to go through Washington, every plan had to have a contingency. We planned too much and when we got there the hostages were gone."

At that point, the troops shifted their attention to the area around the El Venado rapids, where the useless cameras were hidden. Just downriver from the rapids the soldiers spotted about eighty guerrillas while an army patrol farther upstream watched as rebels came ashore with dozens of life jackets, apparently to transport the hostages. The troops, including embedded American Green Berets, tried to set up another cordon. First, they formed a ring around the guerrillas measuring six miles in diameter. Slowly, they crept forward, closing the circle to about three miles.

Keith, Marc, and Tom sensed that they were being hemmed in. Two of their guards, sent ahead of the pack, had already been killed; meanwhile the rebels had moved them downriver, then suddenly changed course and headed back upriver. They could hear aircraft and it felt like their group was being herded from above by helicopters. At one point, Marc found the fresh remains of an MRE ration and licked the salt from an empty packet of peanuts.

"Being pushed, in a way, felt good," Tom said. "We were exhausted, we were ragged, and our supply lines were getting torn up. But it was a good feeling knowing that the guerrillas weren't waltzing around the country-side totally relaxed."

All along, their food stocks were running down.

"We'd take a midday break and make a big tub of coffee and some popcorn because there was no more food," Keith said. By that point, U.S. Special Forces embeds had crept so close to the hostages that, on several occasions, they smelled popcorn.

Still, about twelve hundred feet lay between each of the soldiers in the cordon. And it soon became apparent that the rebels and their hostages had slipped through the porous perimeter. Something had spooked them. Later, an army patrol came upon a pair of wooden boats. Inside were two of the three high-tech cameras.

The insurgents escaped with a vintage feint. They sent a few rebels southwest into the Sierra de Chiriquibete foothills in Caquetá state leaving an obvious trail for the army troops to follow. But the bulk of the guerrillas and all of their hostages moved northeast into Guaviare state along a tributary to the Apaporis. The fifteen hostages were then split into three groups and sent in different directions, with Enrique Gafas keeping custody of Íngrid Betancourt, two Colombian soldiers, and the three Americans. As a further precaution, the rebels stayed off their radios.

By mid-March, the trail of the hostages had gone cold and most of the U.S. Special Operations Forces returned to the United States. Brownfield was livid. The Colombian troops had moved heaven and earth to install the cameras and they had not only malfunctioned, they made things worse by tipping off the guerrillas.

"The bottom line is we lost them," Brownfield said. "I'd been kicking myself in the ass over the cameras. Fuck! We got sloppy! We got caught!"

But as the diplomat fumed, the American hostages rejoiced. The cameras had been placed in a vital FARC transit point, a place so private that it was almost like hiding surveillance gear in somebody's bathroom. On the day the rebel prison warden Enrique Gafas spotted one of the American spy cameras, the blood drained from his face. He looked like he'd seen a ghost.

"The rebels were blown away by that," Keith said. "They were in absolute shock and dismay to see a camera system in a place where they thought they were totally safe."

"That was a changing point for me, for all three of us," Marc added. "Because that's when we started to think that there's some serious American involvement in the pursuit of us."

EVER SINCE HE WAS ELECTED IN 2002, President Álvaro Uribe vowed that under his watch the armed forces would take down at least one member of the FARC's ruling secretariat. He had notched some important triumphs, like the arrest and extradition of Simón Trinidad. And the military had captured or killed a handful of other key FARC leaders, including Martín Sombra, the FARC commander who guarded the three American hostages in 2004 and liked to feed his prisoners boa constrictor stew. These midlevel chieftains were the glue that held the organization together.

Still, there had been no marquee names among the fallen. After forty-four years of fighting, the FARC's seven-man secretariat remained intact, like some unholy priesthood. And with Manuel "Sureshot" Marulanda and the rest of his top commanders still calling the shots, the FARC, though battered, seemed poised to survive and regroup.

But March 2008 would mark the blackest month ever for the FARC, a disastrous four-week period of bloodshed and chaos, and it seemed to signal the fall of the house of Sureshot. The first to feel the heat was Raúl Reyes.

The FARC's longtime spokesman, Raúl Reyes, was a well-known if not especially enlightening character. Pushing sixty, he was a gnomelike figure with a gray beard and glasses and an M4 rifle that was nearly as tall as he was. A Communist labor organizer and a town councilman in Caquetá, Reyes was briefly detained by the army in 1978. Fearing he would be killed for his leftist politics, he joined the FARC and won a series of promotions. He was named to the FARC secretariat and was rumored to be second or third in line to succeed Marulanda. During the peace talks with the Pastrana government, he was a key member of the rebel negotiating team and received visitors ranging from left-wing students to U.S. congressman Bill Delahunt.

Reyes was long on words, short on insight, and overflowing with Orwellian doublespeak. In his telling, FARC prisoners were "detained people," not hostages. Money collected at gunpoint was a "war tax," not an extortion payment. The brutal ways of the FARC were justified because the paramilitaries and the army also committed atrocities. War was a dirty business all around, Reyes said, so why point fingers at the FARC?

After the peace talks collapsed in 2002, Reyes took on a new mission. He became deeply involved in the push to trade hostages for FARC prisoners. He was the commander who sent Simón Trinidad on his ill-fated trip to Quito in an effort to negotiate a prisoner exchange. He was also the one who informed the French middleman in 2003 that his ransom payment for the release of Íngrid Betancourt had been delivered to a flimflam man who had made off with the money. When it came to the hostages, all roads led to Reyes.

But like Enrique Gafas and the First Front rebels holding the Americans, Reyes was getting a little careless. His area of operation included five camps in southern Putumayo state near the Ecuadorian border. But to sleep peacefully, he sometimes crossed the Putumayo River to a spot just inside of Ecuador. Ensconced in a foreign nation, Reyes figured he was untouchable. He began receiving outside visitors, including journalists, revolutionary tourists, and members of Ecuador's newly elected left-wing government.

"More than a guerrilla camp it was a public relations office for the FARC," said Manuel Olate, a member of the Chilean Communist Party, who traveled to the site to interview Reyes. "As we were leaving, other delegations were arriving."

What Reyes didn't know was that a member of his inner circle was feeding information to the Colombian Army for cash. On the evening of February 29, 2008, the informant revealed that Reyes would be receiving a foreign delegation about a mile across the border in Ecuadorian territory. Among his guests were five left-wing university students from Mexico who Colombian authorities later claimed were receiving classes in explosives. With Reyes pinpointed, Uribe gave the green light to attack.

Shortly after midnight, a squadron of Super Tucanos flew toward the Ecuadorian border and hit Reyes's camp with laser-guided bombs. Lucía Morett, one of the Mexican students, woke up to see a tree next to her rough wooden bunk on fire. "It was like a rain of lightning," she said. Morett survived with shrapnel wounds in her back, stomach, and buttocks. But the target was destroyed. Soldiers bagged up the lifeless body of Raúl Reyes, who was clad in a bloody T-shirt emblazoned with the image of Sureshot. The informant later collected a Colombian government reward worth about $2 million.

"Money is what moves things," said José Obdulio Gaviria, a top adviser to President Uribe. "It works because the infiltrator, the Judas, can pinpoint the target to within a few meters."

The cross-border operation that killed twenty-three other guerrillas and "students" brought loud protests from around Latin America. But in Colombia, the death of the FARC spokesman set off celebrations. His demise broke the myth of invincibility of the FARC secretariat and proved that the jungle was no longer an impregnable rebel fortress.

But the families of the hostages fretted. Once again, battlefield triumphs only seemed to derail peaceful efforts to save their loved ones. After the FARC unilaterally released the six politicians to Hugo Chávez—the first breakthrough in years—the hostilities seemed to slam the door on further liberations. Outside intermediaries didn't even know whom to talk to anymore because their main point of contact was lying in a Bogotá morgue. Back in the United States, the relatives of Keith, Marc, and Tom were already deeply depressed because on January 29, Simón Trinidad had been sentenced to sixty years in prison. They feared that the FARC, in a tit-for-tat move, might impose similar sentences on the American hostages. And as if this sequence of cataclysmic setbacks wasn't bad enough, it appeared that regionwide war was breaking out.

Angry over the violent raid into his nation's territory, Ecuadorian president Rafael Correa, a Chávez ally, broke diplomatic relations with Colombia. A few days after the raid, Chávez branded President Uribe a "criminal" and a "lapdog" of the United States and warned him not to try something similar on Venezuelan soil. Then, in a dramatic flourish broadcast on live television, Chávez abruptly ordered his defense minister to move ten battalions, including tanks and aircraft, to the Venezuela-Colombia border.

The crisis was defused at an emergency summit in the Dominican Republic where Uribe, Chávez, and Correa shook hands. By then, both Chávez and Correa had been knocked back on the defensive thanks to three laptop computers and two hard drives that had been recovered at the FARC camp where Raúl Reyes was killed. Thousands of documents, e-mails, and photos on the hard drives revealed a warm and growing relationship between the FARC and top Venezuelan officials, who apparently offered the guerrillas money, weapons, and political support and agreed to help isolate Uribe.

Ecuadorian officials also came across in the documents as FARC supplicants. The e-mails indicated that Interior Minister Gustavo Larrea had met with Reyes and promised to post police and army commanders along the border area with Colombia who would be more tolerant of the FARC. According to the documents, Larrea also seemed to suggest that the FARC should release one of its hostages to the Ecuadorian government to help boost the standing of President Correa. Larrea portrayed these efforts as a strictly humanitarian gesture. But Gaviria, President Uribe's top aide, had another term for what the Ecuadorians were doing: trafficking in hostages.

AMID COLOMBIA'S DUSTUPS WITH ITS NEIGHBORS another calamitous blow to the FARC was nearly overlooked: the mob-style murder of Iván Ríos.

Short, soft-spoken, and with a wispy mustache, Iván Ríos was, like

Raúl Reyes, a little giant within the FARC. Though he privately admitted that the FARC would never win the war, he soldiered on and was rewarded with an appointment to the FARC's ruling secretariat in 2003. But the promotion came just as the FARC began its long, downhill slide. By November 2007, Ríos and his men were isolated in the mountains of western Caldas state. A rebel deserter, who had been part of Ríos's security ring, was feeding information to the military. Troops spent the next three months encircling the rebels and cutting off their supplies. It was then that Pedro Montoya decided to act.

Montoya had joined the FARC as a teenager and gradually worked his way up the ranks to become the main bodyguard for Ríos. But now, as the military moved in, Ríos's men accused Montoya of spying for the army. They considered executing the alleged traitor but were outmaneuvered by Montoya. That same night, he snuck up on the sleeping Ríos, put a pistol to his forehead, and pulled the trigger. He also executed the rebel leader's girlfriend. Then, to prove the identity of the dead guerrilla with the idea of collecting the $2.5 million bounty, Montoya pulled out a knife, hacked off Ríos's right hand, then wrapped the bloody paw in a piece of cloth.

"We killed Ivan Ríos," Montoya announced as the three FARC bodyguards surrendered to a police patrol. Then, as if donating an exhibition piece to the Black Museum of horrors at Scotland Yard, he held out the severed appendage, saying: "Here's the proof."

Stunned officers placed the hand in a Styrofoam cooler for transport back to Bogotá where Ríos's identity was confirmed. Though both men were asleep when they died, at least Raúl Reyes was killed in an enemy attack. Ríos was whacked and mutilated by his aide-de-camp. It was the clearest sign yet that the FARC was cracking.

Then came news that the mighty oak himself had fallen. On March 26, at 6:30 p.m., Manuel "Sureshot" Marulanda, the FARC's maximum leader and the oldest guerrilla commander in the world, died of a heart attack. He was seventy-eight.

Since first taking up arms in 1949, Marulanda had outfoxed his adversaries, built up a 17,000-strong rebel army, and taken the FARC into the twenty-first century. But to the end, he had been a stubborn, ruthless commander. He encouraged war crimes, like kidnapping, and endorsed the rebel move into drug trafficking, then stood by as the overwhelming majority of Colombians turned against the FARC for its cruel ways. He made the enormous strategic blunder of rejecting the olive branch extended by the Pastrana government. When he finally expired, his rebel army had been reduced by half and was light-years away from achieving its ultimate goal of marching into Bogotá. Marulanda had plowed the sea. He died with his forty-something girlfriend at his side amid an army offensive that had squeezed guerrilla supply lines so badly that his bodyguards lacked salt for their food.

"For the first time," said Defense Minister Juan Manuel Santos, "the end of the FARC is in sight."

But unlike Peru's Shining Path, a fanatical Maoist rebel group that had a rigid, vertical command structure and collapsed after the 1992 capture of its chieftain, Abimael Guzmán, the FARC leadership was spread out among seven, semiautonomous blocs. The FARC adopted this structure after the entire rebel leadership was nearly killed in a 1990 military bombardment. And as Marulanda aged, several bloc commanders were groomed to replace him.

The new FARC leader, Alfonso Cano, joined the rebels in the early 1980s and was the organization's chief ideologue. He grew up among a family of Bogotá intellectuals and helped the FARC connect with leftist university students. But he was viewed with suspicion by battle-hardened rebel commanders from peasant stock, and after Cano replaced Sureshot, it was unclear whether he commanded the fealty of all sectors within the FARC. Some higher-ups had pushed for the ascension of Jorge Briceño, better known as Mono Jojoy. He was the group's longtime field commander who was credited with a string of rebel triumphs in the late 1990s.

Given the split loyalties, it was widely believed that Cano would launch new military strikes in order to assert his authority. Goodwill gestures and more unilateral hostage releases by the FARC now seemed out of the question. Thus, a year that began with the discovery of the toddler Emmanuel in Bogotá, the release of six rebel prisoners, and a widening international campaign to free the hostages gave way to fumbled rescue operations, the brief threat of war in the Andes, and the death of the FARC operative who held the keys to freedom for the prisoners. On the surface, the prospect of

Keith, Marc, and Tom getting out of the jungle alive seemed further away than ever.

"I would like to add one more message to those who hold our people," Brownfield said at a somber ceremony at the U.S. embassy marking the fifth anniversary of the kidnappings of the U.S. contractors. "I would say to them that abusing other human beings is not the act of a warrior, or a soldier or a revolutionary; it is the act of a sick and weak institution. You are not soldiers. You are not revolutionaries. Five years is enough. As Moses said to Pharaoh, 'Let our people go.'"

CHAPTER 24

THE UNTHINKABLE

What is acting but lying?
—SIR LAURENCE OLIVIER

THE EXPRESSION "MAN IN THE MIDDLE" refers to a classic electronic deception in which an outsider inserts himself between two communicating parties. The two sides believe they are speaking to each other when, in reality, they are connected to the outside invader who can then delete or modify the original messages or invent new ones. Amid the great unraveling of the FARC—which at first seemed to throw up new roadblocks for the hostages—Colombian authorities realized there were opportunities to be seized. They began to focus on the FARC's communications system and eventually hit upon an ingenious variant of "man in the middle."

The key was the death of Raúl Reyes. In his role as guerrilla spokesman, Reyes had been in constant contact with the top FARC commanders. He was the central switchboard for the rebels and the point man on the hostages. With Reyes out of the picture, the rebel group seemed to operate less like a disciplined military organization and more like a spread-out collection of gangs who often had no idea what their partners in crime were up to.

Besides Reyes, Manuel "Sureshot" Marulanda, who had led the FARC for forty-four years, had also been lost. Thus, the remaining rebel chieftains were uncertain about long-term plans for the hostages. Clarity was difficult to achieve because the rebels knew their cell and satellite telephone calls were being intercepted. Even brief conversations could allow the military to home in on the signals and locate them. In response, FARC commanders often passed along sensitive information through human couriers—a process that could take weeks—or via coded radio messages. Speaking in short bursts, FARC radio operators disguised their instructions in a highly practiced babel of words, numbers, and algorithms.

Army cryptologists had deciphered many of these codes while carefully noting the tone, rhythm, and meter of the radio operators. But rather than passively listening in to the radio traffic, Colombian officials now contemplated actively manipulating the messages. They had nothing to lose. A military operation might get the hostages killed while President Uribe's plan for a "humanitarian cordon" had failed. Thus, Colombian officials gave the green light to use electronic warfare in the hopes of mounting an elaborate sting operation. They would play the rebels, and the rebels would never know they were being played—until it was too late.

"To fool and to trick people is part of the game," said Defense Minister Juan Manuel Santos. "So I told army intelligence to be creative. Be audacious. Think the unthinkable."

Intelligence officers found inspiration in a wide range of sources: from the film *Ocean's Eleven* to the Allied feints leading up to D-Day to the 1976 raid on Entebbe Airport in Uganda in which Israeli commandos disguised as members of Idi Amin's presidential guard freed one hundred hostages. The agents studied past FARC operations, especially the fake bomb threat that allowed the rebels to seize twelve state legislators in Cali— eleven of whom were now dead. Finally, the intelligence team drew motivation from the showy unilateral hostage releases in January and February, operations that were broadcast on live television in which the Venezuelans were cast as heroes while Colombian authorities seemed like hapless by-standers.

"That put more pressure on the army to show some results," said Vice President Francisco Santos, the cousin of the defense minister. "It forced them to take operational risks that they otherwise might not have taken."

Soon, high-tech sharpies from the army's intelligence branch began focusing on radio transmissions between Mono Jojoy, the head of the FARC's Eastern Bloc, and César, the commander of the First Front that was holding Íngrid Betancourt, the three Americans, and eleven police-men and soldiers. The First Front fell under the umbrella of the Eastern Bloc, thus César answered to Mono Jojoy.

To protect themselves, the two men almost never got on the airwaves. Instead, they relied on subordinates to speak for them. Unless hindered by bad weather or military operations, a woman named Andrea sent short-wave radio messages three times a day on behalf of Mono Jojoy to five dif-ferent front commanders, including César. Radio operators for the front commanders then passed the messages to their bosses and later replied to Andrea, who, in turn, relayed the information to Mono Jojoy.

To enhance security, during the initial conference call Andrea in-structed each radio operator to switch to a different frequency. Then, one by one, she spoke to the individual operators in private to impart Mono Jo-joy's orders and to receive information from the fronts. As a result, the guer-rillas of one front—a typical FARC front was made up of between a hundred and four hundred rebels—were detached and largely ignorant of the activities of their rebel colleagues from other fronts.

After studying how the FARC compartmentalized its radio messages, the intelligence team back in Bogotá came up with a modified version of a "man in the middle" attack. They would try to convince the rebels to briefly turn over custody of the hostages to a fake humanitarian mission made up of army commandos who would spirit them to freedom. If the army could perpetuate this alternative reality, no shots would be fired and the mission would make the raid on Entebbe, which left nearly fifty dead, look positively savage.

The intelligence team would wait for a lull in guerrilla communications. Then an army agent posing as Andrea would get on the radio for a fake conference call and instruct the radio operator for César's First Front, a guerrilla nicknamed the Indian, to switch to another frequency. During the initial conference call, other intelligence agents would pose as radio operators from the other four FARC fronts to keep the Indian on the hook. But once they locked onto another frequency and were alone, the fake Andrea—pretending to speak for Mono Jojoy—would send bogus orders through the Indian to César.

"Mono Jojoy and César would think they were speaking to each other," said Santos, the defense minister. "But they would be speaking to us."

When the real Andrea got back on the radio, another intelligence agent, posing as the Indian, would respond in the conference calls and the one-on-one conversations. Finally, to maintain a sense of normalcy, César's more innocuous messages that were unrelated to the hostages would be passed on by army intelligence to Mono Jojoy.

The complicated hoax was a one-shot deal. The wrong accent, a bungled code, a suspicious order would blow their cover. But several factors worked in the army's favor. A fierce military campaign targeting Mono Jojoy kept him on the run and out of radio contact for long stretches, leaving his subordinates largely on their own.

"The key was to keep Mono Jojoy off the fucking air," said U.S. ambassador William Brownfield. "The armed forces drew up a box where they believed Mono Jojoy was located. And they were dropping bombs and moving battalions around. They were just going to town on that box."

Army intelligence officers were confident that their orders would be followed because that was how the FARC worked. Instructions from Mono Jojoy, one of the highest-ranking rebel commanders, were to be obeyed unconditionally. Insubordination was punishable by death. Finally, the recent loss of three of the FARC's top seven leaders—Raúl Reyes, Iván Ríos, and Sureshot—provoked chaos and confusion up and down the chain of command.

As American cryptographer Bruce Schneier noted, man-in-the-middle attacks did not work when the two communicating parties enjoyed a shared history and friendship and recognized each other's voices. Sniffing out the army's ruse required context, but due to the rebel group's command-and-control breakdowns and the deaths of its senior leaders, the FARC guerrillas didn't have any.

"None of this would have happened if Raúl Reyes had not been killed," said one high-ranking State Department official. "He was information central in the FARC for all things relating to the hostages. If Reyes had been vetting the messages . . . he would have recognized right away that something was not correct."

To mimic the key FARC radio operators, intelligence officers selected two female employees whose voices sounded similar to those of Andrea and the Indian. Several male agents were also selected to impersonate the other operators during the radio conference calls. To re-create the ambient sound of the jungle, the intelligence team set up its radio operation at a campsite on a forested 9,500-foot mountaintop near Bogotá. At first, the team simply monitored FARC radio traffic. The female agents studied the voices of Andrea and the Indian and practiced speaking to each other in code. Then, on May 28, they made their move.

The bombing campaign targeting Mono Jojoy had kept Andrea off the air for three straight days. Operators for the front commanders who were expecting Andrea's messages turned on their radios three times a day, and if there was no news within ten minutes, they switched them off. Taking advantage of the silence, the false Andrea went on the air.

She first asked if the radio operators of the five FARC fronts were listening. All five were on board. She then instructed the Indian to speak with her on another frequency. When the two were alone, she told the Indian that from now on the daily conference calls would take place on yet a third frequency. On this new frequency, the team of intelligence agents at the army campsite would mimic the other FARC radio operators. From that point forward, the Indian would be completely isolated from her FARC cohorts and would be speaking directly to the Colombian Army.

Now that the Indian—and in effect First Front commander César—was isolated, the intelligence agents decided to test their system. They were unclear about the location of the First Front's fifteen hostages and whether they were still separated. So the false Andrea sent the Indian a message.

"How is the cargo?" she asked, referring to the prisoners. "How are they distributed? Are you in a position where you could receive an international commission?"

A day later, the Indian replied.

"Greetings," she said. "The cargo is fine. They are separated." The Indian then went on to explain the general location of the First Front's three groups of hostages. It appeared that the FARC jailer Enrique Gafas had moved the Americans into the area around the Itilla River in southern Guaviare state, the zone where César operated. At noon the next day, the false Andrea got back on the radio and told the Indian to bring the prisoners together and to prepare for the arrival of an international commission.

At that juncture, real-life events reinforced the army's work of fiction. Rumors that Íngrid Betancourt was deathly ill prompted the French government to send a jet with a mobile hospital and experts in tropical diseases to Colombia hoping to receive rebel permission to treat Betancourt. Reports of the aircraft's arrival were all over the radio news programs monitored by the rebels, and César would probably surmise that the medics were part of the commission.

Soon afterward, army intelligence officers informed the high command of their ongoing operation to trick the guerrillas. "When they first brought the idea to me, I said: 'My God, it sounds too good to be true,'" said Santos, the defense minister. "But I needed proof that this could work. Otherwise I wouldn't take the idea to the president."

The intel agents delivered. They told Santos that intercepted radio messages indicated that the First Front's three groups of hostages were being marched through the jungle to a single rendezvous point. The fish had taken the bait.

ON JUNE 11, THE FALSE ANDREA, working from the army campsite on the mountaintop near Bogotá, sent another message to César's radio operator. She instructed the First Front commander to keep the information about the international commission a secret and to stay off his satellite phone. Army officers feared that even though their hoax had severed César's radio link to his boss, Mono Jojoy, he might pass the news of the hostage operation to other rebels via his sat phone.

The intelligence officers also blocked Mono Jojoy's legitimate messages to César. When, for example, the real Andrea tried to tell César to maintain tight control over the hostages and to send $250,000 to another FARC unit, her message never got through. Instead, the order was intercepted by the agent impersonating César's radio operator. The false Indian then replied to the real Andrea that the hostages were secure but that due to army operations, sending the money would be impossible.

Incredibly, the scheme was working so well that events were moving almost too fast. With the three groups of hostages converging, the army scrambled to devise a plan to safely extract them from the hands of the FARC.

Recalling the recent arrival of the French hospital plane, the army agents considered mounting a fake medical mission to touch down in the jungle and treat the hostages. But it was also unclear how they would make their getaway without provoking a lethal shoot-out.

General Mario Montoya, the Colombian Army commander, came up with an alternative. He suggested sending a bogus order from Mono Jojoy telling César that a humanitarian mission would transfer the hostages on helicopters to another FARC-dominated region. There, the hostages would meet Alfonso Cano, the newly named FARC leader, who wanted to take stock of the prisoners. The beauty of Montoya's plan was that it presented a plausible pretext for the choppers to lift off with all the hostages on board.

If the effort fell apart, Plan B was for hundreds of troops to move into place to carry out a blitzkrieg version of the humanitarian cordon. Commandos would be airlifted to the area around the rescue site and could be on the ground within eleven minutes of any distress signal. Once surrounded, perhaps César could be persuaded to turn over the hostages.

"It was risk-free for the hostages," Santos said. "If the rebels found out, they would simply not show up at the meeting point. Or if they figured it out during the operation, they might shoot our people but not the hostages."

Soon the Americans found out. The Colombians had put off telling U.S. officials to maintain secrecy. They also wanted to wait until planning and training for the operation were so far advanced that it couldn't be reversed. But eventually U.S. intelligence agents reestablished the general whereabouts of the hostages. Then they figured out that some sort of deception plan was under way, as the three groups of prisoners were moved together. Finally, on President Uribe's orders, Santos invited Brownfield to his house on the evening of June 25 to explain the operation.

"He was flabbergasted," Santos said. "I told the ambassador: 'We're going to do this anyway. You can approve it or not. That's your prerogative. But maybe you can help us.'"

Brownfield agreed that the risk to the hostages was low. He pledged full cooperation but did not push for the inclusion of U.S. Special Forces in the actual rescue mission because he did not want to incorporate outsiders at the last minute into a Colombian team that had been rehearsing for weeks. He thought the plan was ingenious, but it had so many moving parts that he gave it only a 50 percent chance of success.

"Up until the last minute, I was one of the skeptics," he said.

But the Colombians had done their homework. Intelligence officers had closely studied videos of the two Venezuelan-led missions to pick up the six hostages freed by the FARC earlier in the year. Those operations included a mission chief; representatives from Cuba, Venezuela, and Colombia; and European members of the International Committee of the Red Cross who arrived on two Russian-made MI-17 helicopters painted white with orange trim. For maximum authenticity, the army team decided to mount a copycat operation.

"We watched the Venezuelan videos every day. We studied every detail," said one intelligence officer who would play the role of the mission chief.

They would have to move fast. General Montoya first suggested July 12 as the rescue date. Fearing that Mono Jojoy and César would catch on if the man-in-the-middle deception dragged on too long, Santos demanded that the army move up the date. The new deadline was set for July 2. Gathered in a Defense Ministry war room in front of a small-scale mock-up of the rescue site, army officers pondered how to convince the FARC to place its most precious booty in the hands of outsiders. They would have to put together a convincing mise-en-scène.

A crafty FARC veteran in his forties, César seemed likely to sniff out any obvious anomalies. But César's troops were also showing some chinks in their armor. These were the guerrillas who had lost track of Emmanuel, the baby born in the jungle. In addition, César was known to be upset about the recent arrest of his common-law wife, Nancy Conde, the rebel logistics guru who had become entangled in the FBI operation run out of Miami to tap the FARC's communications. He also had a towering ego and, in the end, this was the characteristic in César's psychological profile that intelligence agents decided to exploit.

In subsequent messages, the false Andrea told César that he would personally deliver the fifteen hostages to FARC maximum leader Alfonso Cano. César had never met Cano, and a face-to-face with the FARC's number one would be deemed a huge honor. To enhance César's sense of security—since once aboard the helicopter he would be badly outnumbered by hostages—he was told he could bring along one of his aides. All FARC operations were given code names so César was informed that the prisoner transfer would be baptized in honor of the recently departed Sureshot: Operation Manuel Marulanda.

Next, the intelligence team drew up a cast of eleven characters who would play the roles of the mission personnel. For international flavor, the mission chief was given an Italian accent and the exotic name of Russi. His deputy was supposedly an Arabic speaker from the Middle East while a third team member, who had lived in Australia and spoke English with a Down Under accent, would pretend to hail from Brisbane. Other impersonators included a doctor, three nurses, and a reporting team from Venezuela's state-run Telesur channel, who were issued Roland Hedley–style field vests and Bermuda shorts with multiple pockets. Rounding out the group were two fake guerrillas who would help put César at ease and purportedly held the GPS coordinates for the meeting place with Alfonso Cano. One of the rebel impersonators happened to be an amateur boxer. The other was intimately familiar with the way of the tribe: he had once belonged to the FARC but had switched sides.

The agent playing mission chief Russi was a veteran of dangerous behind-the-lines missions and had some doubts about his cohorts. Before striking out in his new role, he convinced his bosses to pay for acting classes for the entire team. He wanted professionals to help the agents overcome stage fright and fully embody their roles. The players would have to keep cool, improvise, and play their parts with Shakespearian heft if there happened to be a radical turn of events once they were inside the shark tank.

The agents showed up at one of Bogotá's top theater academies and presented themselves as teachers who would be putting on a play to celebrate the hundredth anniversary of their high school. For $2,000, the instructor gave them a crash course in Method acting, and began by urging his students to assume the roles of animals. Russi, the coolheaded mission chief, pretended to be an owl. The agent who would play the hyperactive TV reporter imagined he was a parrot. The professor also told the students to get comfortable in the skin of their characters—to wear the clothes, affect the accents, and call one another by their assumed names. The amateur players passed their first test. Though he wondered about his students' high-tech two-way military radios, the theater professor never caught on that he was teaching a pack of army agents.

Yet after observing this relatively youthful group, General Montoya frowned. Many of the agents looked like they were fresh out of spy school. Recalling some of the grizzled fifty-somethings who took part in the Venezuelan missions, he demanded potbellies and wrinkles. Several members of the team let their beards grow and went in for the geezer effect at beauty salons where gray streaks were added to their hair. Russi, the fake mission chief, who was thirty-seven, received a set of glasses and began slouching like an old man. The agents were especially meticulous about their wardrobe. They even had to dispose of their underwear, which was stamped with the logo of the Colombian Army. Their new threads were sent through washing machines to provide a lived-in look. And Montoya told them to fill their wallets with fake driver's licenses, business cards, and foreign currency.

They all claimed to work for a nongovernmental organization called the International Humanitarian Mission. Army agents mounted a Web site and set up a front office in Bogotá with scripted operators standing by just in case any FARC collaborators called to verify the authenticity of the group. The centerpiece of the organization's green, blue, and red logo was the silhouette of a dove.

As team members practiced their lines, technicians in an isolated hangar stood on ladders and used spray guns to transform two of the military's olive green MI-17 helicopters into innocent-looking white and orange humanitarian aircraft. All over the choppers they pasted logos of the fake International Humanitarian Mission and the universal symbol for no guns allowed—an AK-47 with a red slash through it. The birds now looked like replicas of the choppers involved in the Venezuelan missions.

A team of U.S. technicians then made several key modifications. In case things went wrong and the pilots had guns pressed to their temples, the Americans installed a device in the cockpit so they could, without speaking into their microphones, activate an emergency distress signal that would be picked up back at the forward-operating base in San José del Guaviare. They added electronic beaconing equipment so the choppers and team personnel could be tracked at all times. They also installed a hidden microphone in the camera of the fake reporter to allow officials to listen in while the operation played out. Finally, an American aircraft with electronic jamming gear was scheduled to fly overhead during the operation. That way, should César pull out his satellite telephone at the last minute to verify his instructions with Mono Jojoy, the call would never go through.

All the while, Colombian and U.S. officials were working out the details of a military cordon should the sting operation fall apart. But the members of the fake humanitarian mission were purposely kept in the dark about the details of the contingency plan. The idea was to keep them focused on the success of their own mission.

"We didn't want to contaminate them," said one intelligence officer involved in the planning. "We told them: 'Don't worry about Plan B. Worry about being a good Arab or a good journalist.'"

Brownfield, who had been involved in a series of briefings, delivered a final presentation via video conference on June 30 to the National Security Council. Shortly afterward, the ambassador dialed Juan Manuel Santos, the Colombian defense minister. Washington was on board.

THREE DAYS BEFORE THE HELICOPTERS WERE to launch, the intelligence team received a message from César. The First Front commander wanted to know if he and his lieutenant, Enrique Gafas, could carry pistols aboard the helicopters that would ferry them to the meeting with FARC leader Alfonso Cano.

It was an excruciating call. Armed guerrillas aboard the choppers would increase the likelihood of disaster. But if he were denied permission, it might dawn on César that all was not as it seemed. Besides, army officers knew that FARC rebels *never* went anywhere without their weapons. Even when he received the elegant Queen Noor of Jordan, who ventured into FARC-land during the peace talks in 1999, rebel spokesman Raúl Reyes had kept his M4 rifle by his side. So, after consulting with General Montoya, the intelligence team sent another message to César through the false Andrea: César and Gafas could bring their pistols.

But then the army caught another break. By sheer coincidence, French and Swiss mediators arrived in Colombia to make contact with FARC leader Alfonso Cano in an effort to promote a prisoner exchange. Though Colombian officials were skeptical about their aims, Santos, the defense minister, quickly realized that if the FARC learned about their mission it would reinforce the army's con game. So he made sure that President Uribe's spokesman told the news media about the arrival of the two envoys. The story was broadcast on Colombian radio and, in the wilderness of Guaviare state, the hostages and César heard the reports.

By then, the hostages realized something was about to happen. As they marched to the rendezvous point, they were for the first time during their years of captivity taken through populated areas and along rivers with lots of boat traffic. They camped near villages and the guerrillas brought them new rubber boots, underwear, socks, and backpacks in which to store their gear. Then there was the food. The rebels secured goodies they hadn't eaten in years, including chicken, fresh bread, cookies, ketchup, and mayonnaise. At one point, the rebels even brought the hostages chocolate ice-cream cones.

"We had vanilla-filled shortbread cookies, more rice and beans than we'd ever seen," said Keith, who dubbed their new location Fat Camp. "At every meal, we ate until we couldn't force down another bite, and the guards teased us for not being able to eat any more. It was like our mothers were there urging us to eat."

When the three clusters of hostages finally converged on a farm along the Inírida River in Guaviare, they numbered fifteen: Keith, Marc, Tom, Betancourt, four policemen, and seven soldiers. As they traded news and gossip, they speculated that another unilateral liberation might be in the works. Then, Enrique Gafas broke the news: an international mission with doctors would be arriving to speak with the hostages.

"We started writing letters in case there was an international journalist or a doctor, and we could tell them: 'Please take this to my family,'" Marc said.

Back at the army's mountaintop campsite, the false Andrea continued to manipulate César. In a radio message, she confirmed that on Wednesday, July 2, his rebel unit was to receive the international mission. A TV crew would be filming the operation so he and his troops were to be well armed and impeccably dressed to prove to the world that Colombia's military offensive had not defeated the FARC. And finally, the false Andrea gave César a VHF frequency so he could communicate with the helicopter pilots as they approached the rendezvous point.

But then the intelligence team received another disquieting message from César. He asked if he could bring four more rebels aboard the helicopter as protection from the angry hostages. Army officers figured it might prove impossible to subdue a half dozen guerrillas aboard the choppers without getting into a firefight. This time, they had to hold the line. So the false Andrea sent back a terse message to César: "Impossible."

Just to make sure that César didn't double-cross them, the mission planners decided that just one of the two helicopters would touch down to pick up the hostages. An MI-17 could carry thirty people. With two pilots, two crew members, the army agents, hostages, and César and Gafas, the aircraft would be packed and it would be impossible for César to bring along reinforcements. But in an effort to put César completely at ease, the army agents decided to send him another message, saying that the hostages were to be handcuffed.

THE LAST THING U.S. AMBASSADOR WILLIAM Brownfield wanted to do was jump on an airplane. He'd been holding up to five meetings per day in a cramped, sweltering situation room at the embassy to make sure that everything was on track for the mission, which had been dubbed Operation Check, as in checkmate. July 2 was lining up to be the most important day of Brownfield's thirty years in the U.S. Foreign Service. But on July 1, Senator John McCain, who was locked in a tight race for the presidency with Barack Obama, decided to burnish his foreign policy credentials with a trip to Colombia. McCain planned to visit the colonial resort city of Cartagena on the Caribbean coast. He expected to see the ambassador.

Brownfield wanted to call in sick, but he feared that if he stayed in Bogotá, people would start asking questions. To maintain a sense of normalcy, he flew to Cartagena. "The entire time I'm saying to myself: 'Why am I even here?'" Brownfield said. "I finally got back to Bogotá and went to bed at two thirty a.m. But I couldn't sleep worth a shit."

At the Tolemaida Military Base, meanwhile, the nine intelligence agents of the fake International Humanitarian Mission went through their final rehearsals. To boost their spirits, army commander General Mario Montoya made a surprise appearance. By now, the agents knew that César and Gafas would board the helicopter with pistols, so they devised a seating chart to make sure they were positioned at opposite ends of the helicopter and between the beefiest intelligence officers—including the amateur boxer. Montoya ordered them to pummel the rebels where it hurt. As he grabbed one of the agents to demonstrate a headlock, Montoya said, "After you neutralize him, hit him in the balls."

For added authenticity, the helicopter was supplied with fifteen white jackets for the hostages. FARC leader Alfonso Cano operated in the mountains of western Tolima state, and if that's where the hostages were heading, they would need warm clothes. And just in case things fell completely apart, the agents were issued survival packs, including flashlights, compasses, fishing lines, matches, and flares.

The original plan called for the team to leave Tolemaida on the morning of July 2, the day of the operation. They would land at an isolated farm near San José del Guaviare, then launch Operation Check around midday. But a storm system was moving in, and the choppers had to first cross the eastern ridge of the Andes Mountains to reach the jungle farm. So the team departed on the evening of July 1 just ahead of the bad weather. Before leaving, General Montoya pulled the team together for a group prayer.

"We are doing this for the good of our Colombian brethren," Montoya said. "You are the best of the best and you know that. You can go forward in peace because God is on the side of the good guys. And we are the good guys."

CHAPTER 25

CHECKMATE

All warfare is based on deception.
—SUN TZU

SIX WEEKS OF BRIEFINGS AND REHEARSALS had prepped the army thespians for the most perilous performance of their lives, a death-or-glory road show staged in the heart of FARC-land. As they bunked down inside a rustic farmhouse the night before the operation, the agents oozed confidence. Then they were attacked by Mother Nature's fifth column.

The clouds of mosquitoes, which paid no heed to the agents' deep-woods repellent, were more than just a nuisance. The guerrillas believed the helicopters were flying directly from Bogotá to the pickup point. If the army agents showed up with their faces pocked with insect bites, their entire story might unravel. So they spent a sleepless night eating chicken soup, chain-smoking cigarettes, and shooing away the bugs.

The next morning, as they waited for word to depart, the bleary-eyed team members suffered more mishaps. A softball-sized mango fell from a tree, bonking an agent on the head and giving him a bloody nose. Russi, the fake mission chief, tested a Taser device that they intended to use on César and Enrique Gafas inside the helicopter. He caught a rooster and zapped it with 20,000 volts. The bird collapsed but a few minutes later it jumped up and began squawking.

The team was supposed to be airborne by 11:00 a.m., but takeoff was delayed as army radio operators tried to send another message to César. To provide the FARC commander with a greater sense of security, he would be told that members of the humanitarian mission would handcuff the hostages before putting them on the helicopter. Bad weather blocked the radio signals, but just before midday the army's message got through to the Indian, César's radio operator. The pilots fired up the two white-and-orange Russian helicopters. Prior to boarding, the agents examined their disguises one last time . . . and stopped in their tracks. They were supposed to maintain the façade of city folks arriving from the Colombian capital, yet their boots were splattered with mud. They quickly washed their footwear with sponges and a bucket of water, then climbed up the ladder to the helicopter.

At about the same time, William Brownfield, who had also endured a sleepless night, was conferring with colleagues at the U.S. embassy. He was about to duck into the situation room to monitor the rescue operation when he received a phone call. On the other end of the line was a counterterrorism specialist in Washington who had no clue about the pending mission and wanted to discuss how to deal with the U.S. hostages.

"I say to myself, 'This can't be happening,'" Brownfield said. "In two hours' time we're going to launch the riskiest of operations and I have to talk to some stupid clown about sending down a team of specialists that will be completely irrelevant in another three hours."

Brownfield endured the thirty-minute call, then gathered with his embassy task force. Shortly after midday, his deputy passed the ambassador a message that the helicopters were in the air.

To CALM THEIR NERVES DURING THE forty-one-minute flight, the army agents practiced deep-breathing exercises and rehearsed their lines in their heads. Russi, the fake mission chief, took drops of valerian, a natural calmant often used by President Uribe to manage stress. Yet as he stared out the window at the forest and pasturelands of Guaviare state, Russi couldn't help thinking that their plan was working too well. What if the FARC was staging its own backwoods production? What if the guerrillas were scamming the scammers?

Tension mounted as the helicopter circled above the meeting point designated by César. The coordinates lay on the north side of the Inírida River, which cut through the middle of Guaviare state. The plan called for the team on board the first chopper to make radio contact with César before landing while the second chopper remained in the air. But as Russi and the others peered out of the round, Plexiglas windows of the MI-17, the terrain seemed deserted. The fake journalist got on the radio asking for César but there was no response

The choppers maintained a holding pattern. Suddenly, there was movement on the ground. Armed men appeared to be loading a group of civilians aboard boats. But they were moving to the wrong side of the river. By previous agreement, the hostages were supposed to be dressed in white T-shirts for easy recognition. However, the prisoners had refused to cooperate so none of them were wearing the proper attire. In addition, the rebels failed to comply with their promise to mark the landing zone with smoke grenades.

The agents considered their options. They hadn't even touched down and already things seemed to be spinning out of control. On the other hand, the guerrillas and the hostages were plainly visible from the air. It seemed unlikely that the rebels would give away their position if they thought something was amiss.

"We were asking one another: 'What do we do?'" said the fake journalist. "Since we were already there we decided that we might as well land."

KEITH, MARC, AND TOM MOVED TOWARD the light. For five and a half years they had been hidden away in the impenetrable rain forest, but with the humanitarian mission on the way, the FARC herded the hostages to a clearing beside the Inírida River. They relaxed and soaked up the sun.

Íngrid Betancourt, who held out hope that she might finally be released, kept pestering the guards for information and learned that a helicopter was on the way to transfer the hostages. Betancourt passed on the news to army corporal William Pérez, a self-taught medic who had cared for her during multiple illnesses. Once they were on board the chopper, Pérez suggested, they ought to skyjack the aircraft. Betancourt said nothing. But later she slipped Pérez the two sharp objects she'd managed to hide in her backpack: a fingernail clipper and a scissors.

Shortly after 1:00 p.m., Keith was taking a leak in the bushes when he heard the roar of the two Russian helicopters. One stayed in the air while the other came in low, then settled on the south side of the river next to a field full of waist-high coca bushes. Lines of heavily armed guerrillas in crisp new camouflage uniforms stood at attention while two rebel gunmen pointed M60 machine guns at the aircraft.

The first member of the nine-person team to emerge from the helicopter was the fake Arab, who added one last-minute but crucial detail to his disguise: over his shirt he placed a white bib with a Red Cross logo. The Switzerland-based institution tried to maintain a neutral image in order to safely operate in war zones. Unauthorized use of the organization's logo was prohibited by the Geneva Conventions, but army planners were striving for maximum authenticity and noted that Red Cross personnel had accompanied the Venezuelans on their two missions to pick up FARC hostages. The fake Arab stood for a full minute in the doorway of the chopper so the rebels could plainly see the red bull's-eye covering his chest.

Once on the ground, he pretended he couldn't speak Spanish. He smiled at the guerrillas and wandered around as if awestruck by the natural beauty of the landscape. Next out of the helicopter were the agents impersonating the Venezuelan news team. The fake reporter, who wore a red T-shirt, blue vest, and a bandanna around his neck, immediately launched into his melodramatic lines. "In the middle of the Colombian jungle," he barked into his microphone, "we are here for what will be a historic moment for Colombia and the world!"

Back inside the aircraft, the pilots noticed that some of the guerrillas were surrounding the helicopter. Fearing their cover was blown, they barely resisted the urge to rev the engines and lift back into the air. But they were reassured by the fake cameraman who used his zoom lens to inspect the area for signs of trouble. Finding none, he turned his camera toward the helicopter—the signal that everything was on track and that the remaining agents should deboard.

Unlike the Venezuelan missions in which the choppers shut down and stayed on the ground for more than an hour, the pilots kept the five rotor blades turning. They figured that the wind and commotion would create a sense of urgency, making it less likely that the guerrillas would closely examine the delegates' credentials. The running engines would also allow for a faster getaway. The pilots could follow the action through a microphone hidden inside the TV camera, and if the rebels discovered the deception, Russi would tip off the pilots so they could at least save themselves.

"If he said 'I've lost my wallet,' that meant to take off because the rebels were going to blow them away," said one of the pilots.

Wearing a floppy white hat and affecting his geezer slouch, Russi approached the guerrillas and asked for César. But the rebel sentries seemed suddenly bashful upon meeting the mission chief, and none of them said a word. Moments later, César appeared along with the hostages' main jailer, Enrique Gafas, who was carrying his own video camera. César smiled broadly and extended his hand. It seemed like the FARC was still on the hook. Russi expressed his pride in taking part in the operation, then presented the rebel commander with a book written by former hostage Luis Eladio Pérez, who had been held by César and Gafas. In another move by the agents to reinforce their phony flight plan, the gift was delivered in a Bogotá airport shopping bag.

All the while, the news team scampered about the site, shooting video of the guerrillas and pestering César for an interview. The TV crew's role was to distract César and get in the faces of the other guerrillas to prevent them from concentrating on the events playing out before them. The reporter even feigned an argument with Russi who dressed him down and told him to leave the FARC commander alone. César seemed delighted to be the center of attention and agreed to give the reporter a brief statement. Saying he needed a variety of angles, the cameraman began filming from behind a line of about twenty guerrilla guards. They turned around to face the lens just as the cameraman had planned. Now, most of the rebels had their backs to the helicopter and couldn't monitor what was going on.

After chatting with Russi, César invited the delegates to stay for coffee. It was a gesture of backcountry hospitality but one the imposters feared. Refreshments would prolong their stay and provide César and Gafas with more time to scrutinize their looks, accents, and backstories. Russi took it all in stride.

"I said, 'Sure, let's go,'" he said. "I was ready to have lunch with them and I had a whole speech prepared in which I was going to criticize the government. We had to let things play out."

At that moment, a woman dashed toward César. She was the Indian, César's radio operator who had spent the past month passing to her boss false information fed to her by the Colombian Army. The Indian had just received another bogus message. Foreseeing just such a scenario in which the guerrillas insisted on putting on a spread for their guests, the army's radio operators perched on the mountaintop near Bogotá pulled the final strings of their man-in-the-middle con game. They ordered César to put the hostages aboard the chopper as quickly as possible. Convinced that the instructions came from his boss, Mono Jojoy, César told Russi there had been a change in plans and turned back toward the aircraft.

The hostages watched the disguised army agents with growing disgust. The bastards were joking with the rebels and giving them presents! Two of them wore T-shirts bearing the image of Che Guevara. They seemed like FARC-loving lefties. Any thoughts among the prisoners that they might be liberated quickly faded.

"They were filming us," Betancourt said. "And I was thinking, they just want to tape us so that the world sees that we are alive, and they're going to transfer us to some other place. And this is going to go on and on and on for four more years? Five? Six more years?"

But the final indignity came when the strange visitors insisted on securing the wrists of Betancourt and her colleagues with plastic tie-wraps used by police departments for mass detentions. One by one, the outraged hostages refused to cooperate. One of the soldiers who had been a pillar of strength and a source of inspiration for the other hostages was so upset he threw himself on the ground and began screaming. The army agents were taken aback. It now appeared that the rescue operation might fail because of *too* much attention to detail. In their rush to reassure César by handcuffing the hostages, the agents had provoked a full-blown mutiny among the very people they were trying to save.

AFTER A SEEMINGLY INTERMINABLE WAIT BACK in the sweltering situation room at the U.S. embassy, word came that one of the two helicopters was about to land at the pickup point. From that moment forward, there would be no more communications with the army agents until they had departed guerrilla territory. The plan was for the team to be on the ground for no more than eight minutes. Unaware of the delays caused by the revolt of the hostages, Ambassador Brownfield kept checking his watch.

"Six minutes go by. Ten. Twelve. Fourteen. And there was not a god-damned thing we could do," Brownfield said.

The ambassador had a direct line to Defense Minister Juan Manuel Santos but he didn't call. If he had nothing to offer, he wasn't going to dial the minister simply to express his agony. And there was always Plan B: the encircling of the kidnappers by Colombian and U.S. troops who would then try to persuade César to turn over his hostages.

But as fifteen, then eighteen, then twenty minutes ticked away Brownfield began drafting in his head the message he was going to send to Washington informing his bosses that the mission had fallen apart.

AS ORIGINALLY SKETCHED OUT, THE ROLE of Russi called for a wizened, good-natured mission chief who would cajole and humor César into giving up his human cargo. But once on the ground, the blissed-out César proved to be fully cooperative while the incensed hostages threatened to derail their own salvation. During their brief tutorial in Method acting, the theater coach had stressed the importance of shifting gears. So Russi started scolding the hostages. The tie-wraps, he said, had been demanded by the FARC. If they didn't want to cooperate, well, Jesus Christ, they could stay on the ground for all he cared.

The problem was that most of the prisoners seemed prepared to do just that. As the argument grew louder, the fake Australian delegate, who called himself Daniel, noticed that Keith, Marc, and Tom were off to one side keeping their mouths shut. Maybe the gringos would listen to reason. The phony Aussie sidled up to Keith and told him in English that he knew about his Colombian girlfriend and twin boys. Then, out of earshot of the guerrillas, he pleaded with the Americans to collaborate.

"I don't know who you are but you're not who you say you are," Keith replied as he eyed Daniel's counterfeit ID badge. "You're not Australian. You're lying. You're a Colombian."

Then, the army agent leaned in close and looked Keith, Marc, and Tom in the face.

"Do you want to go home?" he said. "Do you want to see your family? Please, please trust me. I'm going to get you home."

Keith and Tom were the first to submit. "I can only see good with a helicopter," Tom said. "We hadn't been in a helicopter in five and a half years. We'd been in the bottom of boats, on mules, on foot. It all looked good to me."

The logjam was broken. Following the Americans' lead the rest of the hostages grudgingly agreed to be handcuffed by the fake nurse. But then came another delay. Before boarding the chopper, several prisoners approached the news team and tried to lodge a televised protest against the FARC. Keith held his bound wrists in front of the camera while army lieutenant Raimundo Malagón, held hostage since 1998, pleaded for attention. "I've been in chains for ten years!" he shouted.

Though moved by the hostages' desperate words, the fake TV reporter had to pull the plug on their speeches. If all of the hostages insisted on venting the unspeakable truths of captivity, their words would surely enrage César and Gafas who, out of spite, might call off the entire operation. So far the agents' story had held up, but they feared that, any moment now, the effects of the fairy dust would fade away.

ONE BY ONE, THE DEJECTED HOSTAGES boarded the helicopter and plunked down on the two rows of canvas bench seats running along the walls of the fuselage. A man in a Che Guevara T-shirt pulled off their boots and tie-wrapped their ankles. Then, Gafas stepped on board and chose a stand-alone seat next to the door at the front of the chopper. The army's seating chart had Gafas on the bench seats sandwiched between two agents who were to pummel him into submission. So Russi convinced Gafas that he was sitting in the spot reserved for the aircraft technician. He agreed to move. He also gave up his pistol after Russi gestured toward the "no guns" decals plastered to the windows. Farther back in the aircraft, César was wedged between the fake medic and the amateur boxer.

The chopper was moments away from lifting off when the agents remembered the soft drinks. Again mimicking the Venezuelan missions, two members of the team emerged from the chopper and placed two coolers filled with bottled drinks on the ground. Then, with the doorway ladder still hanging down, the MI-17 lifted into the air. The team had been on the ground for exactly twenty-two minutes. As the aircraft gained altitude, one of the agents peered out the window at the guerrillas below and suppressed a strong urge to hold up his middle finger.

Speaking into his microphone from the cockpit, one of the pilots said: "Generators okay." His coded words confirmed to army officers monitoring the mission from afar that all fifteen hostages plus the two guerrillas were aboard the helicopter.

Now, it was time for act three.

As she spoke with the hostages, the fake nurse pretended to be knocked off balance by a patch of turbulence. She landed in César's lap. "Like a gentleman," she said, "he caught me and then said, 'You can ride with me.'"

The phony medic then leaned into the guerrilla, asking him if he had ever flown on a helicopter, if he was airsick, or if the changing air pressure was bothering his ears. With César deep in conversation, the nurse extracted herself from his lap. Then, the boxer moved in for the knockout. He punched the guerrilla in the throat and bashed his head against the wall of the helicopter three times. Russi, the TV journalist, and the medic piled on. César kicked and scratched his attackers and brandished his pistol but that only brought another flurry of blows. The agents kneed him in the nuts, then pulled down his pants to immobilize his legs. At the other end of the aircraft, the fake Arab, the cameraman, and one of the pretend guerrillas wrestled Gafas to the floor.

"Suddenly, this big-ass fight breaks out," Marc said. "All these aid workers were just pounding on César."

At first, the hostages were baffled. But when they saw César and Gafas incapacitated and in their undies, Keith, who had worked his hands free from his tie-wraps, couldn't resist. He and several other hostages pounced on César, and Keith slugged him in the eye. Sitting a few seats away, Betancourt was astounded.

"Something happened, I'm not sure what, and then we saw the commander who for years was in charge of us and had been so cruel and despotic with us, on the floor, naked, and blindfolded."

Gafas was hog-tied, and César was finally subdued with the help of the faulty stun gun and a hypodermic syringe filled with a powerful sedative. The helicopter was heading for home. Fifteen lives had been saved. With their mission accomplished, Russi turned to the now former hostages, smiled, and in nine curt words announced their deliverance.

"We are the Colombian Army, and you are free!"

CHAPTER 26

PASSPORTS

"Here," he said, not really joking. "The bullet
we didn't shoot you with."
—GABRIEL GARCÍA MÁRQUEZ, *News of a Kidnapping*

AFTER RUSSI CUT OFF THE PLASTIC tie-wraps binding the hostages' hands they sang the national anthem and chanted "Uribe! Uribe! Uribe!"

Tom felt like he'd just been released from a tar pit. "It all came together in a heartbeat," he said. "Suddenly, it was like an arrow pierced my brain. It was over. It was done."

"I just felt incredible," Keith said. "Then I thought: 'Man, I hope this Russian piece-of-shit helicopter doesn't crash.'"

By then, the pilots had sent another message back to headquarters: "Anti-ice system okay." That meant César and Gafas had been subdued and everyone on board was safe. At the U.S. embassy, the telephone rang in the situation room. A Special Forces officer picked up the receiver, then turned to Ambassador William Brownfield and relayed the news: "Fifteen pax. All airborne. All good to go."

Brownfield sprinted out of the room toward a waiting vehicle that would take him to the airport. But he had to turn around because he'd left behind his cell phone and BlackBerry. First, he tried calling the French ambassador to let him know that Íngrid Betancourt was free. But no one picked up at the embassy or at the ambassador's residence. Next, he called Steve Donehoo, a consultant who had been hired by Northrop Grumman to serve as a liaison with the families of the American hostages. He got voice mail. Finally, Brownfield tried to call the State Department so Condoleezza Rice could tell President Bush that Operation Check had been pulled off without a hitch. Once again, he was put on hold.

"It was the most important piece of news I'd ever had to tell in my entire life," Brownfield said, "and I couldn't find a human to tell it to."

President Bush eventually got word and put in a call to French president Nicolas Sarkozy. Shortly afterward, Colombian defense minister Juan Manuel Santos revealed the news before an astounded press corps. For the first time in ages, the beat reporters at the ministry broke into sustained applause.

When the two helicopters touched down at the airport at San José del Guaviare, the agents bounded down the steps and hugged army general Mario Montoya. Then the hostages were put aboard the former presidential jet for the short flight to Tolemaida Military Base, with the Americans sinking into the leather seats in first class. A priest on board led them all in a prayer and then Montoya started singing "Glory to the Colombian Army!"

Once on the tarmac at Tolemaida, Santos hugged the most famous hostage, Íngrid Betancourt, and handed her a cell phone. On the other end of the line was Betancourt's long-suffering mother, Yolanda Pulecio.

"Mama, I'm free!" Betancourt shouted into the receiver. "The army rescued me! What they pulled off was the most extraordinary thing. It's for a page in the history books."

By then Brownfield had made his way to Tolemaida and stepped inside the jet to greet Keith, Marc, and Tom. His plan was to usher the Americans aboard a C-130 destined for Bogotá airport, then whisk them to a military base in San Antonio, Texas. But realizing they'd been bossed around for the past five years by armed thugs, Brownfield didn't want to seem pushy. So he stood by as they said their good-byes to their longtime jungle roommates. About five hundred U.S. and Colombian military personnel had gathered at the airport to welcome home the hostages, and when Keith, Marc, and Tom emerged from the aircraft, the contractors were greeted with the military battle cry of "Hooah!"

Aboard the C-130, Keith, Marc, and Tom drank bottles of Lone Star beer provided by Brownfield, a loyal Texan. They had been free men for only an hour and, still accustomed to their patterns of speech with their fellow hostages, kept switching from English to Spanish and back to English. Keith couldn't stop talking. And he wouldn't let go of two souvenirs he'd brought back from FARC-land. In one hand, he held a plastic bag of *fariña*, the daily ration that kept John Frank Pinchao alive during his dash for freedom. In the other hand, he held a thick padlock.

"He was gripping that damned thing and squeezing it and glaring at it," Brownfield said. "He probably told me three times: 'This is the thing they chained me up with every night. I'm never going to let this out of my sight to remind me of who they are, what they are, and what they did to me.'"

Before dashing out of the embassy, Brownfield had put in an urgent request for three new passports. He wanted to welcome Keith, Marc, and Tom back to civilization with a fresh set of credentials, a practical move but one freighted with symbolism: the documents allowed the men to reclaim their identities. With just three hours to make the passports and lacking up-to-date photos, consular officials scanned the proof-of-life images of the thin and haggard-looking American prisoners that had been released by the guerrillas eight months earlier.

Inside the U.S. embassy, diplomats and office workers were shouting and hugging one another while someone placed a can of beer and a bottle of champagne next to the framed portraits of the three contractors that had been positioned on a table at the entrance to the building since 2003.

"I could actually quit now," said one official, "because this is probably about as good as it gets."

IN LOS ANGELES, RONALD SUGAR, WHO had been named chief executive of Northrop Grumman seven months after the contractors were kidnapped, was pulled out of a meeting and told about the rescue operation. "For more than five years, we prayed for the release and well-being of these heroic men," Sugar said. "We shared in the anguish while they were captives, and today we can share in the joy of knowing that they are free men."

Back in the Colombian capital, Íngrid Betancourt was the first freed hostage to appear in public. Ever conscious of her image, she tried to freshen up on the plane ride back to Bogotá by combing her long, unruly hair into a single braid that wrapped around the top of her head like a crown. She emerged from the aircraft, waved to the crowd, and threw her arms around her mother. Then, one by one, the ragged and exhausted soldiers and policemen—many of whom had been held hostage for nearly a decade—addressed hundreds of reporters gathered at the airport. They publicly thanked the army for not forgetting about them and for saving their lives.

Absent from the news conference were Keith, Marc, and Tom, who had been put on a separate plane bound for Bogotá. But in Colombia, the main attraction was Betancourt, who was the last to speak and appeared before the crowd still wearing the knee-high Wellingtons issued by the guerrillas. In her proof-of-life video nine months earlier, she was skin and bones and seemed on the verge of death. But now, she glowed. Recounting the details of the rescue, she gave a lucid and gracious speech in which she praised her onetime political rival, President Álvaro Uribe, called on the FARC to make peace, and urged Colombians to remember the hostages left behind. Though still charismatic, Betancourt seemed to have come out of bondage as a more humble and reflective figure. Asked at the airport about her transformation, she said, "In a kidnapping you leave behind a lot of baggage."

After Keith, Marc, and Tom landed at El Dorado—on the same runway from which their overloaded Cessna had taken off five years earlier—they immediately boarded a C-17 cargo jet bound for San Antonio, Texas, where they would undergo medical and psychological evaluations at Brooke Army Medical Center on the grounds of Fort Sam Houston.

Wearing green flight suits, the men dined on pizza and guzzled Coca-Cola. But during the flight north, they kept pinching themselves. In the jungle, time seemed to stand still. For five and a half years, they had fought off boredom and despair and struggled to distinguish Monday from Tuesday, the year 2005 from 2006. During 1,967 days in captivity, nothing seemed to happen. It was, in the words of Keith, a period when multitasking meant washing one's socks *and* underwear in a mud puddle.

Now, everything was unfolding all at once. They were making a quantum leap from the chains and padlocks of FARC-land to the land of the free. Yet after so much cruelty and so many dashed hopes, it was hard to wrap their heads around the magnitude of the Colombian Army's con job and to comprehend that they were actually free and not simply out on some hallucinatory weekend pass.

"We got jaded, and that carried through to the release. It was like 'Yeah, we're free, but nothing ever turns out the way it should so I'm only going to *kind* of believe it,'" Tom said. "We'd been having lunch as prisoners, eating out of the same pot I've used for the past three and a half or four years and an hour later I'm on an ex-presidential jet flying across Colombia. . . . So much was happening. I just couldn't grab on to it."

The C-17 reached San Antonio just before midnight on July 2. Tom had shed about fifty pounds. Marc had scars on his butt from so many booster shots to treat leishmaniasis. Keith, who had blemishes on his neck from the metal chains, was just getting over malaria. But given their ordeal, U.S. Army doctors at Brooke said the former hostages were in remarkably good shape.

The larger challenge was psychological. After five years of forced hibernation, they were a little groggy and had to regain their bearings in a changed world. They had missed the invasion of Iraq, the 2004 presidential election, Hurricane Katrina. Cell phones now had cameras. Britney Spears had gone off the rails. An African-American named Barack Obama was the front-runner in the race for the White House.

More dramatically, they didn't know where things stood with their marriages, the health of their parents, the development of their children. To avoid an emotional overload, their counselors at Brooke at first allowed them to visit with family members for just forty minutes. They were advised to take baby steps back to reality.

"I tried to imagine myself knocking on my door, with no help, and saying hi to my wife," Tom said. "If there's ever a moment when you need somebody to say 'This is how you want to react with your wife, this is what you can expect,' this was one of those moments."

Patricia Medina flew to San Antonio along with Nicolás and Keith Jr., the twin boys who had never met their father. Keith only knew their voices from their radio messages and now he heard them again.

"I open the door, and I hear: 'Papa! Papa! Papa!'" Keith said. "It was like I had never been gone."

Later, Keith took the boys to the chapel at Fort Sam Houston. Nicolás sat on one of his knees, Keith Jr. sat on the other, and their dad couldn't stop hugging them. His welcoming committee also included his parents, Gene and Lynne Stansell, as well as his two teenaged children, Kyle and Lauren. "It's been five and a half years since I last saw the person who is closest to me in my life," Lauren said. "I'm speechless."

Tom walked around the military base hugging his wife, Mariana. His teenaged son, Tommy, wouldn't let go of his father. Jo Rosano, Marc's mother, had just arrived in Paris to attend an event sponsored by an Íngrid Betancourt solidarity group when she learned about Marc's rescue. She immediately turned around and headed for Texas.

"The first time I saw Marc, he was just perfect," Jo said. "I asked him, 'Marc, how are you?' He said: 'Mom, I'm free!'"

AFTER THREE DAYS OF REST, REUNIONS, and medical treatment, the former hostages appeared at a televised news conference with their families. Freshly scrubbed and wearing blue blazers, they heaped praise on the Colombian Army and President Álvaro Uribe. Also at the podium was Jo, who had been the most vocal of the family members in demanding freedom for the hostages. Now she had a global television audience but suddenly found herself at a loss for words.

"I've been crying for five years, and I'm still crying," she explained, "but these are tears of joy."

Then her son took the microphone. Before Marc had been taken hostage, some of his colleagues viewed him as a lightweight, while even his father had described his son as adrift. But during five years on the dark side, Marc appeared to have drunk deeply from the chalice of wisdom, for he emerged as the most eloquent of the three former hostages. After a sober indictment of the FARC, Marc used most of his five-minute speech to pay tribute to the hundreds of hostages still in the jungle, prisoners who were probably enduring even harsher conditions as the guerrillas clamped down on security in the wake of the rescue operation.

"In this exact moment, right now, they are being punished because we were rescued. I want you guys to imagine that," Marc said. "Right now they're wearing chains around their necks. They're going to get up early tomorrow morning, they're going to put on a heavy backpack, and they're going to be forced to march with that chain on their neck while a guerrilla with an automatic weapon is holding the other end of his chain, like a dog."

He finished with a tribute to the men and women who extricated him from the hands of the FARC.

"You guys, the ones who saved us, the ones who rescued us, are heroes. You've given me my life back, and now I don't have to dream about being free anymore. And it feels so good to be free right now here with all of you."

LIVING TO TELL THE TALE

Freedom is what you do with what's been done to you.
—Jean-Paul Sartre

OPERATION CHECK WAS QUICKLY HAILED AS the greatest military action ever pulled off by the Colombian armed forces. It sparked celebrations across the land, boosted the popularity of President Álvaro Uribe, and enhanced the prospects of Defense Minister Juan Manuel Santos, who resigned nine months later to run for president. Within five days of the rescue, three films about the hostages were in the works. In the words of U.S. ambassador William Brownfield, what the Colombian Army pulled off "was even greater than Entebbe."

Watching it all play out on television, Jorge Sanabria, the disgraced leader of Vulture Company, was ecstatic to learn that the three American contractors—the men his troops had been tracking in the jungle five years earlier—had finally been liberated. But he felt a little melancholy about missing out on the glory.

His timing had been all wrong. Sanabria had graduated from cadet school just as Colombia's military was bottoming out. Then, as the army restructured and found its footing, Sanabria and his men stumbled upon the FARC *guaca*, stuffed their pockets, and blinged their way to ignominy. By the time Colombian troops began taking down members of the FARC secretariat and homing in on the hostages, the troops of Vulture and Destroyer companies were on the run, in the sight of rebel hit squads, or locked up in the stockade for defiling the army's good name.

Yet after the sudden decision to annul the military court's verdict and free the soldiers, Sanabria had trouble recharging his batteries. For a few months, he worked a dead-end job at a brick factory near his hometown of Sogamoso. He followed his doctor's advice and checked in for gastric bypass surgery. Months later, however, he still sported his spongiform body and tipped the scales at more than three hundred pounds. During a lunchtime interview at a Sogamoso restaurant, he inhaled plates of spit-roasted beef, veal, and sausage.

But if the armed forces had taught Sanabria anything it was the art of survival. He had carried on amid the army's darkest hours, endured mission after mission into FARC-land, and later withstood the military's judicial offensive. Now that he was a free man, he wasn't going to agonize over the false turns and the roads not taken. He also remained loyal to his men. Though it had all gone wrong in the jungle, he insisted that his motives were pure: he had allowed his slumdog soldiers to divvy up the FARC loot to help them move up in the world.

"When we fought, they gave their all for me. Thanks to them, I am alive," Sanabria said. "Now, as their commanding officer, I have to respond for what happened and I understand that. But the situation was unprecedented and it was difficult to maintain discipline in the middle of chaos. I don't know if it was all worth it but something good has to come out of all this. God must have some plan."

A few months later, through a friend of a friend who was willing to overlook his legal problems, Sanabria found work as a security supervisor at a Colombian coal mine. As it turned out, he would need a few good men to serve under him. So, just as he rounded up his old mates to take a second crack at the FARC loot a few years earlier, Sanabria recruited some of his buddies from Vulture and Destroyer companies. Though he missed the army, Sanabria and his men once again sported uniforms and weapons—just like old times, sort of.

Former private Walter Suárez, the soldier who discovered the guerrilla cash amid a violent bout of diarrhea, also stuck to a military regimen even though he was no longer in the army. Every day he rose at 4:30 a.m. But instead of reveille followed by push-ups, sit-ups, and a military chow line, Suárez jumped into a white Ford pickup rigged to run on natural gas to save money. In the back sat crates with plastic one-liter bags of milk and cartons of yogurt. The would-be millionaire was now a milkman.

His delivery route took Suárez through the farming communities on the outskirts of Bogotá. Suárez drove slowly, his wife beside him in the passenger seat, as two runners trailed behind, dashing in and out of stores to deliver the goods. But dairy products could be a hard sell. On a recent morning, Suárez arrived so early that many of his regular clients had yet to open their stores. "Nobody here drinks milk," said the owner of one corner grocery as Suárez offered his wares. "They only drink beer." On a good day, Suárez sold seven hundred liters and came away with about twenty-five dollars in profits.

It had been more than five years since he had come out of FARC-land flush with cash that he'd buried beneath a doghouse. Still, the legend followed Suárez, making him a marked man. One evening, a few days after Christmas, five men dressed in camouflage uniforms burst into his apartment carrying pistols equipped with silencers and began shouting: "The money! The money! The money!"

"They said they were guerrillas but that was bullshit," Suárez said.

They tied up Suárez and his wife and turned the apartment upside down. Suárez insisted that he was broke and pleaded with the intruders to check with the landlady. He was living in a ninety-dollar-per-month apartment and was two months behind on the rent. The frustrated burglars finally gave up and roared off on motorcycles. Unfazed, Suárez turned in, then rose before dawn to set off on another milk run.

Frankistey Giraldo, one of the three Giraldo brothers in Destroyer Company, had managed to elude the rebels and the robbers. He used some of his money to open a wholesale grocery store and roared around Bogotá in an SUV with a monster sound system.

"Your image changes," said Giraldo as he cranked the volume on the truck's stereo. "When you have money, people look at you in a different way."

Giraldo also spread his wealth around, buying a house for his parents and giving another $10,000 to his father, a devout Evangelical. His father turned around and donated the money to a preacher in his hometown of Machetá. Unaware of the windfall's sinful origins, the preacher used the cash to buy a plot of land where he put up a Pentecostal church.

Frankistey's little brother, Lenin Giraldo, now known as Jenny following her FARC-financed sex-change operation, had adopted the perfect camouflage. As a buxom hairdresser, Jenny was overlooked by both the Colombian officials who were rounding up the soldiers who discovered the FARC *guaca* and the guerrilla assassins who were trying to shoot them down. She now ran a beauty parlor in Cali.

"Lieutenant Sanabria once declared that the money had been a curse," she said, "but for me it was a blessing."

Though the cloud of further litigation hung over the heads of Jenny and the other former soldiers, as time passed it seemed unlikely that they would be brought back to Tolemaida Military Base for another reckoning before the judge. Only about one-third of the 147 troops had appeared at the original trial, and once liberated, most of them had gone underground. Hernando Castellanos, the lawyer representing the Giraldo brothers, pointed out that the wheels of justice in Colombia turned so slowly that the eleven-year statute of limitations would probably expire before the mess was resolved.

"Someday," said Sanabria as he drained a bottle of beer, "we'll all have a good laugh about it."

WHEN ÍNGRID BETANCOURT STEPPED OFF THE plane at the Bogotá airport on the day she was freed, she gave her husband, Juan Carlos Lecompte, a stiff hug, then the next day flew to Paris with her two children and ex-husband but without her spouse. She had survived six and a half years as a FARC prisoner but, like other former hostages, she was finding it difficult to pull off a storybook homecoming.

"Her love for me may have ended in the jungle," said Lecompte, who soon afterward filed for divorce.

Yet Lecompte admitted that Betancourt's frosty greeting was partly his own doing. While Betancourt's mother sent radio messages to her daughter nearly every day, Lecompte spent long periods without getting in touch. There were also rumors published in gossip magazines, which Lecompte denied, that he was dating a Mexican woman as well as one of Betancourt's cousins. Former hostage Luis Eladio Pérez said a copy had reached Betancourt in the jungle.

"We almost never received magazines," Pérez said. "But one of those high-society magazines arrived and there's Lecompte with a model in Mexico. Of course, Íngrid saw it."

Then, shortly after Betancourt was freed, her jungle liaison with Pérez became public and both she and Lecompte filed for divorce. By then, Betancourt had moved on. She was received in Paris by French president Nicolas Sarkozy: she was granted a private meeting with the pope and took home the Prince of Asturias Award, Spain's equivalent of the Nobel Peace Prize. She ruled out immediately jumping back into politics in Colombia and spent her time writing her memoirs and traveling the world to lobby for the release of the remaining hostages. Nominated for a Nobel Peace Prize, Betancourt fully expected to win and her staff invited reporters to a tentative news conference just in case. But the prize went to Martti Ahtisaari of Finland.

Keith, who came out of the jungle with a fierce animosity toward Betancourt, was relieved she didn't come away with the Nobel. But the Americans, all three of whom resumed working for their old company, Northrop Grumman, faced their own letdowns.

After returning to Merritt Island, Florida, Tom and his wife, Mariana, realized their marriage was over. Mariana found an apartment and Tom found himself wandering around his big, empty "dream house," the home he had never managed to enjoy because his family first moved there just weeks before he was kidnapped.

"The nightmares I have are not about captivity," Tom said. "They're about divorce."

When Marc reunited with his wife, Shane, at Brooke Army Medical

Center in San Antonio, he knew something was wrong because she flinched every time he put his arms around her. A few days after returning to their home in Big Pine Key, Marc filed for divorce, accusing Shane of refinancing their house without his knowledge and running up a massive credit card debt. Soon afterward, Marc moved back to Connecticut to be closer to his parents.

"Marc and Tom were victims of a crime against humanity," Keith said. "They were also victims because their families were torn apart. All these guys ever wanted was to go home and be husbands and fathers again. It kills me what I saw happen to them."

Jo Rosano, Marc's mom, was relieved to see her son extract himself from a troubled marriage, but she had her own fence-mending to do, namely, a public apology to President Uribe for her harsh words during her son's ordeal. With Marc free, she showered the Colombian leader with praise. And at a ceremony at the Colombian embassy in Washington, D.C., a month after the rescue, Uribe made Jo an honorary Colombian citizen.

"I love Colombia and its people," said Jo, who still found it hard to believe that Marc was free. "I can pick up the phone and call my son. Before I had to send messages and there would be no answer back. It's like a dream. I'm still numb. And the three of them have formed a bond that no one can break."

Keith and Patricia got married on the sugar-white coastline of Anna Maria Island, Florida. As they exchanged vows, Keith's eyes filled with tears. They moved into a house with the twins, Lauren, and Kyle located just down the street from Keith's parents in Bradenton. Besides commuting to the Northrop Grumman office in Tampa, Keith used the lessons from the jungle to become a motivational speaker. He addresses corporations and sales conventions on topics like "Survival Through the Unbreakable Bonds of Friendship" and "The Power of Teamwork in Any Situation."

Though their pact to sell their story to Oliver Stone fell through, Keith, Marc, and Tom stuck together in the outside world and inked a joint book deal to write their memoirs. But more than cashing in, the men found themselves savoring life's small wonders.

"I am a person who has redefined his value system because of so much time reflecting," Keith said. "We now have an appreciation for the smallest things, like a glass of water. Just seeing your kid's photo. Or a call from your mom. We want to take out of the jungle that value. . . . Hopefully, it never leaves me."

They also planned to call attention to the plight of the remaining Colombian hostages by taking a motorcycle tour across the United States. Harley-Davidson donated three hogs for the pending journey, which they dubbed the Freedom Ride. And Keith made a surprise return to Colombia to personally thank the men and women in the Colombian military who saved them.

"We will never forget them," Tom added. "It was the best rescue in the history of the world."

BUT FOR THE COLOMBIAN GOVERNMENT, THE glow of Operation Check was already starting to fade. President Uribe was forced to apologize to the International Committee of the Red Cross after news leaked that the army agent who posed as the Arab during the rescue mission had worn a bib with the organization's distinctive symbol.

Weeks later, a far more serious scandal rocked the army. Eleven young men from the Bogotá slum of Soacha had been lured to northern Colombia with the promise of high-paying jobs. But instead, they were executed and presented by army soldiers as enemy combatants. Soon, Colombian investigators began looking into more than a thousand similar cases involving seventeen hundred victims. Now, front-page stories about the heroic army were replaced by photos of the grieving mothers of the dead.

In a way, the Colombian Army was the victim of its own success. Under President Uribe, the number of troops had nearly doubled. Yet government oversight of the armed forces lapsed. Officers came under fierce pressure from President Uribe to deliver on the battlefield, and some of them, in turn, offered GIs promotions, cash rewards, and days off for killing guerrillas or paramilitaries.

"Uribe is calling officers on their cell phones at eleven o'clock at night," said Adam Isacson of the Center for International Policy in Washington. "What's a colonel going to tell him? The only quantitative results he can show are people killed or captured."

Santos, the defense minister and a longtime critic of the body-count mentality, responded by firing twenty-seven military personnel, including three generals. Mario Montoya, the army commander and the hero of Operation Check, survived the initial purge. But his tenure soon became a liability for the Uribe government. The Democrats, who tracked human rights abuses abroad far more closely than the Republicans, now controlled the U.S. Congress as well as the purse strings at a time when Colombia was seeking a major new American aid package. Thus, on November 4, 2008, just hours before Barack Obama was elected president of the United States, the man who directed the sting operation that secured the release of Keith, Marc, and Tom was forced to resign.

"Mr. President," General Montoya said, "after serving my country for thirty-nine years, I arrive today at the end of my journey."

In his exit speech, Montoya praised President Uribe's national security policies, saying they had "changed the lives" of the Colombian people. He was right. The country was far safer than it was in 2003 when the Americans crash-landed on a rugged mountain slope swarming with FARC guerrillas.

The year before, when Uribe first took the oath of office, Colombia registered 2,882 kidnappings. By 2008, the figure had dropped to 437. That same year, a record number of guerrillas—3,027—deserted from the FARC. Shortly after Operation Check, a rebel turncoat hiked out of the jungle alongside Óscar Tulio Lizcano, a former Colombian lawmaker who had been held hostage for more than eight years. In February 2009, the FARC released the last of its kidnapped politicians, though the rebels still held twenty-three police and army troops.

For his efforts, Uribe traveled to Washington in January 2009 where he was awarded the Medal of Freedom by outgoing president George W. Bush. Then he launched a campaign to amend the Constitution so he could run for a third consecutive term in 2010.

"I think Colombia needs to stay with Uribe," Tom said. "He's the best president in probably a hundred years."

Many Colombians shared that view. But Uribe's reelection drive risked damaging his impressive legacy. Some began calling Uribe a right-wing version of the power-hungry Hugo Chávez, who has vowed to rule Venezuela until 2021. In addition, Uribe's implicit message—that without him

Colombia would suddenly fall back into chaos—poked holes in his own argument that Colombia was now a safe and stable democracy.

As Uribe's eight years in office drew to a close, there were some obvious blind spots and blemishes in his record. Though the FARC was diminished, profits from the drug trade would likely keep the organization on the warpath for years. And in spite of all the improvements in security, many rural areas remained off limits. When a visitor mentioned his plans to inspect the site where the Americans' Cessna Grand Caravan had crashed nearly six years earlier, he was warned off by a Colombian Army officer who said guerrillas were in the area.

"I don't recommend that you go," he intoned. "You could get kidnapped."

ACKNOWLEDGMENTS

ALEJANDRA DE VENGOECHEA INSISTED THAT I write *Law of the Jungle* even though we had a baby on the way and I was already spending too much time out in the field or glued to a computer screen. But Alejandra could relate to the subject. Her father—who is now my father-in-law—was kidnapped, twice, by the FARC. *Amorcito: gracias por existir.*

My dear friend David Carr provided encouragement, commented on early drafts, and found me an agent—Flip Brophy—who found me a publisher. Juan Forero, Marcelo Salinas, Ruth Morris, Scott Dalton, Tim Johnson, Quil Lawrence, Zoe Selsky, and Steve Dudley provided photos, advice, and companionship during many excursions into FARC-land.

At the *Houston Chronicle,* my longtime employer until the newspaper industry imploded, Tony Pederson had the foresight to open a bureau in South America and the faith to put me in charge. My editors at the paper, Chris Shively and Darlene Stinson, let me disappear into guerrilla territory and then write long, nuanced stories that provided the backbone for this book.

Former California Microwave pilot Paul Hooper spent many hours with me explaining the world of private contractors. Michael Evans, of the National Security Archive, dug up valuable documents. Alfonso Cuellar and Javier Cruz gave me unfettered access to *Semana* magazine's photo archive, while Danilo Pizarro opened the vault at *El Tiempo* newspaper. Jörg Hiller García put me in touch with El Gordo.

At HarperCollins, my editor, Henry Ferris, was enthusiastic about the story from day one. He took a machete to the clichés and made the good stuff better. Dee Dee DeBartlo hooked me up with Keith, Marc, and Tom. Under tight deadlines, Danny Goldstein helped put all the pieces together.

When I started writing this book I was pretty sure the last chapter would find the three American hostages still wasting away in the hands of the FARC and I'm grateful I was wrong. I would like to express my deep admiration for Keith, Marc, and Tom, as well as for their families, who even in the most despairing of times refused to give up hope and opened their doors to me. And may the many Colombian hostages still stuck in the jungle make it back alive.

Finally, I would like to thank my parents, John and Maxine Otis, for always being there, and for pointing me down the path to the writing life.

NOTES

The vast majority of the information in this book is based on my original reporting—including more than one hundred fifty interviews with the key players—as well as my coverage of Colombia's guerrilla war, the failed peace process, and the hostage crisis for the *Houston Chronicle* over the past thirteen years. Also of enormous value in writing *Law of the Jungle* were several volumes of memoirs published by former hostages as well as the book *Operación Jaque*, which is the Colombian Defense Ministry's official account of the rescue mission. Two short books on the Colombian GIs who found the money, *La Guaca* and *La Guaca Maldita*, were useful. The documentary *Held Hostage in Colombia*, released in 2003, contains the only in-depth interviews with Stansell, Gonsalves, and Howes while they were in captivity. Other sources include U.S. newspaper and magazine articles as well as excellent coverage by the Colombian media, especially *Semana* magazine and *El Tiempo*, the nation's leading daily newspaper.

CHAPTER 1: AIR AMERICA

2   *"Tommy made it look"*: Douglas Cockes telephone interview, December 27, 2007.

2   *Their missions were classified*: Robert D. Kaplan, *Imperial Grunts: On the Ground with the American Military, from Mongolia to the Philippines to Iraq and Beyond* (New York: Vintage Books, 2005), p. 72.

4   *"It was such a change of pace"*: Tom Howes interview, Merritt Island, Florida, May 6, 2009.

4   *"I want to keep these paychecks"*: Paul Hooper telephone interview, December 28, 2007.

5   *"Just a routine flight"*: Howes's quote from 2003 documentary film *Held Hostage in Colombia*, directed by Jorge Enrique Botero, produced by Victoria Bruce and Karin Hayes.

6   *"Any single-engine"*: Jorge Sanjinés interview, Bogotá, February 16, 2008.

7   *"You can't put twenty pounds"*: Ronnie Powers interview, Griffin, Georgia, February 1, 2008.

7   *"a catastrophic aviation mishap"*: Cockes and Hooper letter to James G. Cassady, vice president of Human Resources, Northrop Grumman Corporation, November 14, 2002.

7   *"There was a letter"*: Anne Patterson telephone interview, September 18, 2008.

8   *"With this piece-of-shit"*: Marc Gonsalves, Keith Stansell, and Tom Howes with Gary Brozek, *Out of Captivity* (New York: HarperCollins, 2009), p. xv.

9   *"I was very new"*: Marc Gonsalves interview, Cambridge, Massachusetts, May 2, 2009.

9   *"Out of the blue"*: *Held Hostage in Colombia* documentary.

9   *"Magic Worker"*: Transcript of audiotape played at 2007 Simón Trinidad trial in U.S. District Court, Washington, D.C.

10 *"My gut feeling"*: Howes interview.

10 *"The last thing I remember"*: *Held Hostage in Colombia* documentary.

CHAPTER 2: EL GORDO

12 *"That was inspiring"*: Sanabria interview, Sogamoso, November 23, 2007.

13 *During one 1997 operation*: John Otis, "Colombian army stuck in quagmire against insurgency," *Houston Chronicle*, February 8, 1998.

13 *Even with the draft*: Ibid.

13 *"From the very beginning"*: Jorge Enrique Mora interview, Bogotá, March 10, 2001.

14 *"It was the time of Pablo"*: Carlos Alberto Ospina telephone interview, June 9, 2008.

15 *Unlike orthodox*: John Otis, "Rebel held: Inside Colombia's FARC," *Houston Chronicle*, August 5, 2001.

16 *Even Cincinnati-based*: John Otis, "Critics question Chiquita's claim that it was forced to pay paramilitaries," *Houston Chronicle*, April 2, 2007.

16 *Alluding to the five*: "The Sixth Division," Human Rights Watch, September 2001.

16 *Pastrana's army generals*: Andrés Pastrana interview, Bogotá, November 6, 2008.

17 *"They would tear"*: Freddy Padilla de León interview during helicopter flight over southern Colombia, June 12, 2008.

17 *"I am serious"*: Manuel José Bonett, quoted by DPA wire service, November 1, 1998.

17 *The result was a rout*: "Golpes de Pecho," *Semana*, March 16, 1998.

CHAPTER 3: INTO THE WILD

21   *"How the hell"*: Jorge Sanjinés interview, Bogotá, February 16, 2008.

22   *"It was incredible how damaged"*: *Held Hostage in Colombia*, directed by Jorge Enrique Botero.

22   *"I couldn't believe it"*: Marc Gonsalves, Keith Stansell, and Tom Howes with Gary Brozek, *Out of Captivity* (New York: HarperCollins, 2009), p. xix.

22   *"If all of a sudden"*: John Otis, "Uncertainty, costs weigh on U.S. in Colombia," *Houston Chronicle*, May 15, 2005.

23   *Mercenaries or freelance*: Peter W. Singer, *Corporate Warriors: The Rise of the Privatized Military Industry* (Ithaca, N.Y.: Cornell University Press, 2003).

24   *Blackwater . . . could field*: Robert Young Pelton, *Licensed to Kill: Hired Guns in the War on Terror* (New York: Three Rivers Press, 2006).

24   *Pentagon signed some three thousand*: T. Christian Miller, *Corporate Warriors, and Blood Money: Wasted Billions, Lost Lives, and Corporate Greed in Iraq* (New York: Back Bay Books, 2006).

24   *"That's how the modern world works"*: Marc Grossman telephone interview, February 15, 2008.

25   *"coalition of the billing"*: Pelton, *Licensed to Kill*.

26   *"increasingly everywhere and nowhere"*: William Arkin, "The Underground Military," op-ed column, *Washington Post*, May 7, 2001.

26   *"a lot easier than going before Congress"*: Peter W. Singer interview, Washington, D.C., February 6, 2008.

26   *spent on contractors . . . had doubled*: U.S. State Department, "Report to Congress on Certain Counternarcotics Activities in Colombia," 2007.

26   *"We can't tell you anything"*: Sanho Tree interview, Washington, D.C., February 7, 2008.

27   *"Someone once asked me"*: John Otis, "Despite risks, U.S.-backed crop dusters are on a mission," *Houston Chronicle*, July 17, 2000.

27   *"It was a roll of the dice"*: John McLaughlin telephone interview, January 7, 2008.

28   *"embassy was going bananas"*: Sanjinés interview.

29   *The Cessna disappeared*: Aviation Safety Network Database for crashes in 2003.

29   *"We were always ready to launch"*: Keith Sparks interview, Bogotá, February 15, 2008.

30   *"This is bullshit"*: Santiago Sánchez telephone interview, August 13, 2008.

30   *"Had we gotten there"*: Kevin Christie telephone interview, June 20, 2008.

31   *"We live in a political world"*: Remo Butler telephone interview, September 20, 2008.

31   *" 'That's the FARC' "*: *Held Hostage in Colombia* documentary.

32   *"We crashed right on top"*: Marc Gonsalves interview, Cambridge, Massachusetts, May 2, 2009.

32   *"The little fucks"*: Gonsalves, Stansell, and Howes, *Out of Captivity*, p. 19.

32   *"They were all within"*: Stansell telephone interview, February 27, 2009.

33   *they found the body*: Colombian National Police videotape, Colombian government forensic report.

33   *"The last thing he was going to do"*: Judith Janis telephone interview, February 10, 2008.

33   *"I sensed we were all about"*: Gonsalves, Stansell, and Howes, *Out of Captivity*, p. 26.

CHAPTER 4: THE GREAT DIVIDE

35   *"It was the hardest mission"*: Wilson Sarmiento interview, Bogotá, November 28, 2007.

36   *Suárez was one of five*: Walter Suárez interview, Soacha, December 8, 2007. Of the many Colombian GIs from Vulture and Destroyer companies whom I interviewed, he was the only soldier who asked to remain anonymous. Walter Suárez is a pseudonym.

36   *That was in 1951*: Wade Davis, *One River: Explorations and Discoveries in the Amazon Rain Forest* (New York: Simon and Schuster, 1996).

37   *"In just one Bogotá neighborhood"*: Luis Eladio Pérez interview, Bogotá, January 21, 2009.

37   *"These people did not feel . . ."*: Msgr. Luis Augusto Castro interview, Bogotá, October 15, 2008.

38   *"If the guerrillas can pass out"*: John Otis, "Hostage rescuer now called traitor," *Houston Chronicle*, October 20, 2002.

39   *In 2003 . . . peasant farmers*: United Nations Office on Drugs and Crime annual reports on coca cultivation in South America.

39   *"We are telling peasants"*: Sanho Tree interview, Washington, February 7, 2008.

40   *"I was just about to harvest"*: John Otis, "Legal crops a casualty of drug war," *Houston Chronicle*, October 6, 2002.

41   *Some of them ended up*: John Otis, "Rebel held: Inside Colombia's FARC," *Houston Chronicle*, August 5, 2001.

44   *"we had to greet them"*: Carlos Daza interview, Cali, July 25, 2008.

45   *"It was just rice and monkey"*: Walter Suárez interview.

45   *"It was an anthill"*: Jorge Sanabria interview, Sogamoso, November 23, 2007.

46   *Sanabria had instructed one*: Jörg Hiller García, *La Guaca Maldite* (Bogotá: Grupo Editorial Norma, 2007), p. 33.

NOTES

CHAPTER 5: GOD'S LITTLE GIFT

47 *a real-life action figure:* Stansell portrait drawn from interviews with his parents, Gene and Lynne Stansell, on January 28, 2008; Keith Stansell on February 27 and May 6, 2009; and interviews with other family members and friends.

48 *"He always had to have":* Frank Stansell interview, Tampa, January 29, 2008.

50 *"someone who would have your back":* Kevin Fox interview, Merritt Island, Florida, January 30, 2008.

50 *"He would get a haircut":* Kelly Coady interview, Sarasota, Florida, January 29, 2008.

52 *"I was just tipsy enough":* Malia Phillips-Lee interview, Ocala, Florida, March 18, 2008.

53 *"he felt like I was his mom":* Charlotte Phillips interview, Ocala, Florida, March 18, 2008.

54 *"he was strict":* Lauren Stansell interview, Sarasota, Florida, January 29, 2008.

54 *"kind of cowboyish":* Keith Stansell interview, Bradenton, Florida, May 6, 2009.

55 *"I was a pretty selfish":* Marc Gonsalves, Keith Stansell, and Tom Howes with Gary Brozek, *Out of Captivity* (New York: HarperCollins, 2009), p. 319.

55 *"God's little gift":* Paul Hooper telephone interview, December 28, 2007.

57 *"He said all you do":* Jason Wells telephone interview, February 1, 2008.

CHAPTER 6: BLADE CREEP

59 *"The jungle is beautiful, but it's harsh":* Keith Stansell interview, Bradenton, Florida, May 6, 2009.

59 *"the FARC were jungle rats":* Marc Gonsalves, Keith Stansell, and Tom Howes with Gary Brozek, *Out of Captivity* (New York: HarperCollins, 2009), p. 36.

60 *"We kept getting all these conflicting":* State Department official, telephone interview, September 20, 2008.

60 *"We set up five to ten":* Remo Butler telephone interview, September 20, 2008.

60 *Two scenarios emerged:* State Department official, telephone interview, September 20, 2008.

60 *"We wanted to make sure":* Thomas Shannon telephone interview, August 26, 2008.

61 *"Every time we started to get":* Malia Phillips-Lee interview, Ocala, Florida, March 18, 2008.

62   *Not helping matters:* Robert Novak, "America's Neglected War," op-ed column, *Chicago Sun-Times,* February 20, 2003.

62   *"We had a meeting":* George Gonsalves interview, Hebron, Connecticut, February 10, 2008.

63   *"If you had three active-duty":* Peter W. Singer interview, Brookings Institution, Washington, D.C., February 6, 2008.

63   *In the twelve months:* The story count is according to a research paper by Deborah Avant, a political science professor at the University of California, Irvine, and an expert on government contracting. We spoke in a telephone interview, May 30, 2008.

64   *"A plane was shot down":* Dan Burton quoted in May 1, 2001, House Government Reform Committee hearing transcripts.

64   *"This was clearly one":* U.S. Navy Accident Report, "Redacted SRS aircraft mishap," July 1, 2003.

65   *$8.6 million:* Douglas Cockes telephone interview, December 27, 2007.

65   *"It's easy to blame":* Steve Schooner telephone interview, May 21, 2008.

66   *"annual visit from your cool relatives":* Ronnie Powers interview, Griffin, Georgia, February 1, 2008.

68   *The verdict: blade creep:* Pratt & Whitney Canada accident report, May 26, 2003. Materials Analysis, Inc., report, March 2, 2003.

69   *"I begged him not to go":* Albert Oliver telephone interview, December 17, 2007.

69   *only chance to save Keith:* Betty Oliver telephone interview, December 14, 2007.

69   *U.S. Southern command decided to reactivate:* "Fatal Mission," *New Orleans Times-Picayune,* November 10, 2003. Also U.S. Navy Accident Report, "Redacted SRS aircraft mishap," July 1, 2003.

69   *The reason it got up and running:* Anne Patterson telephone interview, September 18, 2008.

70   *"I know Tommy's commitment":* Sharon Schmidt, telephone interview, January 21, 2008.

71   *The wreckage burned through the night:* U.S. Navy Accident Report, "Redacted SRS aircraft mishap," July 1, 2003.

CHAPTER 7: THREE GRINGOS

74   *"I got pissed off":* Jorge Sanabria interview, Sogamoso, November 23, 2007.

76   *"It wasn't normal":* Wilson Sarmiento interview, Bogotá, November 28, 2007.

76   *"This happens a lot":* Carlos Alberto Ospina telephone interview, June 9, 2008.

77   *Was it the water:* Walter Suárez interview, Soacha, December 8, 2007.

79   *"the crazy stuff":* Tim O'Brien, *The Things They Carried* (New York: Houghton Mifflin, 1990), p. 71.

79 *"Each witness had his own truth"*: Héctor Alirio Forero interview, Bogotá, October 5, 2007.

79 *How much was there*: John Otis, "Cache of cash becomes a curse," *Houston Chronicle*, March 28, 2004.

80 *"When I got my hands on"*: Eccehomo Cetina, *La Guaca* (Bogotá: Intermedio Editores,), p. 64.

80 *"letting a dog run free"*: Interview with Destroyer Company soldier at Tolemaida stockade, March 15, 2004.

81 *Sharing the riches seemed*: Cetina, *La Guaca*.

81 *"You know how the story goes"*: Sarmiento interview.

82 *"People were glaring"*: Suárez interview.

82 *Until recently, pillaging*: This information comes from the article "Pillage" by Thomas Goltz, on the Crimes of War Project Website, www.crimesofwar .org.

83 *After invading Kuwait*: "Iraq seen looting Kuwait of identity," *New York Times*, September 29, 1990.

83 *"I'd walk into Wal-Mart"*: From the 2005 documentary *Soldiers Pay*, directed and produced by Tricia Regan, David O. Russell, and Juan Carlos Zaldivar.

CHAPTER 8: THE LION'S DEN

85 *"Youthful ambitions"*: Portrait of Marc Gonsalves drawn from interview with George Gonsalves in Hebron, Connecticut, February 10, 2008; multiple telephone and personal interviews with Jo Rosano in Bristol, Connecticut, from 2007 to 2009; and telephone and personal interviews with Marc Gonsalves, Cambridge, Massachusetts, May 2, 2009.

88 *"squeezing the shit out of me"*: Marc Gonsalves, Keith Stansell, and Tom Howes with Gary Brozek, *Out of Captivity* (New York: HarperCollins, 2009), p. 99.

89 *"I would count bugs"*: Tom Howes interview, Merritt Island, Florida, May 6, 2009.

89 *became temporarily paralyzed*: Luis Eladio Pérez, 7 *años secuestrado por las FARC* (Buenos Aires: Aguilar, 2008), p. 34.

89 *"I had never wanted to be a priest"*: Gonsalves, Stansell, and Howes, *Out of Captivity*, p. 109.

90 *"But something happened that day"*: Morning Express, CNN, July 11, 2008.

91 *"dumping our hearts"*: Gonsalves, Stansell, and Howes, *Out of Captivity*, p. 141.

92 *"I came to love fish heads"*: Howes interview.

92 *"I liked to talk shit"*: "El Carcelero," *Semana*, March 3, 2008.

CHAPTER 9: BONFIRES

94   *freezing their hind ends*: Olga Rodríguez interview, Bogotá, July 25, 2008.
94   *part publicity stunt*: John Otis, "Colombia rebel leaders on tour of Scandanavia," *Houston Chronicle*, February 3, 2000.
95   *"We could go on like this"*: Alfonso López Caballero interview, May 5, 2001.
96   antipasti *followed by a*: Rodríguez interview.
96   *"high point of the whole peace process"*: Jan Egeland telephone interview, August 20, 2008.
96   *set on fire*: Ibid.
96   *They called him Tirofijo*: Manuel Marulanda interview, La Sombra, Colombia, March 10, 2001. Other information on Marulanda comes from interviews with FARC commanders and Colombian political analysts as well as from two Spanish-language biographies of Marulanda by Arturo Alape: *Tirofijo: Las Vidas de Pedro Antonio Marín Manuel Marulanda Velez* (Bogotá: Planeta, 1989) and *Tirofijo: Los Sueños y las montañas* (Bogotá: Planeta, 1994). I used the information for a lengthy profile on Marulanda in John Otis, "Rebel held: Inside Colombia's FARC," *Houston Chronicle*, August 5, 2001.
96   *"like the arrival of Ho Chi Minh"*: López Caballero interview.
97   *"like an old granddad"*: Egeland interview.
97   *invited a pack of reporters*: Otis, "Rebel held: Inside Colombia's FARC."
97   *"I never went looking for war"*: Marulanda interview.
98   *born Pedro Antonio Marín*: Marulanda interview.
98   *"small towns of utterly grinding"*: David Bushnell, *The Making of Modern Colombia: A Nation in Spite of Itself* (Berkeley: University of California Press, 1993), p. 206.
99   *"It was very well organized"*: Otis, "Rebel held: Inside Colombia's FARC."
99   *killing two nuns*: Early years of the FARC were drawn from numerous interviews with FARC rebels, including Marulanda; with Colombian political analysts; and from the books *Tirofijo: Los Sueños y las montañas*, and Eduardo Pizarro Leongómez, *Las FARC: De la autodefensa a la combinación de todas las formas de lucha* (Bogotá: Tercer Mundo, 1991).
100 *the FARC took a historic decision*: Eduardo Pizarro interview, Bogotá, July 25, 2008.
100 *The other key decision*: Pizarro interview.
101 *"I can operate in peace"*: John Otis, "Colombians forced to pay rebels," *Houston Chronicle*, October 28, 2001.
101 *turning over hundreds of chickens*: John Otis, "Security issues hinder reelection bid," *Houston Chronicle*, May 28, 2006.
101 *raking in $500 million*: The true amount of FARC earnings is unknowable, but Bogotá security analyst Alfredo Rangel as well as government officials used this figure when the FARC was at its peak of power.

102   *If the party gained legs:* History of the Patriotic Union is drawn from interviews with party members, guerrillas, political analysts as well as from Steven Dudley's excellent book *Walking Ghosts: Murder and Guerrilla Politics in Colombia* (New York: Routledge, 2004).

104   *Andrés Pastrana seemed to think:* Portrait of Pastrana and the failed peace talks comes from interviews with Pastrana and my coverage for the *Houston Chronicle*, 1998–2002.

105   *"We are guerrillas":* Otis, "Rebel held: Inside Colombia's FARC."

106   *"it was unbelievable how bad":* Egeland interview.

106   *tossed a surprise party:* Otis, "Rebel held: Inside Colombia's FARC."

107   *"keep them in a cage":* Ibid.

107   *Sureshot walked over:* Ibid.

108   *"testing the waters":* Francisco Santos interview, Bogotá, September 15, 2008.

108   *"I know about kidnapping":* Andrés Pastrana, *La Palabra Bajo Fuego* (Bogotá: Planeta, 2005), p. 378.

108   *set them on fire:* Ibid., p. 379.

CHAPTER 10: COMMUNITY CHEST

110   *Yet as the stacks:* This chapter is largely based on numerous in-person interviews in Bogotá with soldiers from Vulture and Destroyer companies as well as from my reporting for the *Houston Chronicle.* I also drew information and context from two Colombian books about the GIs, *La Guaca* by Eccehomo Cetina (Bogotá: Intermedio, 2003) and *La Guaca Maldita* by Jörg Hiller García (Bogotá: Grupo Editorial Norma, 2007).

110   *"I wanted pesos":* Frankistey Giraldo interview, Bogotá, July 18, 2008.

111   *"I was a real idiot":* Walter Suárez interview, Soacha, December 8, 2007.

111   *The initial gold rush:* David Bushnell, *The Making of Modern Colombia: A Nation in Spite of Itself* (Berkeley: University of California Press, 1993).

112   *Epic search expeditions:* Wade Davis, *One River: Explorations and Discoveries in the Amazon Rain Forest* (New York: Simon and Schuster, 1996).

113   *drained a lagoon:* Report from Colombian news agency Colprensa, "El fantasma de las guacas del Mexicano," 2007.

113   *underground stash of $35 million:* "La intrincada red de caleteros de Chupeta," *El País*, Cali, February 5, 2007.

113   *judge turned him down:* Associated Press, January 16, 2008.

113   *discovered $19 million:* Hiller García, *La Guaca Maldita*, p. 106.

114   *"Army units are spread out":* John Otis, "Cache of cash becomes a curse," *Houston Chronicle*, March 28, 2004.

CHAPTER 11: THE MESSENGER

120 *"I was looking for Íngrid"*: Jorge Enrique Botero interview, Bogotá, February 15, 2008.

123 *"his chummy demeanor"*: Marc Gonsalves, Keith Stansell, and Tom Howes with Gary Brozek, *Out of Captivity* (New York: HarperCollins, 2009), p. 150.

123 *"Ralph was killed"*: Botero's interview with the three Americans make up the bulk of the documentary film *Held Hostage in Colombia*, directed by Jorge Enrique Botero, produced by Victoria Bruce and Karin Hayes.

124 *"'I work for CIAT'"*: Thomas R. Hargrove, *Long March to Freedom: Tom Hargrove's Own Story of His Kidnapping by Colombian Narco-Guerrillas* (New York: Random House, 2001), p. 7.

125 *"I hated that this journalist"*: Gonsalves, Stansell, and Howes, *Out of Captivity*, p. 153.

125 *"I would ask for diplomatic solution"*: *Held Hostage in Colombia* documentary.

125 *"I think the likelihood"*: Ibid.

CHAPTER 12: LAND OF OZ

127 *"It was . . . like entering"*: Jorge Sanabria interview, Sogamoso, Colombia, November 23, 2007.

128 *"when poor people come into money"*: María Bravo interview, Popayán, March 15, 2004.

128 *"sales went up"*: Daniel López interview, Popayán, March 15, 2004.

129 *"we'll pay you fifty dollars"*: "Hubo francachela y comilona," *El Tiempo*, May 23, 2003.

130 *"I lost out"*: "Cache of cash becomes a curse," *Houston Chronicle*, March 28, 2004.

131 *"The dog slept there"*: Walter Suárez interview, Bogotá, December 7, 2007.

131 *a more roundabout route*: Frankistey Giraldo interview, Bogotá, September 5, 2008.

132 *"underneath the floorboards"*: Yaned Daza interview, Popayán, November 15, 2008.

132 *"I got very nervous"*: Aura Gómez interview, Popayán, November 15, 2008.

CHAPTER 13: MIRACLE FISHING

135 *using a photo of Keith*: Malia Phillips-Lee interview, Ocala, Florida, March 18, 2008.

135 *violating the Patriot Act*: "Hostages families fear military rescue," Associated Press, published in *USA Today*, March 8, 2007.

135 *listed as Kyle Phillips*: Kyle Stansell interview, Sarasota, Florida, January 29, 2008.

135 *"give the U.S. government a D-minus"*: "America's forgotten hostages," *Newsweek*, International Edition, February 7, 2008.

135 *upped its reward*: Associated Press, October 13, 2003.

135 *"'What's going on'"*: George Gonsalves interview, Hebron, Connecticut, February 10, 2008.

135 *"write on this napkin"*: Jorge Enrique Botero, *Simón Trinidad: El Hombre de Hierro* (Bogota: Random House Mondadori, 2008), p. 89.

135 *On Washington's dime*: Olga Vega telephone interview, June 11, 2009.

136 *"these guys were not forgotten"*: FBI agent interview, Bogotá, August 7, 2008.

136 *"We were victims of Hollywood"*: State Department official telephone interview, November 17, 2008.

137 *"I was elected to make peace"*: Andrés Pastrana interview, Bogotá, November 6, 2008.

138 *Most of the explosives*: John Otis, "Colombia's cool reaction to attack sign of the times," *Houston Chronicle*, August 11, 2002.

138 *During one ten-hour session*: John Otis, "Colombia leader's work ethic popular," *Houston Chronicle*, December 1, 2002.

139 *warlords had intimidated voters*: John Otis, "Colombia's politics in danger: Many candidates puppets of militias," *Houston Chronicle*, March 10, 2006.

140 *"We were very clear"*: Francisco Santos interview, Bogotá, September 15, 2008.

140 *twenty-nine kidnappers inside*: Diego and Nancy Asensio, *Our Man Is Inside* (New York: Atlantic–Little Brown, 1982), p.14.

140 *named the Blue Angel*: Fernando Araújo, *El Trapecista* (Bogotá: Planeta, 2008), p. 39.

140 *"the rebels would kill him"*: Yolanda Pinto de Gaviria interview, Bogotá, July 15, 2008.

141 *Within Uribe's inner circle*: José Obdulio Gaviria (former presidential aide) interview, August 17, 2008.

141 *Hours before the helicopters*: Description of the failed rescue mission comes from interviews with Yolanda Pinto de Gaviria, José Obdulio Gaviria, and Colombian newspaper and magazine reports.

141 *"We were very naive"*: José Obdulio Gaviria interview.

142 *"Negotiators are not like Superman"*: John Otis, "Colombian kidnappers putting big squeeze on the middle class," *Houston Chronicle*, January 7, 2001.

142 *more than 3,500 abductions*: Kidnapping statistics compiled by the Colombian antikidnapping organization Foundation for a Free Country (País Libre).

143 *entered La María church*: John Otis, "Colombian citizens fight back, refuse to pay ransoms to kidnappers," *Houston Chronicle*, August 8, 1999.

144 *"You have to convince"*: Otis, "Colombian kidnappers putting big squeeze on the middle class."

145 A *self-described crybaby*: Interview with Gloria Polanco, Neiva, Colombia, December 6, 2008

146 *gone on a spending spree*: Interviews with Jo Rosano and Mark Gonsalves.

147 *it was easier for family members*: Interview with Dary Lucía Nieto, psychologist for the Foundation for a Free Country, Bogotá, July 15, 2008.

147 *"My sons are growing up"*: *Held Hostage in Colombia*, directed by Jorge Enrique Botero, produced by Victoria Bruce and Karin Hayes.

148 *"I know outsiders"*: Malia Phillips-Lee interview, Ocala, Florida, March 18, 2008.

148 *"She had hung in there"*: Marc Gonsalves, Keith Stansell, and Tom Howes with Gary Brozek, *Out of Captivity* (New York: HarperCollins, 2009), p. 317.

CHAPTER 14: THE ROUND-UP

150 *"They were idiots"*: Jorge Sanabria interview, Sogamoso, Colombia, November 23, 2007.

150 *The narcos offered Ospina*: Carlos Alberto Ospina telephone interview, June 9, 2008.

150 *One of the first to confess*: "Comandantes dijeron que era un premio," *El Tiempo*, May 22, 2003.

151 *"It made us really sad"*: Wilson Sarmiento interview, Bogotá, November 28, 2007.

151 *"He was screaming like"*: Ana Ferney Ospina interview, Bogotá, March 10, 2004.

151 *busted with the equivalent*: Colombian inspector general report.

152 *"They betrayed the homeland"*: *El Tiempo*, May 21, 2003.

154 *"I was ecstatic"*: John Otis, "Cache of cash becomes a curse," *Houston Chronicle*, March 28, 2004.

154 *she immediately packed up*: Sanabria interview.

154 *The cops forced the Rodríguez brothers*: "Policias sequestraron un soldado guaquero," *El Tiempo*, August 16, 2003.

155 *"I feel safer in jail"*: Otis, "Cache of cash becomes a curse."

155 *One night, fifteen thieves*: Walter Suárez interview, Bogotá, December 7, 2007.

156 *even the general would shake*: Ospina interview.

157 *"In the hands of the guerrillas"*: Héctor Alirio Forero interview, Bogotá, October 28, 2007.

157 *Lombana did two things*: Jaime Lombana interview, Bogotá, March 15, 2004.

157 *"Luck like that"*: María Bravo interview, Popayán, March 20, 2004.

CHAPTER 15: THE EIGHTH PLAGUE OF VALLEDUPAR

158 *Among them stood:* Portrait of Trinidad drawn from numerous 2001 interviews with the rebel leader in the FARC-held DMZ as well as Colombian press reports and Jorge Enrique Botero's book *Simón Trinidad: El Hombre de Hierro* (Bogotá: Random House Mondadori, 2008).

159 *"Ricardo was the most elegant":* Andrés Pastrana interview, Bogotá, November 6, 2008.

160 *"One afternoon":* Gabriel García Márquez, *Living to Tell the Tale* (New York: Alfred A. Knopf, 2003), p. 41.

160 *He fathered twenty-two children:* John Otis, "After prison, singer's popularity thrives," *Houston Chronicle*, March 23, 2005.

162 *"Because he knew us":* New York Times, December 20, 2004.

163 *"branded on our butts":* Trinidad interview, La Sombra, Colombia, March 10, 2001.

165 *"In war, it's not enough":* "Por fin!" *Semana*, January 4, 2004.

165 *"It would piss off the FARC":* Marc Gonsalves, Keith Stansell, and Tom Howes with Gary Brozek, *Out of Captivity* (New York: HarperCollins, 2009), p. 239.

166 *"We don't negotiate":* Myles Frechette interview, Washington, D.C., February 6, 2008.

167 *"Looking back":* Diego and Nancy Asencio, *Our Man Is Inside* (New York: Atlantic–Little Brown, 1982), p. 4.

167 *"The only reason they didn't storm":* Diego Asencio telephone interview, September 23, 2008.

168 *"Reagan's concern was":* Terry Anderson, *Den of Lions* (New York: Ballantine Books, 1993), pp. 105–106.

168 *"Jacobsen's release was":* Ibid., p. 225.

169 *"We never got anywhere near":* William Brownfield interview, Bogotá, October 12, 2008.

170 *"pie-in-the-sky thinking":* Gonsalves, Stansell, and Howes, *Out of Captivity*, p. 240.

CHAPTER 16: JOAN OF ARC

171 *He had to chuck:* Interviews with Juan Carlos Lecompte during several flights over the Colombian jungle in December 2007.

171 *"I leave Fabrice":* Íngrid Betancourt, *Until Death Do Us Part: My Struggle to Reclaim Colombia* (New York: HarperCollins, 2002), p. 53.

175 *"she was the only pure one":* Luis Eladio Pérez interview, Bogotá, April 24, 2008.

175 *by a twenty-eight to two vote:* Juan Carlos Lecompte interview, Bogotá, December 12, 2008.

176   *She sometimes felt more at odds:* John Otis, "Presidential candidate still a hostage," *Houston Chronicle*, April 7, 2002.

176   *"I'm freaked out"*: Ibid.

177   *"It's easy to cry . . .":* Clara Rojas, *Cautiva* (Bogotá: Grupo Editorial Norma, 2009), p. 22.

177   *As he looked into:* Jacques Thomet, *Íngrid Betancourt: Historias del Corazon o Razon de Estado?* (Bogotá: Planeta, 2006).

177   *"They were telling us":* Francisco Santos interview, Bogotá, September 15, 2008.

178   *She apparently told:* Thomet, *Íngrid Betancourt: Historias del Corazon o Razon de Estado?*

178   *Without informing the Colombian:* "Fury as jungle rescue turns to French farce," *The Times* (London), July 28, 2003.

178   *In one message:* The FARC e-mail messages were made public by Colombian officials in 2008 and published in *Semana, El Tiempo,* and other Colombian media.

178   *Paris lost out on $700 million:* Thomet, *Íngrid Betancourt: Historias del Corazon o Razon de Estado?*

178   *only played into the FARC's hands:* José Obdulio Gaviria interview, Bogotá, August 17, 2008.

179   *"They smelled horrible":* Luis Eladio Pérez, *7 años secuestrado por las FARC* (Buenos Aires: Aguilar, 2008).

179   *"How arrogant is that":* Marc Gonsalves, Keith Stansell, and Tom Howes with Gary Brozek, *Out of Captivity* (New York: HarperCollins, 2009), p. 173.

179   *"You're all fakes":* Keith Stansell interview, Bradenton, Florida, May 6, 2009.

180   *"The resentments could explode":* Luis Eladio Pérez interview, Bogotá, April 24, 2008.

180   *"military guys were salt of the earth":* Stansell interview.

180   *"It seemed so absurd":* Rojas, *Cautiva,* p. 87.

180   *the rebels convinced some:* Interview with former hostage Orlando Beltrán, Neiva, Colombia, December 6, 2008.

181   *"those rats were eating":* Marc Gonsalves telephone interview, February 27, 2009.

181   *"She even offered me a job":* Stansell interview.

182   *"Whenever I hear her name":* Stansell telephone interview, November 11, 2008.

182   *"The presence of a woman":* Betancourt's letter to her mother was published in *Semana, El Tiempo,* and other Colombian media and turned into a book, *Cartas a mamá desde el infierno* [Letters to my mother from hell] (Mexico City: Random House Mondadori, 2008).

183   *Early on, the FARC proposed:* Msgr. Luis Augusto Castro interview, Bogotá, October 15, 2008.

184   *"If you don't take the first step":* Álvaro Leyva interview, Bogotá, December 7, 2007.

184 *"would have sold our souls"*: Tom Howes interview, Merritt Island, Florida, May 6, 2009.

184 *Though the two Cartagenas*: John Otis, "Colombia struggles to revive once-thriving tourism industry," *Houston Chronicle*, December 19, 1999.

185 *They urged the government to negotiate*: Gabriel García Márquez, *News of a Kidnapping* (New York: Penguin Books, 1996).

185 *Santos defended his*: Francisco Santos interview, Bogotá, September 15, 2008.

185 *Gaviria had to bend the rules*: García Márquez, *News of a Kidnapping*.

185 *He dined on stuffed turkey*: Mark Bowden, *Killing Pablo: The Hunt for the World's Greatest Outlaw* (New York: Penguin Books, 2001).

186 *Besides, for all his talk*: John Otis, "Talks could signal shift in Colombia's civil war," *Houston Chronicle*, November 27, 2002; and "Colombia warlord's fate a mystery after attack," *Houston Chronicle*, April 29, 2004.

186 *"We felt like insignificant pawns"*: Gonsalves, Stansell, and Howes, *Out of Captivity*, p. 192.

186 *"no one is going to win"*: Carlos Lozano interview, Bogotá, December 18, 2007.

186 *"That's vital for a politician"*: León Valencia interview, Bogotá, February 5, 2009.

187 *"For this president it might rank"*: Lecompte interview, Bogotá, December 12, 2007.

CHAPTER 17: THE DIRTY THIRTY

189 *Sanabria had made it out*: Jorge Sanabria interview, Sogamoso, Colombia, November 23, 2007.

190 *The man dialing long-distance*: Jörg Hiller García, *La Guaca Maldita* (Bogotá: Grupo Editorial Norma, 2007).

190 *"he almost didn't fit into the chair"*: Elmer Arenas interview, Bogotá, November 7, 2007.

191 *"Obviously, the money was important"*: Hiller García, *La Guaca Maldita*, p. 113.

191 *Who was Castellanos*: Reinaldo Castellanos interview, Bogotá, October 25, 2007.

192 *"I missed it"*: Wilson Sarmiento interview, Bogotá, November 28, 2007.

192 *too big of a distraction*: Sanabria interview.

192 *It seemed like an omen*: Interviews with José Emilio Chimbaco and Luz Marina Vargas, Pitalito, Colombia, October 12, 2007.

193 *a special hit squad*: "Los buscan con lista en mano," *El Tiempo*, August 26, 2007.

194 *Sanabria had brought together*: Sanabria interview.

195 *"I thought for sure"*: Carlos Alberto Ospina telephone interview, June 9, 2008.

196 *"Abort mission"*: Hiller García, *La Guaca Maldita*, p. 140.

197 *"They tried and it went badly"*: Ospina telephone interview.

CHAPTER 18: FALL GUYS

198 *made out of grenade shrapnel*: Jörg Hiller García, *La Guaca Maldita* (Bogotá: Grupo Editorial Norma, 2007).

198 *The trial attracted a conga line*: Description of the trial comes from interviews with soldier-defendants and with lawyers for the soldiers, including Pedro Laiton, Jaime Lombana, Héctor Alirio Forero, and Hernando Castellanos.

200 *general's star was rising*: Reinaldo Castellanos interview, Bogotá, October 25, 2007.

200 *Uribe convinced lawmakers*: John Otis, "Colombia's Uribe expected to seek 2nd term," *Houston Chronicle*, February 15, 2004.

200 *"First comes God"*: John Otis, "Security issues hinder re-election bid," *Houston Chronicle*, May 28, 2006.

201 *military's renaissance began*: John Otis, "Colombian army finally gaining momentum over rebels," *Houston Chronicle*, September 12, 1999.

201 *"This was a crucial and dramatic"*: Andrés Villamizar interview, Bogotá, December 9, 2008.

202 *service branches began to cooperate*: Juan Manuel Santos interview, Bogotá, August 21, 2008.

202 *some unexpected downsides*: John Otis, "Skin disease takes toll on Colombian soldiers," *Houston Chronicle*, October 16, 2008.

203 *The resulting scandal*: "Torturas en el ejército," *Semana*, February 19, 2006.

204 *"He preached it harder than anyone"*: Interview with Colombian Defense Ministry official, April 18, 2007.

204 *"If a junior officer"*: John Otis, "Army accused of working with death squads," *Houston Chronicle*, May 6, 2007.

205 *"he did nothing"*: Ibid.

205 *blast killed 119 people*: John Otis, "This was a terrible massacre: Colombian village mourns victims of church bombing," *Houston Chronicle*, May 8, 2002.

205 *shoved, clawed, and climbed*: I was one of the journalists aboard the helicopter.

206 *According to a CIA document*: "Colombia army chief linked to outlawed militias," *Los Angeles Times*, March 25, 2007.

206 *one paramilitary fighter admitted*: Otis, "Army accused of working with death squads."

206 *"This was a clean operation"*: Ibid.

206 *"There was not enough evidence"*: State Department official telephone interview, November 17, 2008.

207 *"That reflects the significant role"*: Details of the Trinidad trial come from interviews with Kenneth Kohl, court transcripts, and notes of the proceedings taken by Washington lawyer Paul Wolf who attended the trial.

208 *"They were starving too"*: Marc Gonsalves telephone interview, February 27, 2009.

208 *"Perhaps I should hate him"*: John Otis, "Case of captured Colombian rebel leader a tangled tale," *Houston Chronicle*, February 1, 2004.

209 *the paws of the beast*: Simón Trinidad trial court transcripts, January 29, 2008.

210 *prosecutors struggled to close the deal*: John Otis, "Case against Colombian may not be a slam-dunk," *Houston Chronicle*, July 4, 2007.

CHAPTER 19: THE ONE WHO GOT AWAY

211 *Born into an impoverished*: Portrait of Pinchao is drawn largely from two lengthy interviews with the policeman in Bogotá, October 22 and 26, 2007, as well as from Pinchao's memoirs: *Mi Fuga hacia la libertad* (Bogotá: Planeta, 2008).

213 *"Prisoner, do not regret"*: José Eustasio Rivera, *The Vortex* (Bogotá: Panamericana, 2001), p. 262. Originally published in 1924 in Spanish as *La Vorágine*.

213 *"your brains, not just your balls"*: Keith Stansell telephone interview, February 27, 2009.

214 *"That was dynamite"*: Luis Eladio Pérez, *7 años secuestrado por las FARC* (Buenos Aires: Aguilar, 2008), p. 83.

215 *Herbin Hoyos launched the series*: John Otis, "Hearing voices can help hostages keep spirits up," *Houston Chronicle*, September 7, 2008.

215 *Patricia was struggling*: I interviewed Medina in person in Bogotá and by telephone on several occasions in 2007 and 2008.

216 *"That took some courage"*: Marc Gonsalves, Keith Stansell, and Tom Howes with Gary Brozek, *Out of Captivity* (New York: HarperCollins, 2009), p. 317.

216 *"Tom felt guilty"*: Luis Eladio Pérez interview, Bogotá, April 24, 2008.

217 *"That's the victory"*: *Morning Express*, CNN, July 11, 2008.

217 *a river began overflowing*: Clara Rojas, *Cautiva* (Bogotá: Grupo Editorial Norma, 2009), p. 81.

218 *Rather than scolding*: Orlando Beltrán interview, Neiva, Colombia, December 6, 2008.

218 *Over the next six days*: Pérez interview.

218 *"No river is straight"*: Paul Theroux, *The Mosquito Coast* (New York: Mariner Books, 1982), p. 179.

219 *"John always seemed to be on the fringe"*: Gonsalves, Stansell, and Howes, *Out of Captivity*, p. 339.

220 *began pissing on the boots:* Pinchao interview.

220 *"he was up to something":* Gonsalves, Stansell, and Howes, *Out of Captivity,* p. 346.

220 *they lowered their offer:* Pérez interview.

221 *"He was the mouse of the group":* Keith Stansell interview, Bradenton, Florida, May 6, 2009.

221 *As recently as the 1940s:* Wade Davis, *One River: Explorations and Discoveries in the Amazon Rain Forest* (New York: Simon and Schuster, 1996).

221 *"I didn't know it was the Apaporis":* Pinchao interview.

222 *He had been dragged underwater:* Pérez interview.

223 *he positioned a joint police-army:* Description of search-and-rescue effort based on interview with Colonel William Ruiz, Bogotá, October 30, 2007.

CHAPTER 20: SIDESHOW HUGO

225 *"Ill-born guerrilla":* Police video clip of Pinchao returning to Mitú was broadcast on Colombian TV news programs.

226 *"He grabbed my arm":* Colonel William Ruiz interview, Bogotá, October 30, 2007.

226 *"Pinchao was able to narrow the search":* FBI agent interview, Bogotá, August 7, 2008.

227 *"The guy was a treasure trove":* William Brownfield interview, Bogotá, October 12, 2008.

227 *"Meeting Mr. Pinchao":* Lynne Stansell e-mail, August 13, 2007.

228 *"'Pinchao! Pinchao! Pinchao!'":* Luis Eladio Pérez interview, April 24, 2008.

228 *"I was profoundly happy":* "Solo saberme mamá me permitió sobrevivir": Clara Rojas, *El Tiempo,* May 11, 2008.

229 *"like hyenas":* Clara Rojas, *Cautiva* (Bogotá: Grupo Editorial Norma, 2009), p. 139.

229 *helping cows give birth:* Ibid., p. 164.

229 *"Clara was going to die":* "El Carcelero," *Semana,* March 3, 2008.

229 *With a 100-watt lightbulb:* Rojas, *Cautiva,* p. 154.

230 *"Clara would stand at the fence":* Marc Gonsalves, Keith Stansell, and Tom Howes with Gary Brozek, *Out of Captivity* (New York: HarperCollins, 2009), p. 209.

230 *"just stare vacantly":* Ibid., p. 206.

230 *He developed leishmaniasis:* Rojas, *Cautiva,* p. 187.

231 *"If Emmanuel dies":* *El Espectador* newspaper, May 22, 2007.

232 *"Who is dying":* Gustavo Moncayo interview, Bogotá, September 10, 2008.

232 *"I'm deeply concerned":* Transcript of President George W. Bush's interview with RCN Television, March 7, 2007.

233 *they raised their AK-47 rifles:* "Así fue la masacre," *Semana,* May 31, 2008.

233 *"Don't gun us down":* Gonsalves, Stansell, and Howes, *Out of Captivity,* p. 217.

234 *"their ideological leader"*: Fernando Araújo made his comments to reporters in New York, and the story was picked up by news agencies as well as BBCmundo.com, the Spanish-language service of the BBC, March 20, 2007.

234 *"Chávez sent his jet"*: Patricia Medina interview.

235 *"They are my brothers"*: Kyle Stansell interview, Sarasota, Florida, January 29, 2008.

236 *"If the two sides"*: Camilo Gómez interview, Bogotá, February 20, 2008.

237 *"Happy fucking Thanksgiving"*: Gonsalves, Stansell, and Howes, *Out of Captivity*, p. 381.

237 *"Mamita," she wrote*: Betancourt's letter to her mother was published in *Semana, El Tiempo,* and other Colombian media and turned into a book, *Cartas a mamá desde el infierno* [Letters to my mother from hell] (Mexico City: Random House Mondadori, 2008).

238 *"I love you very much"*: The FARC-made proof-of-life videos were widely broadcast on Colombian television and on the Internet.

CHAPTER 21: THE MASKED AVENGER

240 *After watching the film*: Stefania Ortiz interview, Cali, July 25, 2008.

241 *"We spent our whole lives"*: Yaned Daza interview, Popayán, November 15, 2008.

241 *"But he said, 'I'm not guilty'"*: Carlos Daza interview, Cali, July 25, 2008.

241 *he slipped back into Colombia*: Jorge Sanabria interview, Sogamoso, November 23, 2007.

243 *"He didn't want to go"*: Aura Gómez interview, Popayán, November 15, 2008.

243 *"'Take me to the hospital'"*: Nancy Valencia interview, Cali, July 25, 2008.

CHAPTER 22: NECK AND NECK

244 *"Every time I swallowed"*: Marc Gonsalves, Keith Stansell, and Tom Howes with Gary Brozek, *Out of Captivity* (New York: HarperCollins, 2009), p. 366.

245 *"Enrique Gafas was bitter"*: Luis Eladio Pérez interview, Bogotá, September 20, 2008.

245 *"I developed a severe distaste"*: *Morning Express*, CNN, July 11, 2008.

245 *vowed to cash in*: Pérez interview.

246 *"We counted the days"*: FBI agent interview, Bogotá, August 7, 2008.

246 *"The two sides were digging in"*: William Brownfield interview, Bogotá, October 12, 2008.

247   *The changing of the guard*: Gonsalves, Stansell, and Howes, *Out of Captivity*, p. 375.

247   *Brownfield was a freethinker*: Brownfield interview.

248   *"What I did was to create"*: Juan Manuel Santos interview, Bogotá, August 21, 2008.

248   *Adding to the FARC's woes*: FBI agent interview; Brownfield interview.

248   *"We had to learn those lessons"*: Brownfield interview.

249   *But the Ninth Conference*: Colombian Air Force communiqué, March 16, 2007.

249   *wearing black T-shirts*: General Alejandro Navas, commander of Joint Task Force Omega, interview, Larandia, November 10, 2008.

249   *Camilo's job was to teach*: Ex-FARC rebel Camilo interview, Bogotá, October 11, 2008.

250   *"how much money had been put on my head"*: Karina's statements are from a Bogotá news conference following her capture, May 20, 2008.

250   *"the solitary men"*: Luis Eladio Pérez, *7 años secuestrado por las FARC* (Buenos Aires: Aguilar, 2008).

251   *But the more Ambassador Brownfield*: Brownfield interview.

251   *"'Don't lock out any options'"*: Ibid.

252   *"They were so bummed out"*: Pérez interview.

253   *"I think they are heroic"*: "Stone: My part in hostage baby saga," *The Observer* (London), January 6, 2008.

253   *But Uribe had it right*: John Otis, "DNA solves mystery over Colombian boy," *Houston Chronicle*, January 5, 2008.

253   *"I already had five children"*: "La Mirada de Emmanuel," *Semana*, January 5, 2008.

254   *Chávez dispatched two Russian-made*: John Otis, "A joyous day for former captives," *Houston Chronicle*, January 11, 2008.

255   *viewed in Bogotá as vindication*: Francisco Santos interview, Bogotá, September 15, 2008.

255   *"Uribe didn't do anything"*: Gene Stansell interview, Bradenton, Florida, January 29, 2008.

255   *Pérez had to shield his eyes*: Pérez interview.

255   *plantains for breakfast*: Orlando Beltrán interview, Neiva, Colombia, December 6, 2008.

256   *they rushed across the tarmac*: John Otis, "4 politicians freed by Colombian rebels," *Houston Chronicle*, February 28, 2008.

256   *"There are a lot of things"*: Pérez interview.

256   *"I have the most beautiful message"*: Ibid.

257 *"That's what kicked things off"*: William Brownfield interview, Bogotá, October 12, 2008.

258 *U.S. troops were embedded*: Ibid.

258 *They learned all sorts of tricks*: Interview with two members of the Colombian Special Forces, Bogotá, December 10, 2008.

258 *"Our guys had more trouble"*: Brownfield interview.

259 *they smoked their uniforms*: Colombian Special Forces interviews.

259 *Brownfield was antsy*: Brownfield interview.

260 *Lying on their stomachs*: Colombian Special Forces interviews.

261 *"I carried photos"*: Ibid.

261 *The commandos fantasized*: Ibid.

261 *"'Is anybody out there'"*: Tom Howes interview, Merritt Island, Florida, May 6, 2009.

262 *"it wasn't real-time"*: Brownfield interview.

262 *The final blueprint*: Ibid.

263 *"We planned too much"*: Colombian Defense Ministry official interview, Bogotá, August 21, 2008.

264 *"Being pushed"*: Tom Howes telephone interview, February 27, 2009.

264 *"a big tub of coffee"*: Keith Stansell telephone interview, February 27, 2009.

264 *a vintage feint*: Brownfield interview.

265 *"The bottom line is"*: Ibid.

265 *"The rebels were blown away"*: Stansell telephone interview.

265 *"That was a changing point"*: Marc Gonsalves telephone interview, February 27, 2009.

265 *if not especially enlightening*: Portrait of Reyes is drawn from numerous personal interviews with the FARC spokesman during the 1999–2002 peace talks.

266 *"it was a public relations office"*: statement from news conference in Santiago, Chile, and quoted by AFP news service, March 7, 2008.

267 *What Reyes didn't know*: John Otis, "Raid that killed rebel chief set up by an informant," *Houston Chronicle*, March 6, 2008.

267 *"Money is what moves things"*: Interview with presidential aide José Obdulio Gaviria, Bogotá, March 5, 2006.

267 *Back in the United States*: Interviews with Gene and Lynne Stansell, January 29, 2008.

268 *Chávez abruptly ordered*: John Otis, "Colombian raid spurs wrath of neighbors," *Houston Chronicle*, March 3, 2008.

268 *Thousands of documents*: "El computador de Reyes," *Semana* special edition, March 4, 2008.

268 *trafficking in hostages*: Gaviria interview.

268 *the mob-style murder*: John Otis, "South American leaders defuse border standoff," *Houston Chronicle*, March 7, 2008.

268 *Short, soft-spoken:* Iván Ríos portrait assembled from numerous personal interviews with the rebel leader during the 1999–2002 peace talks.

269 *Montoya joined the FARC:* Pedro Montoya interview, La Picota Prison, Bogotá, March 27, 2009.

269 *"Here's the proof":* Ibid.

269 *the mighty oak himself:* John Otis, "Colombia confirms rebels' leader has died," *Houston Chronicle,* May 25, 2008.

270 *"end of the FARC in sight":* Juan Manuel Santos news conference, Bogotá, May 25, 2008.

270 *Given the split loyalties:* John Otis, "The demise of rebel hurts but FARC may still be threat," *Houston Chronicle,* May 26, 2008.

271 *"'Let our people go'":* Transcript of Brownfield's speech at the U.S. embassy, February 13, 2008.

CHAPTER 24: THE UNTHINKABLE

273 *babel of words, numbers:* William Brownfield interview, Bogotá, October 12, 2008.

273 *"Think the unthinkable":* Juan Manuel Santos interview, Bogotá, August 21, 2008.

273 *officers found inspiration:* Interviews with Colombian Army intelligence officers, Bogotá, January 28, 2009.

274 *"That put more pressure":* Francisco Santos interview, Bogotá, September 15, 2008.

274 *Soon, high-tech sharpies:* The description of how the Colombian Army set up its sting operation is drawn largely from my interviews with U.S. ambassador William Brownfield, Colombian defense minister Juan Manuel Santos, and Colombian Army intelligence officers who took part in the operation. I also gleaned information from videos made available to me by the Colombian Army, which filmed nearly every aspect of the operation, from planning to execution to the triumphant return of the hostages. Juan Carlos Torres's book *Operación Jaque: La Verdadera Historia* (Bogotá: Planeta, 2008), which is the authorized Colombian Defense Ministry account of the rescue mission, provides a highly detailed blow-by-blow account. Also, I made use of some interviews with army intelligence agents included in the Spanish-language National Geographic TV documentary *Operación Jaque* that aired in October 2008.

275 *"But they would be speaking to us":* Santos interview.

275 *"The key was to keep Mono Jojoy":* Brownfield interview.

275 *man-in-the-middle attacks did not work:* Bruce Schneier, "How a classic man-in-the-middle attack saved Colombian hostages," "Security Matters" column, *Wired,* July 10, 2008.

276 *"None of this would have happened"*: U.S. State Department official telephone interview, August 26, 2008.

276 *Andrea went on the air*: Transcriptions of the conversations between the army intelligence officials and FARC radio operators are included in Torres, *Operación Jaque*.

277 *"too good to be true"*: Santos interview.

278 *"It was risk-free for the hostages"*: Ibid.

278 *Soon the Americans found out*: Brownfield interview.

279 *"He was flabbergasted"*: Santos interview.

279 *"Up until the last minute"*: Brownfield interview.

279 *"We studied every detail"*: Interview with Colombian Army intelligence officer.

279 *Santos demanded that the army*: Santos interview.

280 *Russi was a veteran*: Interview with intelligence officer who played the role of "Russi," Bogotá, January 28, 2009.

282 *used spray guns*: Colombian Army video.

282 *A team of U.S. technicians*: Brownfield interview.

282 *"We didn't want to contaminate them"*: Interview with Colombian Army intelligence officers.

283 *It was an excruciating call*: Torres, *Operación Jaque*, p. 184.

283 *reinforce the army's con game*: Santos interview.

283 *the hostages and César heard the reports*: Keith Stansell interview, Bradenton, Florida, May 6, 2009.

283 *"We had vanilla-filled shortbread cookies"*: Marc Gonsalves, Keith Stansell, and Tom Howes with Gary Brozek, *Out of Captivity* (New York: HarperCollins, 2009), p. 400.

284 *"We started writing letters"*: *Morning Express*, CNN, July 11, 2008.

284 *Andrea sent back a terse message*: Torres, *Operación Jaque*, p. 204.

285 *"'Why am I even here'"*: Brownfield interview.

285 *Montoya ordered them to pummel*: Colombian Army video.

285 *But a storm system was moving in*: Santos interview.

286 *"we are the good guys"*: Colombian Army video.

CHAPTER 25: CHECKMATE

287 *Then they were attacked*: Interview with intelligence officer who played the role of mission chief "Russi," Bogotá, January 29, 2009.

288 *but just before midday*: Juan Carlos Torres, *Operación Jaque: La Verdadera Historia* (Bogotá: Planeta, 2008), p. 242.

288 *washed their footwear with sponges*: Interview with "Russi."

288 *"'This can't be happening'"*: William Brownfield interview, Bogotá, October 12, 2008.

289   *scamming the scammers*: Interview with "Russi."

289   *"we might as well land"*: National Geographic TV documentary *Operación Jaque*.

290   *she slipped Pérez the two sharp objects*: Torres, *Operación Jaque*, p. 225.

290   *"In the middle of the Colombian jungle"*: Colombian Army video.

290   *they barely resisted the urge*: Interview with "Russi."

291   *" 'I've lost my wallet' "*: Interview with Colombian intelligence officers.

291   *feigned an argument*: Colombian Army video.

292   *"I was ready to have lunch"*: Interview with "Russi."

292   *pulled the final strings*: Torres, *Operación Jaque*, p. 225.

292   *"They were filming us"*: *Larry King Live*, CNN, July 9, 2008.

292   *so upset he threw*: Marc Gonsalves interview, Cambridge, Massachusetts, May 2, 2009.

293   *"Six minutes go by"*: Brownfield interview.

293   *Russi started scolding*: Interview with "Russi."

294   *"I don't know who you are"*: Keith Stansell telephone interview, February 27, 2009.

294   *"Do you want to go home"*: Stansell interview.

294   *"It all looked good to me"*: *Morning Express*, CNN, July 11, 2008.

294   *pleaded for attention*: Colombian Army video.

294   *effects of the fairy dust*: Interview with "Russi."

295   *hold up his middle finger*: National Geographic TV documentary *Operación Jaque*.

295   *"Generators okay"*: General Mario Montoya speaking at a post-rescue news conference, Bogotá, July 2, 2008.

295   *" 'You can ride with me' "*: National Geographic documentary *Operación Jaque*.

295   *"this big-ass fight breaks out"*: Gonsalves interview.

296   *"Something happened"*: Post-rescue news conference, Bogotá, July 2, 2008.

296   *"We are the Colombian Army"*: Interview with "Russi."

CHAPTER 26: PASSPORTS

297   *"Uribe, Uribe, Uribe"*: Colombian Army video.

297   *"It was over"*: Tom Howes interview, Merritt Island, Florida, May 6, 2009.

297   *"I just felt incredible"*: Keith Stansell interview, Bradenton, Florida, May 6, 2009.

297   *"Fifteen pax. All airborne"*: John Otis, "Hostage mission took years to plan, execute," *Houston Chronicle*, July 13, 2008.

298   *"It was the most important piece of news"*: William Brownfield interview, Bogotá, October 12, 2008.

298   *Montoya started singing*: Colombian Army video.

298   *"Mama, I'm free"*: Ibid.

299   *"He was gripping that damned thing"*: Brownfield interview.

299   *"I could actually quit"*: U.S. State Department official, telephone interview, November 17, 2008.

300   *"We shared in the anguish"*: Northrop Grumman press release, July 2, 2008.

300   *"you leave behind a lot"*: Post-rescue news conference, Bogotá, July 2, 2008.

301   *"We got jaded"*: *Morning Express*, CNN, July 11, 2008.

301   *"If there's ever a moment"*: Ibid.

302   *"It's been five and a half years"*: Lauren Stansell telephone interview, July 2, 2008.

302   *"he was just perfect"*: Jo Rosano telephone interview, July 18, 2008.

EPILOGUE: LIVING TO TELL THE TALE

304   *"greater than Entebbe"*: William Brownfield interview, Bogotá, July 11, 2008.

304   *Watching it all play out*: Jorge Sanabria interview, Bogotá, September 23, 2008.

306   *was now a milkman*: Walter Suárez interview, Bogotá, August 28, 2008.

307   *"Your image changes"*: Frankistey Giraldo interview, Bogotá, September 5, 2008.

307   *"it was a blessing"*: "El soldado de la guaca que ahora es mujer," *El Tiempo*, April 13, 2008.

308   *"Her love for me"*: John Otis, "New life, difficult transition for ex-hostages," *Houston Chronicle*, July 20, 2008.

308   *"one of those high-society"*: Luis Eladio Pérez interview, Bogotá, April 24, 2008.

308   *"The nightmares I have"*: Tom Howes telephone interview, February 27, 2009.

309   *"Marc and Tom were victims"*: Keith Stansell telephone interview, February 27, 2009.

309   *"I love Colombia"*: Jo Rosano interview.

309   *"redefined his value system"*: *Morning Express*, CNN, July 11, 2008.

310   *"It was the best rescue"*: Ibid.

310   *forced to apologize*: John Otis, "Apologetic Uribe admits Red Cross impersonation," *Houston Chronicle*, July 17, 2008.

310   *a far more serious scandal*: John Otis, "Body-count scandal mars Colombian victories," *Houston Chronicle*, November 3, 2008.

310   *looking into more than a thousand similar cases*: Human Rights Watch letter to President Barack Obama, June 29, 2009.

310   *"Uribe is calling officers"*: Adam Isacson telephone interview, October 28, 2008.

311   *"at the end of my journey"*: News conference, Bogotá, November 4, 2008.

311   *dropped to 437*: Colombian Defense Ministry kidnapping figures.

311 *alongside Óscar Tulio Lizcano*: John Otis, "FARC hostage escapes after 8 years, has captor to thank," *Houston Chronicle*, October 27, 2008.

311 *"stay with Uribe"*: Howes interview.

311 *Uribe's implicit message*: John Otis, "Colombia: A snag in Uribe's re-election steamroller," Time.com, September 2, 2009.

312 *"I don't recommend"*: Interview with Colombian Army officer in Florencia, Colombia, October 29, 2008.

INDEX